Building reputations

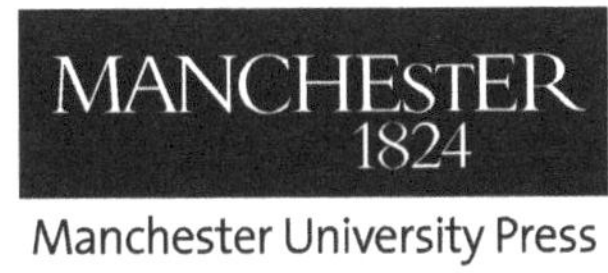

Manchester University Press

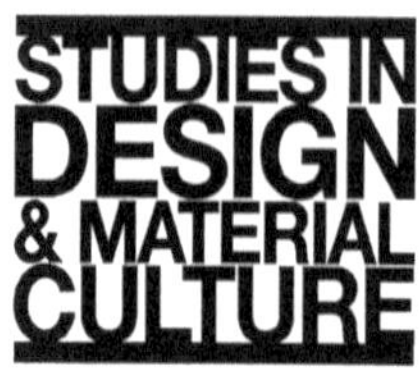

general editor
Christopher Breward
and
Bill Sherman

founding editor
Paul Greenhalgh

also available in the series

Windows for the world
Nineteenth-century stained glass and the international exhibitions, 1851–1900
JASMINE ALLEN

The matter of art
Materials, practices, cultural logics, c.1250–1750
EDITED BY CHRISTY ANDERSON, ANNE DUNLOP AND PAMELA H. SMITH

European fashion
The creation of a global industry
EDITED BY REGINA LEE BLASZCZYK AND VÉRONIQUE POUILLARD

The culture of fashion
A new history of fashionable dress
CHRISTOPHER BREWARD

The factory in a garden
A history of corporate landscapes from the industrial to the digital age
HELENA CHANCE

'The autobiography of a nation'
The 1951 Festival of Britain
BECKY E. CONEKIN

The culture of craft
Status and future
EDITED BY PETER DORMER

Material relations
Domestic interiors and the middle-class family, 1850–1910
JANE HAMLETT

Arts and Crafts objects
IMOGEN HART

The material Renaissance
MICHELLE O'MALLEY AND EVELYN WELCH

Bachelors of a different sort
Queer aesthetics, material culture and the modern interior
JOHN POTVIN

Crafting design in Italy
From post-war to postmodernism
CATHARINE ROSSI

Chinoiserie
Commerce and critical ornament in eighteenth-century Britain
STACEY SLOBODA

Material goods, moving hands
Perceiving production in England, 1700–1830
KATE SMITH

Hot metal
Material culture and tangible labour
JESSE ADAMS STEIN

Ideal homes, 1918–39
Domestic design and suburban Modernism
DEBORAH SUGG RYAN

The study of dress history
LOU TAYLOR

Building reputations

Architecture and the artisan, 1750–1830

Conor Lucey

Manchester University Press

Published by Manchester University Press
Oxford Road, Manchester M13 9PL
www.manchesteruniversitypress.co.uk

Illustrations in this book were funded in part or in whole by a grant from the SAH/Mellon Author Awards of the Society of Architectural Historians

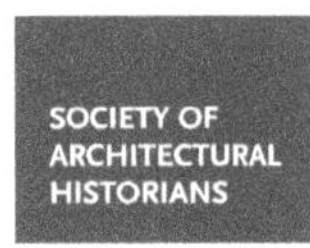

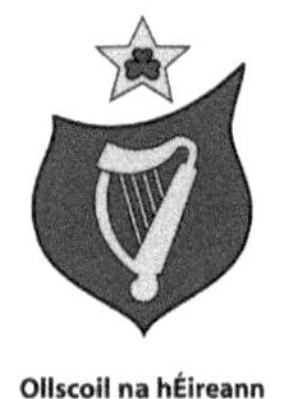

British Library Cataloguing-in-Publication Data
A catalogue record for this book is available from the British Library

ISBN 978 1 5261 1994 0 *hardback*
ISBN 978 1 5261 5957 1 *paperback*

First published 2018
Paperback published 2021

Typeset by Out of House Publishing

In loving memory of my parents

Contents

Plates

Figures

Acknowledgements

This project has been a long time in formation, and emerged from doctoral and postdoctoral research conducted over the course of the past decade. My principal debt is to my doctoral adviser Professor Christine Casey, whose exemplary teaching first inspired my postgraduate studies in the direction of the eighteenth century, and whose consummate research remains for me the archetype of academic scholarship. I am truly fortunate to have her sustained mentoring, support and friendship.

Building reputations was made possible by a three-year postdoctoral fellowship awarded by the Irish Research Council, and jointly funded by the Irish government and the EU (Marie Curie Actions). Scholarships and travel grants bestowed by the Royal Irish Academy and the Paul Mellon Centre for Studies in British Art also facilitated research captured in the text. Generous financial support for image rights and permissions was awarded by the National University of Ireland and an SAH/Mellon Author Award of the Society of Architectural Historians. Various topics presented here were first aired in conferences organized by, among others, the Society of Architectural Historians, the British Society for Eighteenth-Century Studies, the European Association for Urban History and the Association of Art Historians. Themes and ideas explored in Chapter 3 were first published in part in the following journals and edited collections: 'Classicism or commerce? The town house interior as commodity', in Christine Casey (ed.), *The eighteenth-century Dublin town house* (Dublin: Four Courts Press, 2010); 'Pattern books and pedagogies: neoclassicism and the Dublin artisan', in Lynda Mulvin (ed.), *The fusion of neoclassical principles* (Dublin: Wordwell, 2011); and 'British agents of the Irish Adamesque', *Architectural History* 56 (2013). I am grateful to the respective editors and publishers for permission to reproduce this material.

The text first came to fruition during two productive years in the Department of the History of Art at the University of Pennsylvania (2013–15). I am especially obliged to my adviser there, Professor David Brownlee, for his scholarly counsel, professional guidance and warm hospitality. Given the empirical method at the heart of this book, I will be forever indebted to Jim Duffin of the University Archives and Records Center at Penn for his generosity and advice on sources for the history of Philadelphia; and to Jeffrey Cohen, Bryn Mawr College, who provided orientation within the city's historic built environment (and much else besides). In America, thanks are due to: Charles Duff, James Gergat, Alexandra Kirtley, Rosemary Krill, Dean Lahikainen, Bruce Laverty, Carl Lounsbury, Patricia Lowe, Roger Moss, Donna Rilling, Miranda Routh, Susan Schoelwer, Damie Stillman, Sandra Tatman, Aaron Wunsch and to the many curators of house museums from Massachusetts to Georgia who facilitated my inquiries and inspections. A special note of gratitude to the staff and students of the Museum of Early Southern Decorative Arts, Salem, NC, who welcomed me at their 2015 Summer Institute programme in Charleston. Daniella Costa was a wonderful companion through the American South, including eye-opening visits to cities, towns and plantations across Virginia and South Carolina. Mark Reinberger kindly shared with me his important photographic collection of American composition ornament.

The manuscript proceeded apace in the Department of History of Art and Architecture at Trinity College Dublin (2015–16), and was completed at the School of Art History and Cultural Policy, University College Dublin, where I joined the staff on a permanent basis in September 2016 (and was awarded tenure in October 2017). I am grateful for the support and friendship of the academic and administrative staff in both institutions, particularly Yvonne Scott, Director of the Irish Art Research Centre at Trinity, and Kathleen James-Chakraborty, Professor of Art History at UCD (who prudently encouraged the American dimension to my research). Over the years I have benefited from helpful conversation with friends and colleagues across Ireland, the UK and Europe, including Loreto Calderon, Sarah Drumm, Alison FitzGerald, Sarah Foster, Susan Galavan, the late Knight of Glin, Judith Hill, Aideen Ireland, Richard Ireland, William Laffan, Eve McAulay, Patricia McCarthy, Elizabeth McKellar, Edward McParland, Emily Mark-FitzGerald John Montague, Anna Moran, Lynda Mulvin, Finola O'Kane, Michela Rosso, Alistair Rowan, Freek Schmidt, Colin Thom and Ruth Thorpe. Particular thanks are due to Anthony Lewis, who read and advised on my interpretation of Edinburgh's building community (an interpretation already indebted in part to his own research). Critical remarks and suggestions offered by the anonymous reviewers improved the text in myriad ways.

Archives on both sides of the Atlantic have been central to this study, and information gleaned from public collections too numerous to delineate in the bibliography are threaded throughout the text. I would like to single out the following institutions for their outstanding assistance: the Athenaeum of Philadelphia, Edinburgh City Archives, the Historical Society of Pennsylvania, the Irish Architectural Archive, the National Library of Ireland and Philadelphia City Archives. Thanks are also due to the team at MUP, especially Emma Brennan, Commissioning Editor, and Alun Richards, and to Christopher Feeney, my copy-editor. Eileen O'Neill prepared the index with funding generously provided by UCD College of Arts and Humanities.

This book is dedicated to my family with love and gratitude: to my beloved sister Niamh, my brother-in-law Charlie, my niece Eva and nephews Robert and Eoin, and in loving memory of my parents Christine and Michael.

Introduction: a new apology for the builder

> It is not knowing what people did but understanding what they thought that is the proper definition of the historian's task.
>
> R.G. Collingwood[1]

Built in response to a broad range of social and economic imperatives, and subject to both abstract theorizing and the market economy, the brick terraced (or row) house of the eighteenth and early nineteenth centuries remains one of the most potent symbols of architectural modernity throughout the British Atlantic world (Figures I.1 and I.2). Produced in large numbers by artisan communities of bricklayers, carpenters, plasterers and related tradesmen, these houses collectively formed the streets and squares that comprise the links and pivots of 'enlightened' urban city plans. From London, Bristol, Dublin and Limerick to Boston, Baltimore and Philadelphia, this historic building stock continues to play a significant role in the national and cultural identities of these modern cities. Indeed, while civic and ecclesiastical buildings constitute the most conspicuous monuments of the period – under the various rubrics of 'Georgian', 'Colonial' or 'Federal' architectures – the urban house remains central to interpretations of historic space, time and place in both academic circles and in the popular imagination. Despite its ubiquity, however, the brick town house arguably remains one of the most misunderstood and misrepresented building types in the wider discourse on the historic built environment. Disparaged in eighteenth-century architectural discourse as both a jerry-built commodity and an inferior manifestation of the classical hegemony, its form, design and aesthetic character have arguably been marginalized in a burgeoning modern literature focused on the relational effects of urbanism, industrialized capitalism and contracted labour. The building artisan, despite enjoying a position of particular significance in American architectural histories,

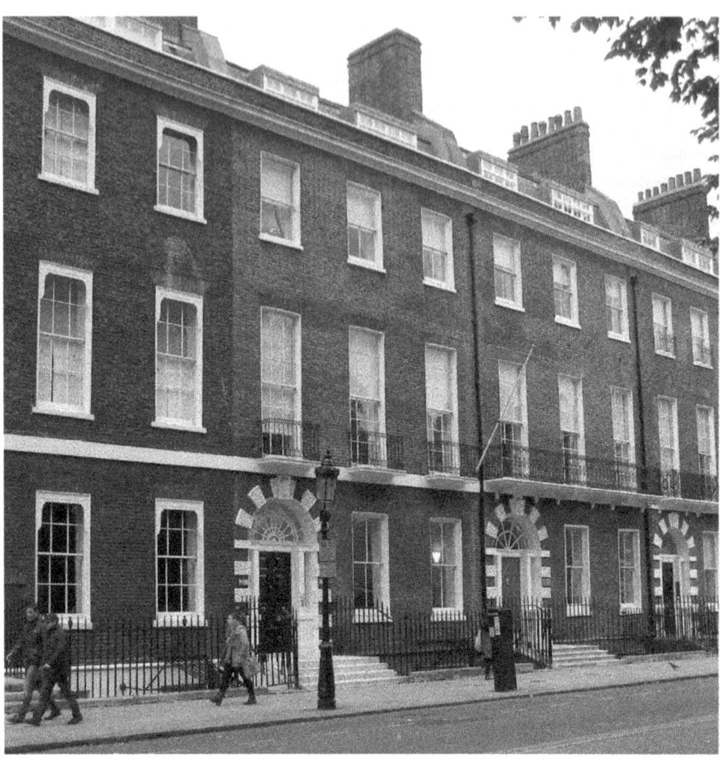

I.1 Bedford Square, London, 1775–83.

has suffered a similar fate. While some individuals have received sustained critical attention and enjoy reputations of distinction in fields as various as architectural pedagogy (the Boston carpenter Asher Benjamin) and interior decoration (the Dublin plasterer Michael Stapleton), the eighteenth- and early nineteenth-century tradesman remains essentially a figure of building production, disassociated from issues relating to design, style and taste.[2]

Taking a cue from Brian Hanson's assertion that the architect-dominated culture of the twentieth century has witnessed 'an enormous, largely unheeded, "dumbing-down" and loss of creativity in the "operative" parts of the building world', this book is an attempt to rehabilitate the reputations of both product (house) and producer (builder), and to establish their rightful places within the architectural firmament.[3] Mindful of Spiro Kostof's observation that 'the same urban form does not perforce express identical, or even similar human content, and conversely, the same political, social or economic order will not yield an invariable design matrix', the present narrative foregrounds commonalities rather than dissimilarities.[4] While geographical or regional inflections are not ignored, the focus here is on processes of making and vocabularies of design

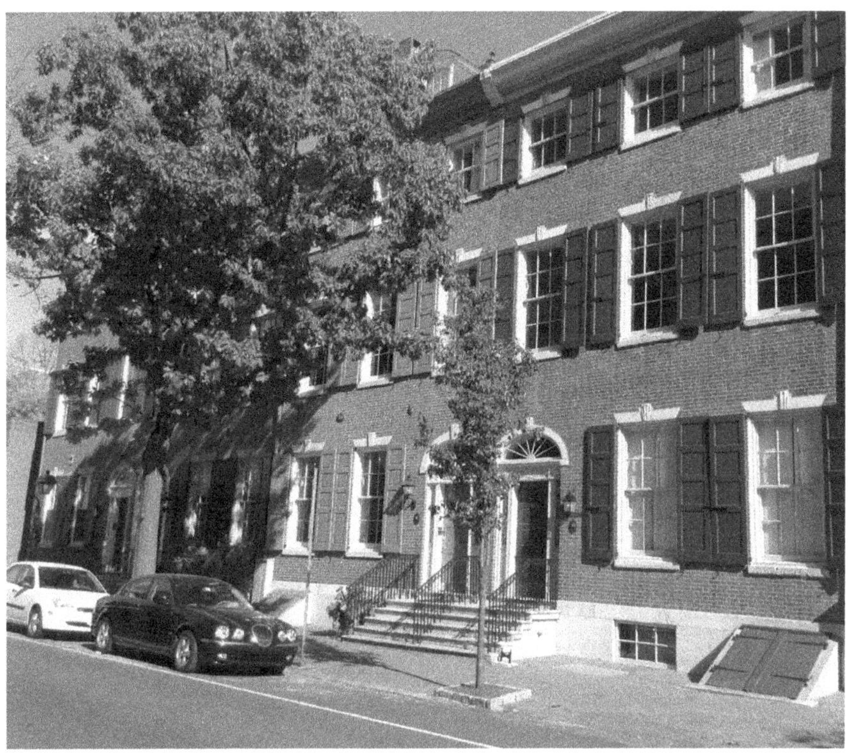

I.2 257-263 South Fourth Street, Philadelphia, built by Jacob Vogdes, carpenter, 1810-12.

common to building producers in cities across the Atlantic world between 1750 and 1830 – widely recognized as a period of critical transformation in histories of architecture in Britain and its colonies. Bookended by the beginning of the modern era in architectural design at mid-century and by the absolute division between 'architecture' and 'building' at the end of the Georgian era, these date parameters also embrace the birth and efflorescence of neoclassicism (the first self-consciously 'modern' architectural style), the emerging autonomy of the building artisan as a building capitalist and the standardization of architectural form based on increasingly industrialized processes in construction and decoration. Opening with a cultural history of the building tradesman in terms of his reception within contemporary social and architectural discourse, subsequent chapters consider the design, decoration and marketing of the elite town house in the foremost cities of the eighteenth-century Atlantic world, focused on London as its cultural and economic hub, Dublin as 'second city' of the nascent British empire and Philadelphia as both the largest city in the colonies and the principal metropolis of early national America.

Architecture and the artisan:[5] a historiographical gloss

Given the interdisciplinary nature of this book, the secondary literature which provides the context for study is wide ranging in scope and methodological approach. Many of these contexts have already received considerable treatment elsewhere: a full analysis of the legal and financial instruments that facilitated property speculation, for example, or the historical implications of house building for early modern urbanization lie beyond the scope of the present narrative. Equally, while classic urban histories of London, Dublin and Philadelphia have informed the text in myriad ways, this account draws more particularly on studies of eighteenth- and early nineteenth-century building production to illuminate the ways in which builders made houses and, in the process, made reputations.[6] Sensible of Peter Borsay's description of the eighteenth-century construction industry as one of the most important elements in the growth of luxury craftsmanship that defined a new urban economy, this study further situates the building tradesman within the wider literature on design, taste and material culture, arguing for his place alongside Wedgwood, Chippendale and other celebrated (and commercially shrewd) tastemakers of the Georgian era.[7]

Despite some disparities in the broader historiographies of house and home, the social production of the built environment has remained a consistent feature of urban house histories on both sides of the Atlantic. Important studies by Linda Clarke and Donna Rilling, for example, have examined the emergence of capitalist modes of building production in London and Philadelphia respectively, considering its impact on the dynamics of social relations, on systems of subcontracting and wage labour, and on the standardization of architectural form through increasingly industrialized processes of construction and materials manufacture.[8] So, while the brick house as a typology remains central to their respective theses, issues of design and taste are necessarily downplayed in favour of establishing complex socio-economic (and, in the case of Clarke, determinedly Marxist) frameworks. James Ayres's study of the construction industry in Georgian England also necessarily foregrounds materials and methods; so while trade cards and bill heads are used extensively to illustrate chapters on individual trades from bricklaying to glazing, their function as marketing tools within the context of genteel real estate consumption is not explored.[9]

More pertinent for the present narrative are histories by Elizabeth McKellar, Carl Lounsbury, J. Ritchie Garrison and others that consider design as a constituent element of house building within artisanal circles.[10] Indeed, Joseph Moxon's *Mechanick exercises* (1703), a guide for building tradesmen, confirms that 'many Master Workmen' in the early modern era routinely produced designs of their own volition, especially those that understood 'the Theorick part of Building, as well as the Practick'.[11] But whereas the complex relationship between design and production in speculative housing markets has long been recognized – in particular the economic and legal imperatives of the ground plan, the role of pattern books and the vocabulary of built examples – the synergy between the business of building and the business of taste has yet to be adequately addressed in this literature.[12] While Sir John Summerson, writing in 1945, acknowledged that eighteenth-century London tradesmen 'could not afford to be behind in questions of taste', our understanding of how builders designed their products and marketed their services within competitive property markets has not substantially evolved in the interim.[13] Dan Cruickshank and Neil Burton, for example, although recognizing that builders, 'being aware of market trends, were intensely aware of the changing nuances of fashion', are nonetheless unequivocal that 'The builders of Georgian cities were highly conventional men; they were not imbued with the spirit of individuality and would happily copy whatever detail was fashionable at the time.'[14] Timothy Mowl's history of Georgian Bristol is equally dismissive: while that city's brick terraces 'often have great charm' they 'rarely represent an original vision', being the product of individuals concerned foremost with making 'a fast sale'.[15]

By contrast, emerging critical and revisionist responses to the established teleological histories of architectural design in eighteenth-century Britain posit new ways of thinking about the artisan's response to canonical tastes. Ignoring the connoisseurial bias embodied in evaluations of terraced houses as the 'lowest denominator' of architectural design,[16] or as examples of 'hit-and-miss builder's classicism',[17] these studies consider adaptation as a form of invention. Elizabeth McKellar's account of the design and building process in late seventeenth-century London, for example, understands the urban house as the product of a culture that 'did not privilege one form over another but instead preferred to operate on the basis of stylistic diversity and eclectic plurality'.[18] This finds a consonance with Bernard L. Herman and Peter Guillery's recent suggestion that the vocabulary of Palladian classicism in England and America was understood as a flexible system of design within artisanal circles, freely adaptable to different circumstances and expectations: 'Classicism did penetrate all levels of society, but not always on an emulative basis, nor as a whole. This was not necessarily because it was poorly understood, rather because it continued to be regarded without deference.'[19] A recent account of the New River Estate in London, built from the 1810s, epitomizes such a balanced approach: while the design of terraces was 'made up of stock forms and details', representing a 'highly standardized surveyor's architecture', the social process by which the estate was realized, and the guidelines that controlled its visual appearance, are delineated without aesthetic bias.[20]

Related to this is the historiography on eighteenth-century building craftsmen. While pioneering studies by Geoffrey Beard, Fiske Kimball and C.P. Curran established a canon of figures that remain central to the present study, recent monographs informed by material culture studies advance new ways of thinking about issues such as agency and volition.[21] A good example is Mark Reinberger's account of the career of English-born ornament manufacturer Robert Wellford, who immigrated to Philadelphia in 1797. Although the serial production (and thus democratization) of domestically produced composition ornament is the focus of his narrative, Reinberger also describes Wellford's products as an 'important conduit for neoclassical imagery from England to America', and outlines his expansion of consumer markets through a network of distributors from Baltimore to Charleston.[22]

The reputation of the building industry

House builders, as we shall see, enjoyed a great degree of design autonomy and social mobility in eighteenth-century Britain, Ireland and North America; but the second half of the eighteenth century also witnessed the emergence of what we now recognize as the architectural profession. John Wilton-Ely, Mark Crinson and Jules Lubbock, and Brian Hanson, among others, have charted the emerging authority of architects on building process in Great Britain during this period, a situation concurrent with the founding of institutions devoted to improving standards in design.[23] Nonetheless, while the formal distinction between the intellectual and manual dimensions of building were becoming increasingly codified, the brick town house represented something of a conundrum. This is confirmed in Robert Campbell's *The London tradesman*, first published in 1747 and intended, as the author notes, to advise parents and guardians 'in what manner to discover and improve the natural genius of their children, before they put them out apprentices to any particular trade, mystery, or profession'. In chapter 31, entitled 'Of Architecture, and those employed in that branch', Campbell asserts the architect's role as both the author of a building's design and the supervisor of the various trades necessary for its construction. However, while Campbell suggests that the architect *should have* a liberal education, *should have* a taste in architecture improved by foreign travel and, above all, *should be* 'eminent in design and invention', he is unequivocal that:

> I scarce know of any in England who *have had* an education regularly designed for the Profession; Bricklayers, Carpenters, &c. all commence Architects; especially in and about London, where there go but few Rules to the building of a City-House.[24]

This perception of the city house as the product of an unfettered building industry – with all of the implied deficiencies in qualities of design and standards of construction – lingered long in the historical interpretation of eighteenth-century urban domestic architecture. Campbell's barely concealed contempt for those who 'commence Architects' was later quoted in a chapter on the building industry in Sir John Summerson's seminal *Georgian London*. Describing how 'One often finds a man described as Mr So-and-so, carpenter, becoming in a very short time So-and-so, Esq., architect', Summerson corroborates the fluidity of professional identity in eighteenth-century England while simultaneously suggesting that the shift in nomenclature from carpenter to architect was both fatuous and unwarranted.[25] Central to his thesis is the distinction between architecture as an intellectual pursuit and building as a commercial enterprise: eighteenth-century builders, by their nature, produced bad or indifferent architecture. At best, the house builder was someone who customarily sacrificed classical manners for commercial gain.[26]

The origins of this invective towards product (house) and producer (builder) are legion and drew opinions from some of the most significant critical voices in eighteenth- and nineteenth-century architectural discourse. In his penultimate lecture to students at the Royal Academy in 1815, for example, Sir John Soane decried the state of contemporary domestic architecture in London. Noting how architects were 'seldom consulted' when 'a neighbourhood of houses is to be new modelled', Soane laid the blame squarely on 'the rapacity of the builders', whose principal concern was 'to raise the largest possible rental'. By such means, he argued,

> our buildings are limited to heaps of bricks with perforations for light and the purpose of ingress and egress, without the least regard to elegance of composition. Thus the character of our architecture and the higher feelings of art merge into the system of profitable speculation.[27]

But those artisans who did aspire to 'elegance of composition' and 'the higher feelings of art' were often mercilessly denigrated for their efforts. While carpenters and housewrights were instrumental in elevating the practice of building into architecture in early national America, in Britain by the 1830s the building artisan was routinely held responsible for a broader malaise in design.[28] A.W.N. Pugin's 'Temple of taste and architectural repository', one of three declarative plates forming a preamble to his polemical treatise *Contrasts* published in 1836, unambiguously complements his assertion that 'Architecture and decoration is a *trade* at present and no great results can be produced while such a system lasts' (Figure I.3).[29] Here the sarcasm is pointed and unrelenting, taking the form of a shop front inundated with advertisements and commercial notices and dedicated ('without permission') to 'The Trade': a lecture on the architecture of the ancient world at the 'Mechanick's Institute' is offered by a 'Mr. Wash, plasterer'; an individual 'just set up as architect' seeks a partner 'who can give him a few hints'; while 'Designs Wanted' include those for

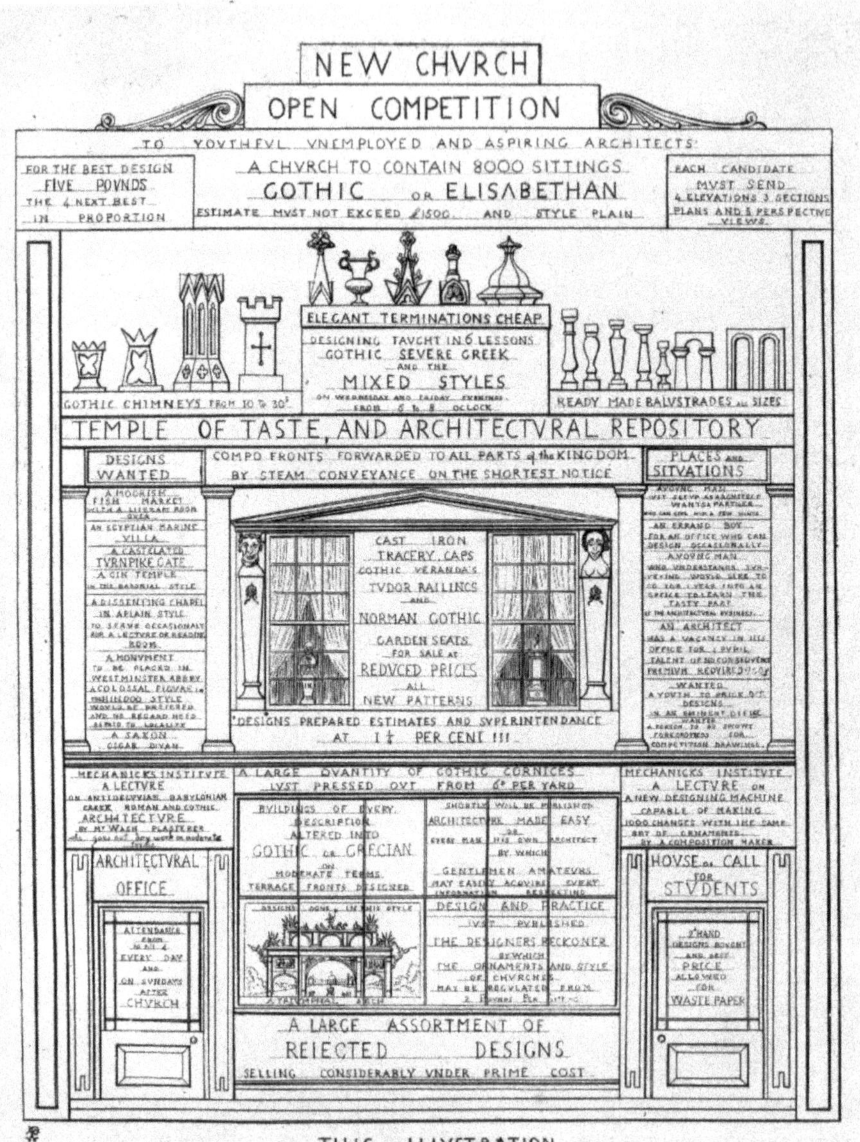

1.3 A.W.N. Pugin, 'Temple of taste, and architectural repository' from *Contrasts* (London, 1836).

a 'Moorish Fish Market' and an 'Egyptian Marine Villa'. Echoing contemporary architectural writer James Elmes's lament that design was then the province of 'non-descripts of every sort, from the plasterer to the paper-hanger', Pugin's 'Temple of taste' mocks the tradesman's grasp of architectural history (making no distinction between 'Antideluvian Babylonian' and the established canons of classical and gothic design), his unwarranted, self-appointed position within the architectural hierarchy (requiring 'hints' from a qualified individual) and his ignorance of the proper semiotics of style (the inappropriate use of 'exotic' modes of design and decoration).[30] In concert with their forgoing of public decorum for private gain, builders misread architectural vocabularies and consequently built in bad taste.

'Builder architect' or 'master workman'?

Notwithstanding the widespread recognition that bricklayers, carpenters, plasterers and others from the building trades were in fact responsible for the brick streetscape that remains such a part of everyday life in cities like Dublin, Limerick, Boston and Philadelphia, modern resources such as the online *Dictionary of Irish architects* or the *American architects and buildings* database contain few biographies of early building craftsmen: the bias remains squarely in favour of the architect or, in American terms, on those retrospectively designated as 'proto-architect'.[31] Indeed, while the artisan inevitably enjoys a more privileged place in histories of early American architecture, the canon suffers from the same art-historical partiality that privileges 'architecture' (read 'bespoke houses') over 'building' (read 'row houses'). Owen Biddle, author of one of the first American-authored architectural books, has long been associated with important public buildings in Federal-era Philadelphia, including the Pennsylvania Academy of the Fine Arts (1805–6; dem.), for which he was the principal building contractor, and the Arch Street Meeting House (1803–8), for which he supplied original designs. Yet despite identifying primarily as a 'house carpenter' throughout his career, his house-building business has only recently been established.[32] A further equivocation is found in the language used by historians of early modern working lives, underscoring the distinction between the polite (intellectual) and vulgar (manual) aspects of the eighteenth-century artisanal world: this is implicit in the characterization of the journeyman's peripatetic existence as 'tramping', defined somewhat sardonically as 'the artisan's equivalent of the Grand Tour'.[33]

At stake here is the distinction between architecture as a profession and building as a trade: the difference between designing houses and making houses. Howard Colvin situates the 'nucleus of an architectural profession' in Britain and Ireland during the accession of George III, distinguishing figures like Robert Adam and Sir William Chambers from both the 'builder architect' of the early modern period and the 'new type of builder' that emerged in response to capitalist modes of building production during the course of the eighteenth century (and who is characterized as 'more of an entrepreneur than a craftsman').[34] But the matter is complicated when America's building traditions are embraced as part of a wider Atlantic world narrative. Jeffrey Cohen, adopting Colvin's terminology, identifies the 'builder architect' as a significant step towards professionalism in colonial America at mid-century: defined as 'usually recently arrived from Britain', such individuals, Cohen argues, represented a challenge to both the 'vernacular-oriented builders' and the 'gentleman amateurs'.[35] This finds accord with Mary Woods's account of what she calls 'the practice of architecture' in early national America, which locates the growth of professionalism in the decades after 1820: architects (in the modern sense) were 'latecomers on the scene' and 'always a very small part of the American building industry'.[36] Anthony Lewis's recent study of the building community responsible for Edinburgh's first New Town, largely built between 1765 and 1795, also argues that *builder* represented a 'a new intermediary stage' between *tradesman* (practice) and *architect* (design).[37]

This brings us to the question of language in eighteenth-century architectural discourse. Omitting definitions for 'builder' or 'craftsman', *The builder's dictionary*, published in London in 1734, variously defines the 'architect' as the 'Chief, and an Artificer or Builder', the 'Master Workman in a Building' and the 'Surveyor, or Superintendent of an Edifice',[38] and thus confirms what Stana Nenadic has described as 'the ambiguous status of architects' at a time when tradesmen were 'branching into new areas of business that included building design and project management'.[39] Indeed, just as 'architect' was evidently a protean term – and indeed a protean figure – so too were the designations of those working in the construction industry.[40] Elizabeth McKellar's account of the building world in early modern London reveals that 'artificer' and 'tradesman' were the most commonly used terms, while 'mechanic', though popular in the American colonies, carried with it derogatory implications and was less prevalent, being defined by Dr Johnson as 'a low workman'. She further notes the distinction that Johnson makes between 'craftsman' (both 'artificer' and 'mechanick') and 'craftsmaster' ('a man skilled in his trade').[41] But Johnson's terminology is in itself very imprecise. An 'artisan', for example, is described simultaneously as 'artist; professor of an art' and as a 'low tradesman', while 'artificer' is 'an artist' but also 'one by whom any thing is made'. Builders and building are equally described in ambiguous terms: Johnson defines a 'builder' as 'he that builds; an architect', but the verb 'to build' as 'to *play* the architect'. Moreover, while the bricklayer is one 'whose trade is to build with bricks', the carpenter is the 'builder of houses'.[42] The matter is further complicated if we refer to Daniel Defoe's *The complete English tradesman* (1726), which notes that

> the said term *tradesman* is understood by several people, and in several places, in a different manner: for example, in the north of Britain, and likewise in Ireland, when you say a tradesman, you are understood to mean a mechanic, such as a smith, a carpenter, a shoemaker, and the like, such as here we call a handicraftsman.[43]

The figure at the centre of this narrative is an individual from the building trades who embraced the business of house building and self-fashioned as an arbiter of architectural and decorative tastes. (In creating this distinction within such a broad occupational category, I acknowledge that this necessarily represented a small minority of the urban work force at any one time.) For the purposes of clarity, and with the aim of assisting the modern reader, the terms 'tradesman' and 'artisan' (and its derivative 'artisanal') have been selected to reflect the nature of the work undertaken by these individuals, based on practical skills typically acquired via indentured apprenticeships and often augmented and refined in drawing schools and builders' academies.[44] The slippery terms 'master builder' and 'speculative builder' which historians customarily use to refer to any person involved in the *business* of property development – as building undertakers generally, and not necessarily building tradesmen by training or profession – are here replaced with the more precise term 'house builder'.[45]

The right to design ... and to good taste

As we have seen, a distinction between architecture (design) and building (production) has coloured histories of the typical town house: although an aesthetic appreciation of the brick terrace has been advanced by historians as diverse as Steen Eiler Rasmussen and Marcus Binney, the emphasis in architectural histories has been on the set pieces of architects John Wood (Bath) and John Nash (London) as paradigms of a neo-classicizing attempt to make architecture *from* building.[46] But semantics aside, at issue was what Anne Puetz has identified as the 'right' to design.[47] In Britain and Ireland by mid-century the importance of design for improving standards in manufacture, and its related economic benefits for domestic consumer markets, had long been recognized.[48] This translated into a type of institution – initially sponsored by private enterprise – formed with the intention of augmenting the typical skills-focused trade apprenticeship and offering premiums for draughtsmanship and innovation: the Dublin Society for Improving Husbandry, Manufactures and other Useful Arts, founded in 1731, was followed by the Society for the Encouragement of Arts, Manufacture and Commerce in London in 1754.[49] Those who attended the drawing schools of the Dublin Society received practical instruction in design and draughtsmanship with the intention of improving their careers in a variety of craft industries. Artisans and apprentices from the building and decorating trades typically enrolled at the School of Ornament and the

School of Drawing in Architecture, but plasterers and stucco-workers also benefited from classes at the School of Figure Drawing.[50] However, while early advocates of design education in Britain and Ireland envisaged a teaching programme that catered for a wide student body, from artists and architects to artisans and 'mechanics', the entitlement to design became, according to Puetz, 'an increasingly contested issue'.[51] So, although the rise in the production and circulation of drawing books, artisanal model books and ornament prints from mid-century arose as a response to 'the very topical demand for artisanal design instruction',[52] the increasing professionalization of architectural design and its preferred control over all aspects of the building and decorating process, from construction and stone-carving to joinery and upholstery, effected a separation between the *design* of architecture and the *making* of architecture. (This was further underlined by the theoretical and hierarchical model espoused by the Royal Academy, founded in 1768.) From mid-century, drawing was increasingly regarded within academic circles as the *mechanical* arm of design: architectural drawing was therefore regarded as the province of the artisan only in so far as it enabled him to comprehend and translate the designs of professionally trained architects.[53] On the other hand, ideologies rarely impinged upon actualities: artisan-led institutions such as the Builder's Evening Academy in Dublin or the Philadelphia Architectural Academy continued to satisfy the demand for design instruction among those tradesmen who aspired to both the *art* and *craft* of building. (The absence in America of an architectural profession *per se* offered further opportunities for the immigrant skilled in drawing plans and elevations 'according to the modern taste in building'.[54])

This formal separation of design and construction remains a persistent problem in histories of the eighteenth- and early nineteenth-century row house. While design historians continue to revise the origins of the division of labour and its impact on invention and manufacture, historians of urban domestic architecture generally, and of building economics particularly, have naturally focused on the off-site standardization of parts and the impact of subcontracting on architectural form – all to the detriment of considering the tradesman's creative agency. Rachel Stewart's recent account of the London house, for example, devotes a chapter to the nonappearance of the 'typical' terraced or row house typology in architectural pattern books and builder's handbooks, concluding that it was 'no doubt because of the limited forms it could take, especially within the speculative market'.[55] But the lack of published exemplars is not in itself evidence that the typical house was not designed. Moreover, although English architectural books fell short of illustrating practicable archetypes, the evidence from a wider range of textual and visual sources reveals how design remained a priority in the building process. Elevation drawings by New York builder John McComb, Jr, the portfolio of Dublin plasterer and house builder Michael Stapleton and the published designs of Boston carpenter Asher Benjamin, among others, confirm that, contrary to Sir John Summerson's suggestion that the expansion of the architectural profession was coeval with 'the repression of the craftsman's initiative', the spirit of invention remained a constituent part of the house builder's arsenal in the decades either side of 1800.[56] Indeed, despite a shared system of building and vocabulary of design – in terms of aesthetics (a standardized classicism), typology (tall brick houses on narrow plots) and process (the system of subcontracting and wage labour) – there is no mistaking the 'typical' brick London house for its counterpart in Philadelphia or Dublin.

As Britain's eighteenth-century consumer culture embraced an ever-widening social demographic, the middling sorts soon bore the brunt of criticism with respect to class-based anxieties about the acquisition of taste: just as luxury consumption threatened the social order, so taste was regarded as the means to curtail its dissolution. Pierre Bourdieu argued that the struggle for social distinction is a primary feature of social life; consequently, taste becomes 'not merely a reflection of class distinctions but the instrument by which they are created and maintained'.[57] Jules Lubbock's history of the discourse on consumer taste in modern Britain reveals that from the middle of the seventeenth century, 'private consumption was seen to have public effects'; this was implicit in the perennial concern for what constituted 'good design', a discourse that 'connected personal consumption to issues of style, design and urbanism' and was ultimately related to 'morality, social order and political economy'.[58] But taste, like design, was a contested jurisdiction. As Lubbock notes, eighteenth-century theories concerning the social, aesthetic and moral implications of taste embraced divergent opinions, from conceptions of taste as 'relative, fluctuating, at the mercy of markets and of fashion', to the notion that it was 'an absolute, immutable quality'.[59] By 1800, the artisan's ability to comprehend good taste was equally subject to conflicting views, from the connoisseur's demand for the subjugation of the artisan's initiative in the creative sphere, to the artisan's insistence on a combination of drawing skills and practical experience as the criteria for good design.[60]

Further longstanding misconceptions about the process of building and decorating urban domestic architecture affect histories of house and home to the detriment of the builder's reputation with respect to good taste. Summerson's classic account of the speculatively built 'brick shell' changing hands from builder to consumer, most recently echoed by Rachel Stewart and Amanda Vickery, requires particular revision: as we shall see, interior decoration – in timber, plaster and paint – was a constituent part of property development from at least the 1780s in London, Dublin and Bath, and in the cities of early national America from 1800 onwards. This posits the house builder as an important arbiter of fashionable taste, and suggests more complex readings of the urban domestic interior as a sign of social and cultural capital in elite consumer circles. It also expands the social demographic for what design historian John Styles has described as 'involuntary consumption' in eighteenth-century Britain.[61]

The British Atlantic world

A holistic approach to the domestic architectures of Britain, Ireland and America necessarily draws on a burgeoning literature devoted to shared cultural and intellectual experiences predicated on early modern transatlantic exchange. With reference to this literature, Daniel Maudlin has recently drawn attention to the development of interdisciplinary initiatives within the humanities, while simultaneously bemoaning the lack of scholarship in the fields of architectural design and the building crafts.[62] But this lacuna is a direct consequence of a dominant thread within that scholarship. Although Maudlin notes a 'shared theme of identity' among scholars of words, ideas and objects, architectural histories have often been concerned with the supposedly representative qualities of style in terms of discrete national or social identities: the 'more purely American' qualities of the Federal style, for example, or the vernacular 'lilt' ascribed to artisanal interpretations of the neoclassical idiom in Ireland.[63] Just as transatlantic studies have helped to 'rethink the ways that national identity has been formulated', so this present study emphasizes cultural contiguity – confirmed by, among other things, the numbers of tradesmen advertising a London training in Irish and American newspapers – and its expression in the urban domestic architectures of the British Atlantic world.[64] But rather than exploring this historic built legacy as a coherent set of 'communicators of meaning and of the values and ideals held by that culture', that is, as signifiers of a shared British identity, this narrative focuses instead on a shared design sensibility among artisans in geographically dispersed urban centres.[65]

While academic studies devoted to investigating networks of cultural exchange between Georgian London and the cities of British North America have gathered momentum in recent years, Dublin has yet to claim a position in this narrative.[66] This omission can of course be ascribed to Ireland's complex social and political relationship with Great Britain and its narration in modern Irish histories: its identity as a separate kingdom throughout the eighteenth century, and its emergence as an independent nation during the course of the twentieth century.[67] But if we acknowledge Ireland's proper place within British history we allow for more nuanced comparative studies of intellectual exchange between centre and periphery. Dublin's proximity to London, for example, compared to the distance between London and Philadelphia (or Boston, or Williamsburg), necessarily informed Irish consumer tastes more precisely and more immediately.[68] Describing the character and processes of building design in the wider Chesapeake area, Carl Lounsbury concedes that the colonies were 'too far away and too different culturally from English society to be merely an unreflective extension of British architectural taste'.[69] By way of contrast, the historiography of Irish architecture during this period has long acknowledged its profound debt to British design authority.[70]

With Ireland securely situated within a broader 'British' narrative, some further correctives need to be introduced. After London, Dublin was substantially larger than any other contemporary British or North American city – with a population more than four times that of Philadelphia, and larger than that of Manchester and Liverpool combined – and sustained a resident aristocracy of peers and nobles, a parliament and a vice-regal court.[71] Socially and architecturally speaking then, the development of London's aristocratic West End during the course of the seventeenth and eighteenth centuries had more in common with Dublin's Georgian streets and squares than with the relatively circumscribed residential district that was home to Philadelphia's post-Revolution elite – known to generations of historians as the 'Republican Court' and clustered around one or two blocks of Second and Third Streets (below High (now Market) Street) – which has recently been the subject of a renewed focus of academic interest.[72]

Related to this is the ever-diminishing distance, figuratively speaking, between London and American towns and cities such as Charleston and Philadelphia. While recent Atlantic world histories tend to reduce early modern transatlantic travel to little more than the crossing of the proverbial 'pond', the physical, cultural and comprehensible distance between Britain and its colonies informed patterns of migration and consumption in ways that were distinct, from the movement of particular social classes to the availability of particular goods and services.[73] This arguably reflects an example of what has recently been identified as significant 'mismatches' in the academic historiographies produced on either side of that pond.[74] Whereas American academics have regarded the rise of a culture of gentility in Colonial America as the expression of an emerging process of Anglicization, English authors such as Peter Guillery are determined to underline those class distinctions central to Britain's strictly hierarchical social order:

> Politeness was in the ascendant in eighteenth-century England, but its roots were in a dominant section of society; the established and prospering members of which would not, as a rule, have been inclined to leave for the hardships of a new country.[75]

Then as now, emigration was as much about economic necessity as social opportunity. This was true also of the builders and decorators who left cities like London and Dublin for Boston, Baltimore and Philadelphia. Using newspaper advertisements to announce a professional formation 'under the first architects' or familiarity with 'the modern taste' in building and decorating, immigrant English and Irish artisans frequently made bold claims to distinguish themselves within a burgeoning marketplace, but such claims are often difficult to substantiate and even harder to reconcile with the empirical evidence provided by the built environment. This relates strongly to what Richard Alan McLeod characterized as one of the longstanding and persistent fallacies in American labour histories: 'since many of the skilled artisans in the United States were foreign-born, all foreign-born artisans, as a generalization, therefore represent highly skilled workers'.[76] But rather than reiterating outmoded narratives about American (or even Irish) provincialism, the focus here is on the cultural and material integration between Britain, Ireland and America, and the important role of immigrant artisans as agents of architectural fashions and decorative tastes originating in London.

Of course the place of the artisan within the wider Atlantic world raises further questions concerning the divergent social and political status of the artisan classes in the British Isles and in both colonial and early national America. Reflecting on the complexity of early modern artisanal identities, Howard Rock notes how a 'legacy of deference' was countered by 'a colonial experience that, based upon widespread land availability and a shortage of labor, allowed craftsmen greater possibilities for economic advancement than was commonly available in England'.[77] In 1782, for example, one visitor noted of the European immigrant that 'He very suddenly alters his scale … and embarks in designs he never would have thought of in his own country.'[78] On the other hand, Eric Foner also identifies certain 'ambiguities and tensions' characteristic of Philadelphia's artisan culture, describing 'the inherent dualism of the artisan's role, on the one hand, as a small entrepreneur and employer and, on the other, as a laborer and craftsman'.[79] The individual central to the thesis of this book is a figure whose practice was formed in craft apprenticeship but whose success was converted into house building, a business that demanded an ability to manage labour relations and complex legal and financial instruments. This had the opportunity of widening the social distance between master and employee, and of countering an emerging ideological bias towards a 'middling' labour class. Other routes towards advanced status, such as the publishing of architectural books, might also be construed as attempts at upward social mobility. Of related significance for this study is the different status enjoyed between individuals in town and country, as well as the formal standing of the individual building trades with respect to one another: while the carpentry trade was universally well regarded, for example, house painting was deemed to require 'very small abilities'[80] and 'no manner of Ingenuity'.[81]

Conclusion: a new apology for the builder

Just as Nicholas Barbon's *An apology for the builder* (1685) argued that builders responded to market demand and, in turn, stimulated the growth of the nation's economy, the purpose of this book is to move a significant step towards rehabilitating the artisan's reputation in design: while reductive images of the 'economic virgin'[82] on one hand and of 'rapacious speculatists'[83] on the other have long been put to rest, the urban house builder as an agent of refined architectural taste is not a familiar narrative in architectural histories, especially in Britain and Ireland. Shaped within the discipline of architectural history, the chapters that follow have therefore been designed to complement recent social and economic histories that have successfully established his financial, legal and managerial competence. Embracing philosopher Charles Taylor's notion of the 'social imaginary' – defined as the 'common understanding that makes possible common practices and a widely shared sense of legitimacy' through a pragmatic vernacular language – *Building reputations* seeks to add further dimension to working lives spent as building producers, by specifically focusing on their design competence and acuity in negotiating the fickle world of architectural taste.[84] In so doing, it contradicts the still common misconception that town house builders necessarily privileged economic pragmatism over architectural niceties, and suggests instead a more complex, nuanced relationship to style and fashion (hitherto the province of a minority of established eighteenth-century individuals).[85] Such a position considers the design process as relational, predicated on developing negotiations between a wide range of network actors, interest groups and end users.[86] Reflecting on patterns of elite consumption in eighteenth-century Ireland, Toby Barnard notes:

> Conventional interpretation would have it that the cultivated … turned to [the craftsman] for nothing except artisanal skills. For their part, the craftsman learnt polite taste from their betters. In actuality, greater reciprocity may have marked the dealings of the self-appointed arbiters of taste … with the craftworkers. Master craftsmen, insisting on what was practicable but keen to demonstrate their virtuosity, helped to determine what was erected. In this, they could display a discriminating fancy or taste, improved by handling imports, seeing engravings or pattern books and by themselves travelling.[87]

Although the potential profit from the business of property development was undoubtedly a significant motivating factor, this book argues that questions of style and taste were a constituent part of that enterprise – that an understanding of style and taste was in fact *essential* to the success of a business catering to the genteel real estate market. Indeed, while the recent inversion of emphasis from house to home in the academic literature on Georgian domestic architecture is both timely and welcome, a significant aspect of urban building production has been accordingly overlooked: genteel lives of polite refinement, vividly captured in recent studies by Amanda Vickery and Hannah Greig, were conducted in houses designed and decorated for the most part by tradesmen.[88]

Of course, not all building tradesmen represented a progressive front. Reflecting on architectural practice in early nineteenth-century America, Mary N. Woods notes how some master artisans had 'no interest in the new styles', preferring instead to preserve established – and approved – modes of building and decorating.[89] With such binaries in mind – tradition/modernity and polite/vernacular – Peter Guillery has recently argued that 'Resistance to fashion can be as significant as susceptibility to fashion.'[90] This book focuses on those individuals who gained a financial competence in the course of their working lives, who turned that competence to competitive advantage by investing in house building and property speculation and who negotiated fashionable architectural tastes in order to make a success of that enterprise. London plasterer Joseph Rose is a representative example of the building tradesman central to this position. In a career spanning more than thirty years he enjoyed the sustained patronage of some of Britain's most revered architects, including Robert Adam, but he also achieved success as a property speculator and interior designer in his own right. Rose was not Adam's counterpart, however, and his apprenticeship to the plastering trade does not stand comparison with Adam's humanist education and formal architectural training in Europe; rather it demands a discrete, impartial assessment. Michael Stapleton and Samuel McIntire, Rose's Irish and American counterparts, are also diminished by specious evaluations. The respective accomplishments of Stapleton, once described unwisely as 'our Dublin Adam', and McIntire, whose 'unique vision of the neoclassical style' continues to generate unnecessary superlatives, require a disinterested appraisal germane to their respective cultural milieus.[91] Conversely, a comparison between the portfolios and sketchbooks of Rose, Stapleton and McIntire can yield important insights into how the taste-conscious artisan adapted and translated Adam's ornamental vocabulary, and how degrees of separation from the source of that language fostered distinct dialects. But rather than reinforcing traditional Anglocentric narratives of centre and periphery, this book makes a case for more complex patterns of cultural production. While America's dependence on 'foreign publications' well into the mid-nineteenth century caused dissent in contemporary architectural discourse, W. Barksdale Maynard reminds us that 'Secondhand ideas need not be less compelling than original ones, and the very acts of translation and emulation shape architecture in fascinating ways.'[92]

Success in business fostered personal improvement. Those who acquired prosperity through industry necessarily, to paraphrase Oliver Goldsmith, caught manners on the way up and cultivated elegance in their appearance and deportment.[93] Marketing themselves as authorities of refined tastes, and risking public ridicule, astute individuals further adopted some of the strategies of genteel retailing as aspects of their 'improved' social identities. As Ann Bermingham has argued, 'In this new urban and urbane commercial culture, where one engaged in public life through economic and intellectual exchange, sociability and refinement were valued as much as wealth.'[94] Given the protean nature of artisanal identity in this period, the building entrepreneur thus emerged as a pivotal figure among the burgeoning 'middling sorts'. As we shall see, a formation in trade was not necessarily an impediment to professional status: reflecting on degrees of business, cultural and intellectual competence among New England carpenters, J. Ritchie Garrison notes that 'social class did not determine a builder's progression to prominence. Performance did.'[95]

As the title suggests, *Building reputations* explores how tradesmen self-fashioned as arbiters of architectural taste. Focusing on the opportunities offered by a burgeoning print culture – in the form of trade cards, pattern books and newspaper advertising – it is concerned with rehabilitating the house builder as an agent of building taste as well as a figure of building production. Just as builders 'virtually dominated the supply of housing', so they correspondingly dictated the form and visual character of those houses.[96] In its widest sense, this book situates itself within an already expansive yet still evolving discourse on domestic architecture; within what Alice T. Friedman has identified as a 'profoundly and irrevocably altered' discipline, committed to creating a 'broader view of architectural value'.[97]

Notes

1 Cited in Peter Collins, *Changing ideals in modern architecture, 1750–1950* (Montreal: McGill-Queen's University Press, 1965), p. 16.
2 In her seminal account of London's seventeenth- and early eighteenth-century development, Elizabeth McKellar acknowledges that the master builder 'is primarily seen as a production figure and not a design figure' in the historiography. Elizabeth McKellar, *The birth of modern London: the development and design of the city 1660–1720* (Manchester: Manchester University Press, 1999), p. 105.
3 Brian Hanson, *Architects and the 'building world' from Chambers to Ruskin: constructing authority* (Cambridge: Cambridge University Press, 2003), p. 21.
4 Spiro Kostof, *The city shaped: urban patterns and meanings through history* (Boston: Little, Brown, 1999), p. 16.
5 'Architecture and the artisan' is the title of a chapter in John Summerson, *Architecture in Britain, 1530–1830* (London: Penguin Books, 1953). It has been chosen deliberately to reflect the nature of this revisionist account of the building trades.
6 John Summerson, *Georgian London* (London: Pleiades Books, 1945; repr. New Haven and London: Yale University Press, 2003); Maurice Craig, *Dublin 1660–1860* (London: Cresset, 1952); and George B. Tatum, *Penn's great town: 250 years of Philadelphia architecture illustrated in prints and drawings* (Philadelphia: University of Pennsylvania Press, 1961).

7 Peter Borsay, 'The English urban renaissance: the development of provincial urban culture c.1680–c.1760', in Peter Borsay (ed.), *The eighteenth-century town: a reader in English urban history 1688–1820* (London: Longman, 1990), p. 165.

8 Linda Clarke, *Building capitalism: historical change and the labour process in the production of the built environment* (London: Routledge, 1992); Donna Rilling, *Making houses, crafting capitalism: builders in Philadelphia, 1790–1850* (Philadelphia: University of Pennsylvania Press, 2001).

9 James Ayres, *Building the Georgian city* (New Haven and London: Yale University Press, 1996).

10 McKellar, *Birth of modern London*; J. Ritchie Garrison, *Two carpenters: architecture and building in early New England, 1799–1859* (Knoxville: University of Tennessee Press, 2006); Carl R. Lounsbury, 'Design process', in Cary Carson and Carl R. Lounsbury (eds), *The Chesapeake house: architectural investigation by Colonial Williamsburg* (Chapel Hill: University of North Carolina Press, 2013), pp. 64–85.

11 Joseph Moxon, *Mechanick exercises: or, the doctrine of handy works* (London, 1703), p. 252.

12 See McKellar, *Birth of modern London*, pp. 116–54; Rachel Stewart, *The town house in Georgian London* (New Haven and London: Yale University Press, 2009), ch. 4; Dan Cruickshank and Peter Wyld, *London: the art of Georgian building* (London: Architectural Press, 1975).

13 Summerson, *Georgian London*, p. 56. Summerson's approach and method has itself been the subject of recent scholarship. See Michela Rosso, 'Georgian London revisited', *London Journal* 26:2 (2001): 35–50; and Elizabeth McKellar, 'Populism versus professionalism: John Summerson and the twentieth-century creation of the "Georgian"', in Barbara Arciszewska and Elizabeth McKellar (eds), *Articulating British classicism: new approaches to eighteenth-century architecture* (Aldershot: Ashgate, 2004), pp. 35–56.

14 Dan Cruickshank and Neil Burton, *Life in the Georgian city* (London: Viking, 1990), p. 118. Dan Cruickshank and Peter Wyld's classic account of Georgian building situates the tradesman's engagement with 'architectural fashion' in a decidedly hierarchical system, suggesting that builders 'universally accepted' the diktat of architects. *Art of Georgian building*, p. 1.

15 Timothy Mowl, *To build the second city: architects and craftsmen of Georgian Bristol* (Bristol: Redcliff, 1991), pp. 96–7.

16 Cruickshank and Wyld, *Art of Georgian building*, p. 1.

17 Mowl, *To build the second city*, p. 105.

18 'The late seventeenth- and early eighteenth-century London house is … a regional dialect of a vernacular variant of the classical language. In our own postmodern age we should have no problem in understanding a culture which did not privilege one form over another but instead preferred to operate on the basis of stylistic diversity and eclectic plurality.' McKellar, *Birth of modern London*, p. 221. Elsewhere she notes that the rules of classicism 'can only be broken if one agrees to abide by them in the first place'. *Ibid.*, p. 118.

19 B.L. Herman and Peter Guillery, 'Negotiating classicism in eighteenth-century Deptford and Philadelphia', in Arciszewska and McKellar (eds), *Articulating British classicism*, p. 188. This echoes Cruickshank and Wyld's earlier comment regarding the 'orderly flexibility of 18th-century architectural classicism', although Herman and Guillery avoid that book's prejudicial tone. Cruickshank and Wyld, *Art of Georgian building*, p. 1.

20 'New River Estate: Introduction', in Philip Temple (ed.), *Survey of London*, vol. 47: *Northern Clerkenwell and Pentonville* (London: Yale University Press, 2008), pp. 185–91.

21 Geoffrey Beard, *Georgian craftsmen and their work* (London: Country Life, 1966); Geoffrey Beard, *Craftsmen and interior decoration in England, 1660–1820* (New York: Holmes and Meier, 1981); C.P. Curran, *Dublin decorative plasterwork of the seventeenth and eighteenth centuries* (London: Tiranti, 1967); Fiske Kimball, *Samuel McIntire, carver, the architect of Salem* (Portland, ME: Southworth-Anthoensen Press, 1940).
22 Mark Reinberger, *Utility and beauty: Robert Wellford and composition ornament in America* (Newark: University of Delaware Press, 2003), p. 15.
23 Hanson, *Architects and the 'building world'*; John Wilton-Ely, 'The rise of the professional architect in England', in Spiro Kostof (ed.), *The architect: chapters in the history of the profession* (New York: Oxford University Press, 1976), pp. 180–208; Mark Crinson and Jules Lubbock, *Architecture: art or profession? 300 years of architectural education* (Manchester: Manchester University Press, 1994); Howard Colvin, 'The practice of architecture, 1600–1840', in Howard Colvin, *A biographical dictionary of British architects 1600–1840*, 4th edn (New Haven and London: Yale University Press, 2008), pp. 15–37.
24 Author's emphasis.
25 Summerson, *Georgian London*, p. 55.
26 Colvin, *Biographical dictionary*, p. 22.
27 David Watkin (ed.), *Sir John Soane: the Royal Academy lectures* (Cambridge: Cambridge University Press, 2000), p. 256.
28 Dell Upton, 'Pattern books and professionalism: aspects of the transformation of domestic architecture in America, 1800–1860', *Winterthur Portfolio* 19:2–3 (1984): 107–50. Despite this, English-born architect Benjamin Henry Latrobe described how 'The business in all our great cities is in the hands of mechanics who disgrace the Art.' Cited in Mary N. Woods, *From craft to profession: the practice of architecture in nineteenth-century America* (Berkeley: University of California Press, 1999), p. 10.
29 Letter from A.W.N. Pugin to E.J. Willson, 1836, cited in Phoebe Stanton, 'The sources of Pugin's *Contrasts*', in John Summerson (ed.), *Concerning architecture: essays on architectural writers and writing presented to Nikolaus Pevsner* (London: Allen Lane, 1968), p. 121.
30 'Lack of taste by clients from commercial backgrounds led to "non-descripts of every sort, from the plasterer to the paper-hanger" being allowed to design, accused the architectural writer James Elmes in his 1821 *Lectures on Architecture*.' Daniel M. Abramson, 'Commercialization and backlash in late Georgian architecture', in Arciszewska and McKellar (eds), *Articulating British classicism*, p. 153. Elmes echoes James Peacock's earlier, satirical admonition of those who entrust design to the 'Fan-painter Toy-Man, Lace-Man, Paper-hanger, or Undertaker'. Jose Mac Packe [James Peacock], *Oikidia, or nutshells: being ichnographic distributions for small villas; chiefly upon oeconomical principles* (London, 1785), p. 53. The vitriol expressed by Soane and Elmes should be understood in the context of the introduction of the system of contracting in gross and competitive tendering in the early decades of the nineteenth century. This had the unwelcome effect of builders regarding themselves as 'the equal of the architect'. Hanson, *Architects and the 'building world'*, pp. 49, 54–8.
31 *Dictionary of Irish architects 1720–1940*, online, www.dia.ie and *American architects and buildings*, www.americanbuildings.org.
32 Conor Lucey, 'Owen Biddle and Philadelphia's real estate market, 1798–1806', *Journal of the Society of Architectural Historians* 75:1 (2016): 25–47.
33 E.J. Hobsbawm, 'The tramping artisan', *Economic History Review* (NS) 3 (1950–51): 313, cited in E.P. Thompson, *The making of the English working class* (London: Pantheon

Books, 1964), p. 241. A more positive spin on 'tramping' characterizes it as 'a labor strategy and means of training young artisans'. Garrison, *Two carpenters*, p. xx.

34 Colvin, *Biographical dictionary*, p. 28. See also Crinson and Lubbock, *Architecture: art or profession?*.

35 Jeffrey Cohen, 'Early American architectural drawings and Philadelphia, 1730–1860', in James F. O'Gorman, Jeffrey A. Cohen, George E. Thomas and G. Holmes Perkins (eds), *Drawing toward building: Philadelphia architectural graphics, 1732–1986* (Philadelphia: University of Pennsylvania Press, 1986), p. 19.

36 Woods, *From craft to profession*, p. 4.

37 A.R. Lewis, 'The builders of Edinburgh's New Town 1767–1795', PhD diss., University of Edinburgh, 2006, pp. 198–9.

38 *The builder's dictionary or gentleman and architect's companion*, 2 vols (London, 1734), vol. 1, n.p. Similarly, there are no entries for trades such as bricklayer or carpenter.

39 Stana Nenadic, 'Architect-builders in London and Edinburgh, c.1750–1800, and the market for expertise', *Historical Journal* 55:3 (2012): 598.

40 A London directory of 1763 categorized architects alongside authors and painters, and had separate listings for 'surveyors of land and buildings' and 'carpenters and builders'. Thomas Mortimer, *The universal director* (London, 1763), cited in Nenadic, 'Architect-builders in London and Edinburgh', p. 598. See also Ayres, *Building the Georgian city*, pp. 8–11.

41 McKellar, *Birth of modern London*, pp. 95–7.

42 Samuel Johnson, *A dictionary of the English language*, 6th edn (London, 1785).

43 Daniel Defoe, *The complete English tradesman* (London, 1726), p. 1.

44 In using this term I am adopting the view of an artisan as someone 'with generally above-average skills and often some degree of education and upward social and economic mobility'. Richard Alan McLeod, 'The Philadelphia artisan 1828–1850', PhD diss., University of Missouri, 1971, p. 5.

45 Dan Cruickshank uses 'builder' rather than 'craftsman'; Linda Clarke underlines the capitalist imperative for building, but insists on 'artisan'.

46 Marcus Binney, *Town houses: evolution and innovation in 800 years of urban domestic architecture* (London: Mitchell Beazley, 1998).

47 Anne Puetz, 'Design instruction for artisans in eighteenth-century Britain', *Journal of Design History* 12:3 (1999): 218.

48 Matthew Craske, 'Plan and control: design and the competitive spirit in early and mid-eighteenth-century England', *Journal of Design History* 12:3 (1999): 187–216.

49 Dublin's lead in state-sponsored design education was regarded as an acute embarrassment in some quarters: 'Ireland, Britain's younger Sister, Seems to have got the Start of her in the Encouragement of all the useful and ornamental Arts. ... should we not be displeased, as a Nation, to be ranked, by Foreigners, after one of our own Colonies?' John Gwynn, *An essay on design* (London, 1749), pp. 91–2.

50 Edward Robbins, Jr attended all three between 1782 and 1785. Gitta Willemson, *The Dublin Society drawing schools: students and award winners 1746–1849* (Dublin: Royal Dublin Society, 2000), p. 83.

51 Puetz, 'Design instruction for artisans', 218. For the broader issue, see Charles Saumarez-Smith, *Eighteenth-century decoration: design and the domestic interior in England* (London: Weidenfeld & Nicolson, 1993), pp. 135–42.

52 Puetz, 'Design instruction for artisans', 220.

53 *Ibid.*, 233.

54 Advertisement of Dudley Inman, a London carpenter, in the *South Carolina Gazette*, 9 February 1765.

55 Stewart, *Town house*, p. 155.

56 Summerson, *Georgian London*, p. 58. Colvin echoes this sentiment, describing Palladianism as 'fatal to the craftsman's artistic self-sufficiency' and how 'Vitruvian precedent took the place of personal inventiveness'. Colvin, *Biographical dictionary*, p. 27.

57 Ann Bermingham, 'Introduction. The consumption of culture: image, object, text', in Ann Bermingham and John Brewer (eds), *The consumption of culture: word, image, and object in the seventeenth and eighteenth Centuries* (London: Routledge, 1995), p. 12. On the shifting boundaries of taste, see John Brewer, *The pleasures of the imagination: English culture in the eighteenth century* (London: HarperCollins, 1997), pp. 87–91.

58 Jules Lubbock, *The tyranny of taste: the politics of architecture and design in Britain 1550–1960* (New Haven and London: Yale University Press, 1995), p. xiv.

59 *Ibid.*, p. xiii.

60 Puetz, 'Design instruction for artisans', 234.

61 John Styles, *The dress of the people: everyday fashion in eighteenth-century England* (New Haven: Yale University Press, 2007). For a critique of Styles's argument see Frank Trentmann, 'Materiality in the future of history: things, practices, and politics', *Journal of British Studies* 48:2 (2009): 283–307.

62 Daniel Maudlin, 'Introduction', in Daniel Maudlin and Robin Peel (eds), *The materials of exchange between Britain and North East America, 1750–1900* (Farnham: Ashgate, 2013), p. 12.

63 Sterling Boyd, *The Adam style in America 1770–1820* (New York: Garland Publishing, 1985), p. 237; John Martin Robinson, *James Wyatt: architect to George III* (New Haven and London: Yale University Press, 2012), p. 105.

64 Susan Manning and Andrew Taylor (eds), *Transatlantic literary studies: a reader* (Edinburgh: Edinburgh University Press, 2007), p. 4, cited in Maudlin, *Materials of exchange*, p. 3.

65 Daniel Maudlin and Bernard L. Herman, 'Introduction', in Daniel Maudlin and Bernard L. Herman (eds), *Building the British Atlantic world: spaces, places, and material culture, 1600–1850* (Chapel Hill: University of North Carolina Press, 2016), p. 2. 'Until a very late period in their development, these colonies each had more communication and connection with Britain than they had among themselves.' Charles N. Glaab, *A history of urban America* (New York: Macmillan, 1967), p. 8.

66 No essays on Ireland in John Styles and Amanda Vickery (eds), *Gender, taste and material culture in Britain and North America, 1700–1830* (New Haven and London: Yale University Press, 2006); or Maudlin and Peel (eds), *The materials of exchange*; or Maudlin and Herman (eds), *Building the British Atlantic world*. Ireland's place in the wider British context is explored in essays included in Olivia Horsfall Turner (ed.), *'The Mirror of Great Britain': national identity in seventeenth-century British architecture* (Reading: Spire Books, 2012), although for an earlier period. John Brewer is unusual in his consideration of the 'other British capitals' – by which he means Dublin and Edinburgh – as part of his narrative of British eighteenth-century culture; nevertheless, London (and England) remains the sole focus. Brewer, *The pleasures of the imagination*, p. 28.

67 S.J. Connolly has argued for Ireland's 'ambiguous status' with respect to Great Britain in the eighteenth century. S.J. Connolly, 'Eighteenth-century Ireland: colony or ancien-régime?', in D.G. Boyce and Alan O'Day (eds), *The making of modern Irish history: revisionism and the revisionist controversy* (London: Routledge, 1996), p. 26.

68 As Toby Barnard reminds us, 'Dublin and its hinterlands had more in common with London in population, wealth and proximity to sources of fashionable design than with (for example) Philadelphia, let alone Williamsburg.' Toby Barnard, *Making*

the grand figure: lives and possessions in Ireland 1641–1770 (New Haven and London: Yale University Press, 2004), pp. 120–1.

69 Lounsbury, 'Design process', p. 85.

70 Murray Fraser, 'Public building and colonial policy in Dublin', *Architectural History* 28 (1995): 102–23; Maurice Craig, *The architecture of Ireland* (London: Batsford, 1982), p. 244. Dublin's architecture as the material expression of its Protestant identity is explored in Robin Usher, *Protestant Dublin, 1660–1760: architecture and iconography* (Basingstoke: Palgrave Macmillan, 2012).

71 L.A. Craig and Douglas Fisher, *The European macroeconomy: growth, integration and cycles 1500–1913* (Cheltenham and Northampton, MA: Edward Elgar, 2000), p. 152, table 7.2. For Philadelphia, see Mary M. Schweitzer, 'The spatial organization of Federalist Philadelphia, 1790', *Journal of Interdisciplinary History* 24:1 (1993): 35.

72 Jeffrey A. Cohen, 'Place, time and architecture: materialized memory and the moment of Latrobe's Waln House', in Alexandra Alevizatos Kirtley and Peggy A. Olley, *Classical splendor: painted furniture for a grand Philadelphia house* (New Haven and London: Yale University Press, 2016), pp. 15–36; Ryan K. Smith, *Robert Morris's folly: the architectural and financial failures of an American founder* (New Haven: Yale University Press, 2014); Amy H. Henderson, 'A family affair: the design and decoration of 321 South Fourth Street, Philadelphia', in Styles and Vickery (eds), *Gender, taste, and material culture*, pp. 267–91.

73 Jennifer van Horn, *The power of objects in eighteenth-century British America* (Chapel Hill: University of North Carolina Press, 2017); Emma Hart, *Building Charleston: town and society in the eighteenth-century British Atlantic world* (Charlottesville: University of Virginia Press, 2010).

74 John Styles and Amanda Vickery, 'Introduction', in Styles and Vickery (eds), *Gender, taste and material culture*, p. 23.

75 Peter Guillery, *The small house in eighteenth-century London* (New Haven and London: Yale University Press, 2004), p. 275.

76 The author continues: this is 'a situation which is not true at least for the Philadelphia area during the first half of the nineteenth century'. McLeod, 'The Philadelphia artisan', p. 19.

77 Howard B. Rock, 'Introduction', in Howard B. Rock (ed.), *The New York City artisan, 1789–1825: a documentary history* (Albany: State University of New York Press, 1989), pp. xxiv–xxv.

78 Gary B. Nash, 'A historical perspective on early American artisans', in Francis J. Puig and Michael Conforti (eds), *The American craftsman and the European tradition 1620–1820* (Minneapolis, MN: Minneapolis Institute of Arts, 1989), p. 2.

79 Eric Foner, *Tom Paine and Revolutionary America* (New York: Oxford University Press, 1976), p. 40, cited in Stuart M. Blumin, *The emergence of the middle class: social experience in the American city, 1760–1900* (Cambridge: Cambridge University Press, 1989), p. 36.

80 Joseph Collyer, *The parent and guardian's directory* (London, 1761), p. 168.

81 Robert Campbell, *The London tradesman* (London, 1747), p. 103.

82 Elizabeth McKellar is critical of how the late seventeenth- and early eighteenth-century craftsman in London has been depicted by historians as an 'economic virgin', whose prime interest was in his handiwork. McKellar, *Birth of modern London*, pp. 94–5.

83 Peacock, *Nutshells*, p. 67.

84 Charles Taylor, *Modern social imaginaries* (Durham, NC: Duke University Press, 2004), pp. 23–4.

85 Daniel Abramson's argument that 'The perspective of commercialization widens understanding of the modernity of Georgian architecture beyond examples of

stylistic abstraction ... and industrial materials', is especially pertinent for this present narrative. Abramson, 'Commercialization and backlash', p. 157. Adrian Forty has noted how 'It is commonly assumed that design would be somewhat soiled if it were too closely associated with commerce ... It has obscured the fact that design came into being at a particular stage of capitalism and played a vital part in the creation of wealth.' Adrian Forty, *Objects of desire: design and society since 1750* (London: Thames & Hudson, 1987), p. 6.

86 Kjetil Fallan, 'Architecture in action: travelling with Actor-Network Theory in the land of architectural research', *Architectural Theory Review* 13:1 (2008): 80–96.

87 Barnard, *Making the grand figure*, p. 118.

88 Amanda Vickery, *Behind closed doors: at home in Georgian England* (New Haven and London: Yale University Press, 2009); Hannah Greig, *The beau monde: fashionable society in Georgian London* (Oxford: Oxford University Press, 2013). Recent histories of the American town house have addressed a broader social demographic. See Bernard L. Herman, *Town house: architecture and material life in the early American city, 1780–1830* (Chapel Hill: University of North Carolina Press, 2005).

89 Woods, *From craft to profession*, p. 56.

90 Peter Guillery, 'Introduction: vernacular studies and British architectural history', in Peter Guillery (ed.), *Built from below: British architecture and the vernacular* (London: Routledge, 2011), p. 3.

91 C.P. Curran, 'Dublin plaster work', *Journal of the Royal Society of Antiquaries of Ireland* 70:1 (1940): 46; Dean Lahikainen, *Samuel McIntire: carving an American style* (Salem, MA: Peabody Essex Museum, 2007), p. 25.

92 W. Barksdale Maynard, *Architecture in the United States 1800–1850* (New Haven and London: Yale University Press, 2002), p. 65.

93 Oliver Goldsmith, *An inquiry into the present state of polite learning* (1759), ch. 11, 'Of Universities'.

94 Bermingham, 'Introduction', p. 12.

95 Garrison, *Two carpenters*, p. 15.

96 Clarke, *Building capitalism*, p. 74.

97 Alice T. Friedman, 'The way you do the things you do: writing the history of houses and housing', *Journal of Society of Architectural Historians* 58:3 (1999): 407–8.

1

Building reputations: a genteel life in trade

While the social and economic histories of the building artisan have long been established, specifically in terms of professional mobility through financial prosperity and the challenges faced by industrialization and systems of wage labour, there has been relatively little appreciation of the house builder as an agent of architectural taste. Now recognized as having possessed both technical and supervisory skills, as well as being a successful employer and businessman, the building mechanic's grasp of design and taste remains historically underdeveloped. At the root of this lacuna lies the apparently antonymous relationship between a life of refinement and a life of trade: a dichotomy between gentility (politeness) and industry (usefulness). But this belies an inherent irony in the history of the Georgian town house: 'useful' people built and decorated houses for 'polite' people. Builders, not architects, raised the houses that formed the 'enlightened' mosaic of streets and squares inhabited by the taste-conscious elite (the subject of Chapter 2); and from the 1780s, the house builder, not the consumer, customarily dictated the design and decoration of the interiors that constituted the requisite backdrop to a life of genteel refinement (discussed in Chapter 3). It follows then that builders had a vested interest in design: at the very least, their success in business depended on the appeal of their product in a flourishing marketplace.

The pertinent question is whether the building tradesman, as a figure of trade and commerce, might successfully negotiate the polite world of architectural connoisseurship: whether it was, in fact, appropriate for tradesmen to dictate polite taste. The 'problem' associated with this perception of the building tradesman was, as we shall see, related to the particular product of his industry: the speculatively built brick house. Loudly condemned in architectural discourse and the public press, its inadequacies were both materially and ideologically related to the circumstances of its production and to the perceived social rank of its producer. But as recent scholarship has emphasized, the 'production-centred definition'[1] of artisanal identity is no longer tenable, and 'the complexity and richness of the lives of early modern craftsmen should not be reduced simply to their labour in the workshop'.[2]

Did artisans from the building industry, from sawyers and lumber merchants to carpenters, bricklayers and house painters, generally belong to the middling or lower ranks of society? As discussed in the Introduction, the use of the term 'artisan' was often imprecise in eighteenth-century social discourse, embracing the different strata of professional organisation that existed between a master craftsman and a jobbing labourer.[3] Indeed, despite its origins in aristocratic court culture, and mediated by its relationship to commerce, gentility facilitated social mobility and blurred social distinctions.[4] Taken together, histories of social class in the eighteenth century confirm the changing patterns of identity and exchange relations predicated on improving material circumstances.

With the terraced house as the focus of this narrative, we are here particularly concerned with those individuals from the building trades who had the ambition to set up in business as house builders, the capital (or means to obtain credit) to facilitate that ambition and the agency and volition to engage with the protean world of architectural style(s). The point of this chapter is to examine the place of the artisan in the wider social spectrum; the textual and visual representations of the house builder in print culture; and the means by which the builder promoted and self-fashioned as an arbiter of architectural taste.

An artisan class?

In his *Anecdotes of the manners and customs of London, during the eighteenth century* (1810), James Peller Malcolm identified four social classes: 'journeyman', 'tradesman', 'opulent tradesman and merchant' and 'nobility'. While the particular descriptions of each class that follow do not permit an easy association with the building capitalist that forms the focus of this study, the fact that the 'opulent tradesmen' is further qualified as one 'that has retired from business' permits the historian some scope to view the late eighteenth-century tradesman in terms other than his 'degrading' manual vocation.[5] In fact, the status of what we may term the 'opulent *building* tradesman' – many of whose names are preserved in the historical record – suggests a social designation akin to the modern middle classes.

Historians of social class in Britain, Ireland and the United States agree on the difficulty in determining a 'middle' class in early modern urban settings generally, pointing to the social and economic mobility embodied in the type of commercial enterprise that formed an important aspect of the eighteenth-century building industry. In his account of the emerging middle classes and their impact on English national identity, Paul Langford notes that, 'When contemporaries talked of the "middle sort", they generally had in mind a wide range of incomes and a great variety of occupations.'[6] Reflecting on the fact that social standing depended on a diversity of circumstances and considerations, from the material (property and employment) to the abstract (politeness and breeding), Langford argues that individual positions were further 'amplified or diminished by the traditions, perceptions, and outlook of the communities in which they were set'.[7]

On the other hand, the artisan is also understood under the rubric of the 'labouring' class or 'working' class, a distinction that creates further difficulties in establishing his place within the social hierarchy. E.P. Thompson's classic account of the formation of the English working classes, citing early nineteenth-century discourses on the place of journeymen and labourers in the social order, confines the generic 'artisan' to this station. Noting that the occupational tables of the 1831 census make 'no effort to differentiate between the master, the self-employed, and the labourer', Thompson is nonetheless anxious to point out that 'there were great differences of degree concealed within the term "artisan", from the prosperous master-craftsman, employing labour on his own account and independent of any masters, to the sweated garret labourers'.[8] This interpretation finds accord with historians of class, taste, gentility and social mores across the early modern English-speaking world.

The difficulty attending the ascription of tradesmen to the middling, as opposed to lower, sorts relates to their lives in trade and commerce. Recent accounts of the eighteenth-century middle classes by Stuart Blumin (on America) and Fintan Lane (on Ireland), underscore this complexity. Lane defines the term middle class as 'an ambiguous locution' generally, but squarely situates the 'self-employed artisan' in Ireland among the *petit bourgeoisie* of small businessmen and independent professionals: the *haute bourgeoisie* being made up of wealthy merchants and industrialists.[9] Blumin, while underlining the distinction between American and European attitudes to social hierarchies, acknowledges a commonly held prejudicial association between types of work and social worth that was observed throughout the anglophone world: 'work with one's hands, even in a skilled and valuable craft', being recognized as 'distinctly degrading'. This was in spite of the 'close identification of middling status with skilled manual work' in cities throughout early national America.[10] What emerges from these collective histories is the fluidity of social class during this period, and the corresponding understanding that 'classes were made not inherited'.[11]

Early to mid-eighteenth-century commentators on socio-economic groupings, including Daniel Defoe and Joseph Massie, placed the 'working Trades' in the middle of a system that was based on occupation, income and patterns of consumption as opposed to inherited social rank.[12] Significantly, the then common linguistic triad of 'higher', 'middling' and 'lower' classes was reconfigured at this time, and 'lower class' was replaced with 'working class'. This was symptomatic of a growing awareness of the social and economic significance of labour, a position given theoretical legitimacy by Adam Smith in *The wealth of nations* (1776). Indeed, just as social commentators became conscious of the new ways in which wealth and status was acquired, censuring its distribution among the widening 'middling' sorts and its effect on social differentials like dress and manners, conversely these positions reflected 'a belief in change and social mutability, rather than in a strictly graded or strictly denoted social hierarchy'.[13] This had wider repercussions in cultural terms. Although historically disparaged as members of the 'lower orders', the labourer and the craftsman were elevated within the social pecking order by eighteenth-century Enlightenment thinking. Nowhere was this more tangible than in America. Politically empowered in the aftermath of the Revolution, artisans emerged as part of what Paul Gilje describes as the 'independent producing class' of the 1790s, the decade when some of the best-known figures in early American architectural history, such as carpenters turned authors Asher Benjamin and Owen Biddle, attained their majority and achieved success and renown in both the manual and intellectual spheres of the building industry.[14] Gary Nash describes how artisans belonged to 'several social ranks' based on the 'overlapping hierarchies' of *craft* (master, journeyman and apprentice) and of *trade* (with 'construction craftsmen' situated among the middle ranks).[15] In a wider British context it seems that the Philadelphia artisan enjoyed greater opportunities for social mobility than his London or Dublin counterparts.[16]

James Ayres's account of the building trades in eighteenth-century Britain unequivocally describes the 'skilled artisan' – that is, someone who had graduated from a formal apprenticeship and operated as both employer and businessman – as the middle class of the building industry.[17] While this might broadly ring true, it requires some qualification. A revealing analysis of social class in the Whitechapel district of London in 1734, for instance, identified 'Artificers, Carpenters, Bricklayers, Glasiers, Painters, etc.' as 'Tradesmen of lower Degree', occupying a position between 'Tradesmen of good Credit, great Dealings, and, most commonly, of good Understanding', and the 'large unruly Herd of Men'.[18] The reality was, of course, more complex and multifaceted. The building world itself boasted its own hierarchy of masters, apprentices, journeymen and labourers: individuals correspondingly enjoyed varying degrees of ambition, literacy and access to capital. Clearly the majority formed the rank and file of the industry, while others developed building businesses and realized a financial competence (or respectable livelihood). But a hierarchy of occupational engagement also existed between the individual trades that constituted the building community. The general opinion of the house-painter, for example, stood in marked contrast to that of the bricklayer, carpenter or plasterer, and parents were advised against binding apprentices for the customary seven years 'to a Branch that may be learned in as many Hours'. Indeed, given the preference for plain finishes throughout the eighteenth century, it was reasoned that with 'the Help of a few printed Directions, a House may be painted by any common Labourer at one third the Expense'.[19]

Apprenticeship indentures to the different building trades demanded varying degrees of capital investment, and the economic obligations and prerogatives of the individual trades were understood. One mid-century source indicates that while a bricklayer might take an apprentice for between £5 and £20, a carpenter and plasterer commanded between £10 and £20,and a timber merchant between £50 and £200. Moreover, while a plasterer needed only £50 to 'set up master', a timber merchant required 'a very genteel fortune to set up', given the necessary credit terms expected of him from house carpenters and master builders.[20] The ability to manage the intellectual and manual dimensions of building projects – a facility requiring both a range of complex legal and financial instruments and the supervision of on-site labour – increasingly determined the character of the eighteenth-century house builder. Acknowledging the economic flexibility inherent in the system of speculative building as it emerged in early modern London, Elizabeth McKellar stresses the importance of literacy and numeracy for success, 'in an industry increasingly organized around contractual requirements'.[21] While administrative skills were crucial for contracting and labour organisation, so financial expertise begat building entrepreneurs, 'the developers of this age'.[22] Donna Rilling's study of the construction industry in early national Philadelphia is also unequivocal that property speculation was the principal, albeit risky, route to professional independence and financial respectability. Rilling further argues that the system of ground rents practised in the city dispensed with 'capital barriers' and facilitated the pursuit of 'competence, society and wealth'.[23] But while a tradesman in possession of these skills might enjoy greater opportunities for social advancement, Paul Langford has suggested that the distinction between the middling and lower sorts rested more particularly on an individual's 'aspiration towards the social and material forms of gentility, and the modest means to achieve them'.[24]

Opportunities to advance professionally differed between the old and new worlds. Roger Moss, for example, has noted the difference between the apprenticeship system in Europe, which observed a rigidly hierarchical system of professional development, and that in the American colonies, where 'No impediment blocked a young artisan from styling himself a master once out of his indenture.'[25] This necessarily impacted on the formal organization of individual shops and businesses, and the relative scale of business enterprises. Donna Rilling has described the fluidity of house carpentry businesses in the early Republic, for example, noting in particular how individuals 'interspersed journeywork on one construction site, with management as a master builder on another'.[26] With the above in mind, Stuart Blumin's description of the middling sorts arguably best describes the building artisan that forms the focus of this present narrative:

> There was, in short, a fundamental, unresolved contradiction in the social standing of the majority of middling folk. The social degradation of manual work circumscribed the status of all artisans, but the independence of many, and the prosperity of a few, strained the very idea of a clearly differentiated set of social levels.[27]

An individual's improved status was not restricted to success in business alone. Societies and associations were of fundamental importance to artisanal identity, and Elizabeth McKellar and Peter Guillery have independently stressed the importance of mutuality among building tradesmen in London throughout the seventeenth and eighteenth centuries.[28] Craft guilds in cities throughout the British Isles regulated artisanal labour and production, and protected the interests of their members, but they also offered the potential for social distinction and bureaucratic advancement: as each city guild returned members to the common council, membership was an important step towards promotion within the arena of municipal politics. While building tradesmen in the American colonies were not hampered by the medieval guild system, craft associations were an increasingly important aspect of the building industry and operated along similar lines of exclusivity, representing only a small percentage of practitioners in any one place. The Carpenters' Company of Philadelphia, formed in 1724, was the foremost trade organisation in the colonies, and its members, according to Roger Moss, 'were in daily social and political association with city and provincial leaders'.[29] In 1795, the Massachusetts Charitable Mechanic Association numbered bricklayers and carpenters among its founding members;[30] this was followed in 1804 by the Associated Housewright Society in the City of Boston, which restricted membership to its particular trade vocation.[31] The Mechanics National Bank, founded in Philadelphia in 1809, represented yet another step towards addressing the specific commercial interests of a burgeoning artisan class. Nor were craft associations confined to the new world. The formation of the Society of Master Builders, Wrights and Masons in Edinburgh around 1790, composed of operatives from outside the city corporations, indicates a shift towards methods of professional organisation conducive to the business of house building.[32]

Given that the rule of decorum demanded 'at least a nominal acceptance of prevailing social distinctions and hierarchies',[33] what was the place of carpenters, bricklayers and plasterers in polite architectural discourse? Indeed, in an era defined by 'the struggle to ensure that commerce served to refine rather to corrupt',[34] how do we reconcile the apparent paradox, argued in this book, of the 'industrious' building tradesman as a pre-eminent arbiter of genteel architectural and decorative tastes? At the outset, it is important to acknowledge that recent scholarship in the fields of consumption and material culture has challenged this polarity. Lawrence Klein notes that while in the earlier part of the eighteenth century 'politeness' was juxtaposed with 'usefulness', it was also commonly understood that 'commercial life itself demanded a kind of politeness'.[35] In an age where social identity was both adaptive and dynamic, the transgression of formal social boundaries gave rise to the phenomenon of what Klein calls 'plebeian politeness': the opportunity to participate in a polite social milieu was in fact increasingly available to a broader spectrum of London's middling sorts.[36] Richard Bushman's account of social refinement in colonial and early national America has also highlighted the relationship between capitalism and gentility, arguing that they were 'allies in the modern economy'.[37] Indeed, reflecting on eighteenth-century concerns about the commodification of culture generally, Ann Bermingham has suggested that the distinction between a liberal and mechanical education, predicated on the foundation of the Royal Academy in 1768, 'was not so much to exclude commerce from art, but to mark the fact that the two were already deeply enmeshed'.[38]

The building artisan in text and image

As a conspicuous member of the modern, commercial city, the building tradesman was well represented in public discourse, both textually and visually. From architectural treatises to polemical broadsides and advice literature, and from commissioned portraits to satirical prints, the representation of bricklayers, plasterers and others reflects the protean nature of eighteenth-century artisanal life generally. Here the contest between aesthetics and utility, and between gentility and industry, is played out in ways both varied and complex. And as we shall see, the business of house building, given its impact on the built environment and predicated on the delicate relationship between producer and consumer, invariably elicited its own distinct responses.

Something of this complexity may be determined by reference to portraits of artisans, in particular those commissioned by artisans. While the expense of a portrait arguably confined the practice to the more commercially successful individual, two discrete approaches emerged: some elected to represent their 'improved' status in the form of elaborate costume and genteel settings, while others chose to be associated directly with their business or occupation. This decision necessarily reflected individual as well as cultural and geographical particulars, but it also addresses shared issues of artisanal identity across the Atlantic world. In his study of occupational portraits in early America, for example, Harry Rubenstein situates the genre within a culture that specifically commemorated the 'artisanal ideal of the productive citizen'. More broadly, however, Rubenstein recognizes that the decision to represent oneself surrounded by the emblems of trade was symptomatic of the 'long tradition of occupational identification and pride which was thoroughly instilled in practitioners of the skilled crafts through apprenticeships, shop culture, and trade associations'.[39] A self-portrait by the Scottish stone carver George Jameson (Figure 1.1), forming the frontispiece to his book of architectural designs published in 1765, epitomizes this confidence in a decidedly artisanal identity: Jameson poses within a workshop environment dressed in suitable labourer's attire (including protective sheepskin collar, sleeves and hat).[40] Just as his book was aimed squarely at the building tradesman and 'gentleman operative' as opposed to the architectural connoisseur, so Jameson emphasizes the manual rather than intellectual dimensions of his practice; illustrating the workbench and tools of the stonemason's craft, for example, rather than the drawing instruments with which he instructed students at his school of architectural draughtsmanship in Canongate.[41]

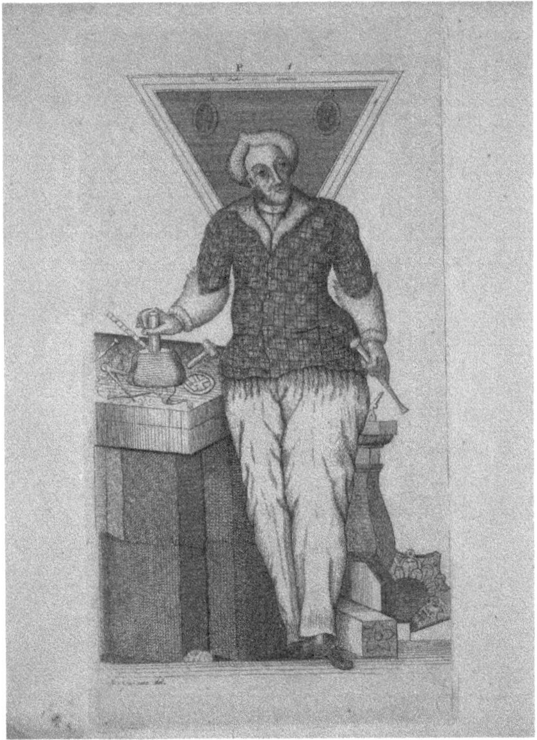

1.1 George Jameson, self-portrait from *Thirty-three designs with the orders of architecture, according to Palladio* (Edinburgh, 1765).

A similar sensibility, this time textual rather than visual, is reflected in Thomas Cubitt's (1788–1855) occupational identity: despite his extraordinary professional success as a developer of new streets and squares across early nineteenth-century London, Cubitt always insisted on the appellation of 'builder' rather than 'architect'.[42]

Formally posed portraits in oils, though rare, illustrate how artisans embraced different strategies of visual representation pertinent to their own sense of place in the social and architectural milieu. In Charles Wilson Peale's portrait of Philadelphia house carpenter Gunning Bedford (1720–1802), the subject is shown seated with an architectural drawing in his hand; behind him is a building under construction. Here both the intellectual and mechanical aspects of Bedford's practice are proudly displayed.[43] English-born joiner William Buckland (1734–74), on the other hand, enjoyed an architectural career of some distinction in Maryland and Virginia, and sought instead to immortalize his elevation into that professional sphere (Figure 1.2). Posed at his drawing table, with a classical edifice as *scaenae frons*, Buckland's portrait stands comparison – compositionally and conceptually – with John Closterman's portrait of Sir Christopher Wren (1711) or Sir Joshua Reynolds's portrait

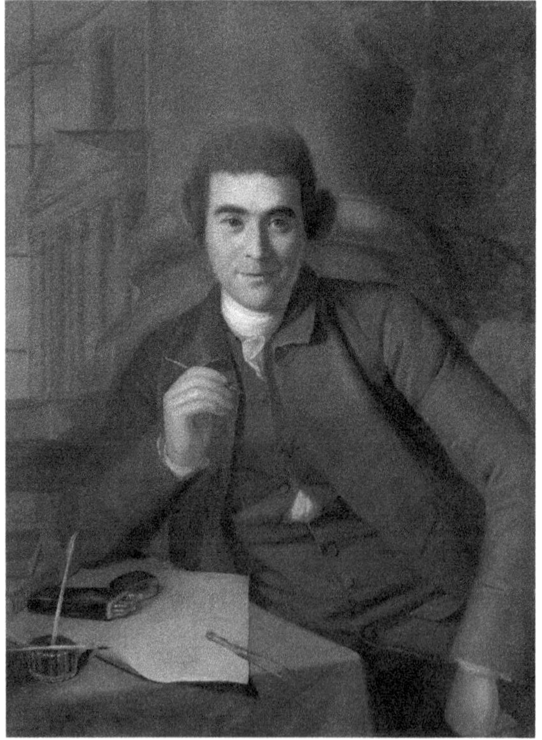

1.2 Charles Wilson Peale, *William Buckland*, 1774.

of Sir William Chambers (c. 1780). Although clearly emulating the conventions of the genre, it has however been suggested that Buckland is shown rather as 'an intelligent workingman' in a modest suit and unpowdered hair, but this is to ignore the fact that English architects by this date occasionally chose similar, less aristocratic attitudes, such as in Reynolds's double portrait of the architect James Paine and his son (1763) (Figure 1.3).[44] (Paine, of course, was himself the son of a carpenter but had benefited from professional instruction at the St Martin's Lane Academy, where the architect Isaac Ware was a prominent member.) Buckland employs the established iconography of architectural portraiture – specifically books, drawings and dividers – and his draughting skills are determinedly 'the essential subject' of his portrait.[45] Semantics aside, by proclaiming a respectable status Buckland's portrait unequivocally celebrates the greater social and professional mobility available to tradesmen in the American colonies. Plasterer and house builder Charles Thorp (d. 1817) enjoyed a meteoric rise through municipal politics in late eighteenth-century Dublin and was elected Lord Mayor in 1800 (Figure 1.4). Commemorated in oils by artist William Cuming, Thorp eschewed all references to his formation in trade and is

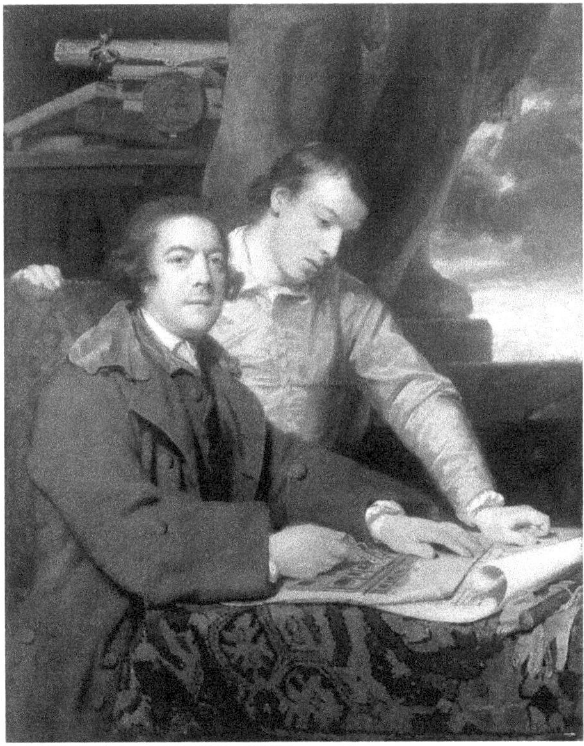

1.3 Sir Joshua Reynolds, *James Paine, architect and his son*, 1764.

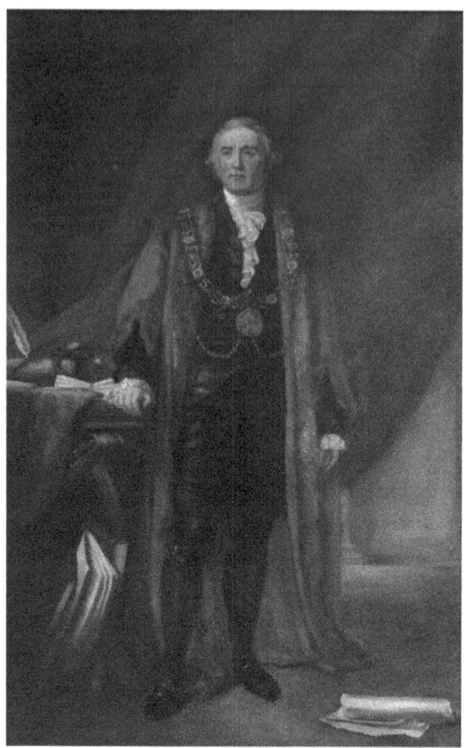

1.4 William Cuming, *Charles Thorp*, 1803.

resplendent in the formal regalia of mayoral office. Significantly, however, he chose to be represented in the rotunda of the Royal Exchange (now City Hall), a building for which he had won the decorating contract in 1776.

Taken together, these portraits illustrate the complexity of artisanal identities within the nascent building industry. Naturally, the means by which building tradesmen chose to represent themselves reflected a range of circumstances and sensibilities particular to the individual and not all aspired to distance themselves from their station.[46] While some like George Jameson and Thomas Cubitt proudly clung to their formative identities in trade, others like William Buckland and Charles Thorp elected to represent the more 'elevated', professional dimensions to their working lives. A finely judged balance between trade and gentility was struck by London 'colour man' John Middleton (d. 1818), whose family portrait was completed c. 1797. While the blue colour of the walls and the decorative borders signified Middleton's trade in pigments, wallpapers and painting materials, the drawing-room setting was a convention of the popular conversation piece genre (Figure 1.5).

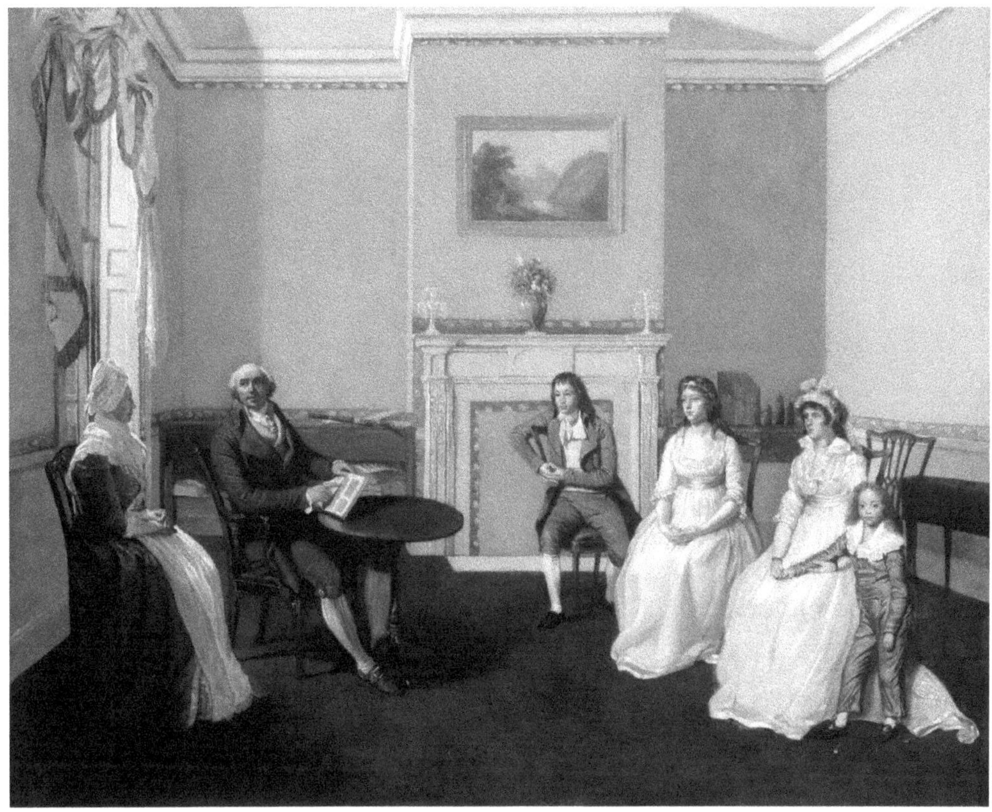

1.5 Anon., *John Middleton with his family in his drawing room*, c. 1797.

'The macaroni bricklayer': the builder ridiculed

Self-commissioned portraits represent one dimension of the visual representation of an upwardly mobile building class, but the multivalent nature of artisanal identities and reputations elicited a variety of responses in print media. Indeed, although titled landowners and city councils appreciated the importance of house builders and real estate speculators to the generation of capital from their estates, criticism of the building world was legion and came from many directions in different guises. While some took exception to the principal product of the building industry – the brick, terraced house – others mocked its producer, specifically the social mobility of this artisan class.

Matthew Darly's caricature of the 'Macaroni bricklayer' (1772) is an instructive example of how ridicule was formed within the visual culture of an emerging public sphere (Figure 1.6).[47] Macaroni was an 'exotic' foodstuff enjoyed by British and Irish grand tourists during the seventeenth and eighteenth centuries, but it soon became a byword for anything conspicuously fashionable. The *OED* defines the macaroni as 'A dandy or fop;

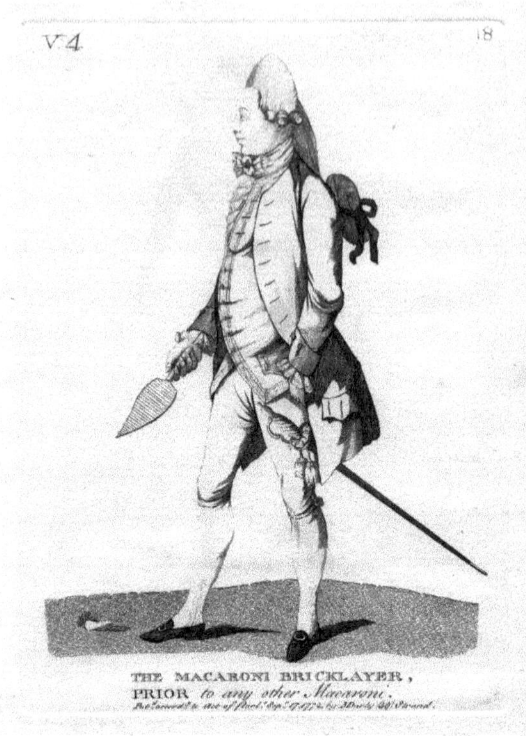

1.6 Matthew and Mary Darly, 'The macaroni bricklayer', 1772.

specifically (in the second half of the eighteenth century) a member of a set of young men who had travelled in Europe and extravagantly imitated Continental tastes and fashions.' By the early 1770s, it was widely recognized as 'a term of reproach to all ranks of people'.[48] Amelia Rauser has noted that while a certain degree of artifice was a prerequisite for polite intercourse, there was a corresponding concern with dressing in a manner appropriate to one's station: in social and cultural terms, the macaroni was regarded as a conspicuous, even dubious member of genteel society; he wore 'an inauthentic social mask' and 'exemplified the dangers of artifice'.[49]

Darly's prints of various macaroni characters drawn from the middling sorts – six sets of twenty-four portraits each were published between 1771 and 1774 – fall somewhere between the grand tourist caricatures of Pier Leone Ghezzi and the street vendors and hawkers popularized in so many *Cries of London* portfolios, including the now famous set by artist Paul Sandby (published in 1765). Shearer West notes how Darly's macaronis represented a wider range of class types drawn principally from the emerging bourgeoisie.[50] Thus, while the 'real macaronis' were part of a privileged aristocratic elite, and conspicuous by their exaggerated forms of dress and social behaviour, the representation of the macaroni grew to embrace a broader social demographic that saw his character 'as ubiquitous in all levels of social life': this in turn suggested a wider class audience. This specificity of individual figures as opposed to generic types situates them within a broader mid-eighteenth-century discourse regarding the nature of character and its representation in visual culture.[51] (Darly's bricklayer, described as 'Prior to any other Macaroni', is evidently a pun on a real person; most likely Thomas Prior, a bricklayer of Great Russell Street, Bloomsbury.[52]) However, while acknowledging that the comedic value of the prints resided in 'the association of a singularity of fashion with specific middle-class professions and behaviors', West locates Darly's representation of London's middling sorts within a political discourse centred on the primacy of private character in public life. Correspondingly, Amelia Rauser interprets the contemporary 'fascination with character', exemplified by the macaroni caricatures, as 'both a cautionary tale and a secret exemplar for the rising middle classes'.[53] In Ireland, according to Martyn Powell, social emulation by the lower sorts also carried political implications: the wearing of London and French fashions by the artisan classes posed 'a challenge to the Ascendancy's distinctiveness'.[54]

It is through this complex cultural lens that we must view Darly's 'Macaroni bricklayer'.[55] What aspects of his character are portrayed here? As social aspirant, his self-fashioning in bourgeois terms – wigs were recognized as a constituent element of a man's public persona – deliberately confounds easy interpretation of his place in the social pecking order: while wigs were worn by the better sort of tradesmen throughout the eighteenth century, a life of production was, as we have seen, generally considered anathema to the performance of gentility.[56] Brandishing both a sword (a fashionable accoutrement of a polite gentleman's wardrobe) and a trowel (the tool of a vulgar trade), the macaroni bricklayer attempts to strike a balance between usefulness and refinement. In his fine clothes he also represents an example of the contemporary concern with what Lawrence Klein has termed 'social transvestitism': he is literally 'wearing the "wrong" clothing for [his] social estate'.[57]

This collapse of social distinction represented by dress was in fact satirized by Robert Campbell's description of the tailor's trade, published in *The London tradesman* (1747):

> There are Numbers of Beings in about this Metropolis who have no other identical Existence than what the Taylor, Milliner, and Perriwig-Maker bestow upon them: *Strip them of these Distinctions, and they are quite a different Species of Beings; have no more Relation to their dressed selves*, than they have to the Great Mogul, and are as insignificant in Society as Punch, deprived of his moving Wires, and hung up upon a Peg.[58]

Campbell's satire was in fact born out of a general recognition among London's tradesmen who had, in the words of Neil McKendrick, 'already recognized the pervasive impact of fashion on the most diverse employment':[59] with dress representing 'the most public manifestation of the blurring of class divisions',[60] the bricklayer's expensive clothing and powdered wig indicate his understanding of 'the role of clothes in this process of social and economic change'.[61] This is surely the point of Darly's humorous print, which tapped into anxieties about the performative nature of dress and how it visually manifested the collapse of the social order.[62] John Kay's caricature of Edinburgh wright Francis Braidwood, published in 1789, makes a similar point using textual association and visual wordplay: in fashionable clothes, walking cane and foppish shoestrings – the most conspicuous item of his ensemble – the artisan literally and figuratively makes an ass of himself (Figure 1.7).[63]

Evidence of a wider antipathy to such display abounds in print media across the British Isles. Correspondents to the *Hibernian Journal*, in a series of letters published between 1776 and 1778, for example, habitually decried how Dublin's artisan class freely embraced such conspicuous, and inappropriate, signs of high fashion:

> Mechanics! Did I say? Why, Sirs, I do not know a Set of more formidable, conspicuous Macaronies in general than our very Apprentices; each of whom ... must have his hair tied up in a Queue or Club of ponderous Magnitude, toupeed, pomatumed, powdered, perfumed, &c. a *la-Mode de Paris* at least once a Week.[64]

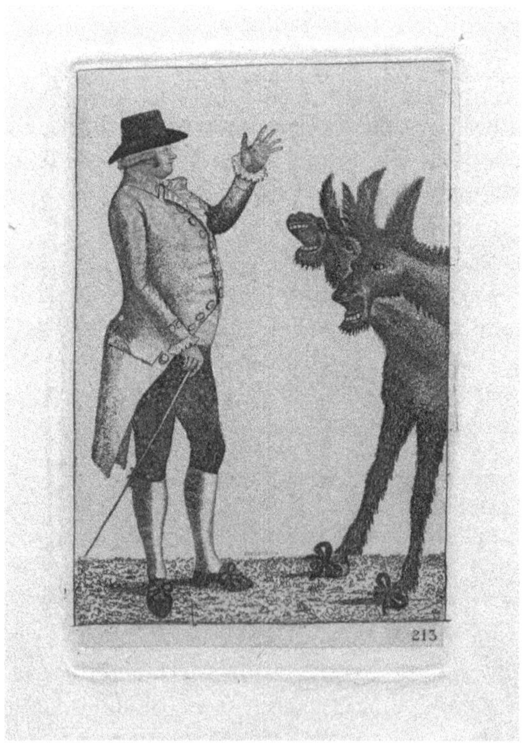

1.7 John Kay, *Francis Braidwood*, 1786.

Another writer wondered if such mimicry constituted 'a proper Education for the sons of Trade? Is it from men whose earliest Notions of Industry are stamped with Luxury, Foppery, and Extravagance, this kingdom must receive its commercial character.'[65] Indeed, the use of the terms 'mechanic' and 'sons of Trade' is arguably not without significance, the former being commonly used in eighteenth-century America 'to specify the limits of legitimate social aspiration' for those employed in manual trades.[66] This brings to mind the withering, retrospective description of eighteenth-century building tradesmen in James Elmes's *Lectures on architecture* (1821), where their lack of appreciation for the unornamented form of the Greek Doric order is equated with their fondness for modish dress:

> Batty Langley, it is true, had a school or academy, but his disciples were all carpenters; a few of them, calling themselves surveyors and builders, and practising carpentry and box-making, were alive in my remembrance; – hating the 'new fancied Doric,' (as they termed it), without a base, as much as they did a shirt without ruffles, or a wig without two good portly curls over each ear, and half a yard of tail behind; scorning its simple flutes without fillets, which they compared to ribbed stockings.[67]

A concern with fancy and, by extension, inappropriate dress is also made explicit in a criticism levelled by architect Sir William Chambers against Robert Smith, his foreman at Milton Abbey, Dorset: in a letter of November 1771, Chambers remarked to Smith, 'I thought your method of going on when I was at Milton a very odd one. Instead of appearing in your work like a Workman I found you always tripping about with your coat & waistcoat on.'[68] In generally advocating 'a simple Plainness' as evidence of 'The Elegance of a Trader or Man of Profession', these forms of public commentary and private admonition clearly addressed the social and moral implications of fashionable dress.[69] This sentiment was echoed in a pamphlet entitled *The miraculous power of clothes*, published in Philadelphia in 1772 (the same year as the 'Macaroni bricklayer'), satirizing the tailor's ability to 'quite literally make the man'. Stuart Blumin has pointed to the text's unambiguous message concerning 'the moral inversion caused by the veneration of exterior appearance rather than inner worth'.[70]

From elsewhere in the building world Darly lampoons the 'The antique architect' and 'The builder macaroni', but here the satire is arguably less pointed and the humour is correspondingly less immediate or appreciable (Figures 1.8 and 1.9): the aged figure of the builder surveys the ground beyond the frame of the image with an eyeglass, no doubt a pun on his role as a *speculator* (a 'builder' during the Georgian period could refer to a merchant or gentleman involved in property speculation, and not necessarily an individual drawn from the building trades); the architect is shown burdened with the trappings of a professional designer, including a book and a fragment of a classical entablature alluding to the increasingly

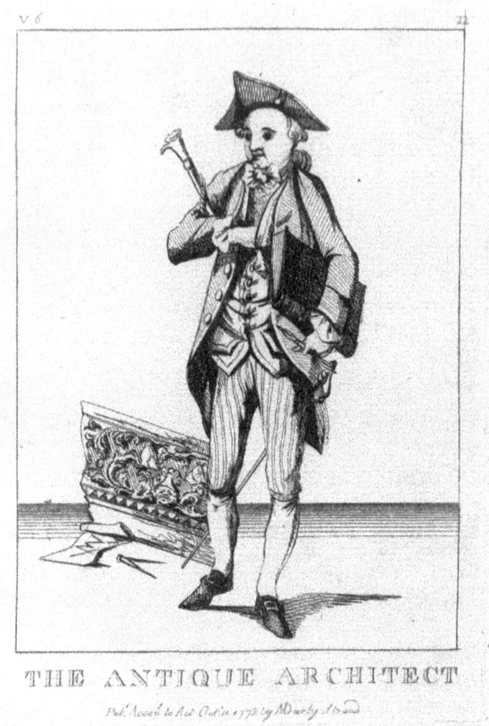

1.8 Matthew and Mary Darly, 'The antique architect', 1773.

bookish nature of architectural design – modern architects such as James 'Athenian' Stuart and Robert Adam published folios of antique archaeology to establish their professional credentials – and by extension the authority *to* design, fostered by grand tourism and a humanist education.[71]

The builder despised … and lionised

With so many building trades at his disposal, from carpenters and plumbers to glaziers and plasterers, why might Darly have selected the bricklayer to satirize? The answer may lie in the prevalence of brick as the material that defined modern domestic architecture in cities throughout the English-speaking world, from London and Bristol to Dublin and Limerick, and across the Atlantic Ocean to Philadelphia, Boston and Baltimore. But it also relates to the low opinion of the bricklayer generally, in terms of the mechanical, professional and commercial aspects of his business. Although the carpenter was an equally significant building capitalist throughout the English-speaking world – and in the American colonies was certainly a more conspicuous building speculator – bricklaying was synonymous with the business of house building. And the house builder, in Britain and Ireland particularly, was the representative figure of public scorn and ridicule.[72] The choice of bricklayer Thomas Prior for Darly's caricature of a

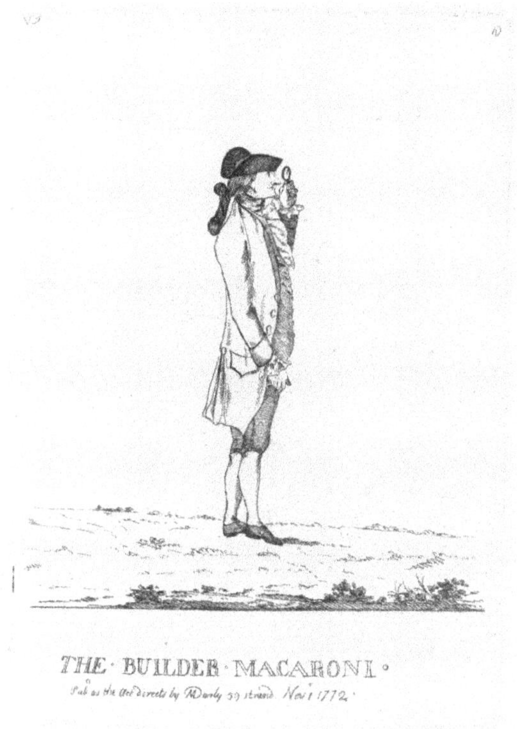

1.9 Matthew and Mary Darly, 'The builder macaroni', 1772.

bourgeois building tradesman – being 'Prior to any other Macaroni' – was evidently calculated on more than a pun: Rachel Stewart describes 'an exceptional level of building demand and supply' in London following the Peace of Paris in 1763, suggesting the bricklayer's pre-eminence among other socially mobile artisans and tradesmen.[73]

Robert Campbell's *The London tradesman*, noted above, published as a guide to the relative merits of the different trades and professions, describes and evaluates the trades associated with the art of building individually. Placing the bricklayer third in the order for building a house – after architect (design) and stonemason ('the first rank of tradesman') – Campbell's opinion is broadly disparaging:

> He differs from the Stone-Mason as much as his materials; his Skill consists, considering him as a mere Bricklayer, only in ranging his Brick even upon the Top of one another, and bedding them their proper Beds of Cements; for it is suppos'd, the Architect directs him in everything relating to Dimensions. But a Master Bricklayer thinks himself capable to raise a Brick House without the Tuition of an Architect: And in Town they generally know the just Proportions of Doors and Windows … and the other common Articles in a City-House, where the Carpenter, by the Strength of Wood, contributes more to the standing of the House than all the Bricklayer's Labour.[74]

A number of points are significant here. Although the architect is the authority on design, the bricklayer '*thinks* himself capable' of building 'a Brick House'. Moreover, while the bricklayer is 'generally' acquainted with the 'just Proportions' (read 'classical proportions') of architectural composition, the sound construction of a brick building is in fact the responsibility of the carpenter. On both counts – design and construction – the bricklayer is found wanting. This stinging denunciation is compounded in the ensuing paragraph, where building speculation, the principal means by which bricklayers and carpenters realized their own financial competence, is wholly denigrated. Acknowledging that bricklaying had the potential to be 'a profitable business', Campbell was unequivocal that success was conditional on the decision by individuals to 'confine themselves to work for others', meaning architects, and 'not launch out into Building-Projects of their own, which frequently ruin them'. In closing, all efforts at impartiality are abandoned and the tone of the text takes a mocking turn: 'It is no new Thing in London, for those Master-Builders to build themselves out of their own Houses, and fix themselves in Jail with their own Materials.'[75] The point of the pun is unambiguous: bricklayers should acknowledge their place in the architectural and building hierarchy; those that seek to rise above their station become the *architects* of their own social and economic downfall. This view was later echoed in Joseph Collyer's *The parent and guardian's directory* (1761), which, although advocating an education for bricklayers in trigonometry, arithmetic and drawing – the better to 'to draw plans, and to survey and estimate buildings, an essential part of the business of a master' – was nonetheless compelled to close with a familiar cautionary note: the individual might with industry realize a profitable business, unless he succumbs to the 'temptation of launching into building projects of his own, by which Bricklayers are frequently ruined'.[76]

At the crux of the 'problem' was the relationship between building economics and building construction. As early as 1703, author Richard Neve had voiced concerns about London's speculative building industry and its impact on the quality of construction: his 'greatest objection' to speculative houses being 'their slightness'.[77] Elizabeth McKellar has argued that it was the shift from timber-frame to brick shell construction during the course of the late seventeenth century that occasioned such concerns: the 'built-in obsolescence' of brick building 'being perfectly suited to the new market conditions' of early modern London.[78] Jules Lubbock's cultural history of taste in Britain, drawing on the so-called 'Luxury Debates' of the early 1700s, considers the complex relationship between commerce and architecture as embodied/represented in the form and spatial organization of London's terraced streets and squares. Admired as much, if not more, for its economic prosperity as for its architectural mien, the city's redbrick houses were, he argues, 'a compromise solution' to 'a long-running battle between the citizens of London and Westminster and the building speculators'.[79] As the greatness of a commercial nation was increasingly measured quantitatively not qualitatively – in the number, rather than design, of houses, streets and shops – so the plain brick terraced house emerged as a 'problem' within architectural discourse.

Much of the concern with the building class *per se* was predicated on the career of builder and economist Nicholas Barbon (c. 1640–c. 1698), whose notorious career as a property developer in late seventeenth-century London pioneered the system of speculative building that characterized the building industry thereafter. Barbon's *An apology for the builder* (1685) represented a first step in free market economics and argued, among other things, that property speculation was a response to the demands of the burgeoning consumer market in real estate. But this view was at odds with a majority opinion that viewed unfettered building development with suspicion.[80] Indeed, Roger North's description of Barbon's practice as 'more in economising ground for advantage … than the more noble aims of architecture, and all his aim was at profit', is widely recognized as a neat encapsulation of both the man and his legacy.[81] In 1724, Jonathan Swift's reflection on the speculative building industry in Ireland blamed the method 'introduced by Dr. *Barebone* at London, who died a bankrupt':

> The mason, the bricklayer, the carpenter, the slater, and the glazier, take a lot of ground, club to build one or more houses, unite their credit, their stock, and their money; and when their work is finished, sell it to the best advantage they can. But, as it often happens, and more every day, that their fund will not answer half their design, they are forced to undersell it at the first story, and are all reduced to beggary.[82]

Such concerns echoed the criticism in architectural discourse throughout the eighteenth century, becoming a leitmotif in treatises, pamphlets and the public press: the redbrick terraced or row house was dubious because it was the province of speculators. Writing in 1756, Isaac Ware lamented 'the art of building slightly', citing evidence of houses having 'fallen in before they were tenanted'.[83] As both architect and authority, Ware was of course at the vanguard of the construction of architectural authority, insisting that design and supervision of a building's construction was the province of the professionally trained architect. But he was also someone with experience in speculative building, having being involved in property development in London in the late 1730s.[84] Referring to the leasehold system adopted throughout the British Isles, Ware argued that 'unless his Grace [i.e. the aristocratic landowner] tye him down to articles', that is to rules and regulations regarding materials and quality of construction, the builder 'does not chuse to employ his money to the advantage'.[85] In Ware's estimation, then, not only should house building be corrected by Architecture (with a capital 'A'), but the building practices of builders should be corrected by controls instituted in covenants and regulations in ground leases: construction, not to mention design, was customarily sacrificed to increase profits. In this, Ware shared Robert Campbell's withering opinion:

> Both Carpenters and Joiners are Undertakers in Building as well as the Master Bricklayer; and are liable to split upon the same Rock of Building Projects: But a Gentleman who wants to build with Security as well as Beauty, would do well not to trust entirely to their Skill.[86]

Mistrust in the intellectual and manual aspects of the business of building also elicited satirical responses. For *Oikidia, or nutshells* (1785), architect James Peacock's elaborate conceit involved the invention of the semi-pseudonymous Jose MacPacke, styled a 'bricklayer's labourer'. This worked on two levels. On the one hand, the status of the supposed author served to underline for the reader the ineptitude of building tradesmen as arbiters of architectural taste generally; by the same token, the advice on topics such as propriety, regularity and proportion – the *sine qua non* of architecture – was 'voiced' by a building tradesman. Described by Eileen Harris as 'a contrary little book', it is often difficult to distinguish between the satirical and didactic voices.[87] Nevertheless, the text is littered with direct attacks on the building industry in general and the house builder in particular. In an appendix that takes the form of a series of 'observations and reflections', with advice for those engaged in building from design to construction, Peacock is unequivocal that if a house 'has perhaps been built for Sale by a Speculator' then 'its durability may be suspicious'. With reference to the prodigious building activity then underway in the Marylebone area of the West End of town, he continues:

> [A] good maxim in building is, 'A little stronger than strong enough;' this, to the speculative adventurer, inured to the maxims and habits of the Mary-le-bone School, is as bad as flat heresy; he goes on calculating his substances, and adapting the qualities of his materials, and the manner of connecting them with such nicety and address, as to decree their dissolution precisely six months after the expiration of his lease.[88]

Implicit and explicit in all of this is the criticism of the speculative builder. The builder turned property developer was not to be trusted with design or construction. But 'builder' was itself a slippery term, as we have seen, and it is clear that the building tradesman became a scapegoat for a wider, systemic issue. Already in the late seventeenth century, the opportunities offered by land and property development attracted figures from outside the building industry. While bricklayers, carpenters, plasterers and others certainly speculated in their own right, and increasingly so by the end of the eighteenth century, the 'builders' and 'master builders' criticized in public discourse also numbered those attracted purely by the potential for capital gain but with no formal training in the building crafts.[89] As Stefan Muthesius has noted, the introduction of building

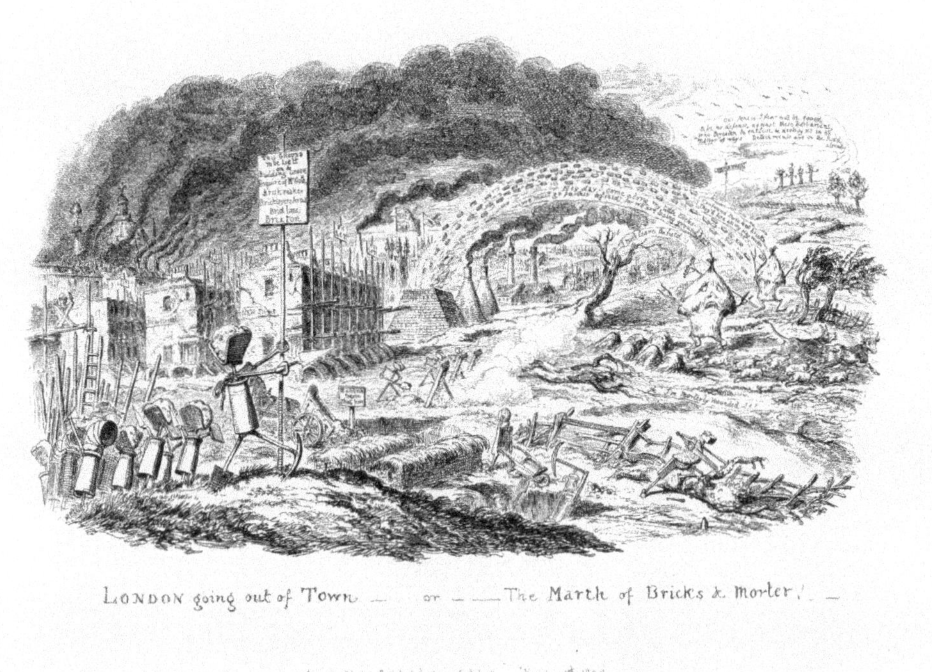

1.10 George Cruikshank, *London going out of town – or – The march of bricks and morter*, 1829.

regulations was an attempt to control builders, speculators and landowners equally.[90]

The invocation of an occupational formation in trade, as opposed to architecture, was also a device used to challenge an individual's character and authority. Professional rivalry inspired architect and polemicist John Gwynn to satirize architect Robert Mylne as 'Mr. Trowel' in his *London and Westminster improved* (1766). This was apparently in response to Mylne describing Gwynn as being 'late of another profession', hinting at his apprenticeship to the carpentry trade and thereby calling into question both his credentials and his reputation.[91] Ironically, both had come up through the building trades – Mylne was descended from a renowned dynasty of stonemasons to the Scottish crown – which made the rebuff more pointed: architectural connoisseurship was resolutely dissociated from the mechanical world of the building tradesman.

This apparently symbiotic relationship between sprawling urbanization, shoddy construction and the greedy builder arguably reached its apogee in George Cruikshank's popular cartoon *London going out of town – or – The march of bricks and morter*, published in 1829 (Figure 1.10).[92] Here the encroachment of the countryside is underway by a series of 'new street' houses formed by legions of building automatons ingeniously composed of shovels, pick-axes and hods. At the centre of the composition a figure erects a sign bearing the legend:

> This Ground to be Lett
> On a Building Lease
> Enquire of Mr Goth
> Brickmaker
> Bricklayers Arms
> Brick Lane
> Brixton

Cruikshank's identification of the builder/developer as 'Mr Goth' is at once an inspired reference to the early modern dialectic between the classical and the gothic, but also, and more pointedly, to the idea of the builder as a vandal, responsible for London's unfettered, jerry-built urban expansion. The geographical identifiers of 'Brick Lane' and 'Brixton' also work on two levels: as wordplay and as a means of situating the culprit in parts of London that were either decidedly working class (the East End) or far from the centres of fashion (south of the river).[93]

In contrast to the mocking satirical tone of Darly and Cruikshank, but sharing their moralistic tone, are the visual and textual representations of building tradesmen in *The book of trades, or library of the useful arts*, first published in London in 1804–5 and revised in many editions into the 1820s. Designed to 'acquaint the rising generation with our various trades', the book was clearly aimed at the offspring of the lower and middling sorts: in this it shares a common purpose with Robert Campbell and Joseph Collyer but dispenses with their often derogatory judgments and appraisals. Representing almost all of the principal trades associated with the building industry, *The book of trades* carefully delineated the techniques and skills of each craft in a decidedly neutral tone of voice: the carpenter is responsible for 'framing and joining pieces of timber, and fitting them up in houses and other buildings'; bricklaying is 'the art of cementing brick … hence its use and importance for building walls, houses, &c.'. Of particular interest here is the invocation of historic precedent: the narrative of the bricklayer's occupation, for example, describes some of England's most celebrated brick-built monuments, including Herstmonceux Castle, East Sussex, and Lambeth Palace, London; by implication, the trade of bricklaying is elevated to the realm of architecture. More significantly, the bricklayer is illustrated in the active (proper?) role of 'building a house': the carpenter, by contrast, is shown preparing the various timber components (Figures 1.11 and 1.12).

Related to these are the textual and visual characterizations found in *Little Jack of all trades*, a children's book first published in 1804 by William Darton (1755–1819), a prominent member of the Society of Friends in London. It was subsequently published in Philadelphia (1808)

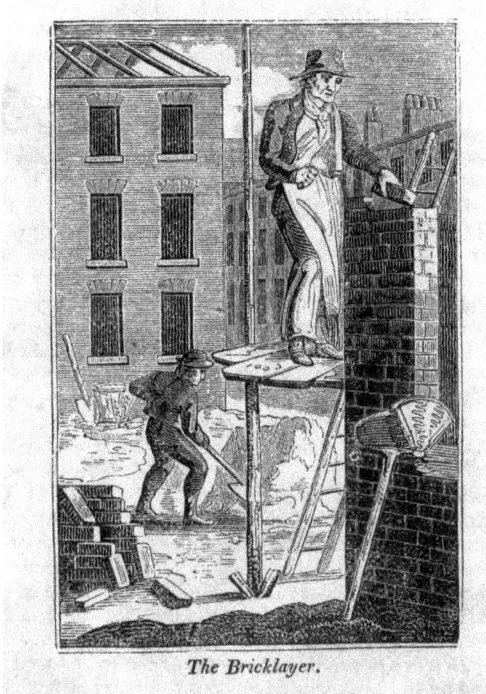

1.11 'The bricklayer' from *The book of trades* (London, 1818).

and Boston (1813), where its emphasis on occupations involving manual labour rather than merchant commerce no doubt appealed to Quaker and Puritan ideals of community and respectability, and where, in the decades following the American Revolution, the artisan enjoyed a new political significance.[94] In illustration, rhyming verse and descriptive explanation, the character and merits of a range of trades are delineated in plain, simple terms in order to appeal to the book's 'little readers'. With individual entries describing a number of building trades, including carpenter, mason and glazier, here it is the brickmaker (Figure 1.13), arguably the lowliest trade in terms of acuity and skill, who is elevated beyond all (reasonable?) expectation:[95]

> Fine cities are London, Bath, Bristol, and York,
> And Dublin and Edinburgh, Glasgow and Cork;
> But what were they once but a heather a swamp,
> Of little mean hovels, dark, dirty, and damp?
>
> Who made these large cities, now tell me, I pray?
> Who but your poor Brick-maker, cover'd with clay.
> Your proud marble monuments shine in cut stones,
> But I rais'd the fame of Great Inigo Jones.[96]

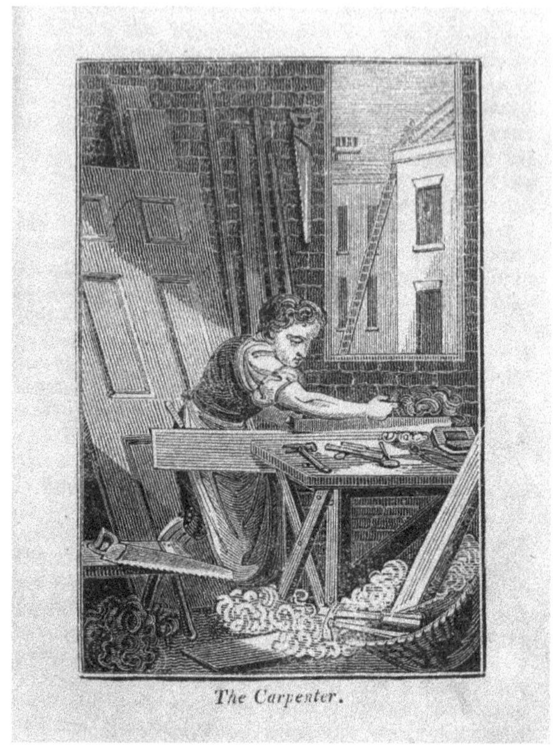

1.12 'The carpenter' from *The book of trades* (London, 1818).

Notwithstanding the fact that cities like Bath and Edinburgh are not substantially built of brick, the point here is that the honest labour of the 'poor Brick-maker, cover'd in clay' is equated with architectural modernity and building quality; and, moreover, with Inigo Jones, an architect of the first importance in eighteenth-century British architectural theory. Alerted to the perils inherent in building construction – 'we are indeed justly alarmed at seeing some climb the ladders laden with hods of mortar, and others standing at an immense height on narrow and tottering planks' – the reader is encouraged to 'be very thankful' to brickmakers 'who thus hazard their lives, in order to build us commodious habitations'. (This commendation is also extended to the carpenters, without whose labours 'We should be obliged to sleep in the open air, and suffer from the cold of winter and the heat of summer.') By contrast, the opening stanza addressed to the bricklayer, who first appeared in the second edition of the book, is cautionary in tone, demanding judgement and mindfulness in everyday practice: 'The firm foundation lay with care, Nor build thy castles in the air'. Here, too, it seems, the dignity of building labour (bricklaying) is contrasted with the potential ignominy of building business (speculation).[97] Unsurprisingly, these depictions of 'honest and useful' tradesmen share a formal vocabulary

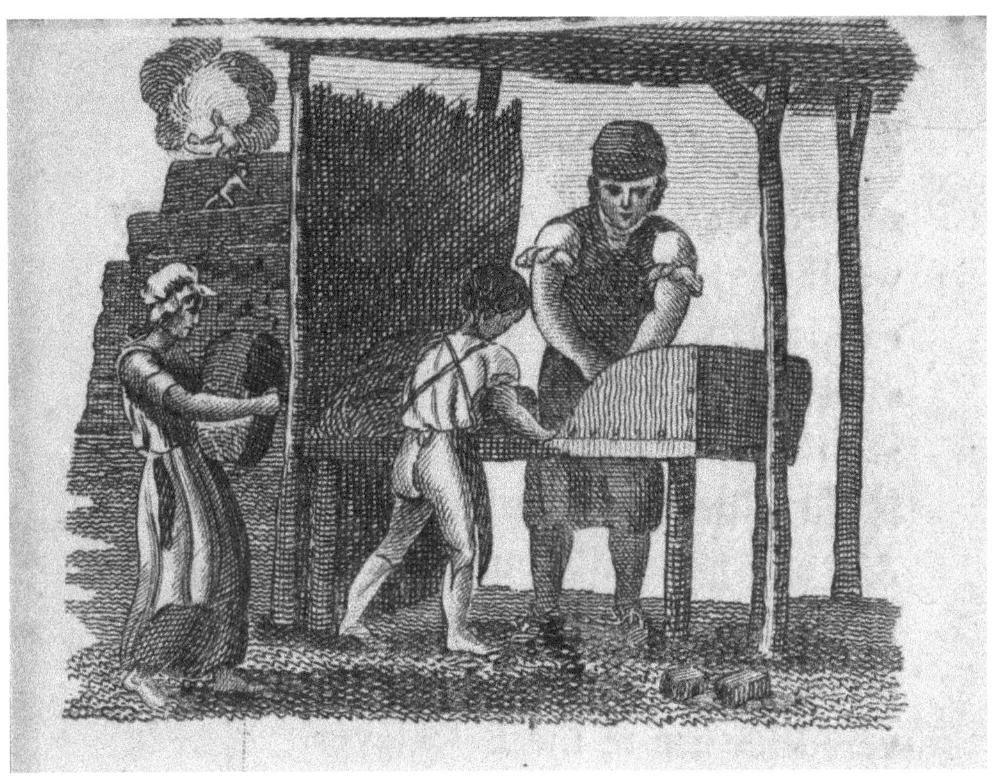

1.13 'The brickmaker' from *Little Jack of all trades* (London, 1814).

with officially sanctioned representations of the building industry, such as the vignette on the membership certificates of the Bricklayers Company of Philadelphia, founded in 1792 (Figure 1.14). While the focus is very much on the working individuals who dominate the foreground, the visual depiction of buildings of different magnitudes – from the humble brick row house to the decorative church steeple – signifies the central importance of the bricklayer for the city's building and architectural industries. This point is further underscored by the brick-wall pattern that provides a literal 'support' for this narrative scene.

Of course, such textual and visual representations of the house builder – from disreputable macaroni to decent labourer – reflect different temporalities, as well as divergent cultural and geographical specificities. But collectively, they speak to the complex ways in which the building tradesmen generally, and the house builder particularly, were perceived in architectural and social discourse. In broader cultural terms, the sardonic view of the producer (house builder) and the product (brick house), and their interdependent relationship, can be read as a symptom of the emerging architectural profession and the politics of design at mid-century.

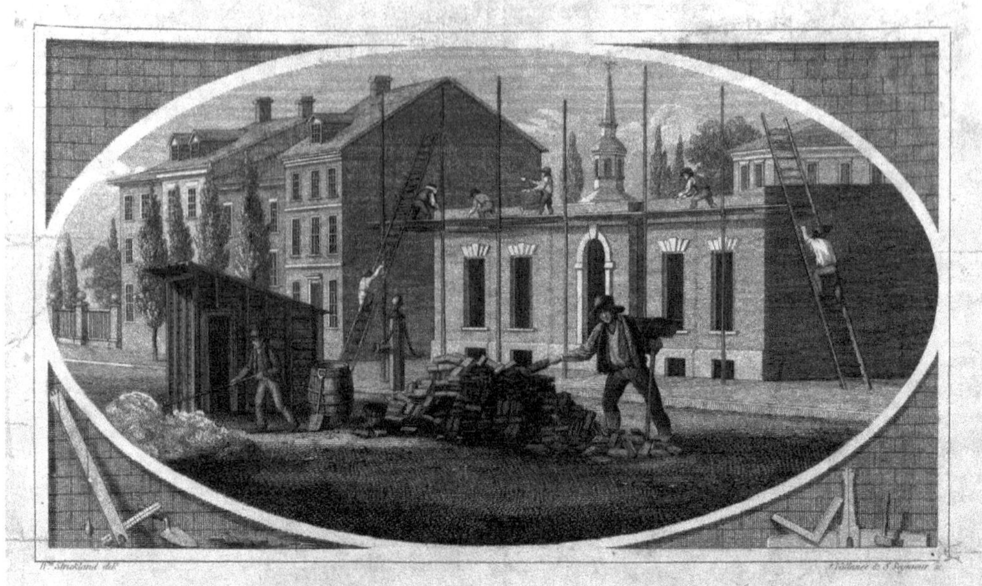

1.14 John Cromwell's membership certificate for the Bricklayers' Company of Philadelphia (detail), 1811.

Conversely, the literature extolling the moral sincerity and honest virtue of the building labourer may be understood in terms of the paradigm shift in building process and labour organization that emerged in the decades either side of 1800, predicated on an increasingly capitalized and industrialized building industry.

A genteel life in trade

Despite the accusations of contemporary and modern discourse, the house builder was necessarily invested in design and architectural taste as a constituent component of his reputation. As we shall explore in the ensuing chapters, this is evident from the way in which builders negotiated the design of the house façade, the decoration of the house interior and the marketing and selling of real estate. Criticism of the building world, as we have seen, neglected to consider the simple economic equation understood by all building entrepreneurs: the success of a building business depended on reputation; and a good reputation could only be achieved through modern, tasteful design and sound construction. Indeed, if brick houses were falling in as regularly as the eighteenth-century public press and architectural critic would have us believe, then we would hardly have the substantial built evidence that has survived down to the present day and which remains a constituent part of the everyday urban character of cities from Bristol to Baltimore. With reference to newspaper advertising, trade cards, broadsides and other aspects of print culture, we now turn our attention to how house builders and decorators distinguished themselves within the commercial marketplace. As Ann Bermingham has argued, 'We need to explore the way in which individuals appropriate cultural forms to their own individual ends, as tools to construct social selves; at times to comply with and at other times to resist institutional and social coercions.'[98]

Taste by association

As London remained the cultural centre of the English-speaking Atlantic World throughout the eighteenth century, so an individual's apprenticeship or tutelage under an English architect, designer or luxury goods manufacturer represented a sign of distinguished accomplishment.[99] Newspaper advertisements attest to the enduring appeal of imported British goods and services, a preference that is now widely recognized as an established characteristic of luxury consumption in eighteenth-century Ireland and America. So endemic was this predisposition to English tastes that one acerbic visitor to Dublin in 1797 decried the lack of encouragement for native 'genius', observing that 'A foreigner is always preferred by the Irish nobility.'[100]

Just as Irish manufacturers and retailers advertised their role as agents for their London counterparts, so building tradesman invoked the names of fashionable English architects to signify their own credentials and thereby generate professional advantage. In 1780, Dublin carpenter Daniel Quigley's reference to 'eight Years in London under the first Architects there, such as Messrs. Adam, Chambers, Paine, Wiatt, &c.' was no vain conceit: although his employment under these figures has not been established, English architects enjoyed extensive Irish patronage throughout the eighteenth century.[101] Daniel Murphy, plasterer, having apparently 'received his education and professional knowledge under the ingenious James Wyatt, Esq; Architect' in England, advised the nobility and gentry of Cork in 1781 that he executed decorative plasterwork 'in the antique grotesque style' as well as 'colouring of the apartments in the manner now practised in the Cities of London and Westminster'.[102] Given Wyatt's extensive country house practice in Ireland from the early 1770s, the significance of this association would not have been lost on Murphy's intended audience.

We find similar approaches among American tradesmen. In Philadelphia in 1773, the enterprising carpenter William Williams, having 'lately returned' from London, advertised his capacity to build in the 'new, bold, light and elegant taste, which has been lately introduced by the great architect of the Adelphi Buildings'.[103] Cleverly designed to appeal to the cultivated and the parvenu alike, who may or may not have understood the reference to Robert Adam's Thameside development, Williams's announcement generates an affinity between accomplished producer and discerning consumer. In 1794, Joseph Bowes announced that he was 'lately arrived from Europe', having spent 'several years past' as a draughtsman in the office of 'the celebrated Robert Adams [*sic*]'. Here, the 'opportunities' gained in the service of 'this Great Man' was Bowes's principal calling card, but he also employed other textual ciphers.[104] While the buildings enumerated by him in London, Glasgow and Edinburgh were certainly beyond the inspection of his Philadelphia audience, this was clearly not the point. Indeed, throughout the eighteenth century, 'London' was habitually a sign of quality and fashion in and of itself: in 1765, Dobie and Clow, 'Builders' of Division-Street, New York, undertook building and decorative work 'after the London Taste'.[105]

The Irish capital evidently enjoyed a reputation as a centre of excellence in craftsmanship and architectural taste in its own right. As 'second city', it boasted a series of superlative public buildings and aristocratic garden squares after the English model, and sustained patronage for London-based architects. In Baltimore in 1789, Joseph Kennedy, a 'Stucco-workman, Plasterer and Plain-painter' from Dublin, performed 'in the most approved and latest Fashions – Having been regularly bred under as good Workmen as any in Ireland'.[106] Carpentry work 'in the modern taste, equal to any now done in the city of Dublin', was advertised in the *Pennsylvania Evening Herald* in 1785. The author of this notice, James Hoban, further distinguished himself by reference to the 'different premiums' he had received for architectural drawing 'from the Dublin Society'.[107] Although a familiarity with the name and function of that improving institution among a general Philadelphia readership must remain a matter for speculation, Hoban's purpose was unambiguous. (This remained an important calling card for Hoban: by 1790, and then resident in Charleston, South Carolina, he described the drawing schools of the Dublin Society as 'one of the first academies of arts and sciences in Europe'.)[108]

While the veracity of these claims should not necessarily be taken at face value – the greater distance between London and Philadelphia compared with London and Dublin, for example, certainly allowed for bolder claims that could not be so readily substantiated – the point of the exercise was to aspire to an improved station within the building industry, and to create an urbane professional discernment based on the ability to work in a fashionable and tasteful manner. Taken together, these self-aggrandizing advertisements confirm that 'aspirants sought incorporation in the class above them, not collaboration with those below them'.[109]

Trade cards and broadsides: marketing taste

The eighteenth-century building tradesman's relationship with print culture was complex and dynamic. It was also, by turns, active and passive. In their study of Georgian sales and marketing techniques, Maxine Berg and Helen Clifford have argued that in an 'economy of persuasion', manufacturers and retailers adopted innovative merchandising and advertising strategies 'to convey messages of discriminating taste'.[110] Building tradesmen were no exception. In Chapter 4 we will see how builders advertised their proficiency as arbiters of architectural tastes, borrowing techniques and strategies from the commercial worlds occupied by the auctioneer and the genteel axis of manufacturing and retailing. Here, we will consider how builders used trade cards to emphasize the politer dimensions of the building business.[111] As culture itself became available to a wider social stratum during the course of the seventeenth and eighteenth centuries, so builders and decorators turned to more sophisticated forms of self-presentation. The purpose of this was twofold: to make publicly visible their trade specialism in order to attract business, and to create professional distinction among their peers. As taste was increasingly understood as the preserve of the consumer, so the entrepreneur understood the relationship between culture, commodification and social performance.[112]

Just as experience in London was frequently invoked to create professional distinction in newspaper advertisements, so the trade card signified professional character, reputation in business and credentials in taste. Forming part of what Berg and Clifford have described as 'a wider context of graphic and print culture ... addressed to attracting individuals to the market place', illustrated trade cards emerged as a key promotional tool of the luxury goods trades during the course of the eighteenth century.[113] Performing various economic functions simultaneously – often acting as advertisement, invoice, receipt and price list at one and the same time – cards and billheads were more important to early modern advertising than newspapers or broadsides.

Following the example of entrepreneurs like Josiah Wedgwood and Matthew Boulton, who avoided the advertising strategies used by 'common shopkeepers' – disparaging newspapers and preferring 'private' displays rather than 'public' shops – the use of trade cards by building tradesmen was evidently a strategy designed to attract and appeal to a particular kind of customer, and to create an impression of the individual that elevated them from the 'lower sort' of common labourers and journeymen. In this manner the trade card became a sign for the builder's shop – in some cases literally. The finely engraved design for Green's bricklayers and builders firm, with its illustration of a three-storey brick building, falls into this category: no doubt a representation of their actual business premises (with sign board), it also signifies their particular trade specialism (Figure 1.15).[114]

Since newspaper advertising rarely relied on images, and then typically in a limited pictorial or figurative sense, the design quality of the trade card and the handbill carried greater currency in terms of marketing taste. Indeed, while the relative expense of printing trade cards meant that not all artisans could afford a bespoke design – and standardized layouts available

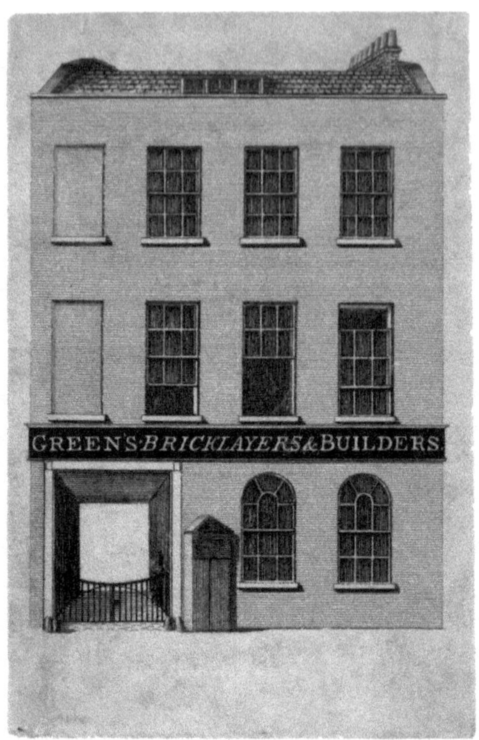

1.15 Trade card of 'Green's bricklayers and builders', n.d.

for customization were already popular by mid-century – Berg and Clifford have argued that their application represented 'a very conscious strategy of promotion'.[115] With this in mind, those bricklayers, carpenters and plasterers who took advantage of the opportunities offered by trade cards might be counted among the more professionally astute: equivalent in size to the modern business card, trade cards served unambiguous networking and promotional purposes.[116] On building sites and in drawing-rooms, not to mention specialist venues such as clubs and societies, the circulation of trade cards conferred personal distinction. Their portability, a key aspect of their commercial function, was akin to titles such as Batty Langley's *The builder's pocket companion* (1747) or William Pain's *The builder's pocket-treasure* (1766).

Cards and billheads took various forms to suit different requirements – being printed on a variety of stock of varying sizes – and embraced the stylistic diversity now regarded as a constituent element of eighteenth-century design: rococo, 'Gothick', Chinoiserie, neoclassicism. Unsurprisingly, Berg and Clifford note an increase in the use of classical iconography from the 1760s, with an emphasis on the 'transcending association with a particular idea of the classical'.[117] A striking example of this is the trade

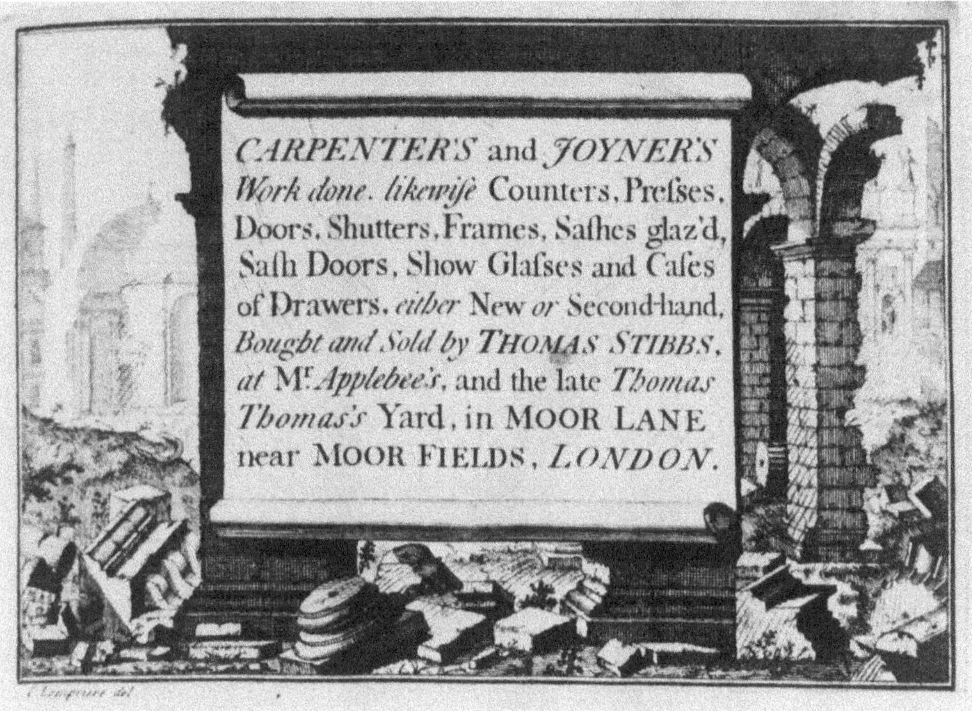

1.16 Trade card of Thomas Stibbs, carpenter and joiner of Moorfields, London, n.d.

card of Thomas Stibbs in Moorfields (Figure 1.16). Against a Roman architectural backdrop of Piranesian grandeur, Stibbs announces his business in 'carpenter's and joyner's work', but also in the decidedly non-genteel trade in second-hand goods 'bought and sold'. Significantly, while the romantic visualization of classical ruins is therefore decidedly at odds with the textual description of Stibbs's actual trade specialism in presses, doors, frames and shutters, this deliberate opacity, it seems, represented an established method used by retailers when 'the commodities for sale were difficult to depict seductively on their own'.[118]

A more direct affinity between the service offered and its visualization – achieving a balance between the semantic fields of image and text – is found in the trade cards of plasterers, reflecting the longstanding process of translation from printed page to decorated surface. Here, too, distinctly individual relationships with architectural tastes and fashionable novelties may be discerned by a close reading of discrete designs. While that of B. Johnson of New Compton Street (Figure 1.17) includes elements of both the rococo and neoclassical ornamental vocabularies, arguably hinting at a lingering conservatism, that of G. Silk of Leather Lane, Holborn (Figure 1.18), is more appreciably modern, being equivalent to the fashionable arabesque cartouches and related framing devices

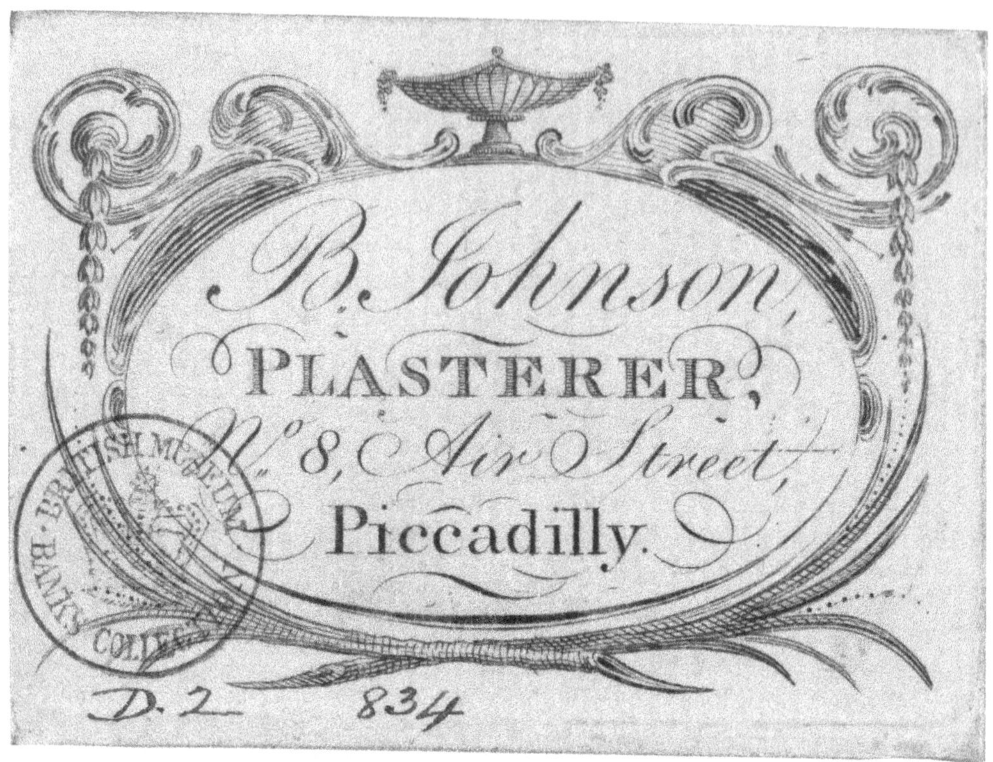

1.17 Trade card of B. Johnson, plasterer of Piccadilly, London, c. 1786.

published by London-based designers such as Michelangelo Pergolesi and Placido Columbani. Such cards also confirm the important association between illustrated trade cards and pattern books, both of which acted as 'transmitters of fashionable forms'.[119] (A Pergolesi design for a 'composition ornament manufactory' in Great Portland Street, London is further testament to this interdependence.) Nor was this level of semantic sophistication confined to the major metropolitan centres, evidenced by the trade card of Alexander McLeod, a plasterer working in the small village of Winkfield, Berkshire (Figure 1.19). Just as the text establishes both his London credentials and his commercial competitiveness, so McLeod's abilities in 'Ornamental Work' are represented by finely engraved figurative and decorative elements. By contrast, London trade cards often took the opportunity to caution potential clients against substandard workmanship or materials: George Hutchison, a painter and gilder of the Haymarket, warned of 'Counterfeits and Interlopers' who 'too often impose on the Publick as Painters, and spoil the Work, to the great Detriment of those that employ them'; Jaques of Holborn, manufacturers of 'every sort of Ornament Work in the Building line', advised customers to 'Beware of Piratical Productions'.

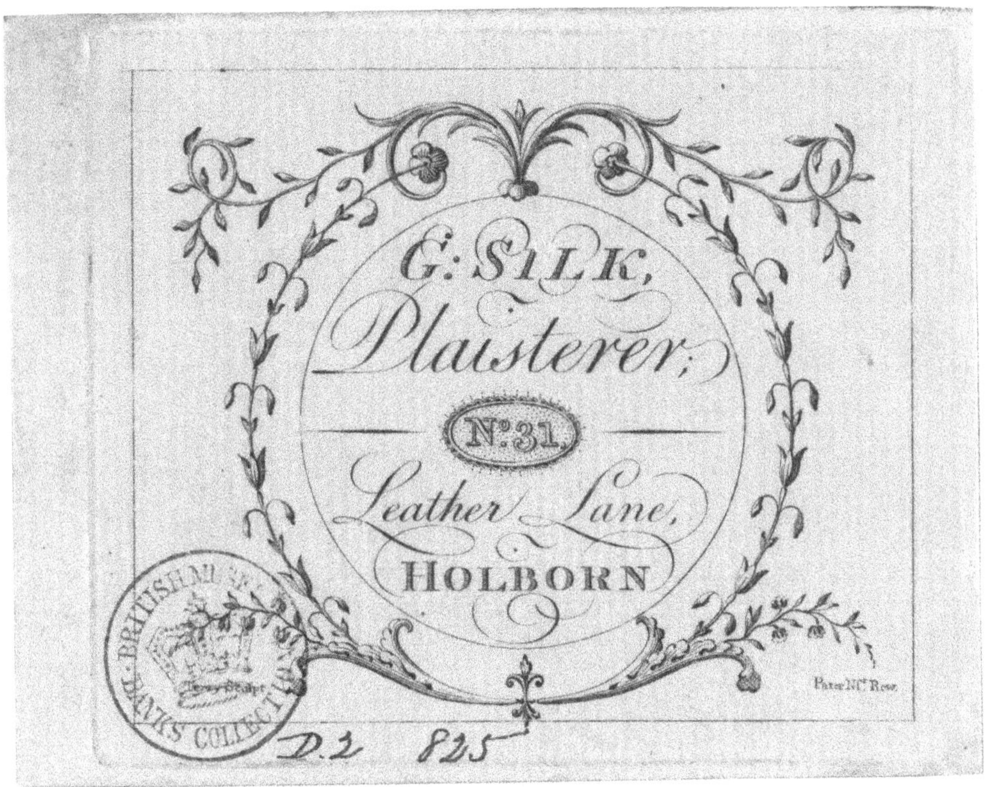

1.18 Trade card of G. Silk, plasterer of Holborn, London, c. 1788.

A decorative emphasis was not confined to the cards of house decorators, and other building trades pursued the persuasive rhetoric of taste making through surprising yet sophisticated combinations of text and image. The trade card of carpenter William Hughes is instructive in this respect (Figure 1.20). In a series of cartouches formed by husk chains and ribbons, that most Adamesque of decorative surrounds, Hughes illustrates both the intellectual (design) and mechanical (construction) aspects of his trade, as well as the product of his business (the house).[120] London bricklayer Edward Weston's card is even closer to those of decorators like Johnson and Silk in its use of the antique grotesque vocabulary: studiously avoiding any allusion to the business or trade of bricklaying, it focuses instead on signifying his understanding of architectural fashion (Figure 1.21). In so doing, Weston not only elevates himself above the everyday practice of 'ranging his Brick even upon the Top of one another', but shifts the emphasis from utility (construction) to beauty (decoration). With arguably no parity, then, between the nature of the business or trade advertised and its visualization in print, the trade cards of Stibbs, Weston and others should be seen as symptomatic of an increasingly 'coherent and codified visual language' that spoke to

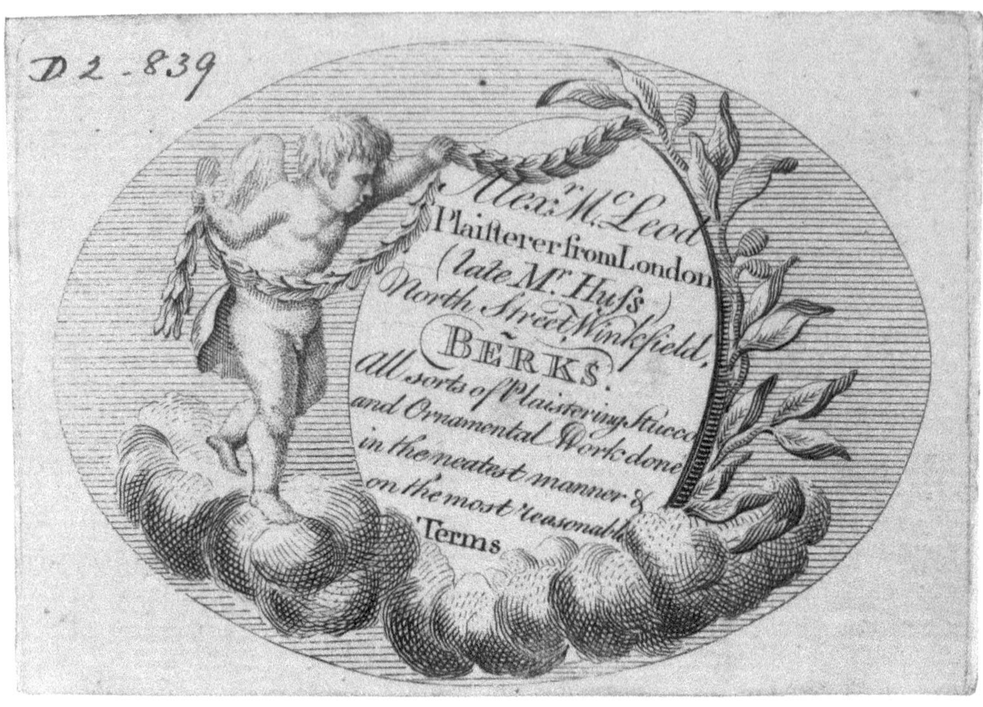

1.19 Trade card of Alexander McLeod, plasterer of Winkfield, Berkshire, c. 1794.

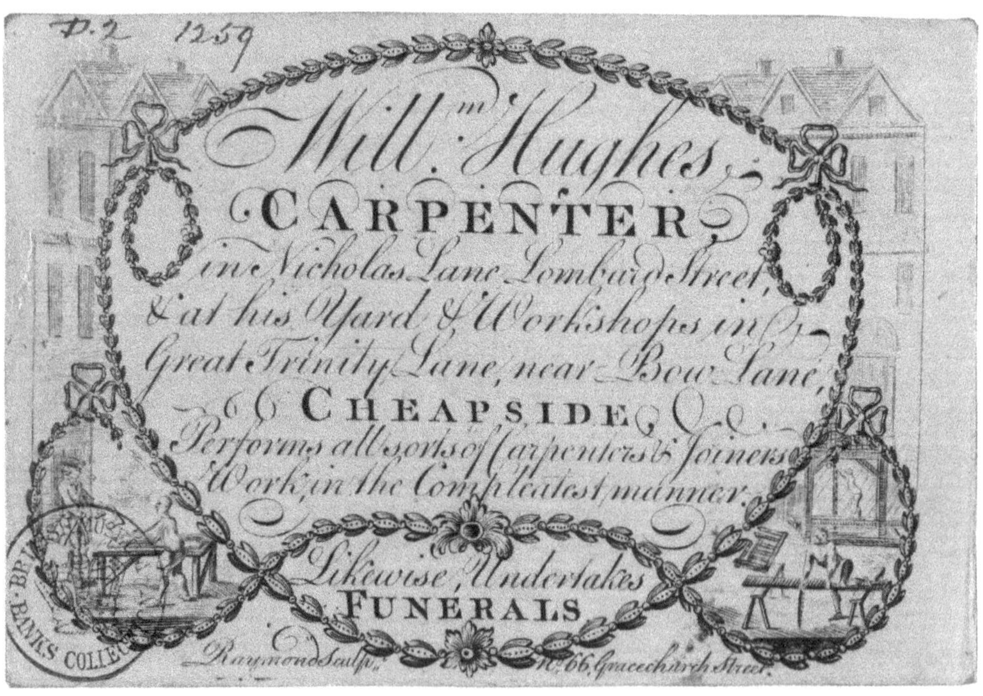

1.20 Trade card of William Hughes, carpenter of Cheapside, London, c. 1791.

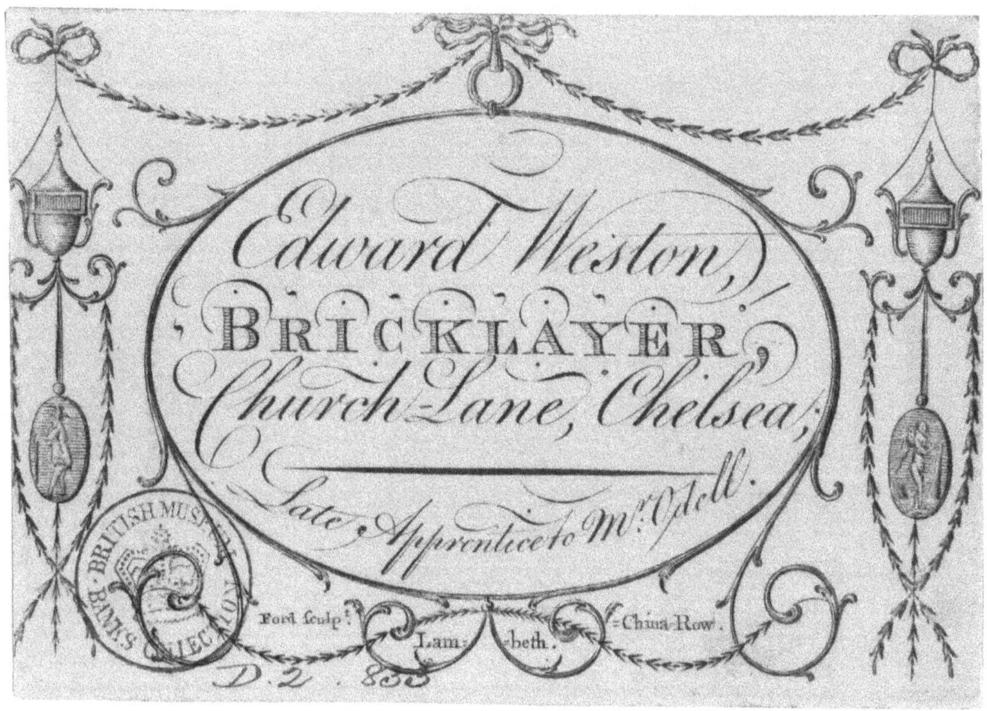

1.21 Trade card of Edward Weston, bricklayer of Chelsea, London, c. 1799.

universal tropes about taste[121] – the preponderance of elegant Adamesque framing devices to advertise trades and businesses of all descriptions at this time being recognized as a graphic convention for representing ideas of quality and taste through more subtle, abstract means.[122]

Cards, handbills and broadsides might often be designed along a more decidedly mercantile bent, yet remain ‘polite’ in tone and visual appearance. The elegant typographic design of William Salmon’s card dispenses with illustrative allusions to style and taste, and focuses instead on itemizing the wide range of prepared ornament available to architect, gentleman and tradesman alike from his shop in Dublin’s Anglesea Street (Figure 1.22).[123] More obviously commercial still is the 1806 broadside of composition ornament manufacturer George Andrews, whose direct appeal to the ‘citizens’ of Boston eschewed visual niceties (both in terms of text and image) in favour of marketing his goods and terms clearly and unambiguously (Figure 1.23). Indeed, while Philippa Hubbard acknowledges that trade cards were, in a consumer economy dominated by complex systems of credit, distinct from the more commercially oriented handbills in terms of ‘quality and select distribution’, she further argues for the place of the trade card in ‘operations of credit’ – namely, as a form of invoice in the recovery of debt – and concludes that their economic

S A L M O N's

Ornament, Chimney Piece and Composition Manufactory,

No. 5, ANGLESEA-STREET, near COLLEGE-GREEN,

D U B L I N;

WHERE Gentlemen, Architects, Surveyors, Builders, &c. may be ſupplied with ornamented Chimney Pieces, Door and Window Cornices; alſo Ornaments for Chimney Pieces, Frontiſpieces, Door Caps, Window Cornices, Door and Window Architraves, Pillaſters, Pannels for Doors and Shutters, Kertouches for Stairs, and every Article in the Building Branch.

Carvers, Guilders, and Cabinet-makers, may likewiſe be ſupplied with all kinds of Ornaments and Mouldings for Glaſs Frames, Gerandoles, Chairs, Tables, &c. &c. on the loweſt Terms.

☞ Iriſh and French Plaſter, prepared and unprepared, at the loweſt Prices.

*** Country Orders punctually attended to.

1.22 Trade card of William Salmon, ornament manufactory at Anglesea Street, Dublin, c. 1795.

To Builders.

Compoſition Ornaments, for ſale

At *No.* 30, *Cambridge-street,* Corner of *Belknap-street.*

GEORGE ANDREWS, *Reſpectfully* acquaints the *Citizens* of Boston, that his *Composition Ornaments* have arrived from his Manufactory, No. 51, Barclay-street, *New-York,* and *City* of *Waſhington,* among which are Tablets of the Likeneſs of the late *celebrated Gen. Hamilton, Eagle, American Arms Tablets,* Likewiſe, *Neptune,* and a great variety of other *Tablets,* and *Ornaments* properly adapted for *Chimney Pieces, Door Caps, Pilasters,* &c. of a peculiarly *Elegant Composition,* which he is determined to sell on moderate terms, if applied for within a few days. Such Gentlmen as have commenced, or purpose Building, will find it to their interest to purchase from him while here, as they can be packed up so as to suit at any time hereafter.

Boston, June 16, 1806.

1.23 Broadside of George Andrews, composition ornament manufacturer of New York, 1806.

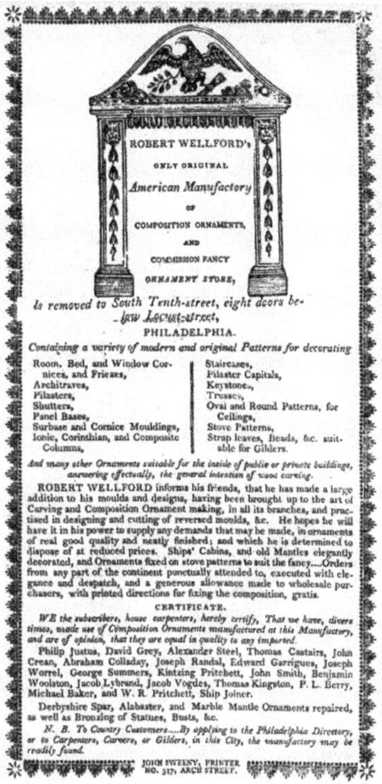

1.24 Handbill of Robert Wellford, ornament manufactory at 10th Street, Philadelphia, c. 1811.

functions were diverse and wide ranging.[124] This is an important point. While the printed cards and handbills of genteel shopkeepers and retailers might well have acted primarily as a form of *aide mémoire*, those of builders and decorators were likely employed in more complex patterns of social and commercial exchange relations: given the particulars of the contracting and subcontracting system – the mechanism by which houses were built – they necessarily addressed a broad spectrum of actors from materials and hardware suppliers to journeymen and labourers.[125] A good example of this is the handbill, dated 1811, of Robert Wellford's 'American Manufactory of Composition Ornaments' in Tenth Street, Philadelphia (Figure 1.24). While the illustration simply demonstrates the application of his prepared ornament (as figurative and decorative additions for architraves, pilasters and window shutters), the text operates on a number of levels: as a list of goods and services provided; as general advertising puff; and, more significantly, as an apparently impartial endorsement of the quality of his stock in a testimonial autographed by eighteen of the city's most distinguished house builders. (Wellford's shrewd use of 'patriotic' imagery, in the form of eagles and other decidedly American symbols, was also part of a wider trend in advertising that would become *de rigueur* by

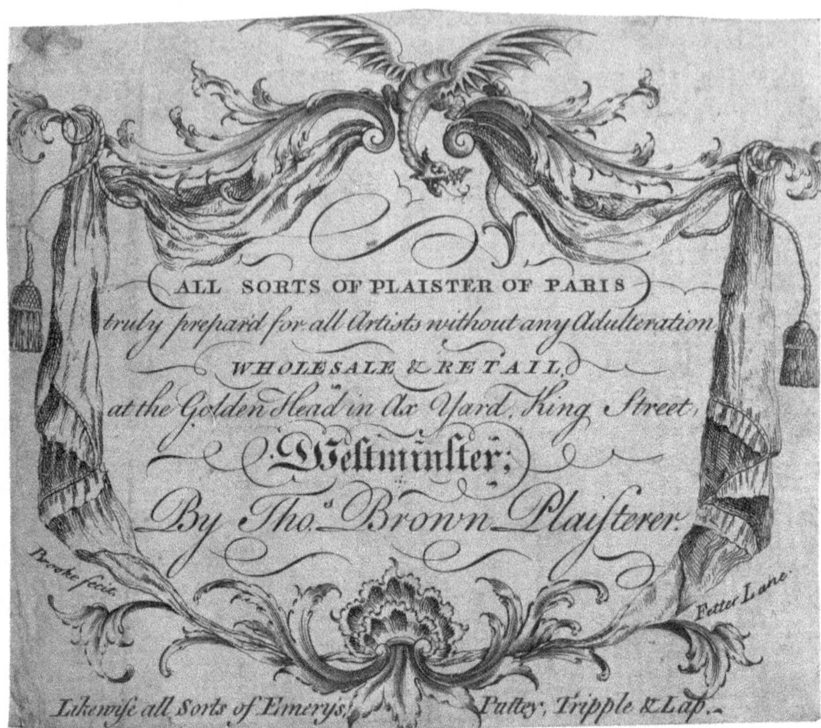

1.25 Trade card of Thomas Brown, plaster of Paris merchant of Westminster, n.d.

the 1820s.[126]) Others employed methods at once both commercially blatant and intellectually subtle. London plasterer Thomas Brown's trade card can, on the one hand, be read as a design intended to simply attract attention, with its elaborate cartouche formed by theatrical drapery and crowned by a dragon (Figure 1.25). Conversely, Brown might have expected that his audience – plasterers in the market for quality materials at retail or wholesale prices – would recognize the significance of the relationship between text and image; the implication being that his products, being 'prepar'd for Artists without any adulteration', were eminently suitable for decorative work of similar visual and technical complexity.

Taken together, the different design priorities displayed here suggest a range of different publics or audiences. But in adopting a codified visual language of taste, the trade cards of building tradesmen complement those of the contemporary shopkeeper, retailer and luxury goods manufacturer. While Michael Snodin has drawn attention to the use of 'stock' designs from mid-century, arguing for less individual agency among artisans and manufacturers in terms of consumer choice, this analysis of builders' cards argues that the selection of styles and ornamental motifs in and of themselves reveals both agency and volition.[127] It is also clear that some were

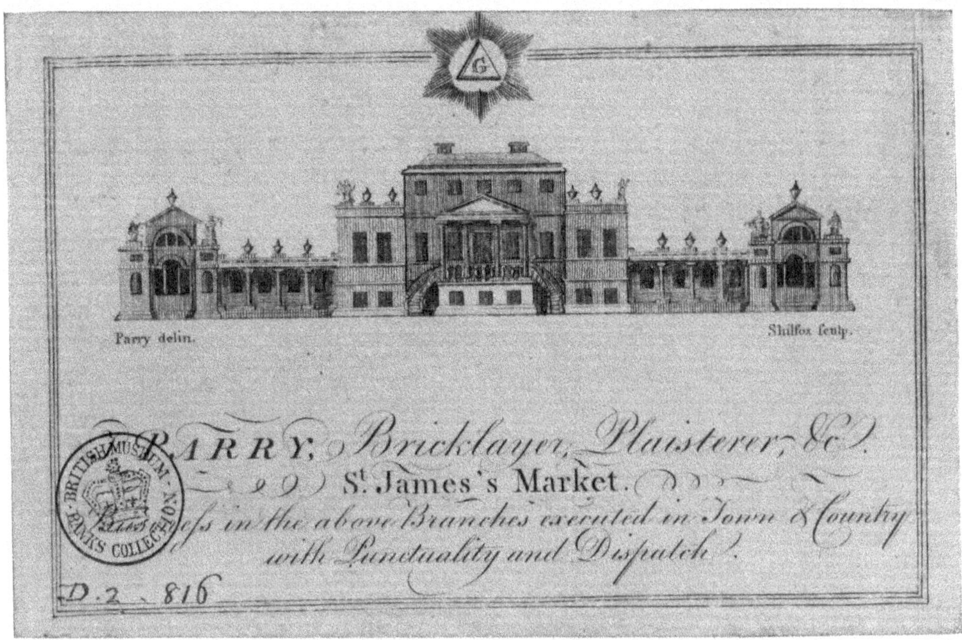

1.26 Trade card of J. Parry, bricklayer and plasterer of St James's Market, London, c. 1789.

directly the product of their respective shops, and thus represented distinctly professional ambitions beyond their immediate vocations. The trade card of J. Parry, a bricklayer and plasterer of St James's Market, is a good case in point: its illustration of a large country pile, albeit a composite from the published designs of John Crunden, William Pain and others, is unambiguously autographed as 'Parry delin.' (Figure 1.26).[128] Moreover, although some historians have generally regarded the elegantly designed trade card as the province of the luxury and semi-luxury retailers of London's West End, being an example of advertising directed at the bespoke client rather than a mass audience, this is demonstrably contradicted by the large number of illustrated cards produced by tradesmen at every level of the urban social spectrum: this includes so-called 'Nightmen' or 'Muckmen', whose job it was to empty the city's cesspools and water closets, and underscores not only the desire to attract genteel clients at every level of commercial life but the pretension to affect the 'polite' means to do so.[129]

Conclusion

Although an eighteenth-century tradesman might possess the outwards signs of gentility, John Locke's treatise on education offers a route into understanding his problematic reception in contemporary social, cultural and architectural discourse. Locke argued that deportment should express an *inner* genteel quality; manners spoke of an *inner* refinement.[130] The implication for the tradesman was that the world of commerce was not inherently genteel – the world of *trade* doubly so? – and that no amount of 'dressing up', either sartorially or through the affectation of elegantly designed business cards, would counter that impression. But with politeness and gentility increasingly available to a broader range of the 'middling sorts' during the course of the eighteenth-century, characters like the macaroni bricklayer are arguably less figures of ridicule – aping the appearance and deportment of their social betters – but rather figures of modernity. The macaroni bricklayer is in fact a prime example of the protean nature of social identity in an increasingly commodified cultural landscape. Working lives begat personal fortunes and dictated architectural tastes: dress and deportment thus represented what J. Ritchie Garrison has described as 'an especially important part of a worker's toolkit'.[131] With this in mind, the bricklayer's fancy attire should be seen as a symptom of what Peter Borsay has defined as the early modern 'urban renaissance', dependent on the growing demand for 'a range of personal aspirations, crucial among which was status'.[132]

Bricklayers, according to James Ayres, 'like many other craftsmen of the time, were permitted professional mobility whilst their social prestige was circumscribed'.[133] But the situation was in fact infinitely more complex. While social decorum upheld class distinctions and hierarchies throughout the period, it could also guide 'the upwardly socially mobile in how to advance inconspicuously'.[134] Dublin plasterer George Stapleton retired to a villa in the Dublin suburbs as a 'Gentleman' in the 1820s, his sons eschewing a life in trade for the medical and legal professions; London builder/developer Thomas Cubitt's son George achieved even greater social distinction, being raised to the peerage as Baron Ashcombe.[135] Cultural refinement was also, as John Brewer notes, 'a social solvent' in other ways, and upward mobility might be reflected in a tradesman's residential address – often cheek by jowl with their aristocratic patrons.[136] In the 1780s, Dublin plasterer and house builder Charles Thorp could count the Rt Hon. Henry Theophilus Clements and Lady Hannah Tynte among his neighbours in North Great George's Street; at the time of his death in 1806, house carpenter Owen Biddle resided in one of the more respectable blocks of Spruce Street in Philadelphia.

Just as certain individuals successfully navigated the boundaries of decorum, so their built legacy was sometimes celebrated rather than castigated in public discourse. Dublin builder John Russell's death notice of 1823, for example, noted that the 'elegant outlet which bears his name owes its origin and present splendid appearance to his enterprising spirit, and few of his profession have contributed more to the improvement of this City'.[137] In 1816, the obituary of Philadelphia house carpenter Jacob

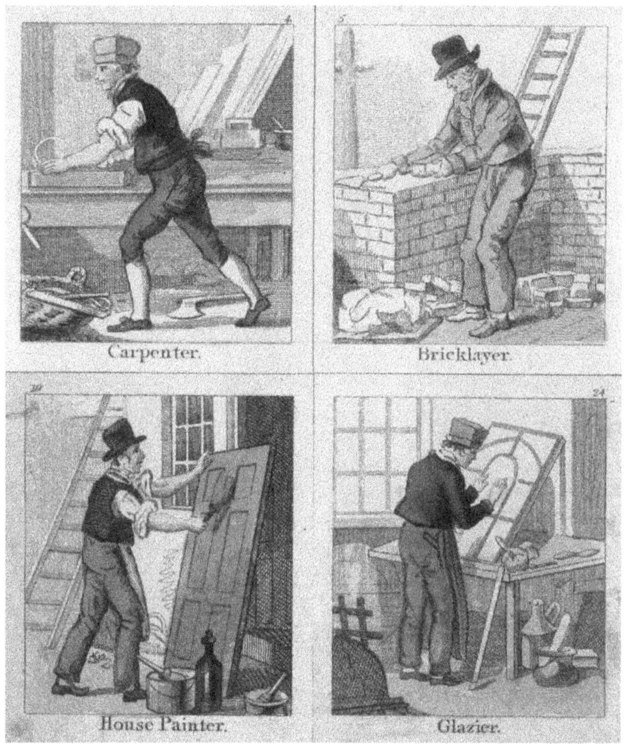

1.27 William Darton, 'Trades and professions' (details), n.d.

Vogdes described him in similarly glowing terms, making particular reference to his practice in domestic architecture: 'A life of industry and integrity had secured to him the esteem and confidence of all who knew him; and to his enterprise and skill, our city is indebted for many of its most ornamental and valuable private buildings.'[138] A more textually sophisticated epitaph acknowledged the relationship between the vulgar and polite dimensions to a life formed in trade: in 1804, the untimely death of 'stucco-plaisterer' John Fallon in Charleston, South Carolina, noted that 'In him the mechanical part of our community have lost one of its brightest ornaments.'[139] Collectively, these endorsements bring to mind Benjamin Franklin's famous maxim: 'He that hath a trade, hath an estate, and he that hath a calling, hath an office of profit and honour' (Figure 1.27).[140]

Notes

1 James Farr, 'Cultural analysis and early modern artisans', in Geoffrey Crossick (ed.), *The artisan and the European town, 1500–1900* (Aldershot: Ashgate, 1997), p. 56.

2 Jasmine Kilburn-Toppin, 'Crafting artisanal identities in early modern London: the spatial, material and social practices of guild communities c.1560–1640', PhD diss., Royal College of Art, 2013, p. 11.

3 Despite the conflation of status – with no distinction made, for example, between master carpenter and journeyman labourer – the 1831 census in Britain shows that the building trades made up the largest group in the occupational tables after agricultural labourers and domestic servants. E.P. Thompson, *The making of the English working class* (London: Pantheon Books, 1964), p. 234.

4 Richard L. Bushman, *The refinement of America: persons, houses, cities* (New York: Knopf, 1992), pp. 28–9.

5 James Peller Malcolm, *Anecdotes of the manners and customs of London, during the eighteenth century*, 2 vols (London, 1810), vol. 2, p. 417.

6 Paul Langford, *A polite and commercial people: England 1727–1783* (Oxford: Clarendon Press, 1989), p. 61.

7 *Ibid.*, p. 62.

8 Thompson, *English working class*, p. 234.

9 Fintan Lane, 'William Thompson, class and his Irish context, 1755–1833', in Fintan Lane (ed.), *Politics, society and the middle class in modern Ireland* (Basingstoke: Palgrave Macmillan, 2010), p. 28.

10 Stuart M. Blumin, *The emergence of the middle class: social experience in the American city, 1760–1900* (Cambridge: Cambridge University Press, 1989), p. 30. See also Gary B. Nash, 'A historical perspective on early American artisans', in Francis J. Puig and Michael Conforti (eds), *The American craftsman and the European tradition 1620–1820* (Minneapolis, MN: Minneapolis Institute of Arts, 1989), pp. 1–13.

11 Jim Smyth, 'The men of property: politics and the language of class in the 1790s', in Lane (ed.), *Politics, society and the middle class*, p. 8. On this point, Smyth is citing Penelope Corfield, 'Class by name and number in eighteenth-century England' (1987), reprinted in Penelope Corfield (ed.), *Language, history and class* (Oxford: Blackwell, 1991), pp. 101–30.

12 Corfield, 'Class by name and number', p. 112.

13 *Ibid.*, p. 128. David Cannadine outlines three different models of social structure that coexisted in the eighteenth-century British mentality: hierarchical or ordained; the triad of upper, middle and lower; and the oppositional high and low. David Cannadine, *Class in Britain* (New Haven and London: Yale University Press, 1998), pp. 24–56.

14 Paul A. Gilje, 'Identity and independence: the American artisan, 1750–1850', in Howard B. Rock, Paul A. Gilje and Robert Asher (eds), *American artisans: crafting social identity, 1750–1850* (Baltimore: Johns Hopkins University Press, 1995), pp. xi–xx.

15 Nash, 'A historical perspective', p. 1.

16 Charles N. Glaab, *A history of urban America*, 2nd edn (New York: Macmillan, 1976), p. 15.

17 James Ayres, *Building the Georgian city* (New Haven and London: Yale University Press, 1996), p. 34.

18 Langford, *A polite and commercial people*, p. 75.

19 Robert Campbell, *The London tradesman* (London, 1747), p. 103.

20 Joseph Collyer, *The parent and guardian's directory, and the youth's guide, in the choice of a profession or trade* (London, 1761), pp. 75–6, 92–3, 266, 276–7.

21 Elizabeth McKellar, *The birth of modern London: the development and design of the city 1660–1720* (Manchester: Manchester University Press, 1999), p. 110.

22 *Ibid.*, pp. 109–10. See also Dan Cruickshank and Neil Burton, *Life in the Georgian city* (London: Viking, 1990), pp. 115–17.

23 Donna J. Rilling, *Making houses, crafting capitalism: builders in Philadelphia, 1790–1850* (Philadelphia: University of Pennsylvania Press, 2001), p. 42.

24 Langford, *A polite and commercial people*, p. 103, n. 29.

25 Roger W. Moss, Jr, 'Master builders: a history of the colonial Philadelphia building trades', PhD diss., University of Delaware, 1972, p. 141.
26 Rilling, *Making houses*, p. 7.
27 Blumin, *The emergence of the middle class*, pp. 35–6.
28 'The contracting system even in the speculative world helped maintain labour relations and an organization of manpower seemingly not that different from the old guild system.' McKellar, *Birth of modern London*, p. 109.
29 Roger W. Moss, Jr, 'The origins of the Carpenters' Company of Philadelphia', in Charles E. Peterson (ed.), *Building early America: contributions toward the history of a great industry* (Radnor, PA: Chilton Book Co., 1976), p. 46.
30 Ian M. Quimby, 'Introduction: some observations on the craftsman in early America', in Ian M. Quimby (ed.), *The craftsman in early America* (New York: W.W. Norton, 1984), p. 7.
31 On American associations in a general sense see Mary N. Woods, *From craft to profession: the practice of architecture in nineteenth-century America* (Berkeley: University of California Press, 1999), p. 11.
32 A.R. Lewis, 'The builders of Edinburgh's New Town 1767–1795', PhD diss., University of Edinburgh, 2006, p. 189.
33 John Styles and Amanda Vickery, 'Introduction', in John Styles and Amanda Vickery (eds), *Gender, taste and material culture in Britain and North America, 1700–1830* (New Haven and London: Yale University Press, 2006), p. 16.
34 *Ibid.*, p. 14.
35 Lawrence Klein, 'Politeness for plebes: some social identities in early eighteenth-century England', in Ann Bermingham and John Brewer (eds), *The consumption of culture: word, image, and object in the seventeenth and eighteenth centuries* (London: Routledge, 1995), p. 373.
36 *Ibid.*, p. 364.
37 Bushman, *The refinement of America*, p. xvi.
38 Ann Bermingham, 'Introduction. The consumption of culture: image, object, text', in Bermingham and Brewer (eds), *The consumption of culture*, p. 5. On the 'symbiotic relationship' between architecture and commerce in eighteenth-century architectural theory see Daniel M. Abramson, 'Commercialization and backlash in late Georgian architecture', in Barbara Arciszewska and Elizabeth McKellar (eds), *Articulating British classicism: new approaches to eighteenth-century architecture* (Aldershot: Ashgate, 2004), pp. 147–8.
39 Harry R. Rubenstein, 'With hammer in hand: working-class occupational portraits', in Rock, Gilje and Asher (eds), *American artisans*, p. 180.
40 Ayres, *Building the Georgian city*, p. 2.
41 For an overview of Jameson's career and its contexts see Anthony Lewis, *The builders of Edinburgh New Town 1765–1795* (Reading: Spire Books, 2014), pp. 27–46.
42 Hermione Hobhouse, 'Cubitt, Thomas (1788–1855)', in the *Oxford dictionary of national biography*, online, www.oxforddnb.com/view/article/6859?docPos=4, accessed 11 June 2015.
43 James F. O'Gorman, 'The Philadelphia architectural drawing in its historical context: an overview', in James F. O'Gorman, Jeffrey A. Cohen, George E. Thomas and G. Holmes Perkins (eds), *Drawing toward building: Philadelphia architectural graphics 1732–1986* (Philadelphia: University of Pennsylvania Press, 1986), pp. 2–3.
44 Woods, *From craft to profession*, p. 13.
45 James F. O'Gorman, 'Some architects' portraits in nineteenth-century America: personifying the evolving profession', *Transactions of the American Philosophical Society* 103:4 (2013): 1–94.

46 'Affluence did not invariably mean abandonment of artisan identity'. Peter Guillery, *The small house in eighteenth-century London* (New Haven and London: Yale University Press, 2004), p. 13.
47 The publication of the 'Macaroni bricklayer' was announced in the *Public Advertiser* on 26 September 1772. It was priced 6d. 'plain' or 1s. 'illuminated'.
48 *The macaroni and theatrical magazine* (October 1772), p. 1.
49 Amelia F. Rauser, 'Hair, authenticity, and the self-made macaroni', *Eighteenth-Century Studies* 38:1 (2004): 101–17.
50 Shearer West, 'The Darly macaroni prints and the politics of "private man"', *Eighteenth-Century Life* 25 (2001): 170–82.
51 West notes that some of the more distinguished types represented in Darly's macaroni series were identified by Horace Walpole as real individuals, although concedes that this did not extend to the wider range of middling sorts. *Ibid.*, pp. 174–5, 181, n. 18.
52 An early authority on British prints suggested a similarity with portraits of George III. See Frederick George Stephens, *Catalogue of prints and drawings in the British Museum*, vol. 4: *1761–1770* (London, 1883), p. 769. A later iteration of this catalogue, however, stated 'Not George III, but a builder named Prior'. See Mary Dorothy George, *Catalogue of the political and personal satires preserved in the Department of Prints and Drawings in the British Museum*, vol. 5, *1771–1783* (London, 1935), p. 83. The source for this is Henry Charles William Angelo (1756–1835), who referred to 'Prior, the builder' as one of the 'bourgeois macaronies' held up to ridicule by Darly. Henry Charles William Angelo, *The reminiscences of Henry Angelo*, vol. 2 (London, 1828; repr. 1904), pp. 267–8. Efforts to identify Prior have yielded little information. A Thomas Prior of the Parish of St George, Bloomsbury, was made a freeman of the Worshipful Company of Tylers and Bricklayers in 1744, having served his apprenticeship to Henry Clement. A Thomas Prior took apprentices in 1754 and in 1766; a third apprentice was bound in 1786 but this may refer to another individual. Cliff Webb, *London apprentices*, vol. 2: *Tylers' and Bricklayers' Company 1612–1644, 1668–1800* (London: Society of Genealogists, 1996), pp. 38, 54, 79. No listing for this combination of name and trade appears in the various London street directories published before 1772, the year of Darly's satirical print. The wedding of the daughter of 'Mr. Prior, Builder', with an address at Great Russell Street, Bloomsbury, was announced in three newspapers in February 1771 (*General Evening Post*, 23 February 1771; *Middlesex Journal or Chronicle of Liberty*, 23 February 1771; *Public Advertiser*, 25 February 1771). References to the 'Macaroni bricklayer' (also referred to as the 'Macaroni trowellist') appear in *Nocturnal Revels*, a scurrilous guide to brothels in London, where his 'athletic and manly form' attracted the attentions of a 'Mrs Br–d–y', and unsavoury aspects of his business practices are suggested. Anon., *Nocturnal revels: or, the history of King's-Place, and other nunneries*, 2 vols (London, 1779), vol. 2, pp. 62–4.
53 Rauser, 'Hair, authenticity and the self-made macaroni', 102. On the broader point see Diana Donald, *The age of caricature: satirical prints in the reign of George III* (New Haven and London: Yale University Press, 1996).
54 Martyn J. Powel, *The politics of consumption in eighteenth-century Ireland* (Basingstoke: Palgrave Macmillan, 2005), p. 62.
55 Given the nature of the Darly portfolios of middling types, it seems clear that the macaroni's reputation for effeminacy and sexual deviancy was not at stake here. For a recent account of the transgressive character of the macaroni, and the 'public cultural concern about masculinity', see Sally O'Driscoll, 'What kind of man do the clothes make? Print culture and the meanings of macaroni effeminacy', in Kevin Murphy and Sally O'Driscoll (eds), *Studies in ephemera: text and image in*

eighteenth-century print (Lewisburg, PA and Lanham, MD: Bucknell University Press, 2013), pp. 241–78.

56 John Styles, 'Manufacturing, consumption and design in eighteenth-century England', in John Brewer and Roy Porter (eds), *Consumption and the world of goods* (London: Routledge, 1993), p. 538; Stana Nenadic, 'Necessities: food and clothing in the long eighteenth century', in Elizabeth Foyster and Christopher A. Whatley (eds), *A history of everyday life in Scotland 1600–1800* (Edinburgh: Edinburgh University Press, 2010), p. 148.

57 Klein, 'Politeness for plebes', p. 374.

58 Campbell, *London tradesman*, p. 191. Author's emphasis.

59 Neil McKendrick, 'The commercialization of fashion', in Neil McKendrick, John Brewer and J.H. Plumb (eds), *The birth of a consumer society: the commercialization of eighteenth-century England* (Bloomington: Indiana University Press, 1982), p. 50.

60 *Ibid*., p. 53.

61 *Ibid*., p. 51.

62 On this point see also Bushman, *Refinement of America*, p. 41; Corfield, 'Walking the city streets', pp. 157–8; Donald, *The age of caricature*, p. 82.

63 For Braidwood, see Lewis, *The builders of Edinburgh New Town*, pp. 136, 144, 147. Some versions of the print bear the legend, 'I say dont Laugh for we are Brothers'. George, *Catalogue of political and personal satires*, vol. 6: *1784–1792* (1938), p. 636.

64 *Hibernian Journal*, 9–12 August 1776. Quoted in Powell, *Politics of consumption*, 61.

65 *Ibid*.

66 Blumin, *The emergence of the middle class*, p. 31.

67 James Elmes, *Lectures on architecture*, 2nd edn (London, 1823), p. 390.

68 British Library, MS 41133, Sir William Chambers letter books, I, 65r.

69 *Hibernian Journal*, 1–3 September 1777, quoted in Powell, *Politics of consumption*, pp. 61–2.

70 Blumin, *The emergence of the middle class*, p. 31.

71 The 'Antique Architect' has been identified as Robert Adam. George, *Catalogue of political and personal satires*, vol. 5, p. 137.

72 Elizabeth McKellar notes that bricklayers counted for a high proportion of speculative builders in early modern London. McKellar, *Birth of modern London*, p. 97.

73 Rachel Stewart, *The town house in Georgian London* (New Haven and London: Yale University Press, 2009), p. 2.

74 Campbell, *London tradesman*, p. 159.

75 *Ibid*., pp. 159–60.

76 Collyer, *Parent and guardian's directory*, pp. 75–6.

77 Richard Neve, *The city and countrey purchaser, and builder's dictionary* (London, 1703), p. 71.

78 McKellar, *Birth of modern London*, p. 85.

79 Jules Lubbock, *The tyranny of taste: the politics of architecture and design in Britain 1550–1960* (New Haven and London: Yale University Press, 1995), pp. 4–5.

80 On Nicholas Barbon, see McKellar, *Birth of modern London*, pp. 12–37; Lubbock, *Tyranny of taste*, pp. 13–15.

81 R. North, *The autobiography of the Hon. Roger North*, ed. A. Jessopp (Madison, WI, 1887), p. 53.

82 Jonathan Swift, *The truth of some maxims in state and government, examined with reference to Ireland* (1724). In October 1769, *The craftsman* magazine reported that bankruptcies among builders in the Marylebone area of London had not dulled the 'rage for building in that parish … carcases which cost the builders … at first hand, from £600 to £1000 each, have lately been sold from only £90 to £200'. Quoted in Stewart, *Town house*, p. 218, n. 20.

83 Isaac Ware, *A complete body of architecture* (London, 1768), p. 291.
84 H.M. Colvin, *A biographical dictionary of British architects 1600–1840*, 4th edn (New Haven and London: Yale University Press, 2008), p. 1088; F.H.W. Sheppard (ed.), *Survey of London*, vol. 36: *The parish of St Paul, Covent Garden* (London: Athlone Press, 1970), pp. 263–5.
85 Ware, *A complete body of architecture*, p. 291.
86 Campbell, *London tradesman*, p. 161.
87 Eileen Harris, *British architectural books and writers, 1556–1785* (Cambridge: Cambridge University Press, 1990), p. 366.
88 James Peacock, *Oikidia, or nutshells: being ichnographic distributions for small villas; chiefly upon oeconomical principles* (London, 1785), p. 65.
89 McKellar, *Birth of modern London*, pp. 42–9.
90 Stefan Muthesius, *The English terraced house* (New Haven and London: Yale University Press, 1982), p. 34.
91 John Bonehill, '"The centre of pleasure and magnificence": Paul and Thomas Sandby's London', *Huntington Library Quarterly* 75:3 (2012): 389. This focused on Mylne's design for Blackfriars Bridge in London, for which Mylne's 'excessive self promotion' evidently attracted 'much ridicule'. Stana Nenadic, 'Architect-builders in London and Edinburgh, c.1750–1800, and the market for expertise', *Historical Journal* 55:3 (2012): 600.
92 For an overview of its conception and formation see Michael Rawson, 'The march of bricks and mortar', *Environmental History* 17 (2012): 844–51.
93 By 1800, the eastern and southern suburbs of the city 'were more than before home to people on lower incomes'. Guillery, *Small House*, p. 27. Cruikshank was a resident of the New River Estate which was building at a 'frantic' pace during the late 1820s, a fact that almost certainly inspired his cartoon. See Philip Temple (ed.), *Survey of London*, vol. 47: *North Clerkenwell and Pentonville* (New Haven and London: Yale University Press, 2008), pp. 185–91.
94 Linda David, *Children's books published by William Darton and his sons* (Bloomington: Indiana University, 1992), p. 11.
95 On brickmaking see Ayres, *Building the Georgian city*, pp. 102–3.
96 First published in London in 1804; subsequently published in Philadelphia in 1808 and in Boston in 1813.
97 The brickmaker shares plaudits with the pavier (whose honest labour preserves us from dust and mud) and the mason (where the orders of architecture, the dialectic between classical and gothic and the magnificence of the modern built environment are invoked).
98 Bermingham, 'Introduction', p. 14.
99 Bernard L. Herman and Peter Guillery, 'Negotiating classicism in eighteenth-century Deptford and Philadelphia', in Arciszewska and McKellar (eds), *Articulating British classicism*, p. 188. On the broader issue, see David Dickson, 'Second city syndrome: reflections on three Irish cases', in S.J. Connolly (ed.), *Kingdoms united? Great Britain and Ireland since 1500: integration and diversity* (Dublin: Four Courts Press, 1999), pp. 95–108; Toby Barnard, 'Integration or separation? Hospitality and display in Protestant Ireland, 1660–1800', in L. Brockliss and D. Eastwood (eds), *A union of multiple identities: the British Isles c.1750–c.1850* (Manchester: Manchester University Press, 1997) pp. 127–46; and Styles and Vickery, 'Introduction', pp. 22–4.
100 Rolf Loeber and Magda Stouthamer-Loeber, 'Dublin and its vicinity in 1797', *Irish Geography* 35:2 (2002): 133–55.
101 *Dublin Evening Post*, 12 February 1780.
102 *Hibernian Chronicle*, 27 August 1781.

103 *Pennsylvania Packet*, 4 January 1773.
104 *Pennsylvania Packet*, 15 October 1794.
105 *New York Mercury*, 11 March 1765.
106 *Maryland Journal*, 6 October 1789.
107 *Pennsylvania Evening Herald*, 25 May 1785. Hoban is best known as designer of the White House in Washington. For an overview of his career, see Ronald M. Birse, 'Hoban, James', in the *Oxford dictionary of national biography*, online, www.oxforddnb.com.ucd.idm.oclc.org/view/article/45956?docPos=1, accessed 1 March 2015.
108 *Charleston City Gazette and Advertiser*, 4 May 1790.
109 Langford, *Polite and commercial people*, p. 67.
110 Maxine Berg and Helen Clifford, 'Commerce and the commodity: graphic display and selling new consumer goods in eighteenth-century England', in Michael North and David Ormrod (eds), *Art markets in Europe 1400–1800* (Aldershot: Ashgate, 1998), p. 189.
111 See also Desmond FitzGerald, Knight of Glin, 'Early Irish trade-cards and other eighteenth-century ephemera', *Eighteenth-Century Ireland/Iris an Dá Chultúr* 2 (1987): 115–32; and Robert Jay, *The trade card in nineteenth-century America* (Columbia: University of Missouri Press, 1987). A range of trade cards from the various building trades is illustrated in Ayres, *Building the Georgian city*, *passim*. Given the focus of his book, Ayres is understandably concerned only with what they reveal about the tools, materials and operations of the different trades.
112 On the commodification of culture and its expression in visual and textual terms, see John Brewer, '"The most polite age and the most vicious": attitudes towards culture as a commodity, 1660–1800', in Bermingham and Brewer (eds), *The consumption of culture*, pp. 341–61.
113 Maxine Berg and Helen Clifford. 'Selling consumption in the eighteenth century: advertising and the trade card in Britain and France', *Cultural and Social History* 4:2 (2007): 146. See also Jay, *The trade card in nineteenth-century America*, p. 4.
114 Here I am taking my cue from Berg and Clifford's observation that 'There was a close connection between the look, design, display of domestic and ornamental consumer ware and its graphic display.' Berg and Clifford, 'Commerce and the commodity', p. 191.
115 Berg and Clifford, 'Selling consumption', 149.
116 Although dimensions vary, a comparison of trade cards at the National Library of Ireland (unsorted collection) and the British Library (Heal and Banks collections) indicates that the majority may be classified within three broad categories of scale: 65mm × 45mm; 95mm × 65mm; and 120mm × 80mm.
117 Berg and Clifford, 'Commerce and the commodity', p. 197.
118 *Ibid.*
119 Berg and Clifford note the similarity between the designs on trade cards and the pattern books 'with which they are so closely associated'. *Ibid.*, p. 196.
120 The simple neoclassical borders, popular by the 1790s, 'outlawed the depiction of any goods, or lengthy lists of them, in the visual simplicity of neoclassical elegance'. Berg and Clifford, 'Selling consumption', 159.
121 Berg and Clifford, 'Commerce and the commodity', p. 197.
122 Berg and Clifford, 'Selling consumption', 159.
123 The trade card of Jaques of Holborn, manufacturers of 'every sort of Ornament Work in the Building line', includes an itemized list of goods on the reverse.
124 Philippa Hubbard, 'The economic functions of the trade card in eighteenth-century Britain', unpublished paper presented at the annual conference of the Economic

History Society, University of Nottingham, 2008 (available online at: www.ehs.org.uk/dotAsset/bb5d50c1–228b-4a2f-9e09–5652a98ad884.doc). See also Philippa Hubbard, 'Trade cards in 18th-century consumer culture: movement, circulation, and exchange in commercial and collecting spaces', *Material Culture Review* 74–75 (2012): 30–46.

125 On the trade card as souvenir and/or reminder of the site of purchase, see Claire Walsh, 'The advertising and marketing of consumer goods', in C. Wischermann and E. Shore (eds), *Advertising and the European city: historical perspectives* (Aldershot: Ashgate, 2000), pp. 79–95; Katie Scott, 'The Waddesdon trade cards: more than one history', *Journal of Design History* 17:1 (2004): 91–100; and Berg and Clifford, 'Selling consumption'.

126 Jay, *Trade card in nineteenth-century America*, pp. 13–14.

127 Michael Snodin, 'Trade cards and English rococo', in Charles Hind (ed.), *The rococo in England: a symposium* (London, 1986), p. 83. See also Ambrose Heal, *London tradesmen's cards of the XVIII century: an account of their origin and use* (New York, 1968), pp. 70, 80.

128 Compare, for example, with John Crunden, *Convenient and ornamental architecture* (London, 1767), plates 37–8, 54–5.

129 Scott, 'The Waddesdon trade cards', 97. For examples of nightmen's trade cards see Cruickshank and Burton, *Life in the Georgian city*, pp. 92–3, where they are illustrated but their significance is not analysed.

130 John Locke, *Some thoughts concerning education* (London, 1693).

131 J. Ritchie Garrison, *Two carpenters: architecture and building in early New England, 1799–1859* (Knoxville: University of Tennessee Press, 2006), p. 45.

132 Peter Borsay, 'The English urban renaissance: the development of provincial urban culture c.1680–c.1760', in Peter Borsay (ed.), *The eighteenth-century town: a reader in English urban history 1688–1820* (London: Longman, 1990), p. 179.

133 Ayres, *Building the Georgian city*, p. 109.

134 Styles and Vickery, 'Introduction', p. 17.

135 F.M.L. Thompson, *Gentrification and the enterprise culture, Britain 1780–1980* (Oxford: Oxford University Press, 2001), p. 90.

136 John Brewer, *The pleasures of the imagination: English culture in the eighteenth century* (London: HarperCollins, 1997), p. 74.

137 *Freeman's Journal*, 21 June 1823.

138 *Poulson's American Daily Advertiser*, 22 October 1816.

139 *City Gazette*, 25 September 1804. Fallon was 'a native of Ireland' and 'late of the city of Washington'.

140 Benjamin Franklin, *The way to wealth* (1758).

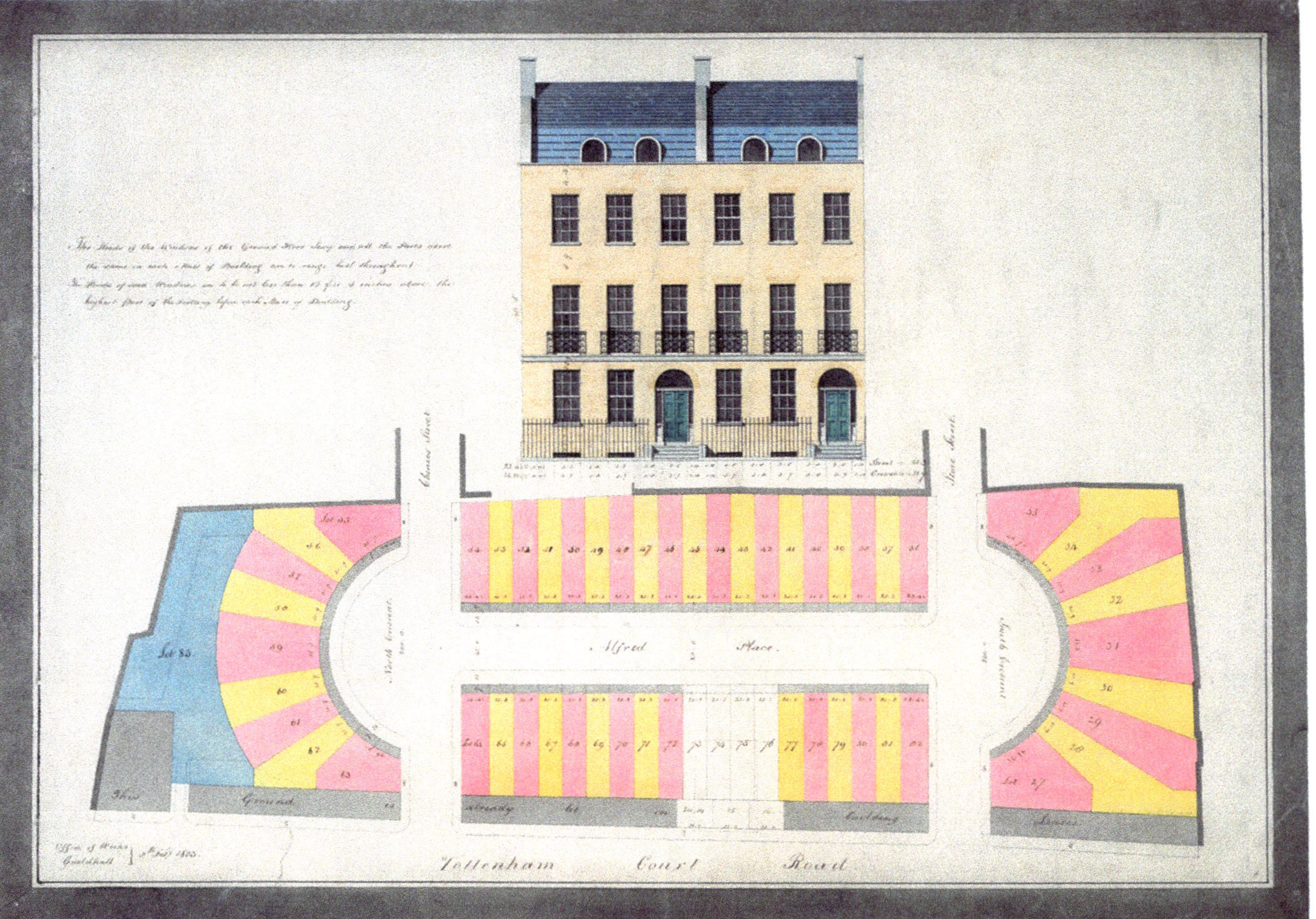

Plate 1 George Dance the younger, plan and elevation for Alfred Place, London, c. 1796.

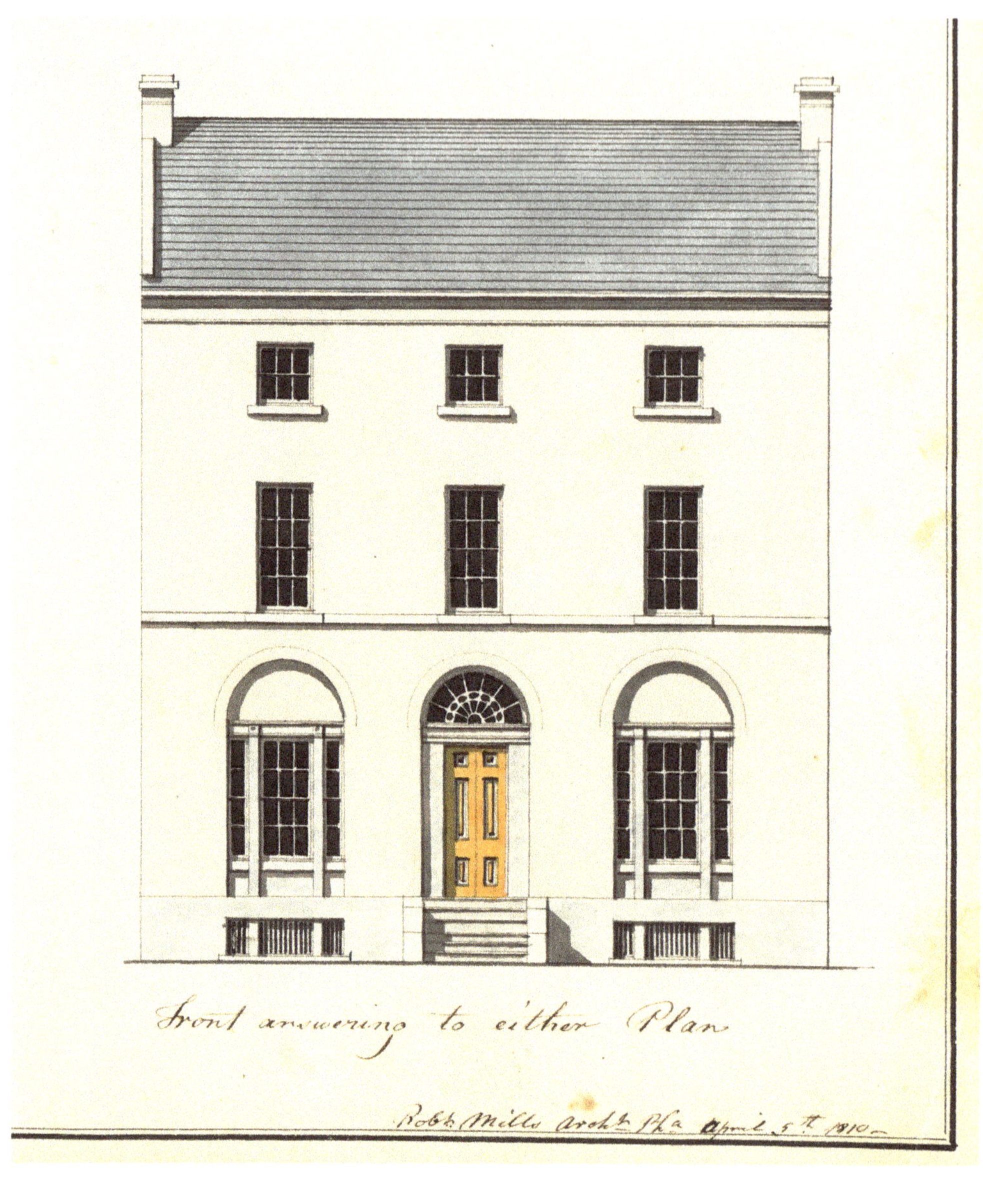

Plate 2 Robert Mills, elevation for Benjamin Chew house, Philadelphia, 1810.

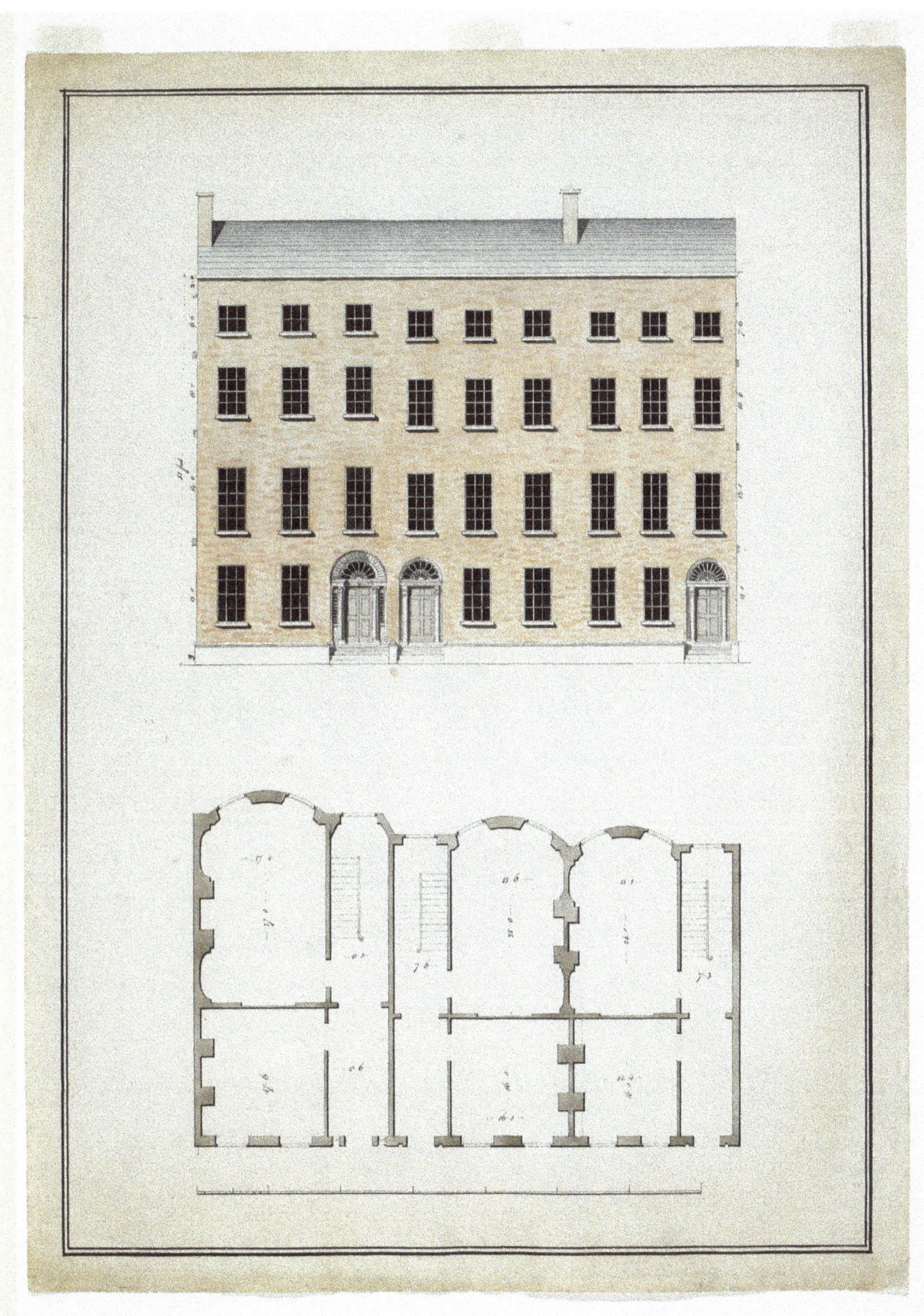

Plate 3 Stapleton Collection: elevation for a row of houses in Dublin, c. 1790.

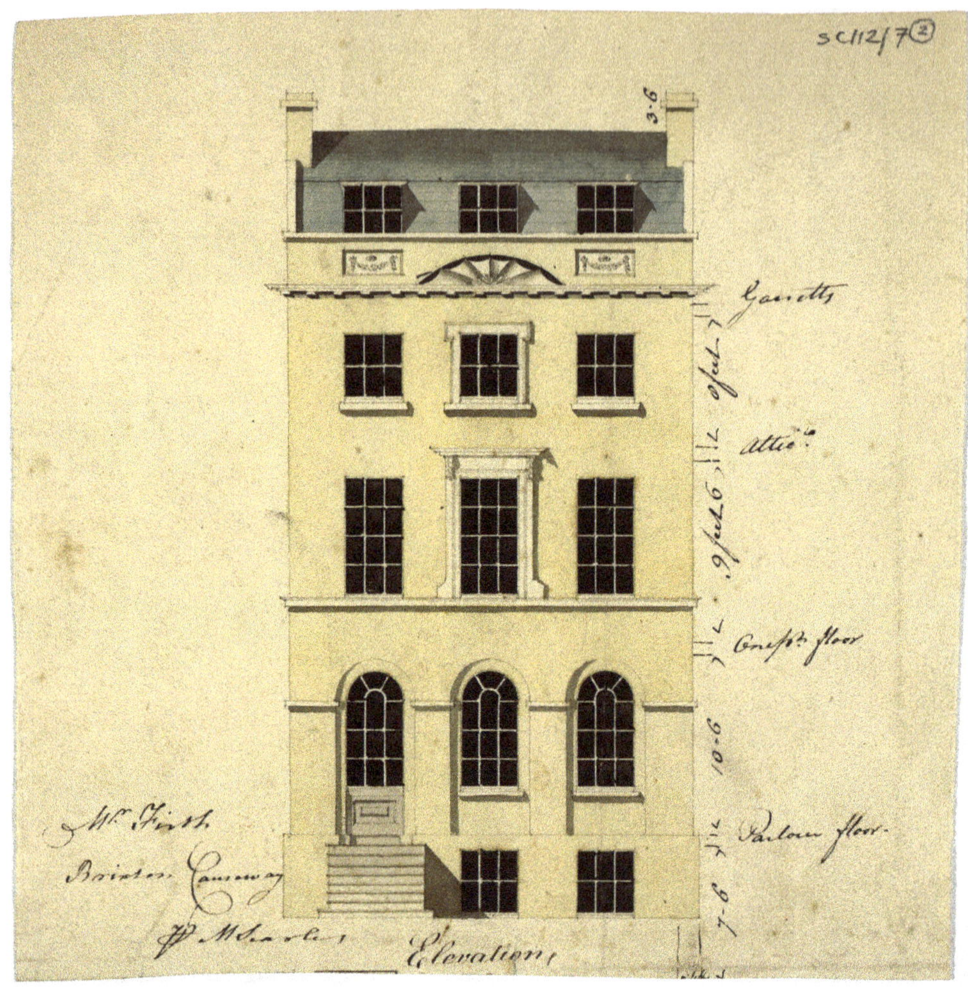

Plate 4 Michael Searles, elevation for a house in Brixton Causeway (Brixton Hill), London, for Mr Firth, c. 1800.

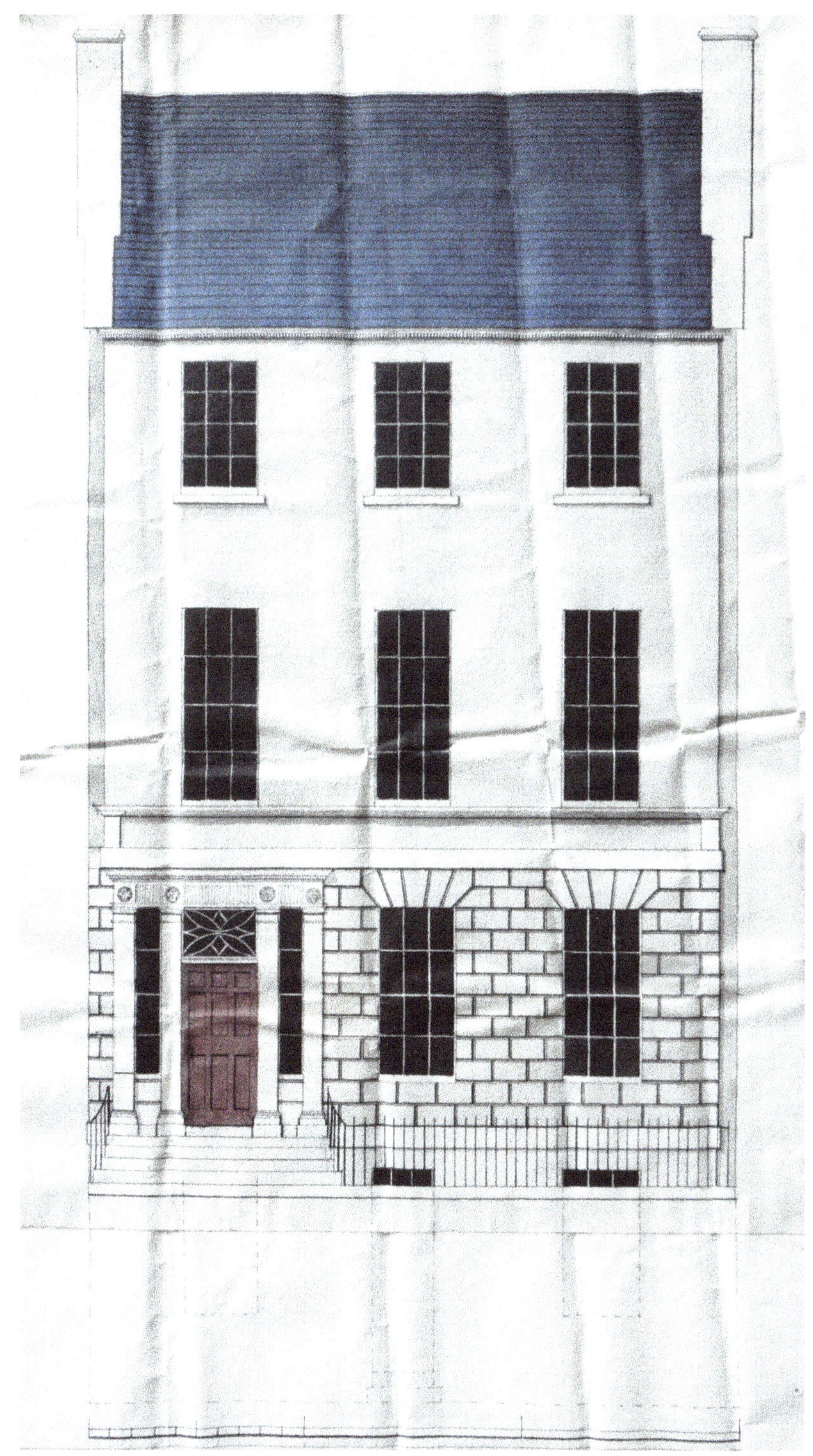

Plate 5 Alexander Balfour, elevation for a house at Queen Street, Edinburgh, 1790.

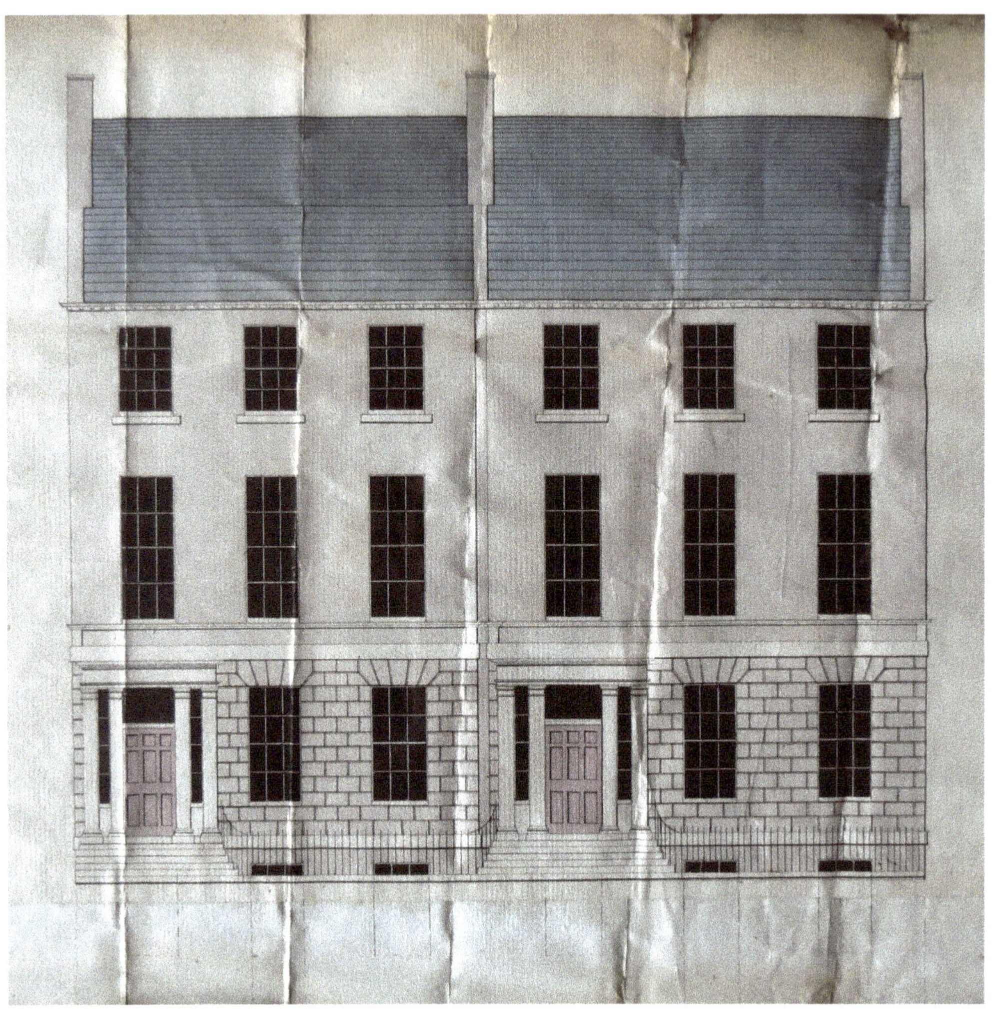

Plate 6 Alexander Balfour, elevation for a pair of houses at Queen Street, Edinburgh, 1790.

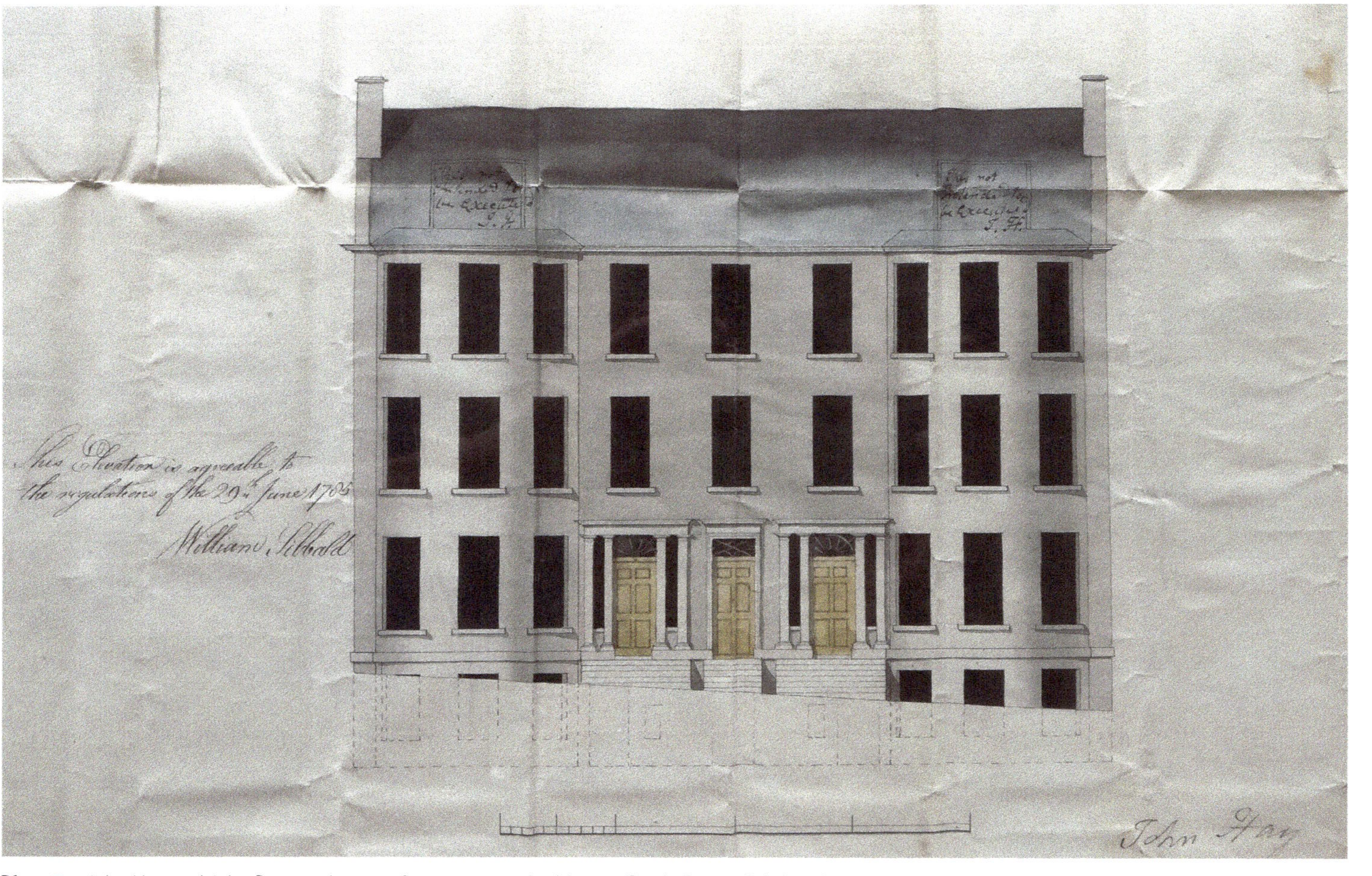

Plate 7 John Hay and John Baxter, elevation for a tenement building at Castle Street, Edinburgh, 1790.

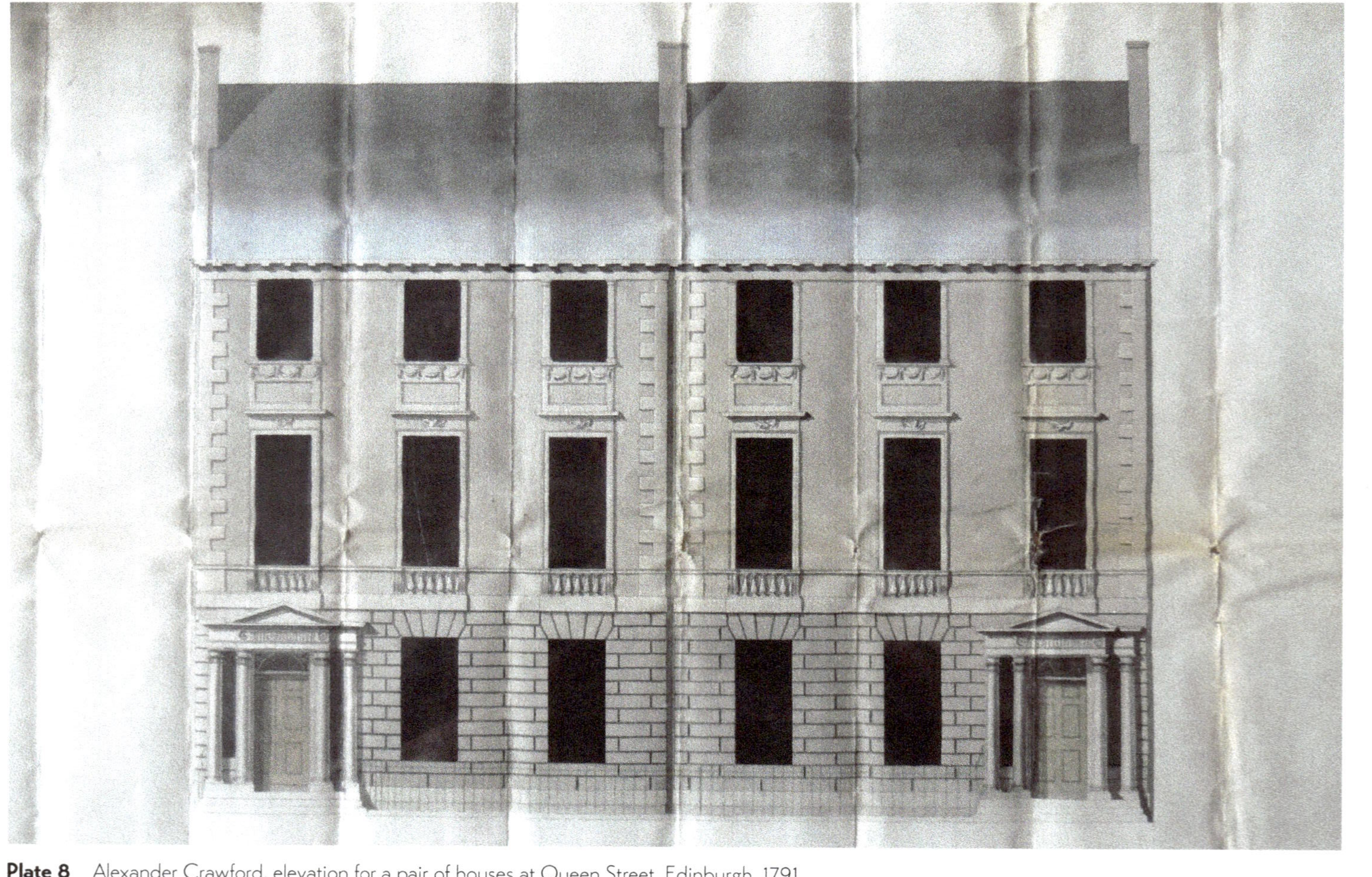

Plate 8 Alexander Crawford, elevation for a pair of houses at Queen Street, Edinburgh, 1791.

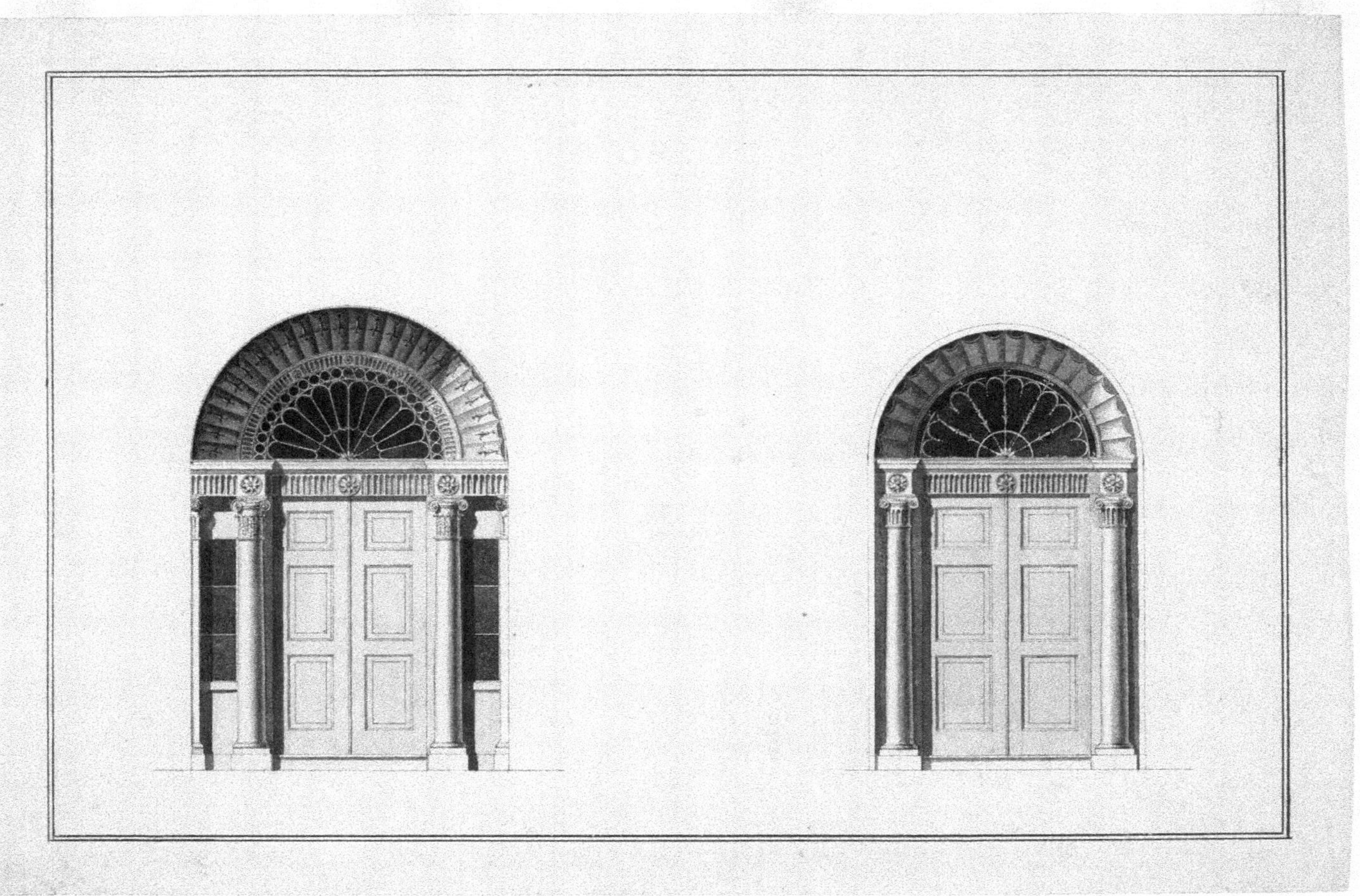

Plate 9 Stapleton Collection: designs for doorcases in Dublin, c. 1790.

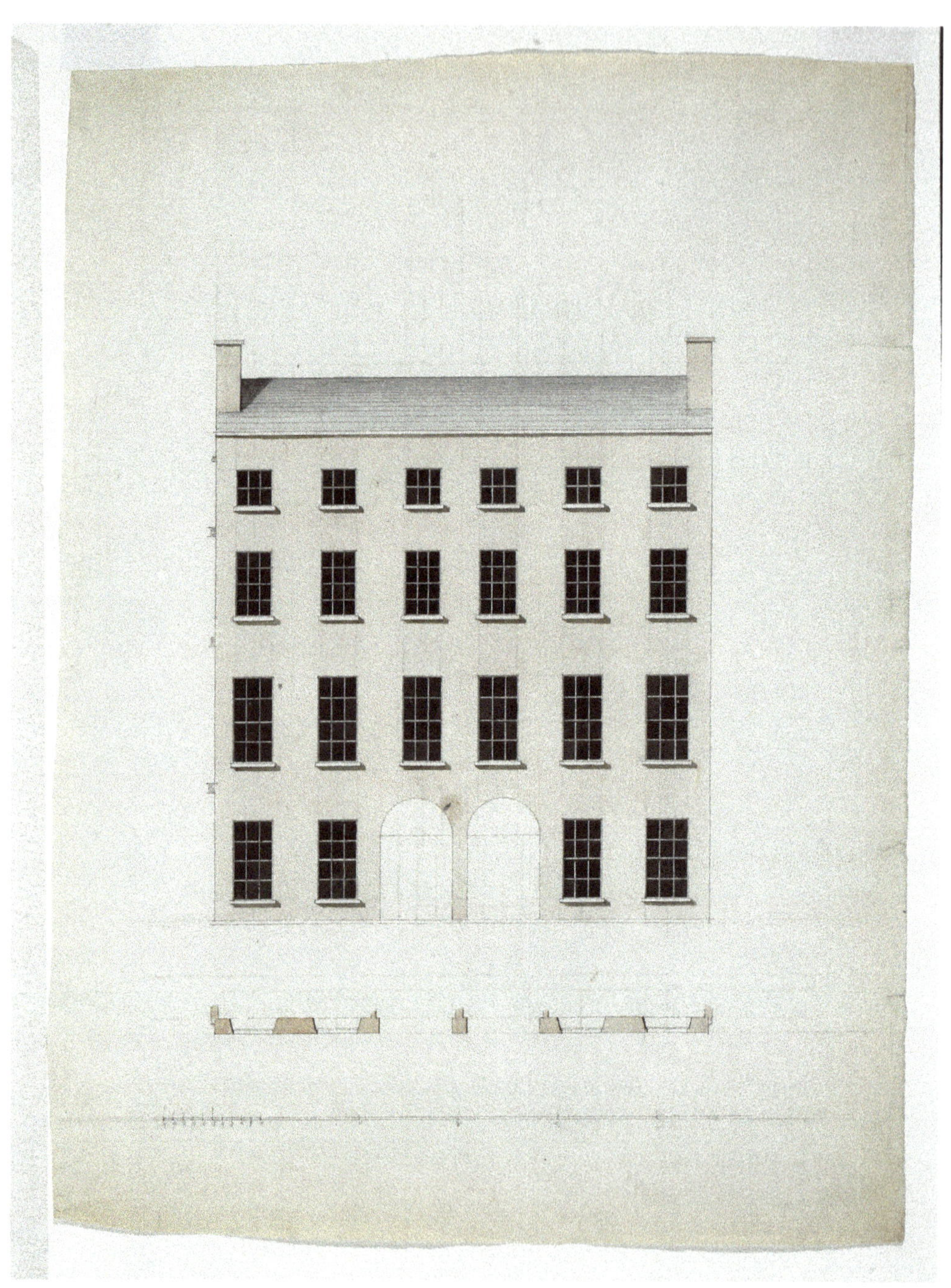

Plate 10 Stapleton Collection: elevation for a pair of houses in Dublin, c. 1790.

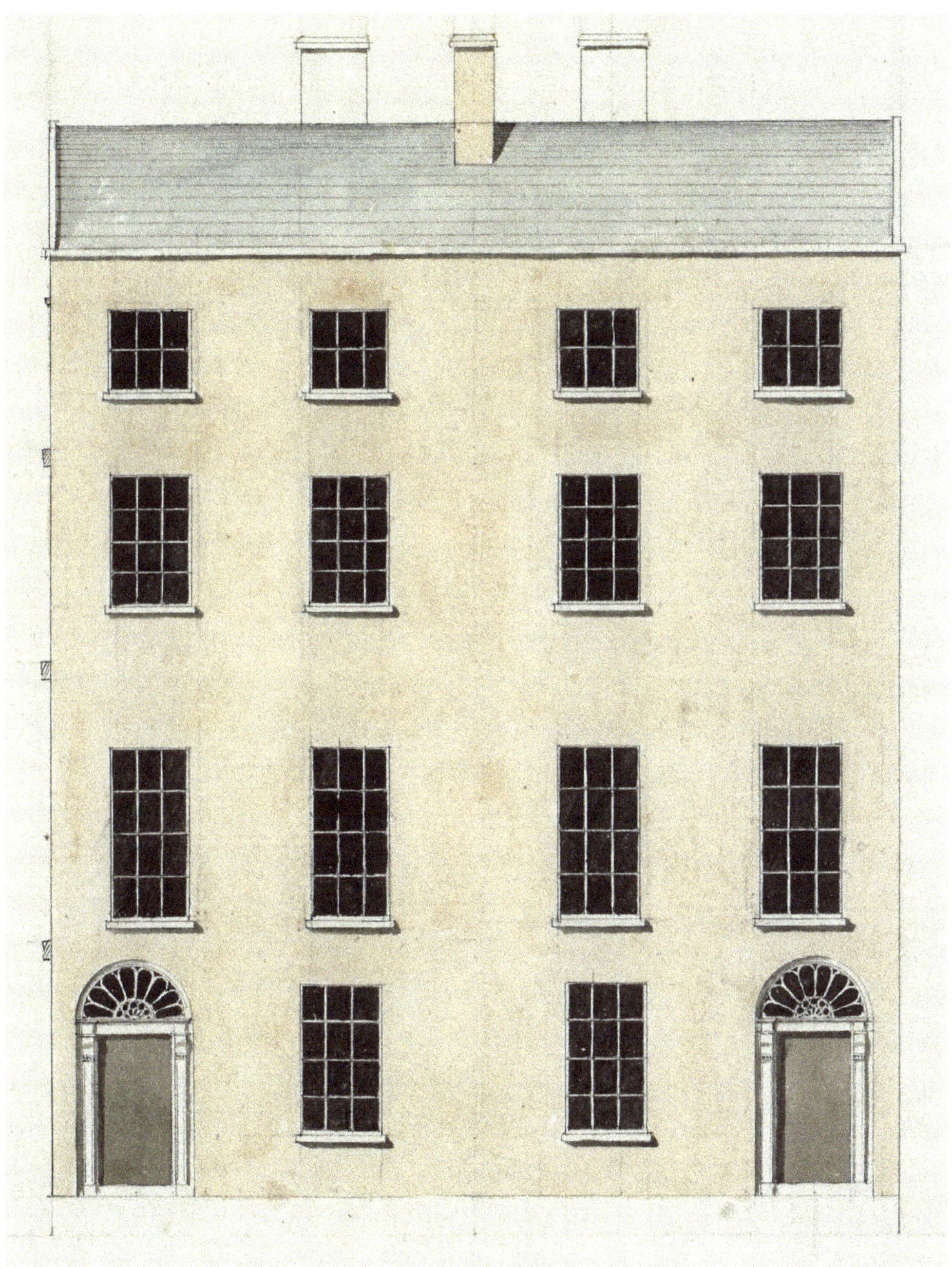

Plate 11 Stapleton Collection: elevation for a pair of houses in Dublin, c. 1790.

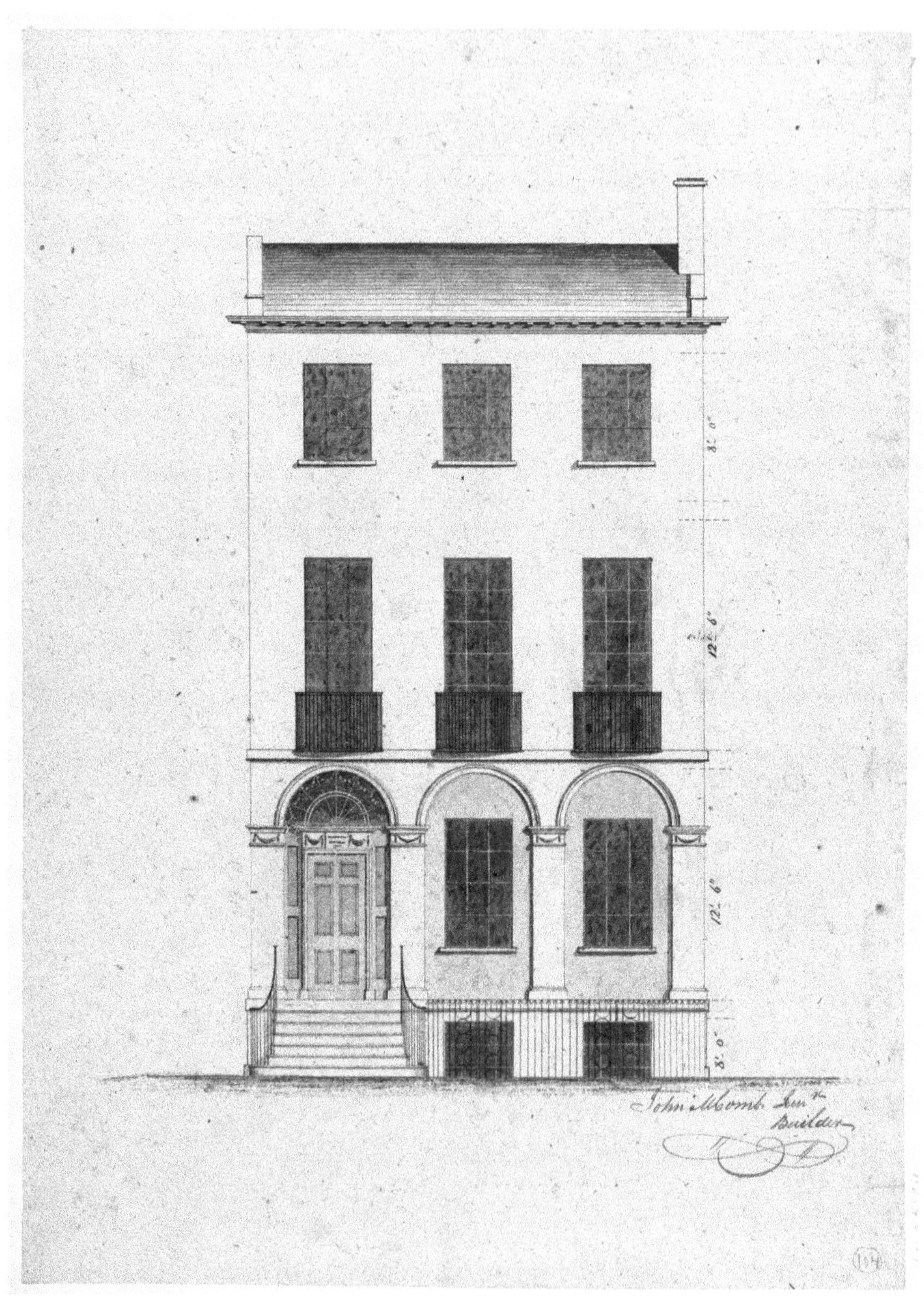

Plate 12 John McComb, Jr, elevation for a house, New York, c. 1800.

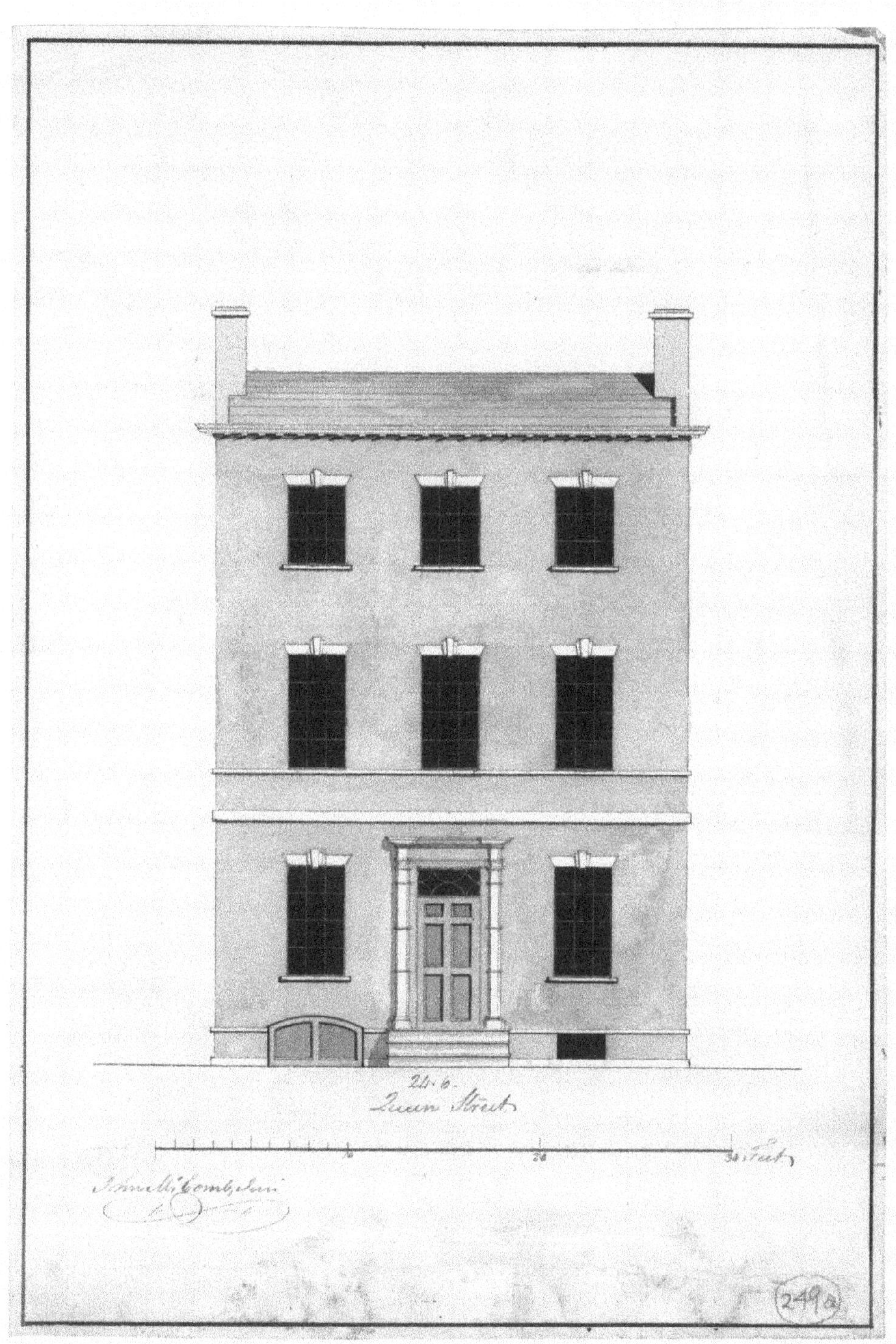

Plate 13 John McComb, Jr, elevation for a house at Queen Street, New York, c. 1800.

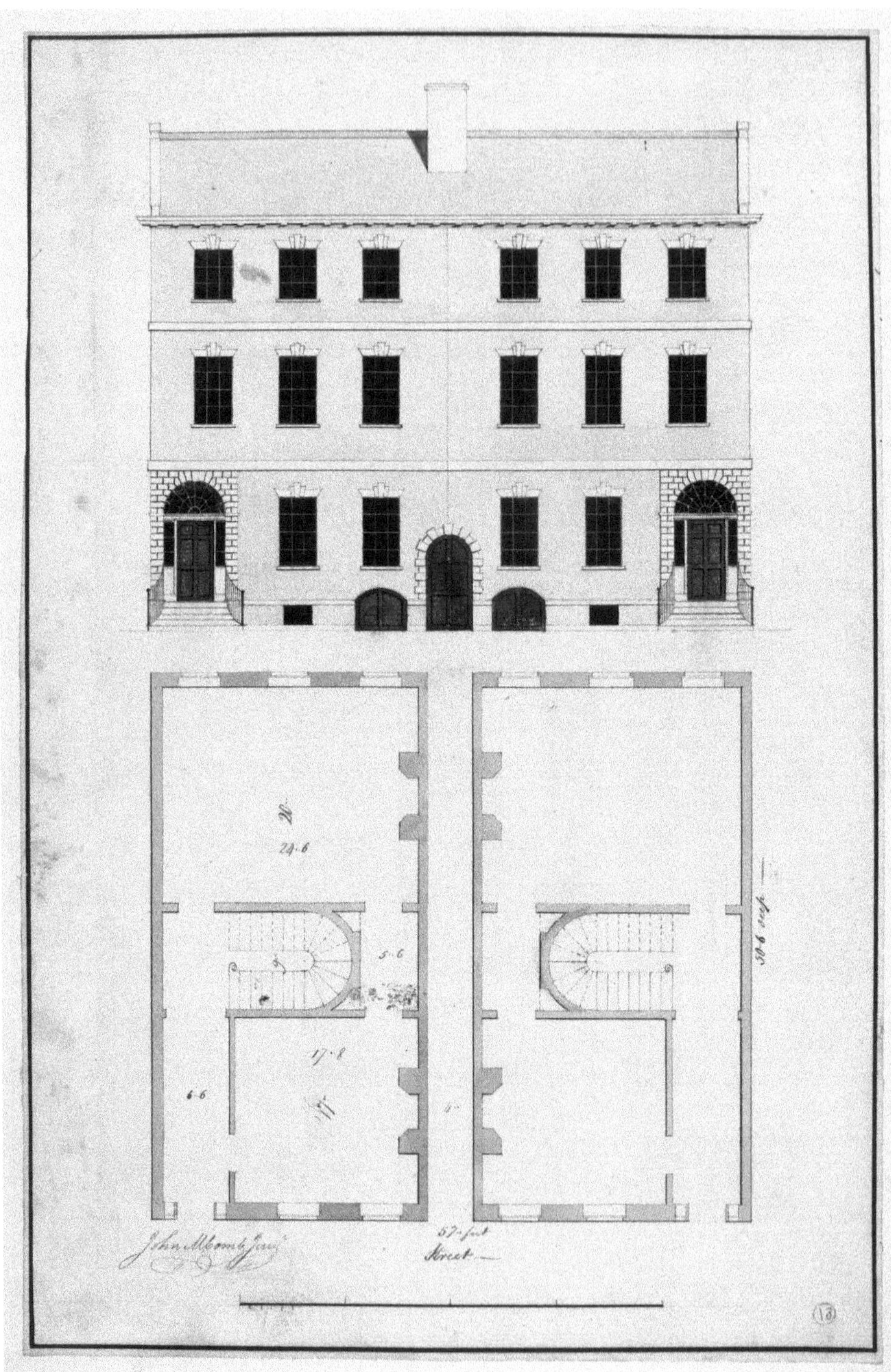

Plate 14 John McComb, Jr, elevation for a pair of houses, New York, c. 1800.

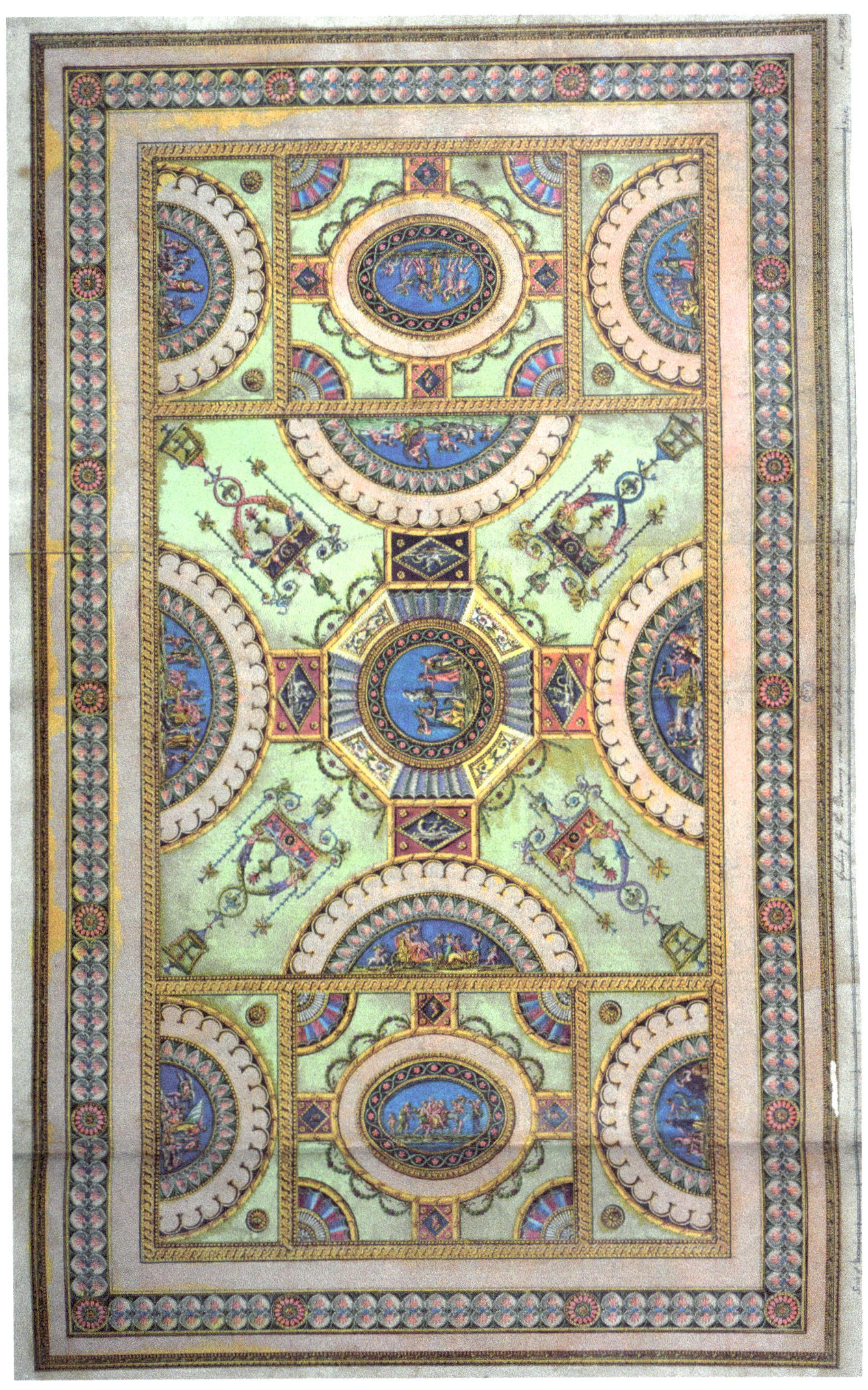

Plate 15 Robert Adam, ceiling design for the drawing-room at Northumberland House, London, 1770.

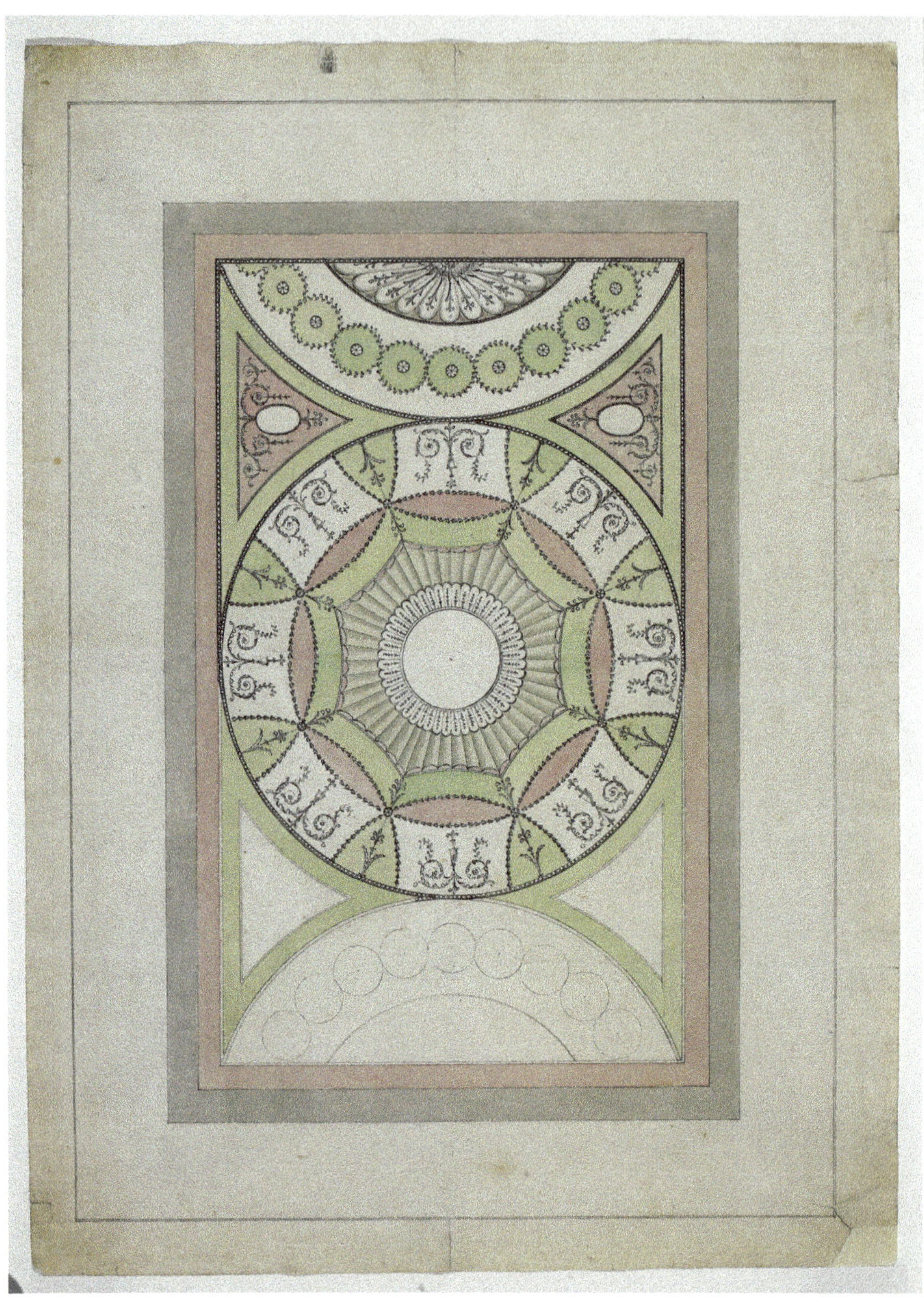

Plate 16 Stapleton Collection: ceiling design for an unidentified house in Dublin, c. 1780.

2

Designing houses: the façade and the architecture of street and square

The built environment as an expression of the social order is a common trope in architectural histories, and early modern architectural discourse was unequivocal in considering the elite town house as the nexus between individual concern (private house) and social obligation (public streetscape). However, while ideologically conceived geometries were dictated by architects, surveyors and, in some instances, civic authorities, the building up of individual urban plots and city blocks was almost entirely dependent on an economically independent and creatively autonomous artisan class. The historical response to this phenomenon has been to consider the individual eighteenth-century house – the typical 'street house' – as being of limited interest: although recent research has shed important light on the semiotic 'illegibility' of the uniform terrace and palace front, historians have traditionally concerned themselves with those paradigms of urban design that made *architecture* from *building*, such as the set pieces of John Wood in Bath from the 1720s onwards, and Robert Adam's attempt to make architectural 'sense' of Edinburgh's burgeoning New Town in the early 1790s (Figure 2.1).[1] Also loudly disparaged are those attempts at architectural coherence by artisan builders, such as the north and south sides of Bedford Square in London, where paired three-bay houses produced the 'tragedy, or rather farce' of a four-bay pediment with five pilasters (Figure 2.2).[2] Broadly speaking, the adversarial view expressed by Robert Campbell in 1747 – that there were 'few Rules to the building of a City-House' – has held firm.[3] Artisan *building* precluded good *design*. But as Peter Borsay has argued, 'how does this tally with the fact that classicism was being delivered to elite consumers by artisan craftsmen?'.[4]

The materials and methods employed in the construction of the typical town house have been amply discussed elsewhere, as have the forces of industrialisation and capitalism that shaped building systems and

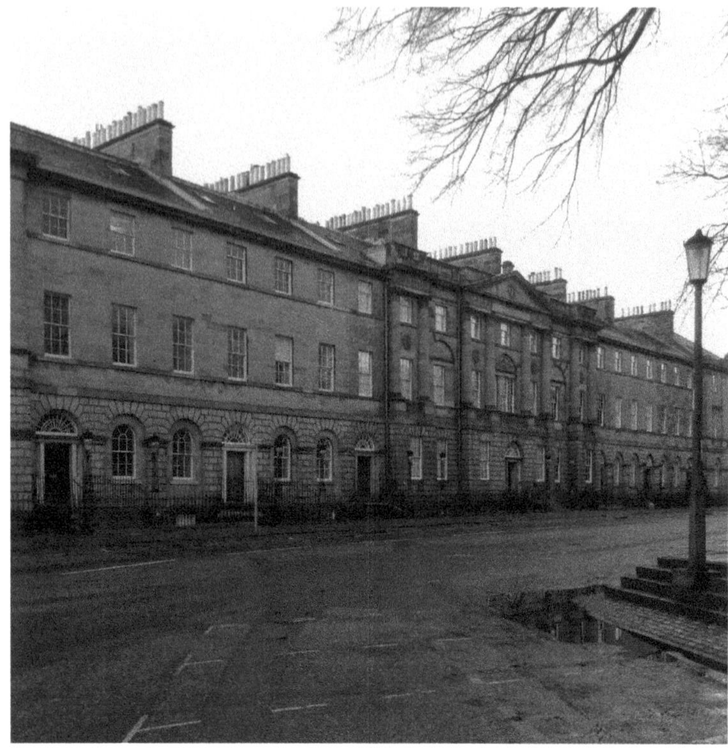

2.1 Robert Adam, Charlotte Square North, Edinburgh, designed 1791.

typologies.[5] The form of the urban house has been variously regarded as a direct consequence of an implicit 'political economy of design', as the material expression of emerging norms of cost behaviour and, despite the potential affront to social order, as a manifestation of an avowed consumer-led preference for decorum by the simplest means possible.[6] Broadly speaking, this literature furthers a characterisation of the town house as a typology that was *made* as opposed to *designed*. The present discussion is intended to complement those literatures with a new emphasis on design, focusing on two related areas: the artisan's relationship to design and taste formed through apprenticeship, building tradition and architectural books; and the designs for town houses produced by artisans in response to the particular socio-economic contexts in which they worked. Just as Alice Friedman has characterized domestic architectural design generally as 'a series of compromises between convention and innovation', so this account considers the design of the town house as a consensus between creative agency and socially constructed regulations and building controls.[7] In the following discussion the commonly invoked term 'vernacular' has been deliberately avoided, particularly for its undertones of low status and cultural conservatism.[8] Clearly this is not what was at stake

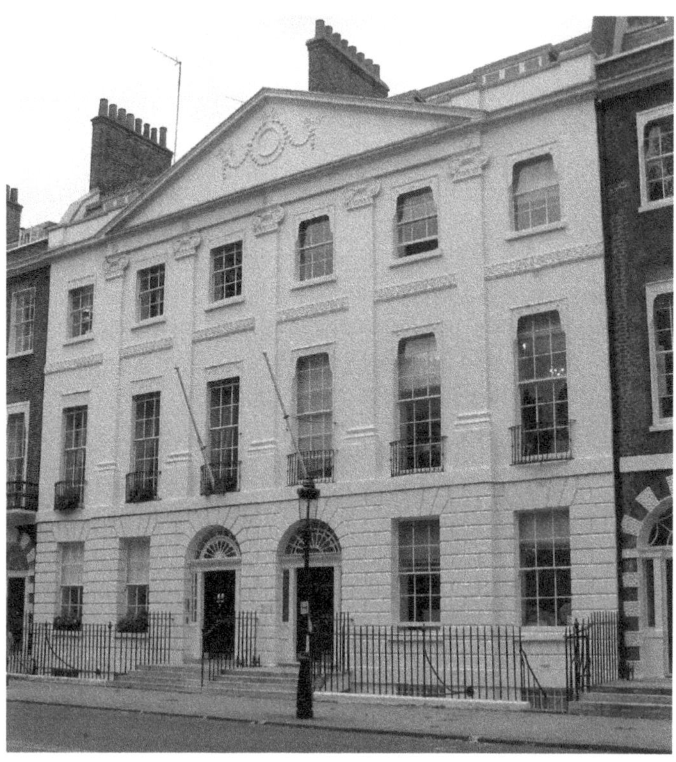

2.2 46–47 Bedford Square, London, 1777–82.

here: as noted in the previous chapter, building tradesmen were quick to embrace the trappings of an elevated social position and to advertise their trade in terms that unequivocally announced their competence in matters of design and of architectural taste.

We are concerned here with those individuals from the building trades who entered the world of (largely speculative) house building and thus made a profound material contribution to the appearance of towns and cities across the English-speaking world. In so doing, this narrative challenges the received wisdom regarding the 'average' builder's supposed 'simplicity of character' and complicit 'readiness to copy rather than indulge in weird decorative invention'.[9] It also resolutely dispenses with the characterization of the eighteenth-century builder as 'essentially a businessman with a financial relationship to design'.[10] Writing in 1761, Joseph Collyer advised that a successful master builder must be 'a good draughtsman'.[11] But while revisionist histories have argued for a broader understanding of the artisan's negotiation of the classical hegemony – not everyone wanted to 'speak' the same classical language – the design of the town house remains something of a contested field in academic scholarship:[12] for London's house builders, the 'standard terrace' represented 'the most robust choice in a risky financial world', being 'infinitely and economically repeatable';[13] in Philadelphia, knowledge of the classical orders or drawing skills 'had little relevance to the construction of row houses'.[14] Almost universally, the form and visual appearance of the town house is attributed to 'the exigencies of speculative building and of legislation'.[15] But who informed that legislation? If, as James Ayres, Stefan Muthesius and others have argued, London's Building Acts codified rather than introduced standards of design, surely the building class was a pivotal agent of that regulation?[16] Following Peter Guillery's recent attempt to invert the derogatory implications of the term 'builders' classicism', this chapter amplifies and extends our understanding of how design was 'a preliminary necessity' within the late eighteenth- and early nineteenth-century building industry.[17]

Design and the artisan

Recent accounts of the 'place' of design in eighteenth-century British culture provide an important context for understanding the builder's relationship to it. Matthew Craske has shown that design by mid-century was understood as 'an essential skill for any individual who wished to raise themselves above the labouring masses', and its popular dissemination in guidebooks and instruction manuals was key to its democratization.[18] This in turn formed part of a public rejection of a 'tradition of classicizing connoisseurship' predicated on aristocratic patronage, and signalled 'a new commercial confidence amongst London's producer classes'.[19] But while the importance of drawing skills for manufactures was widely acknowledged, Anne Puetz has argued that as academic theory emphasized the distinction between invention and execution, 'The underlying assumption (drawing enables designing) became problematic when "design" was understood not as a technical process, but as (the contested issue of) conceptual control.'[20] This had implications for the builder as a designer of architecture.

The traditional route towards proficiency in the building trades was apprenticeship, and although the influence of guilds and corporations receded in significance during the period under review they remained an important step towards certified independence and professional mobility. Draughting skills were a constituent part of a formal apprenticeship for most of the crafts associated with the building industry: stonemasons were required to 'learn Designing, and to draw all the five Orders of Architecture', and the carpenter was expected to 'write a tolerable Hand, and know how to Design his Work'.[21] Anthony Lewis's précis of artisan instruction in Edinburgh, for example, reveals that masons and housewrights were required to make plans, elevations and even pasteboard models of buildings: drawings of the classical orders – in some specific instances 'after Palladio' – represented a typical 'essay' (or 'masterpiece' or 'proof piece') for admission to the corporations as a freeman. Related building trades also had to demonstrate a proficiency beyond the practical demands of their respective skills set: in 1757, apprentice house painter Alex Weir was expected to decorate a house while paying particular attention to the articulation of its classical mouldings and ornaments; in 1783, the glazier Andrew Keay was required to familiarize himself with the relevant pages of Walter Gedde's *Sundry draughts principally serving for glaziers* (1615/16).[22]

As outlined in the Introduction, the artisan could also benefit from other formalized methods of design education. The Dublin Society's School for Drawing in Architecture, founded in 1764, was established with the express intention of providing instruction in technical draughtsmanship, providing 'a proper knowledge of lines and drawing sufficient for mechanics'. Typically drawn from artisan backgrounds, students combined a practical training at their employer's workshop with part-time attendance at the school. In 1772, professional standards were raised when the Society stipulated that 'no person shall be admitted as a scholar ... who is not intended to follow some business wherein a knowledge of Architecture is necessary.'[23] Both the practical and intellectual dimensions of architectural instruction for artisans were recognized in 1787 when the Committee for Fine Arts agreed to a new programme of 'Encouragement for Drawings', divided into two classes: the first class of awards focused on design, and comprised two premiums for plans and elevations of 'a Private Dwelling-house, and another of a Public Edifice, one of each at least'; the second class of prizes had a more practical bent, being for 'Sections of Roofs, Stair-cases, Brackets for Ceilings, &c.'.[24] Private drawing schools also flourished. From 1771, the artist William Waldron – later appointed master of the School of Ornament Drawing – instructed 'Artificers' in the 'several kinds of Ornamental Drawing, after their working hours' at his house in Mabbot Street.[25] Author and stonemason George Jameson operated a school of architectural design from his premises in Canongate, Edinburgh from 1740: students were required to supply their own mathematical instruments and drawing materials, and were awarded a certificate upon completion of a course devoted to 'the first principles of architecture'.[26] In America, the initiative necessarily came from the building trades: in the absence of formal collegiate schools of architecture, design instruction was necessarily artisan-led. A tradition of private drawing academies was already long established in Philadelphia in 1804, when house carpenter Owen Biddle lobbied (unsuccessfully) the Carpenters' Company, the city's foremost trade association, with his plan to open an architectural school.[27] By the end of the eighteenth century, a case of instruments for carpenters customarily extended to drawing pens, porte-crayons and boxes of watercolour cakes.[28]

The absence of institutionalized design education in mid-century London is not easily accounted for – and was indeed lamented by John Gwynn among others – although the scale of house building and architectural publishing in the capital likely addressed the immediate needs of the building community.[29] In the preface to *Rural architecture* (1750), Robert Morris supposed that 'there are already published, and executed, such a variety of town-houses, and so many persons who are daily concerned in the practical part of that branch', that designs from his own hand would likely be considered redundant.[30] But the taste-conscious London artisan also had occasion to engage the services of a professional architect to distinguish his building venture. For 17–18 Cavendish Square, built in the mid-1750s, the partnership of carpenter John Phillips and bricklayer John Barlow solicited designs from the architect Henry Keene in order to secure a 'uniform and continued building' for this exclusive address.[31]

Books of course formed a crucial part of the education of the building industry generally, and subscription lists confirm the high levels of textual and visual literacy among tradesmen and the desire to keep abreast of architectural fashion. As early as 1724, English architect turned author William Halfpenny acknowledged that 'the Town is already burthen'd with Volumes',[32] and the 1779 catalogue of 'Modern Books on Architecture, Theoretical, Practical, and Ornamental', from I. and J. Taylor's 'Architectural Library' in Holborn attests to the capacity of London's publishing industry to accommodate designers and practitioners from across a wide spectrum of professional and trade backgrounds.[33] An 1808 catalogue of the library of New York builder John McComb, Jr itemizes fifty-two titles ranging from Colen Campbell and Robert Adam to William Pain and Thomas Chippendale, and Edinburgh plasterer and builder James Nisbet subscribed to books by his kinsman George Richardson.[34]

The significance of the book for architectural design and pedagogy is, however, another contested field in the historiography of eighteenth-century classicism. Just as builders' manuals and pattern books offered advice on the Palladian idiom rendered for 'the meanest capacity', so they are seen to have fostered an inadequate understanding – or even misunderstanding – of its syntax and vocabulary.[35] But while it is arguable that early titles represented the 'conservative codification' of 'well-trodden and unfashionable forms', the diverse content of the typical eighteenth-century book defies simplistic categorisation.[36] Already from mid-century, builders' guides offered advice and instruction regarding a range of theoretical and aesthetic matters, from the semiotic character of classical ornaments to the relationship between solar orientation and room function; by the 1770s, books by William Pain, George Richardson and others customarily advised on the proportion and decoration of rooms relative to their social importance, and on the distinction between 'ancient' and 'modern' archetypes.[37] Indeed, while the pattern book has in the past been dismissed as 'the comic face of 18th century classicism',[38] and held responsible for the suppression of creative initiative, more recent interpretations have considered its potential to extend the artisan's autonomy and to 'prolong his involvement in the design process'.[39] A further paradox exists in the literature: in 1728, Robert Morris complained of 'insensible singleness' in the design of urban houses, advocating a rational, Palladian classicism;[40] but as builders embraced this 'norm of plain classical appearance', so they were castigated for their creative and intellectual deficit.[41] For social improvers and architectural critics alike this constituted a wider issue with contemporary urban design generally: the city house, in the words of Dan Cruickshank, did not habitually aspire to 'a very high level of architecture'.[42]

Just as the term 'artisan' embraced a range of individual skill and professional competencies, and 'design' enjoyed both technical and conceptual significations, so the respective parts of the building process came to be more formally delineated. By the mid-1770s, *architecture* was the 'art or science of erecting edifices', and *building* the 'art of constructing and raising an edifice' – the former predicated on the invention of 'several designs or draughts', the latter on the 'execution of the design'.[43] Drawing was therefore the practice by which the 'arts' of building – from carpentry and masonry to painting and glazing – were 'subservient to architecture'.[44] As we have seen, in concert with the professionalization of architecture from mid-century, 'the relatively minor social movement which permitted a bricklayer to become an architect was seen as a threat by a later generation of this new professional class'.[45] Himself the son of a bricklayer, the irony was apparently lost on Sir John Soane when he suggested that 'master workmen' were not content 'to follow the directions and be controlled in their charges by the architect'.[46] Individuals were not above criticizing one another in an effort to establish credibility as designers. Professional rivalry, and a more academic classical sensibility, inspired architect John Wood's adverse appraisal of his Bath peer, William Killigrew. By trade a joiner 'who lay his apron aside', Killigrew's designs were categorized by Wood as belonging to a class of 'Workmen' who 'after becoming excellent artists in their own trades, imagine themselves Architects, and so fill the world with Works of Whim and Caprice'.[47] Boasting of the introduction of a 'new system of architecture' in Boston in 1806, the authors of *The American builder's companion* (1806) cautioned that 'Old fashioned workmen who have for many years followed the footsteps of Palladio and [Batty] Langley, will, no doubt, leave their old path with great reluctance.'[48]

Design and the 'street house'

House building in the cities of the eighteenth- and early nineteenth-century Atlantic world was a largely speculative exercise. Though specific conditions differed from city to city, the general principle remained constant: a tract of ground was surveyed and divided into individual building lots; each lot of ground was then acquired (through sale or lease) at an annual rent by a building speculator (often, but not exclusively, a building tradesman); and a house was erected on the ground, usually within a prescribed period of time and often subject to clauses relating to design and construction. Once completed, the house was offered for sale (or lease) on the open market. Beneficial to landowner and builder alike, the system of speculative building has been described as 'a delicate balancing act' between maintaining high standards of design to secure high-status tenants and offering favourable conditions for developers with short-term interests.[49]

As a type, these houses are now widely described as the products of a proto-capitalist building industry: erected by master builders operating at their own capital risk, they were dependent on a complex system of contracting and subcontracting and of evolving patterns of labour organisation and wage agreement. The 'typical' three-bay brick house was already established as a typology by the end of the seventeenth century, and the emerging industrialization of the building industry during the course of the eighteenth century meant that house construction became increasingly 'a matter of assembling various pre-ordered parts', in the form of timber joists and scantlings, and door and window frames.[50] And as the products of a building industry, they are largely understood as 'objects of production, exchange and profit'.[51] This 'modern' quality prompted Danish architect Steen Eiler Rasmussen to describe London's terraced houses as 'refined industrial products', and arguably explains the sustained emphasis on economic pragmatism in the historiography thereafter.[52] At the same time, it is clear that these buildings satisfied the demands of the elite housing market. Although some of the grandest town houses were designed as discrete architectural statements in their own right, in cities like London and Dublin the nobility and gentry were generally content to purchase or lease a tradesman-built brick terraced house for their city residence (or to erect one in a similar form). So, while this 'reduced' classical style was predicated on increasingly standardized processes of building design and technology, and on the economically driven system of speculative development, it can also be interpreted as the expression of a cultivated, genteel sensibility – the house-buyer privileging public obligation (street) over private concern (home). Uniformity or monumentality of the street elevation, a visual effect increasingly demanded from enlightened architectural discourse and exemplified at the Royal Crescent at Bath and Charlotte Square in Edinburgh, depended on either an imposed architectural design from the outset, or a scale of operation that meant that all buildings in a street or terrace were constructed at the same time by a single controlling hand.[53]

In the previous chapter we saw how the brick house became synonymous with jerry-building, and the bricklayer, by extension, the focal

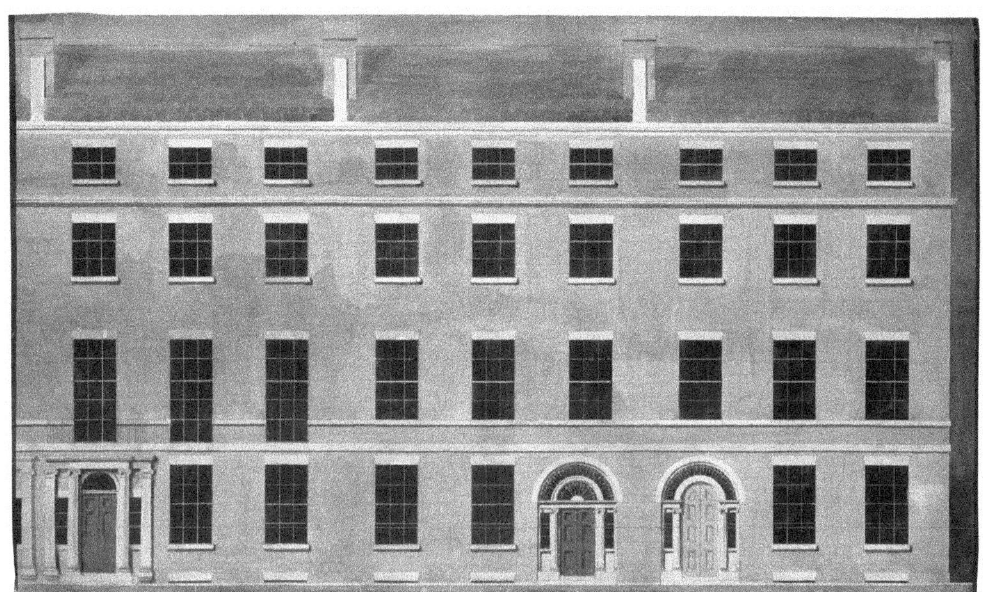

2.3 Royal Academy lecture drawing of Mansfield Street, London.

point of criticism concerning standards of design and construction. Such views were a feature of British architectural discourse from Isaac Ware and John Gwynn at mid-century, to John Soane and James Elmes at the close of the Georgian era. But while Ware condemned 'the art of building slightly', and Soane dismissed London's terraced houses as 'so many brick-heaps piled one after the other', it is important to remember that architects of the first importance, such as Robert and James Adam (at Mansfield Street), William Chambers (in Berners Street) and George Dance the younger (the Minories), also undertook speculative building projects that negotiated, rather than radically overhauled, the 'standard' brick typology (Figures 2.3, 2.4 and Plate 1); and their counterparts in early national America, such as Benjamin Henry Latrobe (Decatur House in Washington) and Robert Mills (Benjamin Chew House in Philadelphia), routinely designed bespoke houses in a plain brick idiom (Plate 2).[54] Brick construction, of course, enjoyed a better reception in the colonies given the tradition of timber-frame building that persisted throughout the eighteenth century. As brick replaced timber in New York in the wake of new building regulations, for example, one nineteenth-century citizen described how 'This interference on the part of the Legislature has introduced much neatness and regularity to the general aspect of the dwelling-houses.'[55]

The brick aesthetic was also impugned throughout the period under review. In 1756, Isaac Ware thought the colour of red brick

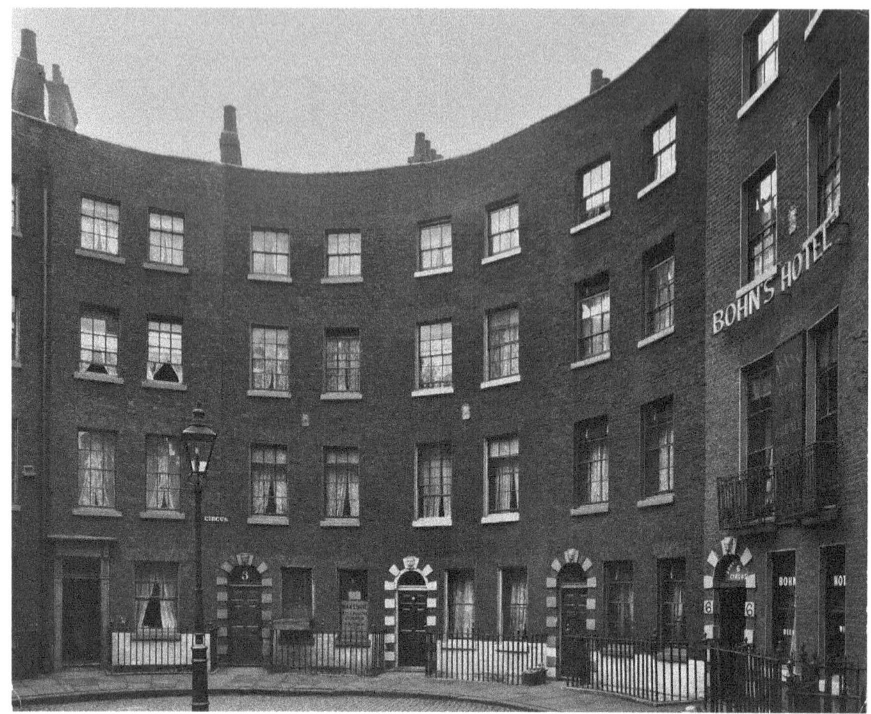

2.4 George Dance the younger, The Circus, London (dem.), 1767–74.

'fiery and disagreeable to the eye', and preferred the chromatic harmony achieved between a visual field of grey stocks and the customary use of stone ornaments in the form of window pedestals and rusticated plinths.[56] This point of view soon became orthodoxy: Ware's opinion was later reproduced verbatim in *The builder's magazine* (1774–78) and Peter Nicholson's *The new practical builder* (1823), and so sustained an appraisal of the brick terrace in architectural discourse that was at odds with architectural practice.[57] But in other cities across the Atlantic world, red brick enjoyed a different reputation. Dublin's late eighteenth- and early nineteenth-century terraces were often built with grey stock bricks that were 'colour washed red' with Venetian Red and Spanish Brown pigments,[58] and an elevation drawing in the Stapleton Collection captures the attractive visual and material properties of red brick in an impressionistic manner that emphasizes its qualities of colour and texture (Plate 3).[59] A similar augmentation of stock brick finishes was observed by an early nineteenth-century English visitor to Manhattan, who noted that 'The inhabitants of New York inherit the taste of their Dutch ancestors for fresh paint; every house of any pretension is annually coated with scarlet or grey, the divisions of the bricks are picked out with white.'[60]

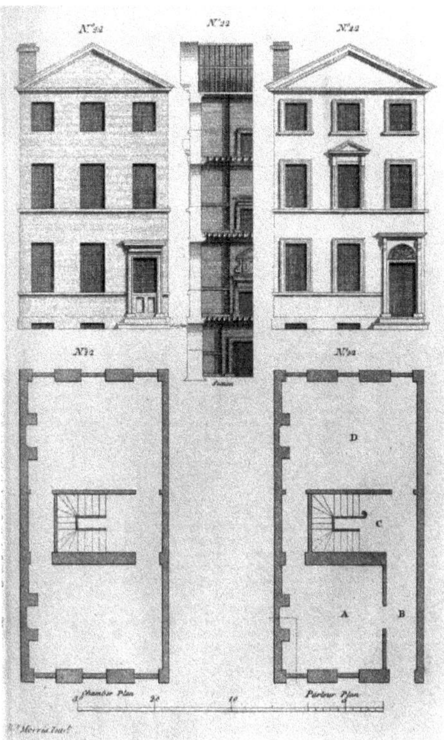

2.5 Elevation for 'a small town house' (plate 46) from Robert Morris, *The modern builder's assistant* (London, 1757).

As the visual countenance of London's streetscape became increasingly a matter of public concern, at least in terms of critics such as John Gwynn and James Peacock, so the design of the street house became a matter for the authors of books aimed at the building industry. In a recent, illuminating account of the London house in eighteenth-century English architectural literature, Rachel Stewart notes the lack of designs for the 'typical' brick terraced house: published designs for town houses generally ignore the narrow confines of the standard city plot and propose buildings of considerably grander scale and pretension.[61] For this reason, they may be said to complement, materially and figuratively, the discourse on the elite urban mansion and its requisite magnificence; a position shared by the admittedly limited Irish counterpart to this literature, such as William Stitt's *The practical architect's ready assistant* (1819).[62] Of the numerous designs examined by Stewart, two might be singled out as credible innovations within the established terrace idiom: Robert Morris's 'small Town House' published in *The modern builder's assistant* (1757) and John Carter's design 'for a private Gentleman' in *The builder's magazine* (1774) (Figures 2.5 and 2.6). While Morris's elevation is casually dismissed by

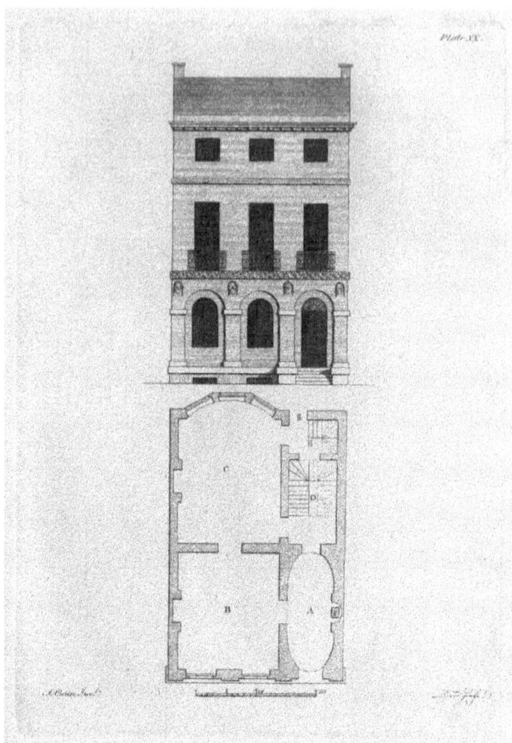

2.6 John Carter, 'A design of a town house for a private gentleman' (plate 20) from *The builder's magazine* (London, 1774–78).

Stewart as 'unremarkable' – although its 20 feet frontage arguably indicates a serious attempt at addressing the design of the typical house – Carter's design is seen as evidence of the potential for making architecture from building.[63] Indeed, both in plan (elliptical hall) and elevation (blind arcade at street level), it augments rather than radically readdresses the characteristic form yet achieves a formal distinction befitting a noble household.[64] Yet despite representing a clever compromise between economic pragmatism and architectural connoisseurship, Carter's published designs are not afforded the same attention as those of 'leading architects' such as Robert Adam and James Paine.[65] Also overlooked are the designs of figures such as surveyor turned architect Michael Searles, whose 'remarkable skill in the design of modest urban housing' was clearly indebted to the prototypes of Carter, John Crunden, William Pain and others (Plate 4).[66]

A qualitative appraisal of these pattern book designs is one matter. But in suggesting that the typical terraced house was 'generally not written about or designed for', Stewart discounts a broader literature (in the form of 'estimators', 'ready reckoners' and books of mensuration), and overlooks the wider geographical sweep (that is, beyond the confines

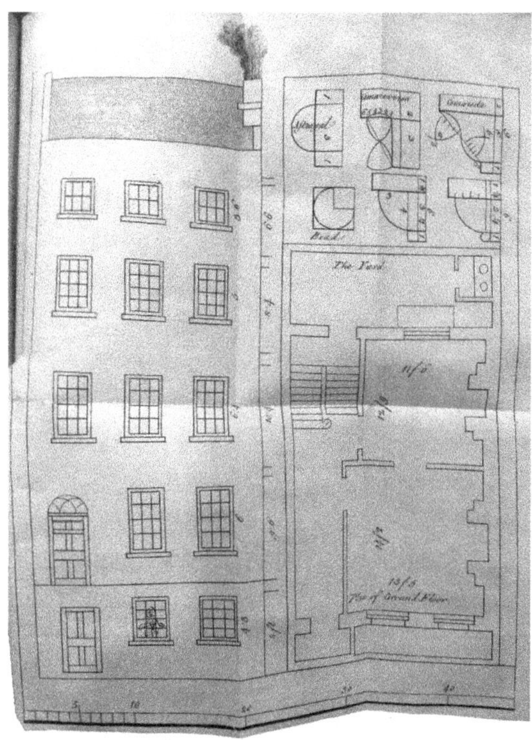

2.7 House elevation from John Leadbeater, *The gentleman and tradesman's compleat assistant* (London, 1770).

of London) of eighteenth- and early nineteenth-century British architectural culture.[67] In her appraisal of the design for a four-storey, three-bay house in John Leadbeater's *The gentleman and tradesman's compleat assistant* (1770), for example, Stewart argues that the rudimentary elevation reflects the fact that 'in its standard form the terrace house did not really need designing, just building' (Figure 2.7).[68] However, while admittedly laconic in detail – the design and textual description are decidedly meagre – there is a clear emphasis on the importance of proportional relationships between storey heights and window opes, and of their relative distribution with respect to one another. So, instead of focusing on what the design *is not* – it is neither a radical departure from the norm nor an inventive exercise within an established idiom – better to consider what it *is*: a careful delineation of the composition of a typical façade for the purposes of achieving 'the true Proportioning [of] the several Stories, and the Members thereto belonging'.[69] It might further be argued that the lack of prescriptive detail in Leadbeater's elevation acknowledges the individual builder's creative autonomy with respect to the articulation of the standard brick envelope.

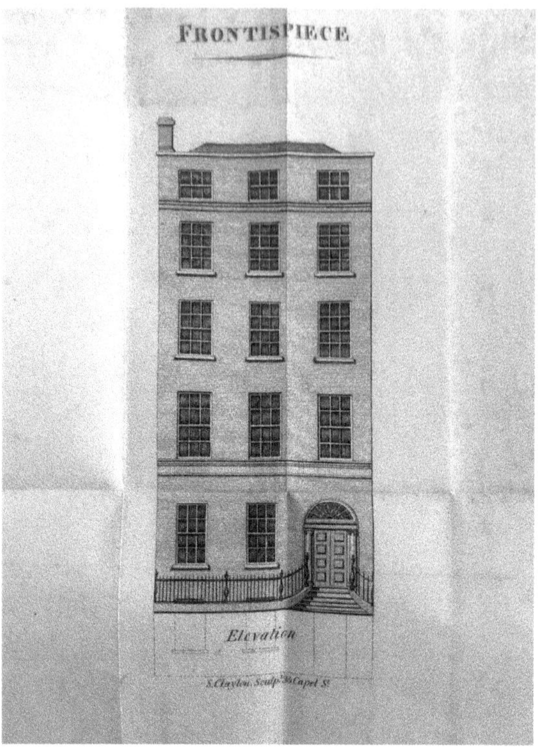

2.8 House elevation from Thomas Humphreys, *The Irish builder's guide* (Dublin, 1813).

Dublin measurer Thomas Humphreys's published estimate for 'a permanent and substantial dwelling-house in a genteel part of the city' was also accompanied by an elevation, this time pictorial rather than schematic (Figure 2.8). Indeed, while *The Irish builder's guide* (1813) arguably codified already established methods of building – and the content is largely concerned with itemizing the different costs of building 'first rate' houses in Belfast, Cork, Dublin, Limerick and Waterford – the model presented as a general frontispiece to the book is by turns conservative and creative. Just as Christine Casey has recently noted that 'a cornice is an event' in Dublin's Georgian terraces, so the augmentation of the customarily plain elevation with a decorative cornice and string course of stone or brick is clearly Humphreys' own invention.[70] In spite of his 'not having been educated in any of our elegant Classical Seminaries' – being rather 'bred to the study of Mechanism' – Humphreys's experience as a builder in 'the different cities and principal towns in Ireland' clearly informed the decision to create an arguably more urbane, yet still cost-effective, archetype for his intended reader.[71]

Across the pond, books had a more immediate impact on building aesthetics.[72] While Carter's design for *The builder's magazine* might have

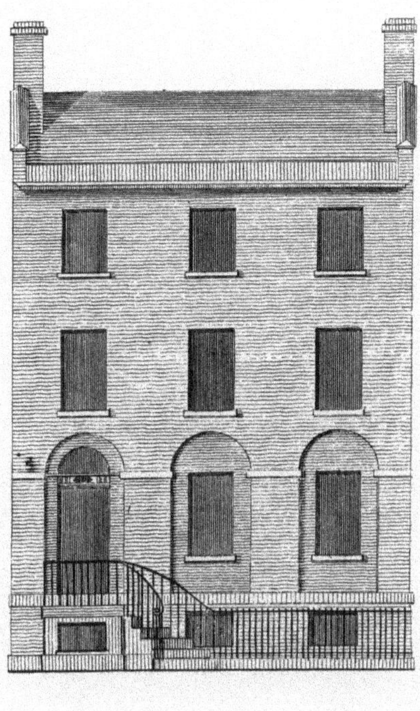

2.9 'Elevation for a small townhouse' (plate 33) from Asher Benjamin and Daniel Raynerd, *The American builder's companion* (Boston, 1806).

been an anomaly in an *English* context, it was certainly influential in the wider *British* context, providing the inspiration for, among other buildings, Charles Bulfinch's design for 13–17 Chestnut Street in Boston (1804–5), Asher Benjamin's design 'for a small town house' in *The American builder's companion* (1806) (Figure 2.9) and the town house designs of New York builder John McComb, Jr (discussed below).[73] Benjamin is an especially significant character, customarily regarded as a key figure in the development of the architectural profession in early national America.[74] As terrace or row architecture in Boston was in its infancy, his published designs 'for houses in Town' illustrate a range of responses to the city's particular social demographic. Benjamin's refinement of Carter's design retains the ground-floor arcade, omits the enriched string courses and applied ornaments and adjusts the proportions of solid to void to more common American archetypes. A carpenter by trade, Benjamin addressed his book to America's burgeoning building industry and clearly had an eye to established systems of building and construction. But its adaptation towards, arguably, a more economic type may equally be interpreted as a rationalization of architectural form: the blind arcade, after all, was not a

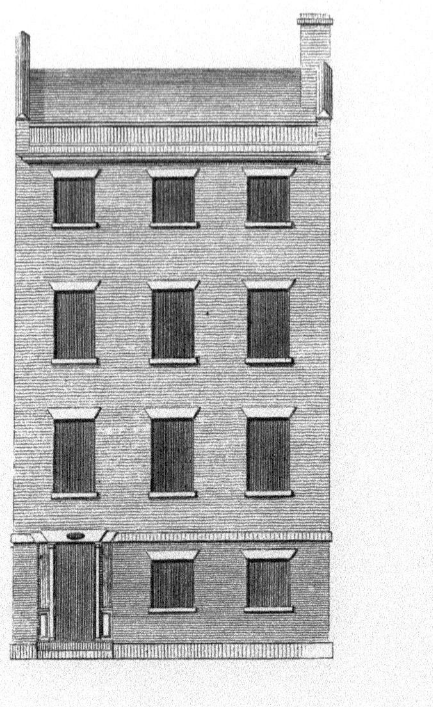

2.10 'Elevation for a townhouse' (plate 34) from Asher Benjamin and Daniel Raynerd, *The American builder's companion* (Boston, 1806).

typical feature of early nineteenth-century town houses in Boston and so must be understood as a constituent element of Benjamin's *design* and a matter of his *taste*.

Although not appending any further descriptive titles – none, for example, are described as being suited for 'a gentleman' or other social station – Benjamin's town house designs clearly provide examples of single- (25 feet) and double-plot (54 feet) street houses similar to those built in the fashionable Beacon Hill district, including 11–23 Hancock Street (c. 1806), customarily attributed to him.[75] Textual description focuses instead on the spatial organization of rooms and the hierarchy of the individual storeys: a design for a three-bay house boasts a 'parlour floor' complete with dining-room, china closet and library (Figure 2.10). Benjamin's origins in trade yet simultaneous concern for aesthetic effect is revealed by the particular attention paid to the relative proportion of material components, specifically window glass; that of the principal storey, for example, being 'eleven by sixteen inches, twelve lights each window'. Inspired by English paradigms, and modified to suit elite tastes and building customs in the cities and towns of New England, the publication of designs such as these was clearly part of Benjamin's self-advancement from 'housewright' in 1803 to 'architect and carpenter' by 1806. They also formed part of a wider culture of architectural publication that sought to protect the craftsman's place in a burgeoning building market, to elevate him among his journeymen peers and to counter the claim that design (and taste) was the sole province of an emerging architectural profession.[76]

House builders as designers

Just as the measuring literature published in Britain and Ireland, coupled with the architectural literature published in early national America, has revealed a broader range of practicable exemplars available to the eighteenth- and early-nineteenth century builder, so elevation drawings by artisans across the Atlantic world reveal the extent to which design was regarded as a constituent component of the business of urban house building. Here we must make a distinction between the myriad types, and functions, of architectural drawings. While describing the process of elite house design in late seventeenth-century London as 'incremental, empirical, and not solely paper based', Elizabeth McKellar found evidence of the use of plan drawings within speculative development.[77] Recognizing the 'unique capacity' of the plan 'for crystallizing in graphic form a complex set of legal, financial and environmental relationships which ensured its use',[78] she nonetheless concludes that they were 'inferior to the written word' and 'by no means universal nor critical in the design formulation of a development'.[79] Within a working milieu where drawings clarified cost computation rather than aesthetic form, evidence for the elevation is negligible for this early period. Donna Rilling, describing the building world of early nineteenth-century Philadelphia, is also unequivocal that the finely rendered elevation drawing was 'an unnecessary elaborate inclusion' among the requisite legal and financial documentation demanded of builder developers.[80]

A more universal form of 'design' was precedent.[81] Leases issued in the 1720s by developer William Hendrick for ground in Dublin's Smithfield specified buildings 'in all respects of equal height, storeys and ornaments to the houses now finishing fronting Queen Street';[82] on London's Bedford Estate, the builders of Charlotte Street were required to 'put a Portland Block Cornice above the Two pair of Stairs Window in a line with the other Houses adjoining'.[83] And as late as 1808, the sale of a building lot on Ninth and High (now Market) Streets in Philadelphia between John Ducker, carpenter, and Jacob Keyser, plasterer, bound Keyser to Ducker's original agreement that 'no other Building should be erected on the same in front of High Street other than of Brick and of the same Highth and no higher as the messuage erected … at the South East corner of the said High Street and Ninth Street'.[84] These kinds of instructions provide evidence of a traditional yet enduring approach to design that relied on widely understood conventions of form and construction, and an expectation of a 'workmanlike' product using good-quality materials.[85] It was indeed the system employed to build the Royal Crescent at Bath (completed c. 1775), one of the most widely celebrated examples of eighteenth-century urban design.[86] As outlined in Chapter 1, journeymen artisans also shared knowledge about design and construction through social clubs, craft societies and professional clustering; forming what Stana Nenadic has recently described as 'communities of interest'.[87]

Simultaneously, however, the use of elevation drawings was emerging as a key device for achieving architectural coherence in urban design, particularly in those cities where building guidelines had long been in place: by mid-century, drawing was in fact recognized as an advisable, if not always compulsory, step in the building process.[88] Bristol adopted early the methods of regulation that contributed to the ideal of the harmonious street elevation. Storey heights for houses in the more polite parts of the town, such as Queen Square, were already a feature of property development at the beginning of the eighteenth century; by the 1710s, building leases for relatively modest tributaries such as Orchard Street were equally prohibitive, and by mid-century house builders were increasingly expected to work to an approved drawing.[89] In 1768, an agreement for building two houses in the fashionable suburb of Clifton required the contracted builders – a partnership between Joseph Grindon, tiler and plasterer, and Henry Hawkins, house carpenter – to build 'agreeable in every Respect to the plan and Elevation' prepared by architect Thomas Paty.[90] Ground leases for Bath Street (laid out in 1787) specified houses with 'best' stock brick façades ornamented with pilasters, fasciae and sill courses in stone, 'as per Elevation'.[91] By the close of the century, an elevation drawing was both a means to ensure design fidelity and a device to attract prospective building entrepreneurs (discussed in Chapter 4). A notice 'To Builders', requesting tenders for three 'Capital Houses' near Finsbury Square in London in 1790, noted that interested parties 'inclined to contract' could appraise the 'Plans, Elevations and Particulars'.[92] As the practice of paper designs grew, so the house builder responded accordingly.

The following account builds on the notion that Matthew Craske and others have advanced: that design 'enabled men to make the transition from a trade, to the profession of architecture'.[93] Focusing on the façade – as the locus of both public interest and architectural discourse – the remainder of this chapter will examine designs produced for town houses and terraces (or rows) by the artisan builders of the first New Town in Edinburgh; by the renowned Dublin plasterer and house builder Michael Stapleton; and by John McComb, Jr, the foremost 'builder architect' in Federal-era New York.[94] Individually and collectively, these finely rendered elevations in ink and watercolour signal drawing as a form of intellectual capital and demonstrate the graphic skills acquired through apprenticeship and in drawing schools and builders' academies. In broader terms, these drawings confirm a shared interest among building tradesmen across the British Atlantic world in the creative manipulation of established typologies of form and ornament in an era of increasing standardization through building rates and industrialized manufacture.

Edinburgh's builders and the houses of the first New Town

The first New Town in Edinburgh, built from 1767 to a design by architect James Craig, has long been admired as the material expression of enlightenment urban planning. Together with the Northern New Town (planned 1801–2), the Western New Town (built piecemeal from 1805) and the Moray Estate (feued in 1822), it constitutes an urban landscape memorably described as 'the most extensive example of a Romantic Classical city in the world'.[95] But this is Enlightenment design in orthographic terms only. In an effort to attract developers and stimulate building progress, and in the absence of any reasonable assurance of demand, early Building Acts of 1767 and 1768 had not imposed any rules regarding the design of individual houses and their relationship to the wider streetscape: acknowledging that 'as people's taste in building is so different', speculators were instead granted what was later deemed to be an immoderate degree of design autonomy.[96] (Although Craig evidently favoured a formal visual coherence achieved through a careful balance between uniformity and variety, there is no evidence that he was charged with the responsibility for the design of street elevations; Robert Adam's elegant palace front designs for Charlotte Square, the principal ornament of the first New Town, were conceived only in 1791 and commenced building in 1795.) In response to the building variety that emerged, the town council inaugurated a series of guidelines and restrictions: an Act of 1781 specified a standard three-storey façade for the principal streets (exclusive of basements and garrets), and from 1785 applications for building ground had to be accompanied by an elevation of the intended house.[97] Thereafter, building tenders were typically rejected for, among other transgressions, proposing an irregular numbers of storeys, or for inserting 'Stormont' (dormer) windows in the garret storey; features typical of the multiple-occupancy dwellings common in the older parts of the city, but gradually regarded as inappropriate for the foremost thoroughfares of this modern and 'rational' urban setting.[98]

Edinburgh, then, is a city whose late Georgian streetscape has been appreciated in aggregate: the individual houses, and the people responsible for building them, having only very recently attracted objective, academic attention. A.J. Youngson's seminal account of *The making of classical Edinburgh* (1966), despite its suggestive title, discerned 'a strong tendency in the direction of monotony and lack of distinction' in houses built before Adam's commission by the town council.[99] But arguing against the received notion of the New Town as a sort of 'Mayfair-on-Forth'[100] – a Scottish equivalent to London's elite residential terraces and squares – Anthony Lewis's recent study of the New Town considers its formal properties as less a celebration of 'a static order and social hierarchy' and more a place of 'dynamic, changing social order'.[101] Conceived by the town council as an expression of its 'North British' identity, the city's building industry, in terms of economic, creative and political agency, was a vital constituent of its urban evolution. In 1777, a complaint of architect James Craig about the 'ridiculous' designs of mason William Smith was not entertained by the city council, who argued that 'if the Builders do not get fair play it will retard the finishing of the [New Town] plan'.[102] The scale of building production undertaken by the typical house builder was also inevitably more attractive to developers, investors and a corporate body mindful of the risks associated with the real estate market.

Scores of surviving drawings from the mid-1780s to the early 1790s bear witness to an artisan community with varying degrees of architectural ambition, and competing interests were played out in formal building terms: designs for large-scale tenements with dormer windows and gable ends, for example, continued to be envisaged, and indeed built, on many of the foremost streets of the New Town, including George Street and Queen Street. Here, it might be argued, building tradition trumped both enlightened planning and architectural decorum. But the city's house builders could also cite precedent in preserving a typology that predated the 1785 Act and contributed to a visual continuity with an existing building stock that dated from the foundation of the New Town. (Nor did George Square (1766–79) in the Old Town, described as both 'the first truly modern house building project in Edinburgh' and 'the most ambitious scheme of unified architectural character yet attempted', represent a paradigm of academic classicism to which builders might aspire: of cherrycock-pointed Craigmillar rubble, and composed of modest houses of varying width and height, its aesthetic 'mediocrity' was decidedly at odds with the model of genteel urbanism envisaged for the New Town.[103]) Development proceeded apace. By the early 1780s, St Andrew's Square and the western blocks of George, Queen and Princes Streets were substantially built; a decade later, Hanover and Frederick Streets were almost complete, Castle Street had commenced building and the design for Charlotte Square had been commissioned and approved.[104]

While the designs produced by Edinburgh's builders demonstrate a competence with the principles of classical composition generally – though sometimes, it must be said, with little regard for context – others were more discerning. Lewis has shown how Robert Adam's design of 1771 for Baron Robert Ord's house in Queen Street – specifically its tripartite doorcase and ground-floor rustication – was emulated by a number of house builders in the 1780s and 1790s; in other words, subsequent to

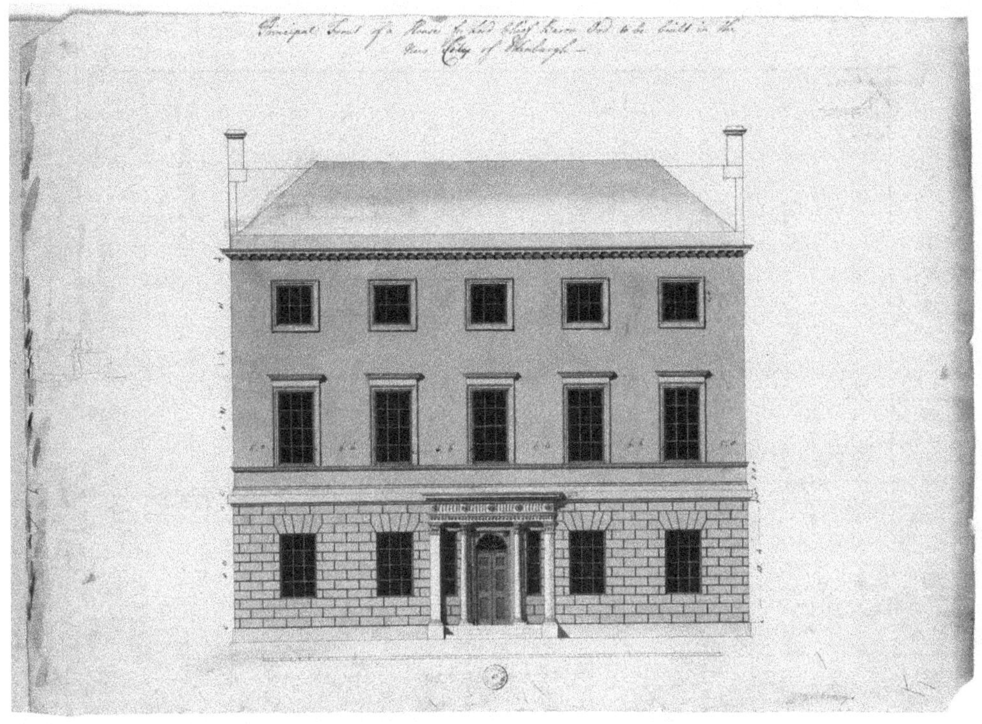

2.11 Robert Adam, elevation for Baron Robert Ord's house at Queen Street, Edinburgh, 1771.

the institution of building regulations by the town council (Figure 2.11).[105] Of course, adaptation or imitation from the built environment constituted one of the prevailing methods by which artisans appraised themselves of innovations in construction and fashion, and adapting a façade designed by a renowned architect might well be construed as a businesslike approach to architecture. This is certainly true of designs produced by the mason Alexander Balfour in 1790, where subtle variations in terms of window proportions and the flattening of architectural elements (columns to pilasters) barely conceal his debt to Adam's original design for Baron Ord (Plate 5). But there is arguably more invention here than first meets the eye. This is best determined by an elevation for a pair of houses produced by Balfour for Queen Street in the same year (Plate 6). Although clearly conceived as a pair, of particular interest here is the manner in which the discrete properties have been emphasized with a shallow break-front to each three-bay façade – defined by a vertical break along the party wall – and the termination of the sill course at either end with a pedestal moulding. These designs by Balfour cleverly achieve the type of continuity and uniformity desired of the late eighteenth-century terrace, while simultaneously retaining the visual appeal of the single property. Although confined to late eighteenth-century London, Rachel Stewart's recent study of town house architecture has shown that 'purchasers and tenants generally chose between houses on the basis of subtle differences within general sameness'.[106] But Balfour's elevations for Queen Street indicate that the decision to affect 'differences within general sameness' was as much the province of the builder as it was the client. Moreover, these drawings contradict the notion that the design of the house was solely contingent on the financial risks associated with speculative building, and complicates the long-held assertion that, within the confines of a Georgian street or square, it was 'neither necessary nor expected that each house should be an individual work of art'.[107]

While Balfour effectively offered two iterations of the same (arguably derivative) elevation, the design of the façade was generally predicated on the location of the property within the New Town. Craig's plan, although historically castigated as a 'mechanical and symmetrical' gridiron, effectively catered to a broad social spectrum:[108] Princes Street and Queen Street were built up on one side only in order to allow uninterrupted picturesque views of Fife and the Firth of Forth, and of the Castle and Old Town respectively; the modest houses of Thistle Street and Rose Street, by way of contrast, were intended for shopkeepers, merchants and 'the better class of artisans'.[109] Designs by the building partnership of John Hay, mason, and John Baxter, slater, for a house in George Street (1786) and a tenement building in Castle Street (1790), for example, reveal the different approach to the design of elevations in a residential thoroughfare and a major tributary, or cross street, where bow-fronted tenements were common (Figure 2.12 and Plate 7).[110] Interestingly, the habitual diminishing of window sizes relative to the spatial hierarchy of the typical town house is dispensed with in the design of the tenement building: as a multiple-occupancy dwelling, albeit one intended for the gentry classes, it was evidently deemed appropriate to maintain a consistency of scale on each of the three principal storeys.[111] In 1790, mason Robert Wright submitted to the council a bow-fronted design intended for Frederick Street, arguing that 'being a cross street the Petitioner finds it necessary to adopt a plan that will he thinks strike the attention of the public, as the Houses of these streets often stand empty long after they are finished, which is not only a loss to the Petitioner but also to the Town of Edinburgh'. As well as proffering a credible architectural solution to a problem identified with selling real estate in the less obviously fashionable areas of the New Town, Wright was unequivocal that 'the ground plan has given universal satisfaction to people of Taste'.[112]

Elevations for pairs of houses by the stonemason Alexander Crawford (d. 1793), produced in 1790 and 1791, reveal discrete solutions to the design problem posed by houses in pairs. Although arguably dependent on Adam's elevation for Baron Ord, one design substantially elaborates

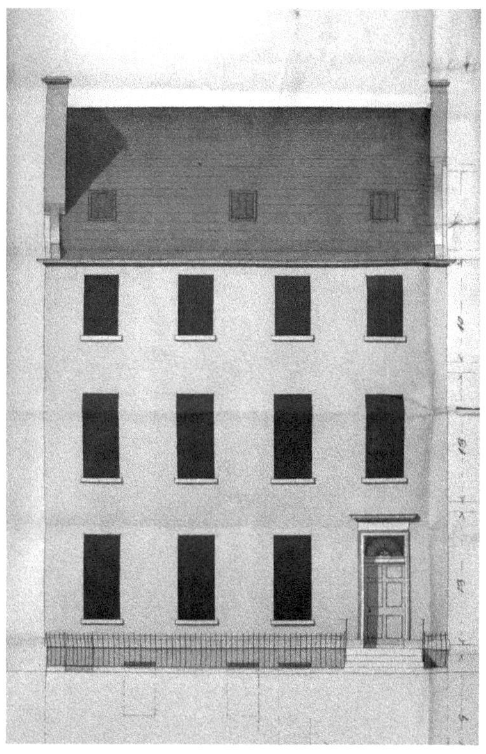

2.12 John Baxter and John Hay, design for a house in George Street, Edinburgh, 1786.

on this model, with balustrades to the windows of the *piano nobile*, an enriched, ornamental apron to the second-floor windows, a pedimented tripartite doorcase and a fringe of quoins to the upper storeys (Plate 8). Crawford may also have been inspired by Alexander Balfour's earlier design for paired houses that skilfully retained an individual character – both developments were intended for Queen Street – and his paired elevation is a singularly decorative solution. But context and building precedent were also important. In 1786, the partnership of Hay and Baxter approached the town council in order to amend an earlier proposal for a house on the north side of George Street, since 'at that time it was proposed that the Lodging on the opposite side of the street was to have a similar front – But now that the proprietor of the house on the opposite side has given up the idea of introducing pilasters, the Petitioners now humbly propose to build their House with a plain front similar to the other Houses there'.[113]

Edinburgh's house builders were clearly obliged to design. And as the town council moved increasingly towards the better regulation of building in the New Town, so it might be argued that builders depended or relied on approved models to the detriment of their own creative invention. But in the absence of design specifications *per se*, and cognizant of the 'people

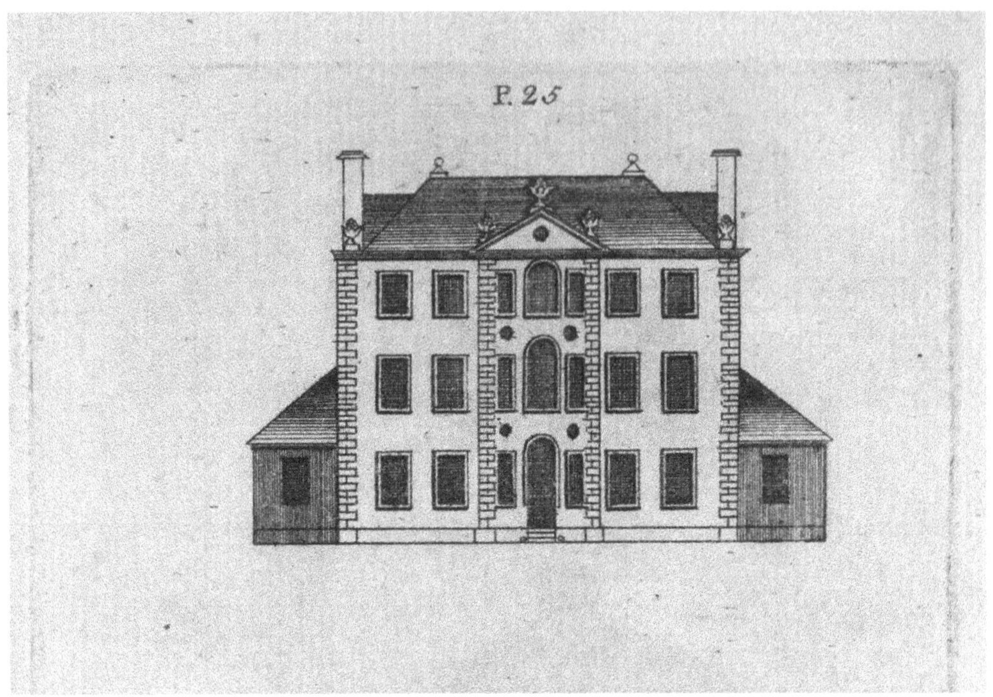

2.13 Elevation for an urban dwelling (plate 25) from George Jameson, *Thirty-three designs with the orders of architecture, according to Palladio* (Edinburgh, 1765).

of Taste' who constituted the real estate market, the impetus for builders like Alexander Balfour and Alexander Crawford was to create architectural distinction of increasing delicacy and refinement. Their creative invention lies in the subtle manipulation of architectural details (door surrounds, string courses, balustrades) and of the material textures of dressed stone (rustication, and courses of smooth and tooled ashlar) that announces individual speculations yet simultaneously maintains a balanced harmony in terms of the wider urban composition.[114] Compared with designs for urban dwellings published by Edinburgh mason George Jameson in 1765, they also express the more considered approach to street architecture that had emerged in the interim (Figure 2.13).

Despite the obvious attention paid by masons and wrights to the architectural aesthetic, the formation of these houses within a culture of *building* continues to elicit criticism among historians of eighteenth-century urbanism. A recent example is Charles McKean's curious reprimand of the work of 'ambitious plasterers', whose façades in George Street display a 'decorative fungus' of carved ornament.[115] But it is important to understand this within the context of architectural criticism generally. Writing in 1934, Steen Eiler Rasmussen criticized the builders of London's terraced houses for their 'superficial' use of classical architectural form and ornament, a position that arguably says more about modernist anxieties about decoration:[116] a similar view prompted post-war English architectural critics to praise 'the value of restraint in the use of exterior ornament' and the 'civic urbanity' of Dublin's 'plain designed Georgian facades'.[117] McKean's statement ignores the significant historical fact that the house in question – identified as the present 115 George Street – was built for Lady Balcarres, a member of Edinburgh's elite, who in 1789 contracted with plasterer and master builder James Nisbet to design and build a house that would be 'one of the most substantial compleat and elegant of any of that size in the New Town'.[118] It also pointedly ignores the fact that classical architectural detail is customarily decorative rather than tectonic; and this is as true of Robert Adam's elevation for Baron Ord as it is of Alexander Balfour's adaptation of that same design for own his speculative buildings.

As a delicate balancing act between production and consumption, and set against the increasing jurisdiction of Edinburgh's town council, the houses of the first New Town demonstrate how the making of *architecture* from *building* should not be confined to the palace front or the uniform row. In the elegant words of Anthony Lewis, 'Despite the fact that not every house in the New Town was the same and built by one man or one building company, the builders of the New Town could demonstrate a common, collective aim to make the new streets beautiful.'[119]

Michael Stapleton and the Dublin house

Unlike Edinburgh's New Town, the redbrick streets and squares of Georgian Dublin are admired less for any perceived quality of architectural beauty than for a sense of place consistent with the visual coherence of its historical built environment; its eighteenth-century brick terraces being recently described as 'the most singular feature of the city's fabric'.[120] (In his castigation of London's brick terraces in 1945, Sir John Summerson discovered that equivalent and 'monotonous' rows of houses survived 'to a really distressing degree' in Dublin.[121]) A number of elevations from the portfolio of plasterer and house builder Michael Stapleton (c. 1747–1801), however, reveal that the city's house builders were more sensible of design than customarily allowed in the literature. Indeed, given the pronounced architectural reticence of Dublin's eighteenth- and early nineteenth-century terraces, the existence of a corpus of drawings relating to their design might surprise those for whom the city's historical street pattern represents the prioritizing of 'mathematical – profitable – plots first and architecture – conditionally – later'.[122] Though he is best known as an exponent of Robert Adam's neoclassical decorative style (discussed in Chapter 3), the inclusion of Stapleton's name in a 'Certificate of the Principal Architects and Builders of this City' in 1794 indicates his standing and reputation among Dublin's building community, and the drawing collection includes five elevations for town houses that exhibit all of the characteristics of the standard eighteenth-century form in Dublin.[123]

The elite houses of Dublin, like London, and unlike Edinburgh's New Town, were raised on privately owned estates that demonstrated varying degrees of architectural ambition. The Gardiner estate, where Stapleton built a number of houses in Mountjoy Square and Mountjoy Place, was arguably the most ambitious – but on paper only. Grand-manner set pieces in the form of palace fronts and uniform terraces were typically realized in two dimensions only, and the individual houses of streets and squares largely conformed to a plain, unarticulated typology long endorsed by architects, builders and developers: architect Richard Castle's elevation for Doneraile House in Kildare Street (built 1746–50), for example, illustrates this preference for a bespoke house.[124] While the reasons for this are complex and multifarious – economic pragmatism, lack of consumer interest, a preference for a reticent classicism – the controls stipulated in building leases were correspondingly slight.[125] As a result, the city's building industry negotiated classical paradigms to suit established practices and tastes, and its terraced architecture relied on materials for much of its formal congruity.[126] Leases for Mountjoy Square, where Stapleton built three adjoining houses between 1789 and 1793 (all now demolished), stipulated façades of 'red stock brick' that were expected to rise to 47 feet in height and range 'exactly with the parapet of the adjoining buildings'; a further requirement stipulated 'no Bow windows or other projections beyond the window stools and doorcases'.[127] As houses were raised up from the individual plots, so a consistent parapet height became the sole *design* principle: in 1791, a deed of lease for a prominent corner site at the northeast side of Mountjoy Square, contiguous with Belvedere Place and perpendicular to Fitzgibbon Street, required the leaseholder to observe only that the fronts of the houses in Mountjoy Square would 'range exactly with the parapet of the buildings' on the north side of the square; those in the adjoining streets needed only to be 'good and substantial dwelling houses four stories in height'.[128] Curiously, given the singular importance attached to the height of houses in the square, there was no corresponding stipulation regarding the proportions of the individual storeys, a specification that might have affected a more discerning compositional regularity across terraces built piecemeal by individual speculators. Leases for Merrion Square on the aristocratic Fitzwilliam Estate requested only that houses should be raised 'three storeys and a half high above the cellars', and evidently relied on the fact that the design of the domestic house was already by degrees standardized and self-regulating – a plainness and approximate uniformity by default – hence the lack of explicit instructions.[129] A good example of this principle in practice is represented by 80–87 Merrion Square South, involving a business partnership between William

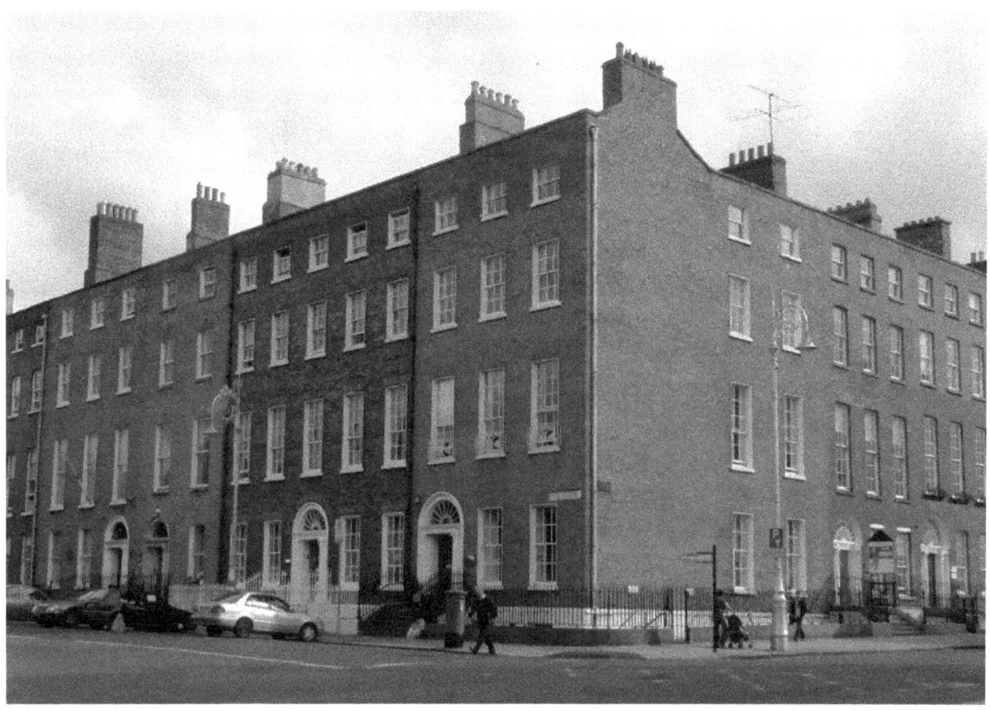

2.14 Merrion Square South (left) and Merrion Street, Dublin, c. 1789–93.

Hendy, John Gibson and John Donnellan, described as 'Copartners in the Trade of Carpenters and Builders' (Figure 2.14).[130] Presenting a unified appearance to the square, the houses are in fact of varying breadth and spatial dimension: while the majority are of standard three-bay frontage, albeit of varying width (between 27 feet 2 inches and 33 feet 2 inches), one (number 85) has a narrow two-bay frontage (a mere 22 feet 6 inches), and another (number 86) is a double-fronted, five-bay house (of 40 feet 9 inches frontage).[131] Collectively, a visual harmony across the entire property is achieved by a consistent parapet height, a symmetrical fenestration pattern and doorcases of identical form and design.

In the absence of strict guidelines, Dublin builders may have turned to the literature aimed at the building trades in order to determine the proportions of storeys relative to the hierarchical composition of the façade. Dan Cruickshank has shown that a number of systems were in operation at mid-century: while architects turned authors Robert Morris and Isaac Ware advocated Palladio's 'ideal' proportions and ratios based on mathematical and geometrical extensions of the cube, circle and square, in practice such theories 'found only limited expression'.[132] William Pain's *The builder's companion* (1769) provided a simple rule of thumb: 'It is a general Rule in Buildings, to diminish the Stories in their Height one sixth Part; that is, the second Story to be a sixth Part less in Height than the first, and the third Story to be a sixth Part less in Height than the second.'[133] There is an interesting, if unsurprising, correspondence to the schematic elevation in Leadbeater's *The gentleman and tradesman's compleat assistant* where the diminution of storey heights obeys this system. The storey heights outlined in two undated house-building specifications composed by Dublin measurer Bryan Bolger (c. 1758–1834) also correspond with Pain's formula, confirming the importance of the book in eighteenth-century building culture generally. Significantly, however, Stapleton designs annotated with figures depart from this rule of thumb method; the attenuated drawing-room dimensions, for example, being akin to more 'enlightened' architectural exemplars, including the Royal Circus in Dublin (1790), and Robert Adam's designs for the Royal Terrace, the Adelphi (1768) and Frederick's Place (1775).[134] This suggests that the design of the terraced house in Dublin was rooted as much in an *architectural* culture with an emphasis on aesthetics and theoretical principles, as it was in a *building* culture habitually circumscribed by legal, construction and economic considerations.[135]

This is confirmed by close inspection of a Stapleton design for three adjoining properties (Plate 3), which illustrates how building proportions were carefully adapted to houses of identical height – stipulated by leases issued by the Gardiner Estate – but of varying plot width (between 23 feet and 27 feet). Ostensibly an exercise in exploring the maximum potential revenue from a site – the individual houses invariably conform to the standard 'two-room' plan ubiquitous from mid-century – this deceptively simple drawing reveals that there was equal concern for proportion and symmetry in the elevation, the cornerstones of Palladian classicism. The different storey heights represented on either side of this design (14 feet for the drawing-room storey of the larger house; 13 feet for the two smaller properties) demonstrate how the composition of the façade, including the proportions of windows and doors, was in fact at the service of the formal spatial organisation of the interior.[136] A related design illustrating Adam-style doorcases and fanlights of different dimensions underlines the aesthetic significance of the door as the sole ornamental inflection of the typical façade across the city (Plate 9). This is corroborated by building leases issued for Baggot Street on the Fitzwilliam Estate in 1790, which stipulated a 'doorway ornamented with Cut Stone so as to render [the intended house] Handsome to the front of said street'.[137]

A number of the Stapleton designs suggest an understanding of the system of house 'rates' or 'sorts' – the set of specifications regarding the construction, size and cost of urban houses introduced in London by a series of prescriptive (if often ignored) Building Acts during the course of the seventeenth and eighteenth centuries.[138] In the wake of the Great Fire, the City Rebuilding Act of 1667 had, among other things, specified wall thicknesses and room heights, with the 'third sort' of house – intended for 'fronting high and principal streets' – being equivalent to the late Georgian typology under discussion.[139] The so-called 'Black Act' of 1774, named for its supposedly pernicious influence on the quality of urban design thereafter, did not in fact prescribe any rules regarding design *per se*, being principally concerned with enforcing earlier Acts regarding fire prevention, standards of construction and the system of rates.[140] Despite this classification system not being formally adopted in Ireland, elevations in the Stapleton Collection illustrate the divergent aesthetic demands made of 'first' and 'second' rate houses and share some similarities – conceptually, if not strictly in formal terms – with the four types illustrated in Peter Nicholson's *The new practical builder* (1823).[141] (Nicholson's text is significant as an example of practice informing theory, being a codification of house typologies already longstanding in building custom.) A 'first-rate' design in the Stapleton Collection is for a pair of three-bay houses (Plate 10).[142] Here, the proportion is almost a perfect square (a ratio of 1:1), with a combined frontage of 50 feet and measuring approximately 52 feet from base to parapet. However, while it departs from the 2:3 proportion common in London houses – a departure necessitated by the fact that Dublin houses expressed the garret as a discrete storey – the wall plane delimited by the first- and second-floor levels is square in area, and the proportions of windows follow Palladian ratios of 1:1, 1:2 and 2:3.[143] The pleasing balance of solid to void coupled with the uniform pattern of fenestration across each storey is appropriate for houses intended for the better sort of residential street or square: the symmetrical alignment of the doorcase necessarily demanding a generously sized entrance hall suitable for a house of this calibre (first-rate houses were expected to occupy a cubic capacity of 900 square feet). Another design suggests a 'second-rate' designation (without accompanying plans it is not possible to establish the area that would unambiguously determine its rate), the houses being of a narrower, two-bay proportion not dissimilar to Stapleton's self-built houses in Harcourt Street (1786–89) and increasingly common after 1800 (Plate 11). Here the ground-floor windows are slightly misaligned with those of the upper storeys, and the doorcase more markedly so; evidently a concession to the spatial organization of this storey and a clear example of form following function. (The three classes below 'first-rate' houses in Nicholson's schematic elevations also sacrifice window alignments at ground-floor level, the plan taking precedence over the façade.)[144] A further plan and elevation of adjoining houses of different heights and widths indicates the adaptability of the typology on a site of 40 feet width that was clearly not part of an elite residential enclave where uniform parapet heights would have been imposed: Stapleton's advertisement for a 'single roomed house' in Harcourt Street in 1789, described as being 'very suitable for a single Lady or Gentleman', confirms that the building community customarily adapted to the various demands of the elite housing market.[145]

While it must be conceded that these designs of houses in pairs or threes were conceived without reference to the appearance of their neighbouring properties, the rendering of exposed timber joists between the storeys in all of the Stapleton drawings nonetheless indicates that they were fully understood to form part of a larger terrace or row. In that sense they recall the evolution of urban design in eighteenth-century Britain and Ireland, a process described by Peter Borsay as the 'subtle but significant shift in emphasis away from the individual dwelling towards unit development'.[146] Despite its admittedly taciturn appearance, we must accept the Dublin house as being as carefully designed as its Edinburgh analogue.

John McComb, Jr and the New York house

Unlike its British and Irish counterparts, uniform rows of houses were not a common feature of the American urban landscape before 1800. Whether realized, such as Robert Mills's designs for Philadelphia (Franklin Row, 1809) and Baltimore (Waterloo Row, 1816), or paper-bound, such as Alexander Parris's designs for Portland, Maine (1806), the terrace or row 'always remained the exception' in the Federal era.[147] Early attempts at the palace front, such as architect Charles Bulfinch's Tontine Crescent in Boston (designed in 1793–94), which introduced 'a wholly unfamiliar aspect of urban elegance to the town',[148] also met with resistance: acquiring land for an affluent new suburb of the city in 1795, the Mount Vernon proprietors 'thought in terms of free-standing houses' rather than in terraces or squares like those of London, Bath, Edinburgh or Dublin.[149] In American cities, where residential zoning was still in its infancy, its wealthiest citizens elected instead to create visual distinction in terms of scale and ornament: a bigger house signified a bigger claim of social capital.[150] A series of elevations by 'builder architect' John McComb, Jr (1763–1853) display a range of responses to the task of designing a bespoke house within the row house idiom; here, too, we can determine the American dependence on the English pattern book, described as 'a perfectly natural practice for someone of McComb's date and training'.[151] Interestingly, while the drawings of houses in Edinburgh and Dublin reflect in varying degrees the visual properties of their respective materials – the silver-grey hues of sandstone in Edinburgh and the mellow tones of red brick in Dublin – the McComb elevations are uniformly rendered in shades of grey. In the absence of any comparable upstanding houses from his oeuvre, we might assume that McComb envisaged the typical red brick construction to have been painted, as described by visitors to the city (noted above):[152] as stone tables or basements are clearly delineated as ashlar blocks in at least two elevations, it seems clear that brick was the default building material.[153] But it may also reflect the influence of the graphic conventions of architectural *engraving* on architectural *drawing*, where the pattern of brick construction was elided in favour of emphasizing form and ornament.[154]

McComb's designs for domestic architecture were clearly intended for the better end of the market and articulate his eclectic approach to the classical idiom. The son of a mason turned builder-architect, his formation in design was likely through apprenticeship and the building site, and refined by architectural literature: as noted above, his personal library extended to volumes on a variety of topics, ranging from engineering and fortifications to decoration and furniture. Damie Stillman characterizes McComb's buildings as representing 'a later colonial-Adamesque style', and identified a disparity between his paper designs and his executed work, noting how his familiarity with English neoclassicism was in practice 'subdued in favour of a more conservative approach'.[155] This conservatism did not go unnoticed. Writing in 1824, James Fenimore Cooper complained that 'the Americans have not yet adopted a style of architecture of their own. Their houses are still essentially English.'[156] But while there is certainly some truth in this statement – the domestic architecture of Federal-era New York belonging to a shared *British* architectural culture – it is also significant that there is more variety in McComb's portfolio of designs than in those of his Dublin or Edinburgh peers. As essentially bespoke houses, or bespoke pairs or rows, his creative opportunity was distinct from that of house builders in the cities of Britain and Ireland, where the design of the urban house was, as we have seen, often circumscribed by regulations and covenants. As in Philadelphia, many early Federal-era houses in New York were two storeys over basement with a dormered pitch roof, creating a variable street elevation uncommon in the better parts of cities like London and Dublin.

In early nineteenth-century New York, a city 'plainly commercial in character', the contest between public and private interests stimulated the Common Council to address the haphazard development of Manhattan's street patterns, four-fifths of which, above Houston Street, had yet to be urbanized. A commission appointed in 1804, and augmented in 1807, reported that 'a city is composed principally of the habitations of men, and that strait sided and right angled houses are the most cheap to build and the most convenient to live in'. But having failed to inaugurate 'several significant planning considerations' regarding land usage or the heights and volumes of buildings, 'any area' of its now famous grid, devised in 1811, 'was equally open for the construction of a mansion or a foundry'.[157] Moreover, the introduction of fire regulations aside, 'housing restrictions aimed at improving the quality of urban housing were not adapted in the United States until the mid-nineteenth century'.[158]

Although it seems that competitive house-building businesses in New York had up to six properties in progress at any one time,[159] the elite house was, as in Boston and Philadelphia, an event in the urban landscape, and so formally and conceptually distinct from the homogeneous character of streets and squares in the cities of Britain and Ireland during the last

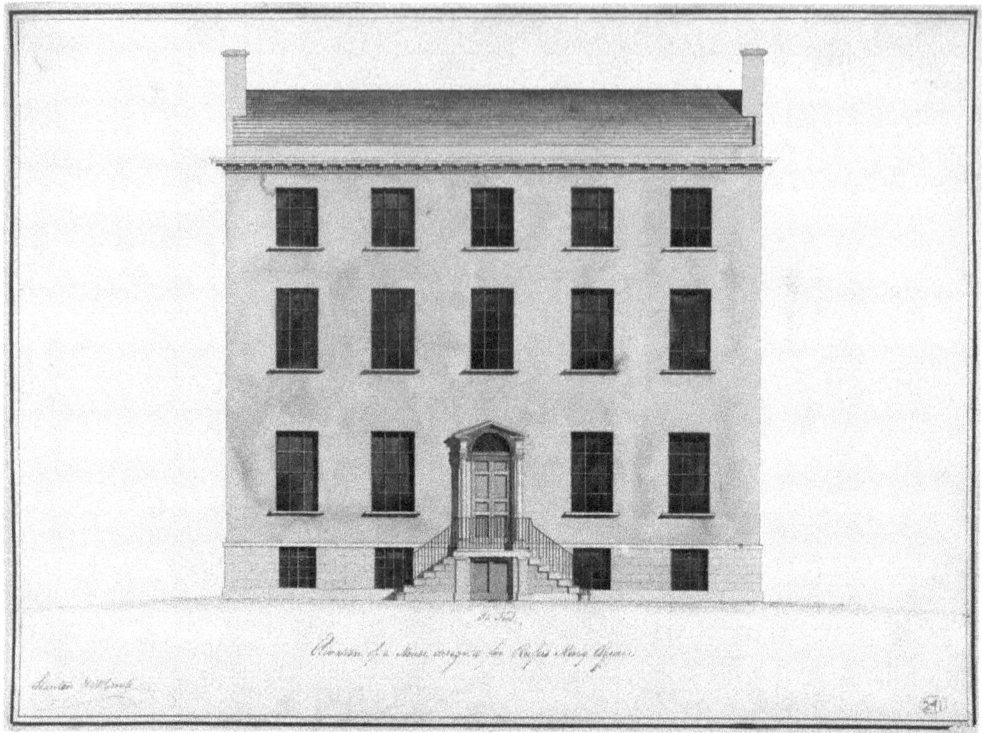

2.15 George Stanton and John McComb, Jr, 'Elivation of a House design'd for Rufus King esq.', Broadway, New York, c. 1794.

quarter of the eighteenth century. A good example of this is McComb's design for lawyer and diplomat Rufus King (c. 1794): a large five-bay house of 54 feet frontage, the stern modernity of its façade loudly announced King's pre-eminence in both the cultural and political arenas of New York society (Figure 2.15).[160]

A design for an unidentified three-bay house, autographed as 'John M'Comb Builder', is a good example of how a common typology was adapted to local needs and tastes (Plate 12). While the practice of creating a visual distinction between the ground and first floor (or *piano nobile*) was usual in London and Dublin houses after 1750, this was not something observed by American builders or, evidently, demanded by American consumers: the ground floor (or 'first floor' to use the American nomenclature) of even the grandest Philadelphian town houses, for example, customarily being reserved for the best reception rooms.[161] However, while the storey heights of McComb's design depart from English (and Irish) models where the first floor is typically taller, McComb creates a visual distinction with tall (almost floor to ceiling) windows at this level. This may suggest that the design was intended for a client who demanded a greater degree of architectural pretension. An unrelated plan drawing for lawyer and politician John B. Coles's house at 1 State Street (dem.), indicates that the 'drawing room' was situated on the first floor ('second story'), in the manner of an English or Irish town house.

Of course, McComb's elevation is clearly inspired by John Carter's town house design published in *The builder's magazine* (described above), and likely predates Asher Benjamin's iteration of the same source.[162] But subtle differences indicate how McComb customized Carter's published design in accordance with local building practices and, presumably, real estate expectations: while he retains the blind arcade at ground-floor level, for example, he omits the round-headed windows, which, though popular in London through the speculative developments of Michael Searles and James Burton, were never common in New York (the taller proportion of the windows in the attic storey is a further concession to practice rather than theory). The spandrel ornaments and fluted, second-storey string course of the English design are also here discarded, and surface decoration is instead confined to an enriched door lintel and impost moulding of a type of generic classical ornament in stucco or reconstituted stone already familiar in the better terraces of London and, after 1800, Boston.[163] On the other hand, fanlights were uncommon in New York before the 1820s, and rarely took the large semi-circular form illustrated here.[164] A similar design with two separate entrances (Figure 2.16) – catalogued as a two-family residence but more likely representing a mixed-use property – features the rectangular toplights that remained popular in that city into the 1820s; examples of which can still be seen in houses on Charlton Street and Vandam Street (built from 1817).

Other designs for single houses reveal the creative tension that arises between the observance of architectural protocol and the pragmatic demands of the building site. A design for an unidentified house in Queen Street, while only 24 feet 6 inches in width, asserts the ideal, if impractical, location of the door at the centre of the façade (Plate 13). Without an accompanying plan it is not clear what particular spatial organization was envisaged here – unidentified plans for three-bay houses in McComb's portfolio invariably place the door to the right or left of the composition – but it seems unlikely that he would have followed Isaac Ware's model (published in *A Compleat body of architecture* in 1756) and given over the front part of the ground floor entirely to the hall, a solution rarely attempted in London and, as Rachel Stewart has noted, 'out of step' with Ware's own advice that 'neither magnitude nor elegance' was required of entrance halls in city residences (Figure 2.17).[165] An almost identical design (with accompanying plan) on the verso represents a more pragmatic response to what was likely the same brief: the street parlour commands a generous 17 feet 8 inches of the 25 feet street frontage, with the entrance hall, positioned at left, confined to a mere 5 feet 6 inches in breadth.[166]

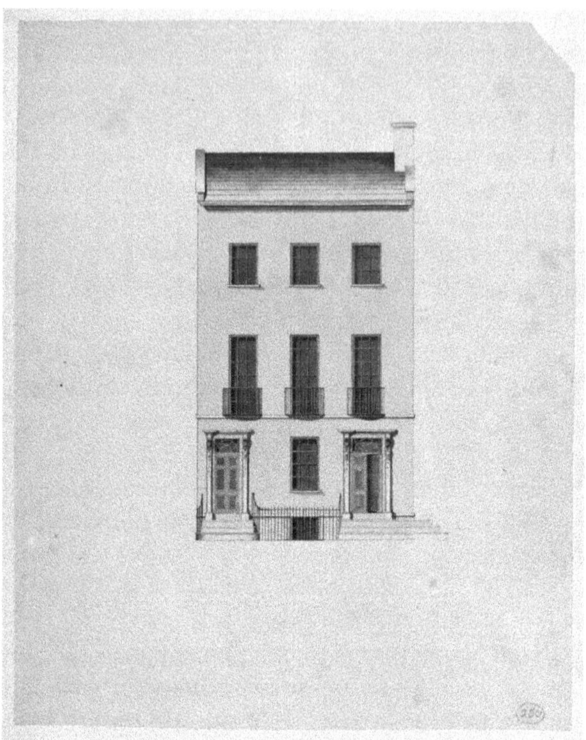

2.16 John McComb, Jr, design for an unidentified house, New York, c. 1800.

Although the uniform row was not a feature of New York's urban landscape until the 1820s, a number of designs reveal McComb's response to the problem posed by houses built in pairs or threes. Here we can witness the contest between idealism and rationalism; that is, between the dictates of English pattern book typologies and the economic realities of the American real estate market. While it is difficult to determine the evolution of his approach to row house design, given that the properties remain for the most part unidentified (and undated), architectural features such as string courses and stone lintels enriched with voussoirs indicate an earlier inception: after 1800, New York houses, like their Dublin counterparts (and the later row houses of Boston and Philadelphia), favoured austere, plain brick facades.

One ambitious design comprising three individual properties takes the form of two three-bay houses flanking a five-bay house (Figure 2.18).[167] Here, the larger centre house (50 feet) is articulated with a rusticated blind arcade at street level and a giant order of Ionic pilasters; the façades of the end houses (25 feet each) are differentiated with a pedimented breakfront, creating a visual terminus akin to a pavilion. A further distinction is made between the tripartite Adam-style doorcase of the larger property and the William Pain-style

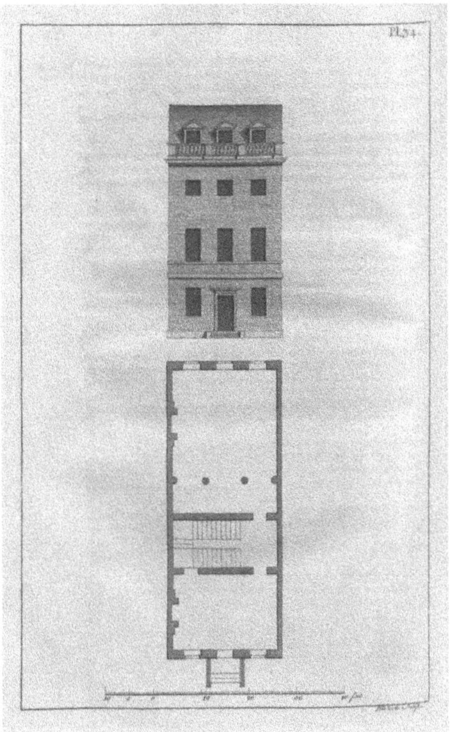

2.17 Design for a town house (plate 34) from Isaac Ware, *A complete body of architecture* (London, 1756).

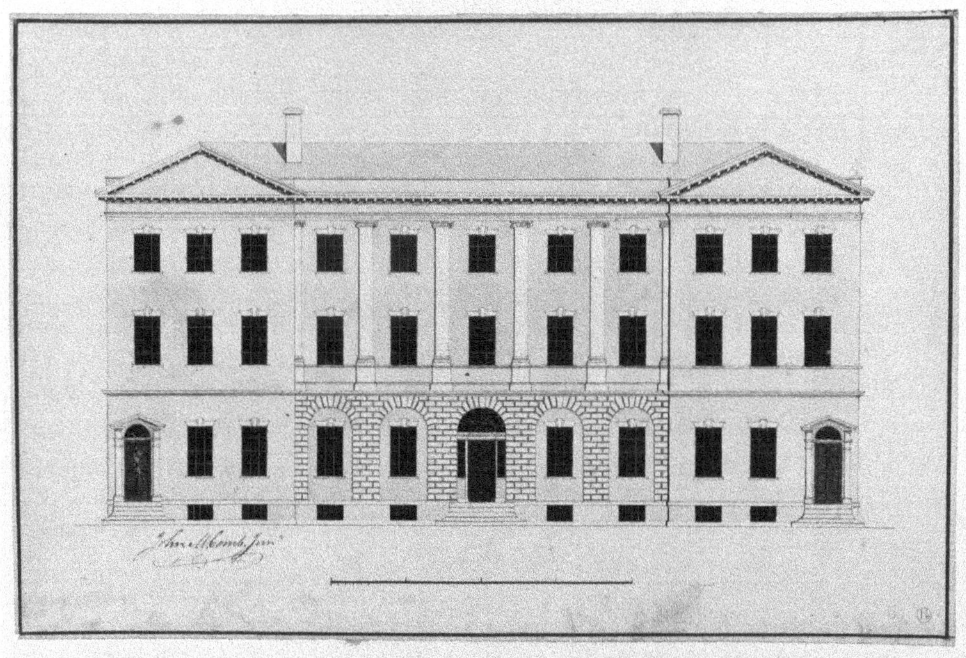

2.18 John McComb, Jr, design for a row of houses, New York, c. 1800.

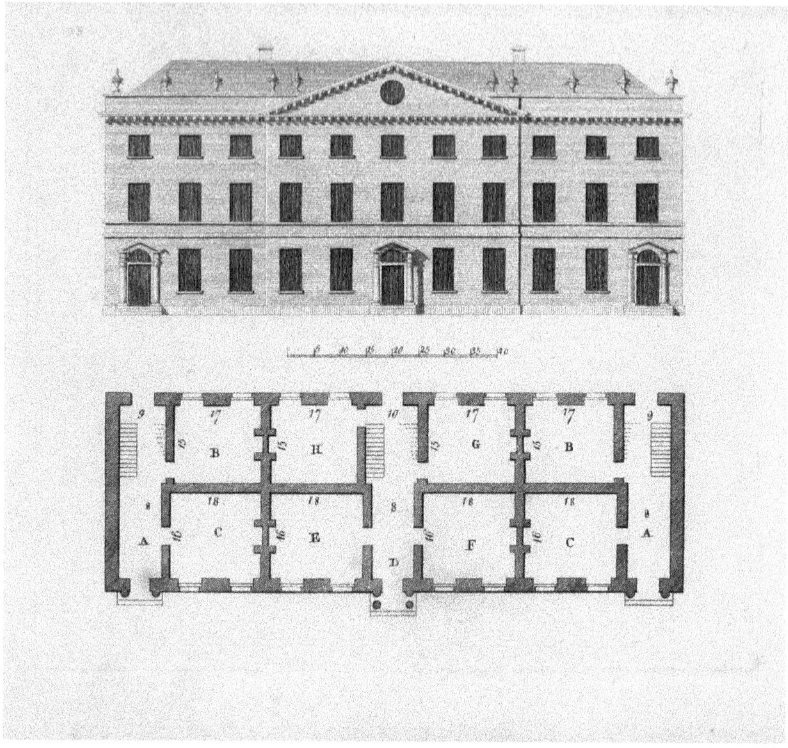

2.19 'Designs for three town houses, making one regular elevation' (plates 28 and 29) from John Crunden, *Convenient and ornamental architecture* (London, 1767).

doorcases of the flanking houses. Interestingly, this design is a composite and borrows its form and vocabulary from two different printed sources: the configuration of two three-bay houses flanking a larger, five-bay house is derived from John Crunden's *Convenient and ornamental architecture* (1767), while the articulation of the middle house is clearly indebted to a design from William Pain's *The practical house carpenter* (1794) (Figures 2.19 and 2.20).[168] But this is more than a mere agglomeration of sources, a cut-and-paste paper architecture: a uniformity of storey heights and modillion eaves cornice is observed across the combined frontage, and the careful articulation of string and sill courses on each breakfront and their relationship to the pedestal of the pilaster order is adroitly managed. Although dependent on an architectural vocabulary that could be described as *retardataire* – Pain's books often reproduced plates whose first outing was decades earlier – McComb's design achieves a harmonious balance between the contemporary demand for houses of different size and cost, and the obligation to create an architecture with a responsibility to the public realm. We might also learn from Carl Lounsbury's assertion that 'searching English architectural books for design precedents may be a useful exercise in connoisseurship, but far more

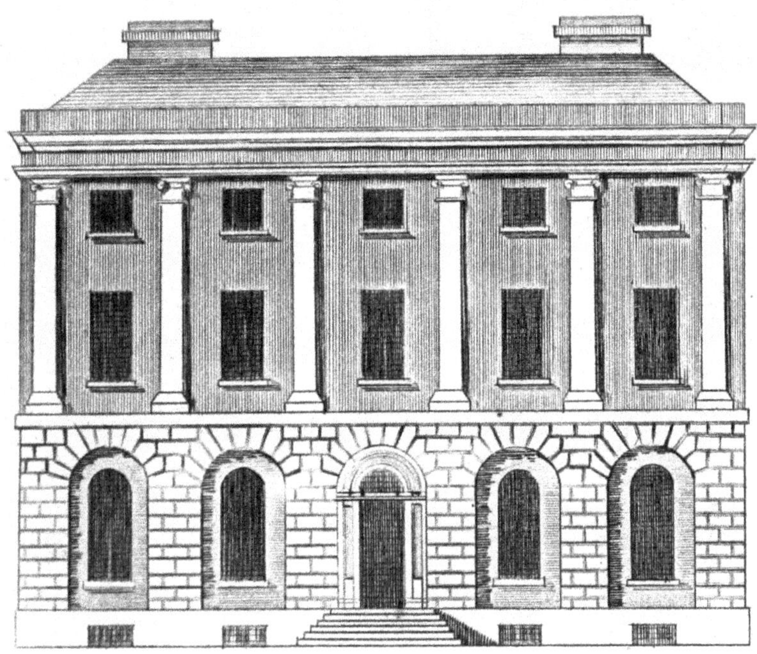

2.20 Elevation for a town house (plate 116) from William Pain, *The practical house carpenter* (London, 1794).

valuable is the study of how the academic concepts promoted in these books were integrated into the colonial design process'.[169]

More modest, and likely earlier in date, is a design for a pair of three-bay houses with a shared central passage leading to a yard or back passage (Plate 14). Here, the string courses, the taller pitch of the roof and the splayed lintels are obvious signs of McComb's debt to American building tradition. An unusual variant on the rusticated plinth is noteworthy, if somewhat gauche: here confined to the door surround (more typically to the entire ground-floor façade) but clearly related to the volume of the entrance vestibule directly behind (seen in the accompanying plan). A later elevation was evidently intended for a pair of houses in a grander residential setting: here the modernity of the design is expressed in the simple rectangular window openings with projecting sills and a parapet which would have concealed the low-pitched hip roof at street level.[170]

In the variation displayed in McComb's portfolio we find the opposite of Charles Lockwood's assertion that row house design in early nineteenth-century New York 'was little more than the embellishment of doorways and windows in the currently fashionable style'.[171] In the number of drawings devoted to this typology we also find a particular response to a socio-economic imperative.[172] Although Donna Rilling's study of Philadelphia's early national building industry found little evidence of the use of drawings in that city's speculative housing market, describing them as 'superfluous' within a building culture that understood 'widely known conventions' of construction and ornament, John McComb, Jr clearly used the elevation drawing as a means to distinguish his practice from the common herd of house builders in New York.[173]

Conclusion

A century after Joseph Moxon recommended that 'the fashion and form of each Front', and its articulation in terms of 'Facias, Rustick Quines, Architraves, Friezes and Cornices', should be determined in 'Draughts or Designs of the Uprights or Orthographyes', house builders had fully embraced the creative potential of the architectural elevation.[174] But while architecture and building are certainly 'different aspects of the same phenomenon', the design of the town house is not something that the builders of Georgian England or Federal America are thought to have necessarily concerned themselves with: the increasing industrialization of the building industry is habitually regarded as an impediment to creative imagination rather than something that builders negotiated.[175] Taken together, however, the variety of designs produced by Stapleton, McComb and their Scottish counterparts confirms the quality of artisanal invention in the decades either side of 1800.

These designs are of course, following Adrian Forty, responses to the conditions of their making: in Edinburgh, the guidelines and regulations imposed by the town council; in Dublin, the importance of proportional relationships in a city where unarticulated brick was the norm; and in New York, the adaptation of English pattern book archetypes to suit local tastes.[176] But taken together, these drawing collections confirm the distinctive quality that the classical idiom enjoyed in discrete parts of the British Atlantic world, and are a further testament to individual creative agency. And while Robin Evans characterized presentation drawings as 'projections of a plausible outcome for a set of instructions and proposals already defined elsewhere but not yet accomplished', the extraordinary fidelity between these projections on paper and the buildings in brick (or stone) – not least at Mountjoy Square in Dublin and Queen Street in Edinburgh – is further testament to a widespread congruence between the designing and making of urban domestic architecture during the late eighteenth and early nineteenth centuries.[177]

Peter Guillery has recently argued that London's terraced house 'was not a revolutionary invention, but the product of an evolving interplay between tradition, the profit motive, legislation and fashion'.[178] This is certainly true of terraces and rows throughout the wider British culture of building. But working with and against the regulations and guidelines imposed by private landowners and city councils, carpenters, bricklayers and plasterers turned house builders invented within the parameters of those limitations. It is in the subtle differentiation of form and ornament within the already flexible system of Palladian classicism, and within a typology of tall houses on narrow plots, that we find the *architecture* of the town house. This is *design*.

Notes

1 For a recent and illuminating discussion on the dissimulation of the elite town house see Rachel Stewart, *The town house in Georgian London* (New Haven and London: Yale University Press, 2009) pp. 116–35. However, although ostensibly devoted to the 'typical' speculatively built terraced house, Stewart's text focuses on the 'better sort' of house designed by architects like Robert Adam.

2 Dan Cruickshank and Neil Burton, *Life in the Georgian city* (London: Viking, 1990), p. 126. On this anomaly, and how it might have been rectified, see Andrew Byrne, *Bedford Square: an architectural study* (London and Atlantic Highlands, NJ: Athlone Press, 1990), pp. 25–6.

3 Robert Campbell, *The London tradesman* (London, 1747), p. 158.

4 Peter Borsay, 'Why are houses interesting?', *Urban History* 34:2 (2007): 341.

5 See, for example, Linda Clarke, *Building capitalism: historical change and the labour process in the production of the built environment* (New York: Routledge, 1992); James Ayres, *Building the Georgian city* (London: Yale University Press, 1996); Cruickshank and Burton, *Life in the Georgian city*, pp. 98–189. For America, see Donna Rilling, *Making houses, crafting capitalism: builders in Philadelphia, 1790–1850* (Philadelphia: University of Pennsylvania Press, 2001).

6 Jules Lubbock, *The tyranny of taste: the politics of architecture and design in Britain, 1550–1960* (New Haven and London: Yale University Press, 1995), p. xi; Ingrid Jeacle, 'Accounting and the construction of the standard house', *Accounting, Auditing and Accountability Journal* 16:4 (2003): 582–605; Stewart, *Town house*.

7 Alice T. Friedman, 'The way you do the things you do: writing the history of houses and housing', *Journal of the Society of Architectural Historians* 58:3 (1999): 406–13. According to Patrick Joyce, custom can be 'innovative and adaptive'. Patrick Joyce, 'The historical meanings of work: an introduction', in Patrick Joyce (ed.), *The historical meanings of work* (Cambridge: Cambridge University Press, 1987), p. 20.

8 Peter Guillery describes the artisan as 'culturally conservative' and characterizes his output as vernacular. Here he adopts Jill Lever and John Harris's definition: 'Designed by one without any training in design guided by a tradition based on local needs, materials and construction methods. Unconcerned with national or international styles, vernacular architecture is essentially local and conservative.' Peter Guillery, *The small house in eighteenth-century London* (New Haven and London: Yale University Press, 2004), p. 2.

9 Cruickshank and Burton, *Life in the Georgian city*, p. 117. Although describing an earlier period, Elizabeth McKellar is critical of how London's building craftsmen have been depicted by historians as 'subservient to the architect in both economic and design terms once the [role of professional architect] begins to emerge'. Elizabeth McKellar, *The birth of modern London: the development and design of the city 1660–1720* (Manchester: Manchester University Press, 1999), pp. 94–5.

10 John Wilton-Ely 'The rise of the professional architect in England', in Spiro Kostof (ed.), *The architect: chapters in the history of the profession* (New York: Oxford University Press, 1977), p. 193.
11 Joseph Collyer, *The parent and guardian's directory* (London, 1761), p. 93.
12 Bernard L. Herman and Peter Guillery, 'Negotiating classicism in eighteenth-century Deptford and Philadelphia', in Barbara Arciszewska and Elizabeth McKellar (eds), *Articulating British classicism: new approaches to eighteenth-century architecture* (Aldershot: Ashgate, 2004), pp. 187–225; McKellar, *Birth of modern London*; J. Ritchie Garrison, *Two carpenters: architecture and building in early New England, 1799–1859* (Knoxville: University of Tennessee Press, 2006), p. 17; Carl Lounsbury, 'Design process', in Cary Carson and Carl Lounsbury (eds), *The Chesapeake house: architectural investigation by Colonial Williamsburg* (Chapel Hill: University of North Carolina Press, 2013).
13 Stewart, *Town house*, p. 119.
14 Rilling, *Making houses, crafting capitalism*, p. 75.
15 Stewart, *Town house*, p. 122.
16 James Ayres has argued that the houses of Bloomsbury Square in London (1661) – 'the forbear of the terraced house' – informed the guidelines instituted by the post-fire Building Act of 1667; summaries of its legislation having introduced a 'profoundly classical' system of proportion. Ayres, *Building the Georgian city*, p. 14.
17 Peter Guillery, 'Georgian: builders' classicism', in Denna Jones (ed.), *Architecture: the whole story* (London: Thames & Hudson, 2014), p. 252.
18 Matthew Craske, 'Plan and control: design and the competitive spirit in early and mid-eighteenth-century England', *Journal of Design History* 12:3 (1999): 190.
19 *Ibid.*, 200.
20 Anne Puetz, 'Design instruction for artisans in eighteenth-century Britain', *Journal of Design History* 12:3 (1999): 232.
21 Campbell, *London tradesman*, pp. 158–60. Apprentices to the bricklaying trade were recommended to learn arithmetic, geometry, trigonometry and drawing. Collyer, *Parent and guardian's directory*, p. 75.
22 A.R. Lewis, 'The Builders of Edinburgh's New Town', unpublished PhD diss., University of Edinburgh 2006, pp. 177–8.
23 John Turpin, *A school of art in Dublin since the eighteenth century* (Dublin: Gill & Macmillan, 1995), pp. 49, 51.
24 Royal Dublin Society, *Proceedings of the Royal Dublin Society* 23 (2 November 1786–26 July 1787), 135.
25 *Dublin Chronicle*, 15 October 1771.
26 Anthony Lewis, *The builders of Edinburgh New Town 1767–1795* (Reading: Spire Books, 2014), pp. 41–2.
27 Jeffrey A. Cohen, 'Building a discipline: early institutional settings for architectural education in Philadelphia, 1804–1890', *Journal of the Society of Architectural Historians* 53:2 (1994): 139–83.
28 George Adams, *Geometrical and graphical essays* (London, 1791), pp. 9–11.
29 For contemporary criticism, see John Gwynn, *An essay on design* (London, 1749), pp. 91–2. Although state-sponsored education in architectural design was inaugurated only in 1768, with the foundation of the Royal Academy, there were other options for London artisans: under Sir Christopher Wren, the Royal Works had prioritized 'an empirical understanding of building' and offered a route towards professional mobility for carpenters, masons and joiners; the St Martin's Lane Academy (1735) was patronized by Frederick, Prince of Wales, and numbered architect Isaac Ware as a member. Mark Crinson and Jules Lubbock, *Architecture: art of profession?*

300 years of architectural education in Britain (Manchester: Manchester University Press, 1994), pp. 15–34.

30 Robert Morris, *Rural architecture: consisting of regular designs of plans and elevations for buildings in the country* (London, 1750), n.p.

31 Cited in 'Cavendish Square', in Philip Temple and Colin Thom, *Survey of London*, vols 51 and 52: *South-East Marylebone* (London: Yale University Press, 2017), available online at www.ucl.ac.uk/bartlett/architecture/sites/bartlett/files/chapter07_cavendish_square.pdf, p. 54, accessed 29 May 2017.

32 William Halfpenny, *Practical architecture* (London, 1724).

33 For the 'Architectural Library' see Eileen Harris, *British architectural books and writers, 1556–1785* (Cambridge: Cambridge University Press, 1990), pp. 59–60.

34 Damie Stillman, 'Architectural books in New York: from McComb to Lafever', in Kenneth Hafertepe and James O'Gorman (eds), *American architects and their books to 1848* (Amherst: University of Massachusetts Press, 2007), p. 164. James Nisbet is a named subscriber to George Richardson's *New designs in architecture* (London, 1792).

35 Richard Neve, *The city and countrey purchaser, and builder's dictionary* (London, 1703), p. xvii.

36 Guillery, *Small house*, p. 64. According to Guillery, this approach is discernible from the 'asymmetrically fenestrated and gabled front elevation' accompanying Joseph Moxon's *Mechanick Exercises* (London, 1703).

37 *The builder's guide* (Dublin 1758), by 'F.P., Builder', describes how 'all the principal Chambers of Delight, all the Studies and Libraries be towards the *East*, the Morning being a Friend to the Muses' (p. x). George Richardson's *A new collection of chimney-pieces* (London, 1781) includes advice regarding how to select a design appropriate to room function – grand rooms should have ornaments at a large scale, of simple forms and bold relief (pp. 7–8).

38 Dan Cruickshank and Peter Wyld, *London: the art of Georgian building* (London and New York: Architectural Press, 1975), p. 83. They describe the content as 'a peculiar mixture of the works of the pompous, the ignorant, the ambitious and the plagiarist as well as the shared experience of unpretentious craftsmen'.

39 Christopher Woodward, '"In the Jelly Mould": craft and commerce in 18th century Bath', in Neil Burton (ed.), *Georgian vernacular: papers given at the Georgian Group Symposium, 28 October 1995* (London: Georgian Group, 1996), p. 5. Dell Upton has made the important point that architectural books 'could only be used as a supplementary reference by someone who had a command of basic carpentry and design techniques'. Dell Upton, 'Pattern books and professionalism: aspects of the transformation of domestic architecture in America, 1800–1860', *Winterthur Portfolio* 19:2–3 (1984): 114. As early as 1952, Hugh Morrison argued that craftsmen in the colonies 'departed freely – and usually intelligently – from their sources, altering a detail here or a dimension there in accordance with necessity, invention, or taste'. Hugh Morrison, *Early American architecture: from the first colonial settlements to the national period* (repr. Oxford: Oxford University Press, 1987), p. 291.

40 Robert Morris, *An essay in defence of ancient architecture* (London, 1728), p. 69.

41 Stewart, *Town house*, p. 120.

42 Cruickshank and Burton, *Life in the Georgian city*, p. 125; see also Damie Stillman, *English neoclassical architecture*, 2 vols (London: Zwemmer, 1988), vol. 1, p. 180.

43 *The builder's magazine* (London, 1774–78), pp. 22, 91.

44 Ayres, *Building the Georgian city*, pp. 20–1, citing Abraham Rees, *Cyclopedia: or, an universal dictionary of arts and sciences*, 5 vols (London, 1778–88), vol. 1, n.p.

45 Ayres, *Building the Georgian city*, p. 9.

46 As a result, London's first 'grand essays of the speculative system of building', such as Grosvenor Square and Cavendish Square, had rapidly descended into 'streets of monotonous and, it may be added, of ill-constructed houses'. Moreover, while the design of earlier houses revealed 'an imitation of Palladio' and bore witness to the fact that 'Inigo Jones was not quite forgotten', the new terraces constituted 'so many brick-heaps piled one after the other'. David Watkin (ed.), *Sir John Soane: the Royal Academy lectures* (Cambridge: Cambridge University Press, 2000), p. 256. For the American version of this, see Upton, 'Pattern books', 119–20.
47 John Wood, *A description of Bath*, 2 vols (London, 1765), vol. 2, p. 317.
48 Asher Benjamin and Daniel Raynerd, *The American builder's companion* (Boston, 1806), p. viii.
49 Cruickshank and Burton, *Life in the Georgian city*, p. 111. In mid-century Bristol, the percentage of established master craftsmen engaged in speculative building has been estimated at 70 per cent. However, by the 1780s, 'when projects became more numerous and ambitious', this had fallen to 30 per cent and developers increasingly leased sites to mere 'journeymen carpenters and working masons', a fact that has inevitably been linked to the relatively reduced standards in design and construction of some of the later residential terraces. J.R. Ward, 'Speculative building at Bristol and Clifton, 1783–1793', *Business History* 20:1 (1978): 8–9.
50 McKellar, *Birth of modern London*, p. 78.
51 Howard Davis, *The culture of building* (Oxford: Oxford University Press, 2006), p. 12.
52 Steen Eiler Rasmussen, *London, the unique city* (London: Jonathan Cape, 1934, repr. 1960), p. 229. Rasmussen's apparent appreciation of the town house aesthetic is in fact self-contradictory: while arguing that the facades signify 'pronounced aesthetic ideals' (p. 235), he suggests that classical moulding and ornaments were used 'in a rather superficial way, both literally and figuratively' (p. 242).
53 'Regularity suits large-scale development because it facilitates measuring and pricing, even perhaps price-fixing. Standardisation was driven by economies of scale for the producers, not by consumer demand.' Guillery, *Small house*, p. 51.
54 Isaac Ware, *A complete body of architecture* (London, 1756), p. 291; Watkin (ed.), *Royal Academy lectures*, p. 256.
55 Unidentified source in Charles Lockwood, *Bricks and brownstone: the New York row house, 1783–1929, an architectural and social history* (New York: McGraw-Hill, 1972), p. 27.
56 Ware, *A complete body of architecture*, p. 61.
57 Peter Nicholson, *The new practical builder, and workman's companion* (London, 1823), pp. 346–7; *Builder's magazine*, p. 60.
58 Susan Roundtree, 'Brick in the eighteenth-century Dublin town house', in Christine Casey (ed.), *The eighteenth-century Dublin town house* (Dublin: Four Courts Press, 2010), p. 75.
59 Elsewhere, the plain brick finish is rendered in watercolour tints of red, pink and brown.
60 Unidentified source in Lockwood, *Bricks and brownstone*, p. 8.
61 Stewart, *Town house*, p. 159.
62 William Stitt's designs also ignore the typical town house, providing instead estimates for 'building and completing a Mansion House' and for 'building a House 66 by 56 feet square'. William Stitt, *The practical architect's ready assistant* (Dublin, 1819) pp. 156–98, 200–28.
63 This street frontage corresponds with that of the house estimate published in *The builder's guide* (Dublin, 1758), pp. 102–4; and with the design in John Leadbeater, *The gentleman and tradesman's compleat assistant* (London, 1770).
64 Stillman recognizes Carter's design as a response to 'the enormous influence of the Adam manner'. Stillman, *Neoclassical architecture*, vol. 1, p. 201.

65 Stewart, *Town house*, p. 166.
66 Cruickshank and Burton, *Life in the Georgian city*, p. 129. For Searles see W. Bonwitt, *Michael Searles: a Georgian architect and surveyor* (London: Society of Architectural Historians of Great Britain, 1987).
67 Stewart, *Town house*, p. 138.
68 *Ibid.*, p. 155.
69 Leadbeater, *The gentleman and tradesman's compleat assistant*, p. 242.
70 Christine Casey, 'Dublin's domestic formula', in Casey (ed.), *The eighteenth-century Dublin town house*, p. 49.
71 Thomas Humphreys, *The Irish builder's guide* (Dublin 1813), p. vi. Unusually, Humphreys proposes five storeys over basement, rather than the customary four.
72 'If there was an overall national character to American architecture … it was one borrowed from England. The means whereby Americans learned about English architecture were modern – that is, publications and mass-produced, accurate illustrations. … Americans were more reliably informed about the buildings of London than about those in Boston, Baltimore, or Charleston.' Michael Lewis, 'Owen Biddle and *The young carpenter's assistant*', in Hafertepe and O'Gorman (eds), *American architects and their books*, p. 160.
73 Sterling Boyd, *The Adam style in America 1770–1820* (New York and London: Garland Publishing, 1985), pp. 228–9. See also Jack Quinan, 'Daniel Raynerd, stucco worker', *Old-Time New England* 65:3–4 (1975): 1–21.
74 Jack Quinan, 'Some aspects of the development of the architectural profession in Boston between 1800 and 1830', *Old-Time New England* 68:1–2 (1977): 32–8; Upton, 'Pattern books'.
75 Keith N. Morgan, *Buildings of Massachusetts: metropolitan Boston* (Charlottesville: University of Virginia Press, 2009), p. 113.
76 Upton, 'Pattern books', 107–50.
77 McKellar, *Birth of modern London*, 120.
78 *Ibid.*, p. 126.
79 *Ibid.*, p. 132.
80 Rilling, *Making houses*, p. 79.
81 See Ayres, *Building the Georgian city*, pp. 1–16; McKellar, *Birth of modern London*, pp. 138–54; Cruickshank and Burton, *Life in the Georgian city*, 218; C.W. Chalklin, *The provincial towns of Georgian England: a study of the building process, 1740–1820* (Montreal: McGill-Queen's University Press, 1974), pp. 188–203.
82 Brendan Twomey, *Smithfield and the parish of St. Paul, Dublin, 1698–1750* (Dublin: Four Courts Press, 2005), p. 19.
83 Stewart, *Town house*, 120.
84 Philadelphia City Archives, Deeds E.F./33/28.
85 Rilling, *Making houses*, p. 76; McKellar, *Birth of modern London*, pp. 147–8. Architect Robert Mills's design for Waterloo Row, Baltimore (1817–19), with its triplet windows set in blank relieving arches, was quickly adapted to houses of reduced scale and social pretension, as at 10–18 West Hamilton Street (1820–22), erected by builder Robert Cary Long, Sr. See Mary Ellen Hayward and Charles Belfoure, *The Baltimore rowhouse* (New York: Princeton Architectural Press), p. 33. This is now recognized as evidence of a shared approach to design across the British Atlantic world. See 'Introduction', in Daniel Maudlin and Bernard L. Herman (eds), *Building the British Atlantic world: spaces, places, and material culture, 1600–1850* (Chapel Hill: University of North Carolina Press), p. 4.
86 Walter Ison, *The Georgian buildings of Bath from 1700 to 1830* (1948; repr. Bath: Kingsmead Press, 1978), pp. 231–3.
87 Stana Nenadic, 'Architect-builders in London and Edinburgh, c.1750–1800, and the market for expertise', *Historical Journal* 55:3 (2012): 597–612.

88 Ayres, *Building the Georgian city*, p. 20. In 'An Estimate for Building a New House', William Pain advised that 'It is necessary, to convey a better Idea of the Work, and also prevent Disputes, previous to the erecting any Building, to draw Plans of every Floor, and Elevations of each Front'. That said, the 'Two Designs, Plans & Elevations of Gentlemens Houses' illustrated in the text bear no resemblance to the typical town house typology. William Pain's *The builder's companion, and workman's general assistant* (London 1769), p. 10.
89 Walter Ison, *The Georgian buildings of Bristol* (1952; repr. Bath: Kingsmead Press, 1978), p. 153. These were often amended in practice.
90 Bristol Records Office, Haynes Collection HA/D/281.
91 Ison, *Georgian buildings of Bristol*, p. 25. See also Roger H. Leech, *The town house in medieval and early modern Bristol* (Swindon: Historic England, 2014), pp. 53–4.
92 *Public Advertiser*, 27 May 1790.
93 Craske, 'Plan and control', p. 191.
94 Isaac Ware suggested that 'An elevation shews the house, and every one who builds with taste desires it should be seen: the inside he contrives for use and his own convenience, but the outside is decorated for shew, and to please the eyes of others.' Ware, *A complete body of architecture*, p. 99.
95 Henry-Russell Hitchcock, quoted in Colin McWilliam, David Walker and John Gifford, *Edinburgh*. The Buildings of Scotland (New Haven and London: Yale University Press, 1984), pp. 18–19.
96 A.J. Youngson, *The making of classical Edinburgh, 1750–1840* (Edinburgh: University of Edinburgh Press, 1966), p. 81.
97 Lewis, 'Builders of Edinburgh New Town', p. 38.
98 *Ibid.*, p. 40.
99 Youngson, *Making of classical Edinburgh*, p. 93.
100 Charles McKean, 'The incivility of Edinburgh's New Town', in W.A. Brogden (ed.), *The neo-classical town: Scottish contributions to urban design since 1750* (Edinburgh: Rutland Press, 1996), p. 39.
101 Lewis, 'Builders of Edinburgh New Town', pp. 12–13. The context for the following analysis of elevation drawings is indebted to Anthony Lewis's research.
102 *Ibid.*, pp. 71–2, citing Edinburgh City Archives (hereafter ECA), Miscellaneous Council Papers 1778, Petitions and Miscellaneous Council Papers, 1/1/1768–31/12/1779, D0015R.
103 Youngson, *Making of classical Edinburgh*, p. 68; Gifford *et al.*, *Edinburgh*, p. 251. Dorothy Bell, *Edinburgh Old Town: the forgotten nature of an urban form* (Edinburgh: Tholis Publishing, 2008), p. 222.
104 Stillman, *Neoclassical architecture*, vol. 1, p. 226; Youngson, *Making of classical Edinburgh*, p. 92.
105 Lewis, *Builders of Edinburgh New Town*, p. 111.
106 Stewart, *Town house*, p. 117.
107 *Ibid.*, p. 123.
108 Youngson, *Making of classical Edinburgh*, p. 77.
109 Gifford *et al.*, *Edinburgh*, p. 321. The uninterrupted view from Princes Street was in fact threatened as early as 1770 and protected only in 1816. Youngson, *Making of classical Edinburgh*, pp. 87–91.
110 The pair of bow-fronted tenement buildings at Adam Square in the Old Town (dem.), designed by the architect John Adam in 1761, are customarily regarded as the source for the artisan-designed bow fronts of the New Town in the 1780s and 1790s. Ian R.M. Mowat, 'Adam Square: an Edinburgh architectural first', *Book of the Old Edinburgh Club* (NS) 5 (2002): 93–101.
111 Castle Street was built with 'high-class main door tenements and a few houses'. Gifford *et al.*, *Edinburgh*, pp. 291–2.

112 Lewis, 'Builders of Edinburgh New Town', pp. 77–8, citing ECA, Town Council Minutes 20/1/1790.
113 *Ibid.*, pp. 78–9, citing ECA, Town Council Minutes, 5/4/1786.
114 See for example the present numbers 57–61 Castle Street.
115 McKean, 'The incivility of Edinburgh's New Town', pp. 41–2. The particular house is identified in Lewis, 'Builders of Edinburgh New Town', p. 213.
116 Rasmussen, *London*, pp. 191–2.
117 Eleanor Butler, 'The Georgian squares of Dublin', *Country Life* (5 August 1945), 200; Elisabeth Beazley and Sam Lambert, 'An Irish appetiser', *Architect's Journal* 144:10 (1966): 568.
118 Lewis, 'Builders of Edinburgh New Town', pp. 204–5, citing National Library of Scotland, Acc 9769/22/1/13.
119 *Ibid.*, p. 79.
120 Christine Casey, *Dublin*. The Buildings of Ireland 3 (New Haven and London: Yale University Press, 2005), pp. 1–2.
121 John Summerson, *Georgian London* (London: Pleiades Books, 1945; repr. New Haven and London: Yale University Press, 2003), p. 126.
122 Niall McCullough, *Dublin: an urban history* (Dublin: Anne Street Press, 1989), p. 29. Arthur Gibney erroneously maintained that the 'repetitive design patterns' of Dublin's town houses dispensed with 'the need of drawings and descriptive specifications'. Arthur Gibney, 'Studies in eighteenth-century building history', PhD diss., Trinity College Dublin, 1997, pp. 67–8.
123 National Archives of Ireland (hereafter NAI), Bryan Bolger Papers, unsorted bundle titled 'Various accounts re Measuring – Measurements by others'.
124 David Griffin, 'The building and furnishing of a Dublin townhouse in the eighteenth century', *Bulletin of the Irish Georgian Society* 38 (1996/7): 25–39, fig. 1.
125 See Casey, 'Dublin's domestic formula'. The influence of insurance rates was likely another significant factor: already by the 1720s, premiums for timber houses were twice as much as those for brick houses. Rowena Dudley, 'Fire insurance in Dublin, 1700–1860', *Irish Economic and Social History* 30 (2003): 24–51.
126 Conor Lucey, 'Building dialectics: negotiating urban scenography in late Georgian Dublin', in Gillian O'Brien and Finola O'Kane (eds), *Portraits of the city: Dublin and the wider world* (Dublin: Four Courts Press, 2012), pp. 91–109.
127 Registry of Deeds, Dublin (hereafter RD), 412/522/271151. There was in fact some variation demanded from building heights in response to the particulars of the topography: leases for the east side of Mountjoy Square in 1796 specified houses of 52 feet, 'from the Top of the Base to the Coping of the parapet'. RD, 502/431/325824.
128 RD, 438/316/282915.
129 NAI, Pembroke Papers, 2011/2/2/10.
130 RD, 473/317/303209.
131 The latter represents an ingenious solution to the problem presented by a shallow plot (only 20 feet 8 inches deep): in an attempt to preserve the necessary accommodation for a polite family, the spatial orientation of the house is parallel, rather than perpendicular, to the line of the street.
132 See Cruickshank and Burton, *Life in the Georgian city*, pp. 134–49.
133 William Pain, *The builder's companion* (London, 1769), p. 2.
134 Compare the storey heights of the *piano nobile* in the collection of architectural drawings, National Library of Ireland, Stapleton designs AD 2353 (14 feet and 13 feet) and AD 2223 (13 feet), with Robert Adam's Royal Terrace, Adelphi (14 feet) and Frederick's Place (13 feet 9 inches) in London, and Queen Street, Edinburgh (14 feet); and with Bedford Square, London (14 feet 6 inches). Compare too with the first-floor storey height advocated by John Leadbeater (10 feet 4 inches).

135 There is in fact much variety in elevations designed by Robert Adam: the relative scale between drawing-room and attic storey heights in Royal Terrace, Adelphi (2 feet 6 inches more than Pain's formula) is considerably more than at Frederick's Place (1 foot 3½ inches taller than Pain's formula).
136 Although Robert Campbell bemoaned the fact that 'there are but few rules to the building of a town house', he conceded that 'in towns [bricklayers] generally know the just proportion of doors and windows'. Campbell, *London tradesman*, p. 10.
137 Quoted in Eve McAulay, 'Some problems in building on the Fitzwilliam estate during the agency of Barbara Verschoyle', *Irish Architectural and Decorative Studies* 2 (1999): 105.
138 These were the most prescriptive Building Acts in terms of their influence on architectural form.
139 'Mansion houses' intended for 'citizens or other persons of extraordinary quality' belonged to a fourth sort and faced no design restrictions.
140 Guillery, *Small house*, pp. 282–4; C.C. Knowles and P.H. Pitt, *The history of building regulation in London 1189–1972* (London: Architectural Press, 1972), p. 50.
141 Ayres, *Building the Georgian city*, p. 15.
142 The three houses in the previous drawing (AD 2352) are all first-rate houses, in terms of ground-floor footprint.
143 These ratios are based on measurements made from the drawing.
144 Stefan Muthesius, *The English terraced house* (New Haven and London: Yale University Press, 1982), p. 181.
145 Stapleton designs AD 2223; *Saunders's News-letter*, 27 April 1789. A 'single-roomed house' refers to a house with a single reception room on the ground and first floors; a 'two-room' house was the typical form in Dublin and London from mid-century.
146 Peter Borsay, 'Introduction', in Peter Borsay (ed.), *The eighteenth-century town: a reader in English urban history 1688–1820* (London: Longman, 1990), p. 21.
147 Damie Stillman, 'City living, Federal style', in Catherine E. Hutchins (ed.), *Everyday life in the early Republic* (Winterthur, DE: H.F. du Pont Winterthur Museum, 1994), p. 166.
148 Walter Muir Whitehill, *Boston, a topographical history* (Cambridge, MA: Harvard University Press, 1968), p. 52.
149 *Ibid.*, p. 62. See also Morgan, *Buildings of Massachusetts*, pp. 100–1.
150 See Robert James Gough, 'Towards a theory of class and social conflict: a social history of wealthy Philadelphians, 1775 and 1800', PhD diss., University of Pennsylvania, 1977. For an early example of occupational clustering in New York see Bruce M. Wilkenfeld, 'New York City neighborhoods, 1730', *New York History* 57:2 (1976): 165–82.
151 Stillman, 'Architectural books in New York', p. 167.
152 Two houses in Harrison Street (formerly 315–317 Washington Street), a street of modest two-storey (with dormers) brick houses, are given to McComb, Jr. The architect lived at number 317 'for many years'. Barbaralee Diamonstein-Spielvogel, *The landmarks of New York* (Albany: State University of New York Press, 2011), p. 86. The well-known house at 7 State Street (1794), a brick building with stone dressings, remains an attribution only. *Ibid.*, p. 80.
153 Gilchrist draws attention to two designs – uniformly of grey washes – whose basements are 'walled in stone' [024] or 'indicated as being in stone' [096]. Agnes Addison Gilchrist, 'John McComb, Sr. and Jr., in New York, 1784–1799', *Journal of the Society of Architectural Historians* 31:1 (1972): 10–21.
154 Elevations of Adelphi in London, for example, illustrate the Royal Terrace as if it were a monumental stone entity.

155 Damie Stillman, 'John McComb Jr.', in Adolf K. Placzek (ed.), *Macmillan encyclopaedia of architects*, 4 vols (London: Collier Macmillan, 1982), vol. 3, p. 134.
156 James Fenimore Cooper, *Notions of the Americans* (repr. New York: State University of New York, 1991).
157 Edward K. Spann, 'The greatest grid: the New York plan of 1811', in Daniel Schaffer (ed.), *Two centuries of American planning* (Baltimore: Johns Hopkins University Press, 1988), pp. 11–39.
158 Richard E. Foglesong, *Planning the capitalist city: the colonial era to the 1920s* (Princeton, NJ: Princeton University Press, 1986), pp. 62–3.
159 Elizabeth Blackmar, *Manhattan for rent, 1785–1850* (Ithaca, NY: Cornell University Press, 1989), p. 186.
160 The design is very close to John Crunden, *Convenient and ornamental architecture* (London, 1767), plate 19.
161 Exceptions to this rule include the Powel House, Philadelphia (1765) and 913 East Pratt Street, Baltimore (1810).
162 Stillman, 'Architectural books in New York', p. 166.
163 For example: Portland Place and Fitzroy Square by Adam in London; Finsbury Square by Dance in London; Beresford Place and Royal Circus in Dublin; Bowdoin Square in Boston. McComb's design for the John B. Coles house is illustrated in Stillman, 'City living, Federal style', p. 147, fig. 8.
164 Lockwood, *Bricks and brownstone*, pp. 11–13.
165 Stewart, *Town house*, 147.
166 Illustrated in Agnes Addison Gilchrist, 'Notes for a catalogue of the John McComb (1763–1853) collection of architectural drawings in the New-York Historical Society', *Journal of the Society of Architectural Historians* 28:3 (1969), fig. 7.
167 Catalogued as an unidentified public building.
168 The Pain design is a refinement of a design originally published in William and James Pain, *Pain's British Palladio* (London, 1786), plate 12. Titles by Crunden and Pain were available from New York booksellers by 1800. See Janice G. Schimmelman, *Architectural treatises and building handbooks available in American libraries and bookstores through 1800* (New Castle, DE: Oak Knoll Press, 1999).
169 Carl Lounsbury, '"An elegant and commodious building": William Buckland and the design of the Prince William County courthouse', *Journal of the Society of Architectural Historians* 46:3 (1987): 228–40.
170 Gilchrist, 'John McComb, Sr. and Jr., in New York, 1784–1799', fig. 11.
171 Lockwood, *Bricks and brownstone*, p. xiii.
172 There are in fact fourteen designs for town houses. Gilchrist, 'Notes for a catalogue', 209.
173 Rilling, *Making houses*, p. 76.
174 Moxon, *Mechanick exercises*, p. 252.
175 Davis, *Culture of building*, p. 8.
176 Adrian Forty, *Objects of desire: design and society since 1750* (London: Thames & Hudson, 1987), p. 8.
177 Robin Evans, 'Architectural projection', in Eve Blau and Edward Kaufman (eds), *Architecture and its image: four centuries of representation* (Montreal: Canadian Centre for Architecture, 1989), p. 19.
178 Guillery, *Small house*, p. 66. More recently, and following Pierre Bourdieu's concept of the 'field', Guillery recognizes 'all architectural design as emerging from social relationships tempered by individual creativity'. Peter Guillery, 'Introduction: vernacular studies and British architectural history', in Peter Guillery (ed.), *Built from below: British architecture and the vernacular* (London: Routledge, 2011), p. 4.

3

Decorating houses: style, taste and the business of decoration

The neoclassical style in Britain and Ireland, and its American counterpart, known as the Federal style, remained the dominant language of interior design practised during the late eighteenth and early nineteenth centuries. Emerging in architectural circles during the 1750s, its efflorescence and dissemination within artisanal communities was facilitated by a burgeoning print culture, by the movement of immigrant tradesmen and by new building and decorating technologies. Opposed to the architectonic Palladian classicism fashionable in early Georgian Britain, neoclassicism was characterized by an eclectic and inventive use of classical sources, both antique and modern, and by an increasingly delicate and refined approach to composition, ornament and colour (Plate 15). By 1800, it was the characteristic style of elite urban interiors from London to Charleston and from Dublin to Boston. But while classicism was certainly the 'common spatial and decorative language' across the wider Atlantic world, and through economic and technological standardization exhibited a sameness that became a signifier of British architectural culture generally, the traces of artisanal innovation were hardly eradicated.[1]

Unlike the bricklayer and carpenter, artisans who practised the more refined building trades, such as plasterers, joiners and decorative painters, have generally enjoyed a better reputation in the historiography of late eighteenth- and early nineteenth-century architecture. While architects like Robert Adam and Charles Bulfinch remain central to the narrative of neoclassicism in Britain and America respectively, craftsmen are also recognized as pivotal agents of its wider cultural and material reach. But as with the design of the terraced house, art-historical appraisal of the artisan's comprehension of Robert Adam's pioneering decorative style has often been misunderstood. Alistair Rowan remarked that lesser architects and artisans adopting his ornamental lexicon typically 'lacked an understanding of its syntax',[2] and for Geoffrey Beard, craftsmen 'faced with the complex intricacies of neo-Classicism ... might well have been found lacking without careful supervision'.[3] On the other hand, recent interpretations of the artisanal relationship to classicism (and neoclassicism), influenced by cultural-historical perspectives, tend to prioritize context over connoisseurship. In *Building the British Atlantic world* (2016), Daniel Maudlin and Bernard Herman recognize how the artisan was 'highly responsive to the forward impulse of modernity and the consumer drive for fashionable good taste', an impulse 'facilitated by the dissemination of ideas through migration (of craftsmen and connoisseurs), trade (the transatlantic shipping of books about buildings and supplies of building components), and through a high level of personal correspondence'.[4] Recently published monographs on the Irish plasterer Michael Stapleton and the American carpenter Samuel McIntire, both long recognized as key exponents of the neoclassical style in Ireland and America respectively, consider their individual interpretation or negotiation of Adam's decorative manner in terms consistent with their particular pedagogic formation and socio-economic circumstances (Plate 16).[5]

Of course, the neoclassical decorative style has also been recognized as a visualized sign of economic modernity. In his seminal *Art in an age of revolution, 1750–1800* (1989), Albert Boime described neoclassicism as 'the first art movement in history to be packaged, advertised and sold on the market as a profitable investment',[6] and Joseph Rykwert characteristically described Robert Adam's organisational abilities as 'the manufactory of virtu'.[7] In building terms, the industrialization and commercialization of classical ornament provided the artisan with an opportunity to preserve his autonomy within a professional space increasingly occupied by architects: the nature of contracting and subcontracting also allowed the house builder, though the employment of qualified plasterers and joiners, to dictate the quality and extent of interior decoration. While the architectural character and proportion of the interior remained essentially classical in derivation throughout the eighteenth century, the design of superadded features, such as enriched plaster ceilings and cornices, was more immediately subject to the vagaries of fashion. Endorsed by architects for both its aesthetic and pragmatic qualities – possessing a coveted sculptural quality at a fraction of the cost – decorative plasterwork emerged as one of the most effective visual and material means to reflect new architectural tastes within an increasingly standardized brick shell. Nowhere was this more tangible than in the speculatively built town house, the architectural typology that remained the preserve of the building artisan. And as we shall see, interior decoration formed an integral part of property speculation by the closing decades of the eighteenth century. Decorated by tradesmen as part of a commercial enterprise, and therefore independent of 'polite' architectural patronage, the neoclassical interiors of elite town houses from Dublin to Philadelphia were realized in response to circumstances distinct from those encountered by classically trained architects and their classically schooled patrons.

Related to this is a distinction between *in situ* hand-modelling (building craft) characteristic of the early Georgian era, and the moulded and applied work (building manufacture) that became more common from mid-century; a development in both materials and techniques predicated on new plaster technologies, specifically the adoption of quick-setting gypsum in place of traditional lime-based mortars. In the extensive literature on decorative plasterwork this has been understood as marking the beginning of a wider malaise in craft production. Implicit within this criticism, and still prevalent within the broader historiography, is an art-historical bias that venerates the 'organic' hand-modelled sculptural work of early eighteenth-century baroque and rococo styles, often attributed to individual 'hands', at the expense of the 'mechanical' neoclassical style, assembled from pre-cast components. However, while such methods necessarily produced 'repetitive ornament that was wholly prepared in advance and applied *en série*', it is clearly a mistake to think of building craft as separate from building technology.[8] As Howard Davis has recently argued, technology need not be 'unartistic' or 'in opposition to craft processes': indeed, as an expression of the relationship between people and tools, 'building culture is itself, in one sense, a technological system'.[9] From a design-historical perspective we might also understand the relationship between a new plaster technology (gypsum) and a decorative style dependent on repeat patterns (neoclassicism) as being fundamentally reciprocal.[10] Facilitated by a flourishing trade in architectural books and by new and sophisticated building systems and technologies, the house decorator emerged as a key agent of the neoclassical taste within the context of urban domestic architecture.

The artisan Adamesque

Although classicism had been the *sine qua non* of architectural design in Europe since the Renaissance, the neoclassical style that emerged in the middle of the eighteenth century was more archaeologically and ideologically oriented. Trained in the drawing schools and academies of continental Europe, and inspired by excavations at Pompeii and Herculaneum, architects such as Robert Adam and Sir William Chambers developed a fashionable classical taste consonant with the enlightened aims of grand tourism.[11] Of these, it was the 'kind of revolution' embodied in Robert Adam's eclectic and inventive approach to the classical idiom that transformed elite domestic interiors from the late 1750s to the close of the century, replacing architectonic *ornaments* with applied *decorations*.[12] But there was more to this phenomenon than archaeology, fashion and visual elegance, particularly given its association with this particular stratum of

Georgian society. In *Fabricating the antique: neo-classicism in Britain, 1760–1800*, Viccy Coltman considers the scholarly origins of this decorative style, and its subsequent expression in material terms. With reference to Pierre Bourdieu's theories of cultural capital and the *habitus* – broadly defined as a system of acquired patterns or 'dispositions' of thought, perception and action – Coltman posits a symbiotic relationship between eighteenth-century public school pedagogies and the citation and transposition of antique artefacts and ornamental motifs in contemporary British and Irish interiors. Describing the dominance of classical languages and literatures within contemporary school curricula as a process of 'Romanization', and reflecting on different processes of intellectual translation, Coltman conclusively defines neo-classicism as 'a style of thought'.[13]

As we saw in Chapter 2, recent studies concerning the design instruction of artisans in early modern Britain have emphasized the extent to which the use of commercially available publications, in the form of ornament prints and pattern books, reflected both contemporary craft practice and formal design instruction.[14] During the 1780s, the Dublin Society acquired books by London-based designers of neoclassical ornament such as George Richardson and Michelangelo Pergolesi for use in their drawing schools, emphasizing the importance attached to English pattern books as paragons of architectural taste for emerging designers and practitioners in Ireland.[15] Given that books and prints formed one of the principal instruments by which builders and craftsmen assimilated new decorative styles, it is pertinent here to consider Bourdieu's contention that 'a work of art has meaning and interest only for someone who possesses the cultural competence, that is, the code, into which it is encoded'.[16] Given the hierarchical paradigm that persists in the historiography of classical architecture in Britain and Ireland, it is important to examine the artisan's perception of neoclassicism in response to what Bourdieu defined as 'determining structures'; namely, class and education.

Neoclassicism and the book

The revival of classical taste across continental Europe from the middle of the eighteenth century relied in no small way on the print medium, resulting in what Viccy Coltman has described as the 'packaging of antiquity in book form'.[17] Although Paris and Augsburg remained the foremost centres of ornament print production throughout the period, English architectural books became important agents of neoclassical decoration and furnishing across the wider British Atlantic world.[18] But while the publication of Robert and James Adam's *The works in architecture* in 1773 was certainly 'vital within the patterns of social consumption as a signifier of élite taste', the builder decorator acquainted himself with the neoclassical idiom through a wide variety of printed media.[19] The auction of the contents of the celebrated English plasterer Joseph Rose's premises in

April 1799, for example, records titles aimed at every class of reader from the bibliophile to the bricklayer.[20] While Rose's longstanding professional association with the Adam architectural practice and his Grand Tour to Rome and Venice in 1769–70 set him apart from the average house decorator, the volumes from his studio library nonetheless reflect the diversity of published material available to, and utilized by, the eighteenth-century artisan. As well as publications by Adam and Chambers, Rose's library included Robert Wood's *The ruins of Palmyra* (1753) and James Stuart and Nicholas Revett's *The antiquities of Athens* (1762), as well as antiquarian titles such as Pietro Bartoli's *Admiranda romanarum antiquitatum* (1693) and Bernard de Montfaucon's *L'Antiquité expliquée et représentée en figures* (1719). Dublin plasterer Michael Stapleton – Joseph Rose's nearest Irish equivalent – had in his possession a similar if less comprehensive range of books and prints, including George Richardson's *A book of ceilings in the stile of the antique grotesque* (1776), James Gandon's *Six designs of frizes* (1767) and Thomas Martyn and John Lettice's translation of the first volume of *Le antichita di Ercolano*, published in 1775 as *The antiquities of Herculaneum* and a key sourcebook for decoration *all'antica*.[21]

In fact, by the 1770s books aimed exclusively at the building industry had already embraced the vogue for neoclassical decoration. Quite apart from Adam's lofty objective of 'capturing the spirit of antiquity', these were concerned with rendering the style accessible to architect and artisan alike. As early as 1769, and thus preceding the publication of *The works in architecture* by some four years, Matthias Darly's *The ornamental architect, or young artist's instructor* presented 'Antique Ornaments' in a manner that 'most capacitys, by practice and attention, may draw'; in this respect, Darly claimed it 'the most usefull Workmans Book extant'.[22] A similar sentiment was expressed in the preface to William Pain's *The practical builder* (1774), which included 'a great Variety of useful and elegant Examples' of the 'very great Revolution' in architectural taste 'vainly sought in any other practical Treatise'.[23] While the didactic intention implicit in these titles is now generally understood to reflect demand for artisanal instruction from those operating outside of Britain's major metropolitan centres, it also points to a more inclusive relationship to the grammar of neoclassical ornament.[24]

With this in mind, it is clear that the design education of artisans – predicated on the pattern book as both practical and pedagogical tool – fostered a viable, working knowledge of the neoclassical decorative style. But an equivalent understanding of the semiology of classical ornament is less easily determined. Building accounts for Powerscourt House, Dublin dated c. 1777–80, and corresponding to the period in which Michael Stapleton was engaged to decorate the principal reception rooms, certainly reveal the extent to which he was at least cognizant of a range of motifs and their representative qualities: here, an 'Ornamental Ceiling' for an unspecified room was to incorporate four 'Oblong Pannels [with] dancing figures alluding to the use of the Room' and 'Round the Large Circle Boys & Sphinxes Emblems of Love and Immortality'.[25] It is also perhaps significant that plasterers, including Joseph Rose and Edward Robbins of Dublin, numbered among the subscribers to George Richardson's *Iconology* (1779), a neoclassical interpretation of Cesare Ripa's celebrated *Iconologia* (1603). In the preface to *Iconology*, Richardson suggested that:

> An assiduous study of allegory, would be the most effectual means of rendering the ornaments that adorn the sides and ceilings of the apartments of the great, expressive and significant: it would enable the artist to suit his decorations to the place he designs to embellish, and to a variety of circumstances relative to both the apartment and the possessor; would thus render his art singularly entertaining, and intelligible to reason, taste and judgment.[26]

Nonetheless, the apparent levels of literacy enjoyed by Rose, Robbins and Stapleton cannot be assumed to represent the 'norm' within house-decorating circles. A singular impediment to this is the arguably inappropriate selection of classical figurative scenes, in the form of plaster bas-reliefs, as focal points for ceiling compositions and mural decorations: available for ready purchase from so-called 'plaster shops' and one of the most characteristic ornamental devices of the neoclassical interior in Dublin, it appears that they were often employed without regard for their richly associative meanings. Indeed, the unlikely appearance of the figure of Pan with a hermaphrodite (from *Le antichità di Ercolano*, vol. 1, plate XVI) in a variety of properties decorated by Michael Stapleton, for example, including 5 Ely Place, 9 Harcourt Street and 17 Stephen's Green, not to mention the variety of spaces from entrance halls and staircases to dining-parlours and drawing-rooms, suggests the arbitrary use of a stock repertoire; a supposition given further credence by the general congruity between classical allusion and room use in the figurative bas-reliefs and painted insets employed in the decorative schemes of Robert Adam and other classically literate architects. But while the published designs of John Crunden, William Pain and others contain no corresponding explanatory texts, indicating their intended use in the hands of house-decorators indifferent to neoclassical rhetoric, advice on the signifying properties of classical ornaments was a feature of the wider literature aimed at the building industry. Designs for entablatures published in *The builder's magazine* (1774–78), for example, were customarily indexed to particular room functions, including 'a Drawing or Dining-room' and 'a Lady's dressing-room' (Figure 3.1).[27] *The American builder's companion* (1806), composed by carpenter Asher Benjamin and plasterer Daniel Raynerd, was the first widely circulated book in early national America to offer textual advice on the selection of ornaments/motifs appropriate to a variety of room types, from the hall and staircase ('solidity and strength') to the dining

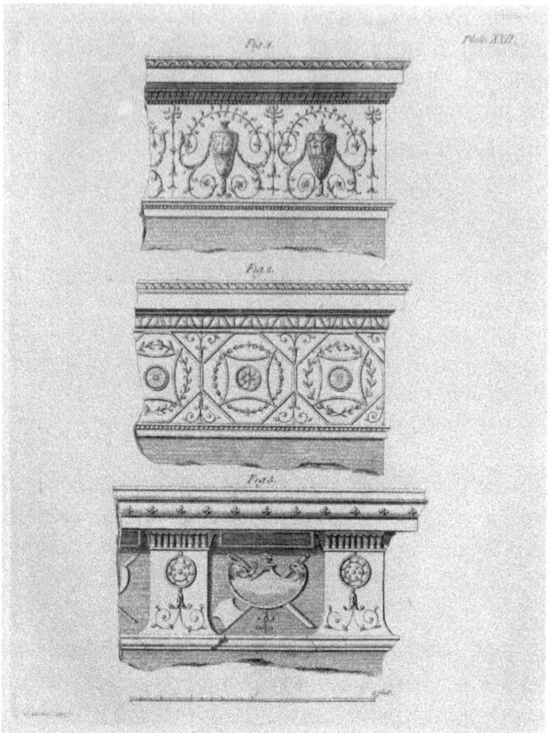

3.1 'Designs for entablatures for rooms' (*top to bottom*: drawing- or dining-room; lady's dressing-room; and hall) (plate 22) from *The builder's magazine* (London, 1774–78).

room ('any thing that denotes eating or drinking').[28] With this in mind, we might instead interpret the occasionally indiscriminate use of allusive classical imagery as evidence of a different engagement with neoclassicism, concerned principally with generating credible, albeit generic, 'antique' decorative effects.[29]

Mindless replication or creative adaptation?

While the study of drawings represents an important avenue of academic enquiry in architectural histories, illuminating both an architect's design methodology and creative accomplishment, the portfolios of eighteenth-century building tradesmen have received little comparable attention; a situation that reflects both the privileged role accorded the architect and the perceived acquiescence of the building tradesman within this hierarchical paradigm.[30] As a result, the biographies of artisans have often emphasized their roles as executors *of* design at the expense of their careers *in* design. However, while customarily employed to execute the designs of others, a situation reflected in the content of albums and drawing collections associated with the plastering firms of Michael Stapleton (the 'Stapleton

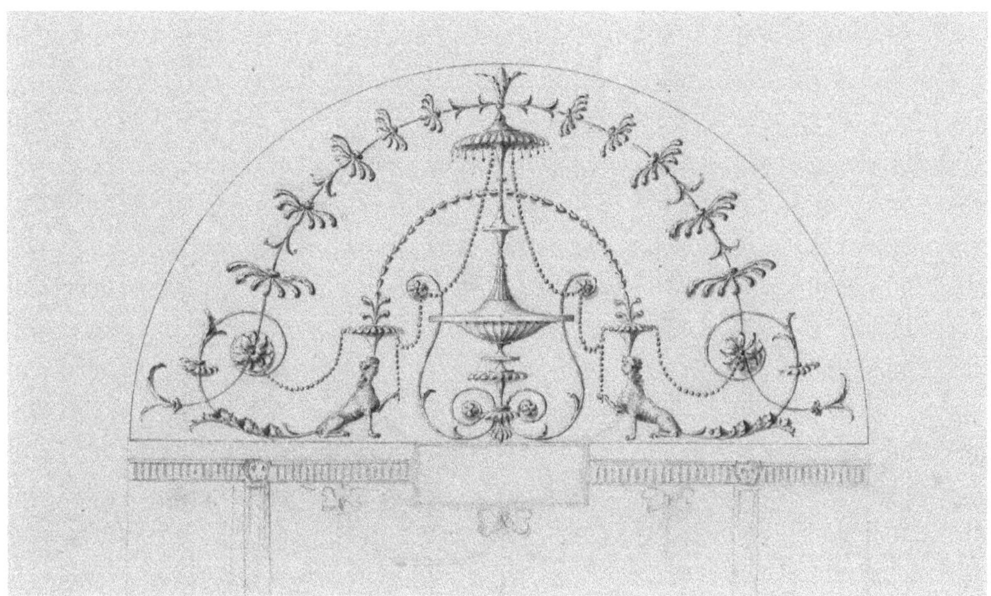

3.2 Design for a decorative overdoor from the Stapleton Collection.

Collection') and Joseph Rose (the 'Sketch Book of Rose' and the 'Sketches of Ornamented Frizes'), it is abundantly clear that these same individuals were capable of setting out a competent design of their own invention.[31] It also confirms the constituency of design for practice and hints at a superior aesthetic sensibility among certain classes of the artisan community. The Stapleton Collection comprises 158 drawings and includes finely executed presentation designs in ink and watercolour together with more rudimentary sketches in pencil.[32] While the designs are identifiably by a variety of hands, it represents an important working compendium assembled during the thirty years of Stapleton's practice (Figure 3.2).[33] The auction of Joseph Rose's studio and property, held over two days in April 1799, itemized sixty-one individual lots of drawings, including more than 300 ceiling designs.[34] The contents of Samuel McIntire's portfolio of drawings, though less preoccupied with interior decoration than his London or Dublin counterparts, also reveals a proficiency with the rudiments of the neoclassical idiom, including a concern with creating an integrated visual effect (one of the hallmarks of the Adam style) (Figure 3.3).

Designs for ceilings form the principal category within the Stapleton Collection, and typically feature simple geometric compositions, often based around ovals, diapers or chamfered octagonal forms set within rectangular frames. Objectively, the 'Stapleton' designs with more complex patterns are derived from the publications of George Richardson and others (Plate 16); the autographed designs contained in the 'Sketch Book

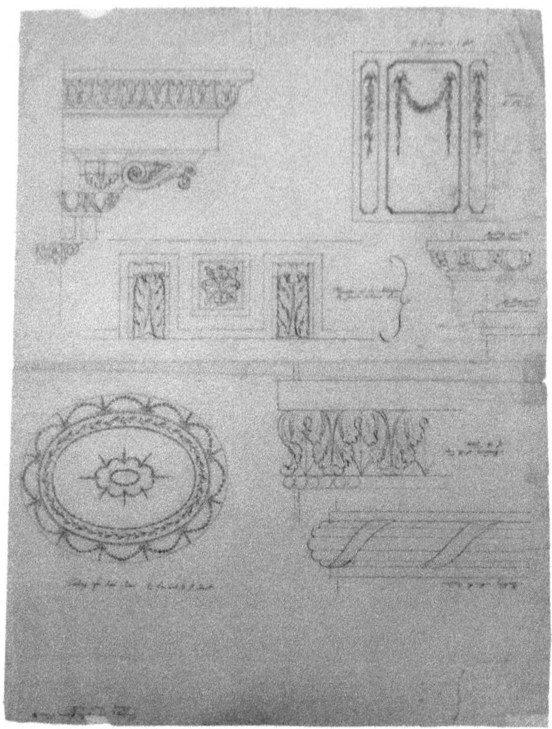

3.3 Samuel McIntire, designs for the oval room at the Derby Mansion, 215 Essex Street, Salem, MA (dem.), 1795–98.

of Rose', though small in number, demonstrate a similar aptitude on Rose's part, leading Geoffrey Beard to conclude that 'there is nothing that led to unusual innovation' (Figure 3.4).[35] But this point demands qualification. The artisan's reliance on pattern book sources in fact stands comparison with contemporary architectural practice: ceiling designs by Robert Adam, Sir William Chambers and James 'Athenian' Stuart have been traced to identifiable (and typically engraved) antique sources; their 'original' designs being often very slight variations on those prototypes.[36] Based on their formation in the drawing schools and academies of continental Europe, designs from their hands are qualified as credible transliterations from the classical canon to the domestic British interior. But the artisan has not been afforded the same latitude: instead, those whose designs can be traced to published exemplars are seen at best as derivative; more often, as noted above, the practice has been understood as evidence of a reduced intellectual capacity for design. The point of difference appears to rest on a distinction between primary and secondary source materials: a difference between designs adapted from archaeological books and designs adapted from pattern books. But given the shared interest in creating decorative

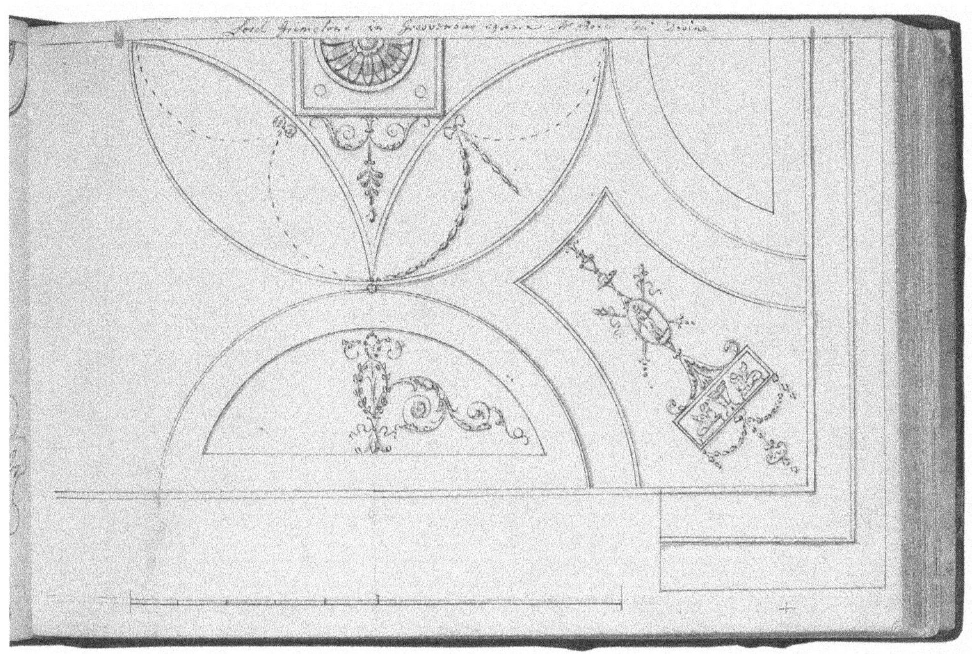

3.4 Joseph Rose, Jr, ceiling design for 'Lord Grimston's in Grosvenor Square' from the 'Sketch Book of Rose'.

schemes that signified a notional 'spirit of antiquity', why should one practice of adaptation be privileged over another?

The direct replication of plate 2 from George Richardson's *Ceilings* across three different houses in Dublin during the 1770s and 1780s – at 32 St Stephen's Green (by Edward Robbins, discussed below), at 34 North Great George's Street (by Francis Ryan, a named subscriber to the book) and at 52 St Stephen's Green – can certainly be interpreted as an example of artisanal acquiescence to architectural authority. But published designs were not typically regarded as sacrosanct. While the authorship of the celebrated interiors at Belvedere House, Great Denmark Street (completed c. 1786) remains open to question – although it is certainly the work of plasterers Robert West or Michael Stapleton or both – the designs illustrate how creative invention was realized through the manipulation of printed sources. The composition of the ceiling in the so-called 'Diana' drawing-room is an imaginative combination of plate 35 (nos. 184 and 185) and plate 30 (no. 144) from Michelangelo Pergolesi's *Original designs of vases, figures, medallions, pilasters, and other ornaments in the Etruscan and grotesque styles* published in instalments between 1777 and 1792. (An original drawing, now lost, also included elements from plates 30 (nos. 145 and 146) and plate 34 (no. 177) which were evidently discarded prior to its translation from paper to plaster.)[37] The

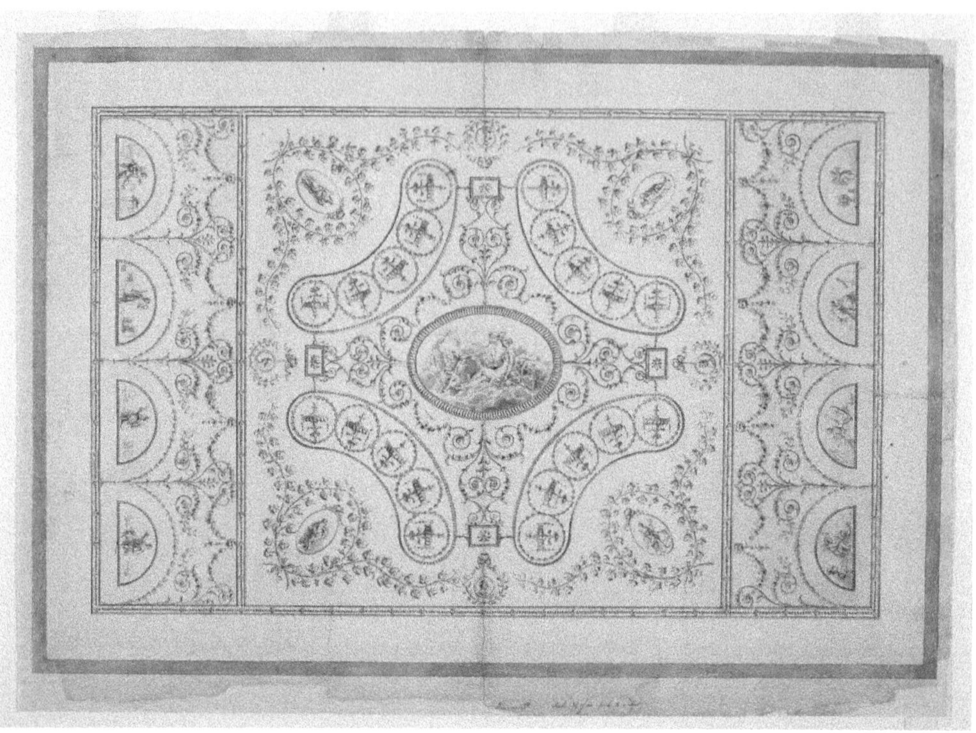

3.5 Ceiling design for the Venus drawing-room at Belvedere House, Great Denmark Street, Dublin, c. 1786.

ceiling of the 'Venus' drawing-room, on the other hand, exhibits a less doctrinaire approach to orthodox 'antique' models (Figure 3.5). Edward McParland established the principal source for this composition as plate 32 of George Richardson's *A book of ceilings*, together with the addition of ornaments from the Adam brothers' *The works in architecture* (vol. 1, part 5, plate 8).[38] Joseph McDonnell later identified the remaining elements of the design to be citations from continental European sources: the figurative centrepiece depicting 'Vénus Couronnée par les Amours' is copied from an engraving by Gilles Demarteau (published in 1773) after a painting by François Boucher; the putti in the lunettes of the outer panels, representing astronomy, painting and sculpture, are replicated from an engraving of the painted decorations in the Petite Galerie at Versailles by Pierre Mignard.[39] In such instances it seems clear that house decorators were concerned more with the abstract, ornamental properties of printed designs, taking Richardson's advice that 'by blending particular parts, with others', his readers 'might form new designs according to their fancy'.[40] This in fact accorded with the type of instruction approved for students of both the fine and applied arts: premiums awarded by the Society of

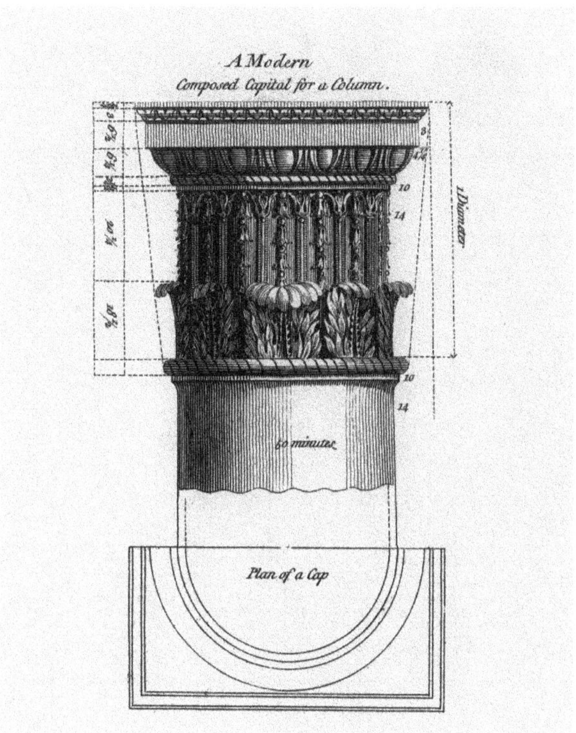

3.6 Design for 'A modern composed capital for a column' (plate 22) from William Pain, *The practical builder* (London, 1774).

Arts, for example, were often based on designs and ornaments 'taken from various prints'.[41] Moreover, designs for 'Modern Composed' capitals and entablatures in William Pain's *The practical builder* (1774) represented for an artisanal audience an example of the artistic licence advocated by the Adam architectural practice, who in 1773 criticized the 'minute and frivolous' attention paid by modern architects to the rules and proportions of the classical orders (Figure 3.6).[42]

Perhaps unsurprisingly, academic interest in vernacular interpretations of the neoclassical style has generally focused on the extent to which its mechanical nature was compromised. Writing in 1967, C.P. Curran preferred those specimens of Stapleton's oeuvre where the customary geometrical forms and cast ornaments were combined with foliated enrichments modelled by hand. According to Curran, these Dublin ceilings reflected the 'good taste and charm with which [Stapleton] married natural and more formal ornament', a trait perhaps best exemplified by several designs in the Stapleton album of drawings, and by the now lost decorative schemes for his speculative houses in Harcourt Street and Mountjoy

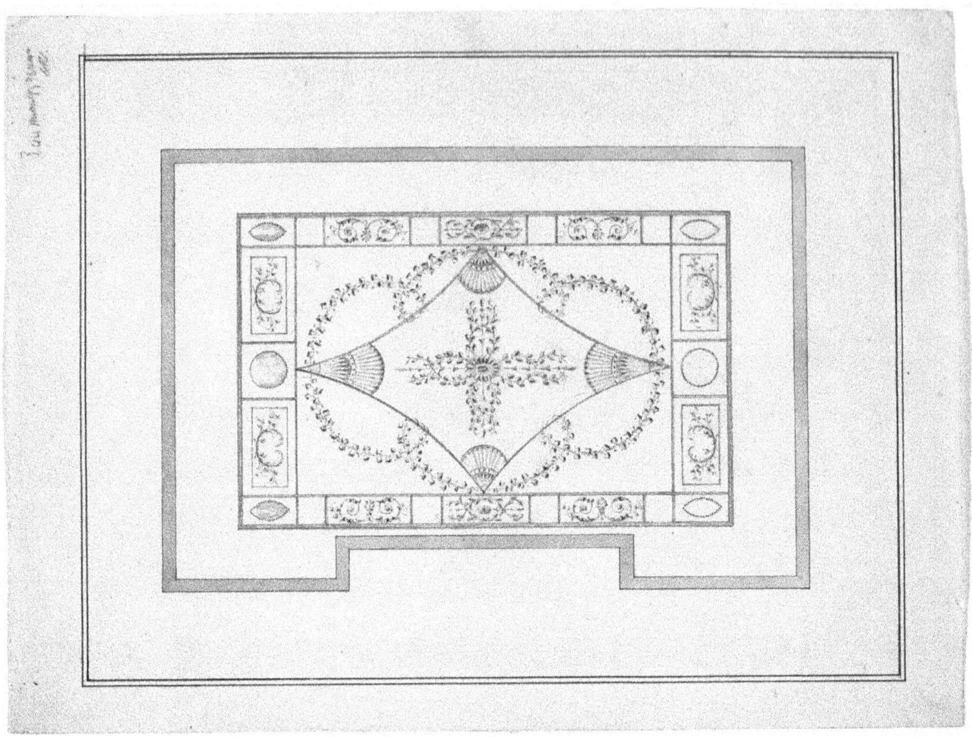

3.7 Ceiling design from the Stapleton Collection.

Square (Figures 3.7 and 3.8).[43] Sir Charles Herbert Reilly admired a similar quality in the houses of the Royal Crescent in Bath, describing their neoclassical interiors as 'beautiful in a similar but rather stronger manner than that one is accustomed to connect with the name of Adam', being 'very like similar work in Dublin' with its 'occasional touch of very effective naturalistic ornament' (Figure 3.9).[44]

Such adaptations of Adam neoclassicism allow us to look beyond the 'surface of apparent stylistic and spatial sameness' of a shared British architectural culture, towards a greater diversity of creative agency.[45] At Homewood in Baltimore (1802), an important expression of the 'Americanization of the neoclassical villa', the carved enrichments of the chimneypieces are derived from William Pain's decidedly utilitarian octavo volume *The practical house carpenter* (1797), and not, for example, George Richardson's more appreciably Adamesque folio *A new collection of chimney pieces ornamented in the style of the Etruscan, Greek, and Roman architecture* (1781).[46] But while this certainly reflects the limited circulation of the larger volumes published by London-based ornament designers such as Richardson, Pergolesi and others in

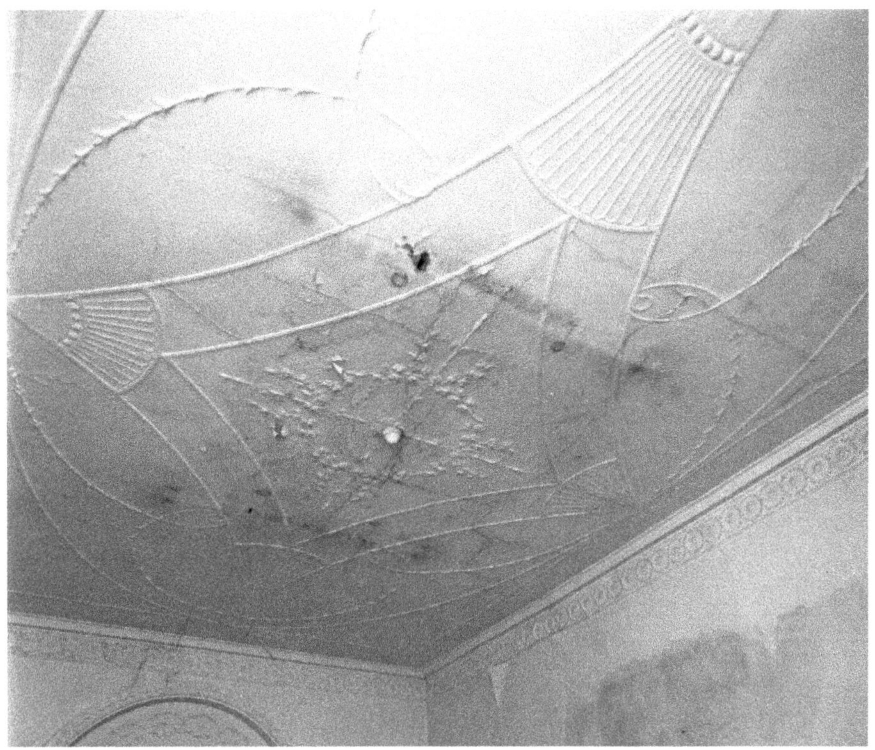

3.8 Ceiling of front drawing-room at 4 Harcourt Street, Dublin (dem.), c. 1786.

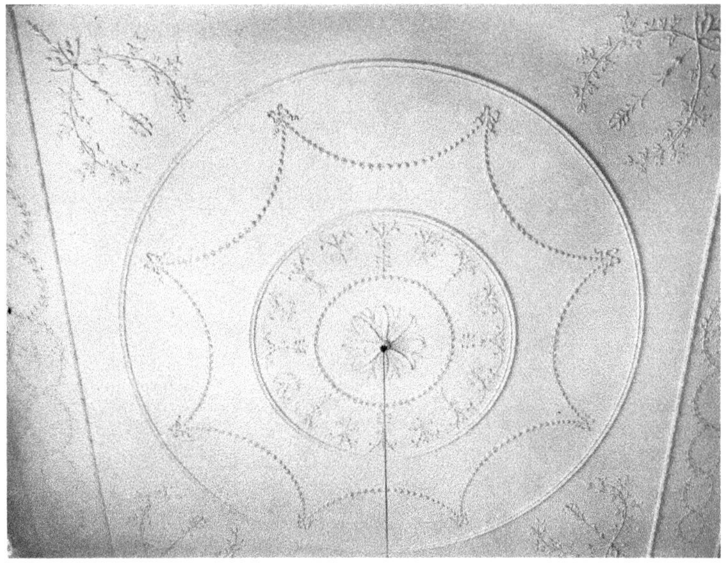

3.9 Ceiling of front drawing-room at 5 Royal Crescent, Bath, c. 1775.

America at this time, it also underlines the important role of the building artisan for creating a plausible neoclassicism from the sources readily available to the trade.[47] Although American carver Samuel McIntire's neoclassical vocabulary apparently relied as much on built precedent as it did on print media – of the six architectural titles recorded in an inventory of his estate in 1811, builder's handbooks such as *Pain's British Palladio* (1786) represented the only identifiable printed source devoted to the Adam decorative vocabulary – his interiors for the houses of wealthy merchants in early nineteenth-century Salem number among the most accomplished examples of the Federal style in New England.[48] Indeed, Owen Biddle's justification for composing *The young carpenter's assistant* in 1805, describing the limited usefulness of many of the imported British architectural books for the American artisan, suggests further ways to understand the less appreciably Adamesque character of town house interiors in Boston and Philadelphia compared with those in London and Dublin.[49]

While the Stapleton and McIntire drawing collections signal a claim for creative ambition and intellectual capital and so may be compared with those of Joseph Rose, unlike Rose's albums they are not organized or annotated in any coherent manner. This distinction perhaps reflects the functional nature of the Stapleton and McIntire portfolios as opposed to Rose's apparently retrospective compendia. Of these, the 'Sketches of Ornamented Frizes', a Moroccan-bound manuscript volume of finely drawn frieze designs compiled in 1782, is particularly interesting. Comprising 331 individually numbered designs over 106 pages, the compositions are described as being from 'original models' in Rose's possession, many of which 'were made from the designs of the most eminent architects'. Organized by motif (bucranium, patera, anthemion and palmette) rather than by architect (Adam, Chambers, Stuart and Wyatt), and boasting two indexes – including an 'Index for different Rooms' – it seems certain that the book was intended for publication, its layout being comparable to the large folio volumes of designers like Michelangelo Pergolesi but also to the trade catalogues of ornament manufactories like Jee and Eginton of Birmingham (Figure 3.10). Featuring accomplished designs of the family business (Joseph Rose & Co.) alongside those of London's most renowned architectural practices, it would certainly have rivalled popular titles such as Placido Columbani's *Variety of capitals, freezes and corniches* (1776), one of the few Adamesque pattern books that enjoyed commercial distribution in the colonies.[50] Instances of artisan turned author, and by extension as arbiter of new modes of architectural taste, were especially significant in America: in 1806, Boston 'stucco worker' Daniel Raynerd achieved the rare distinction of being the first American author of published designs for decorative plasterwork (Figure 3.11).

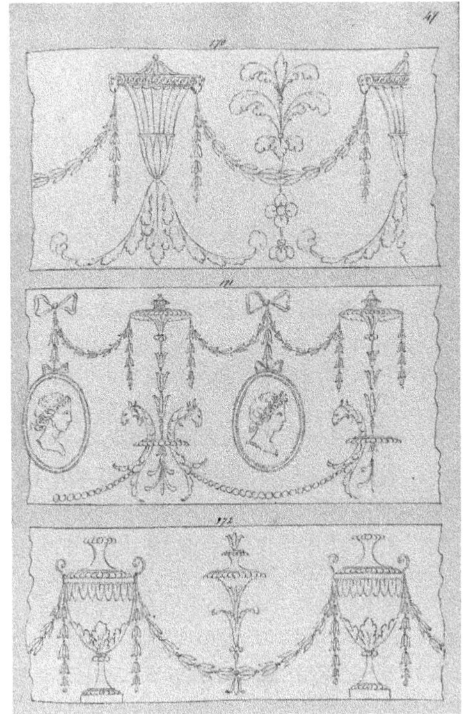

3.10 Frieze designs by Joseph Rose, Jr, from 'Sketches of Ornamented Frizes', compiled 1783.

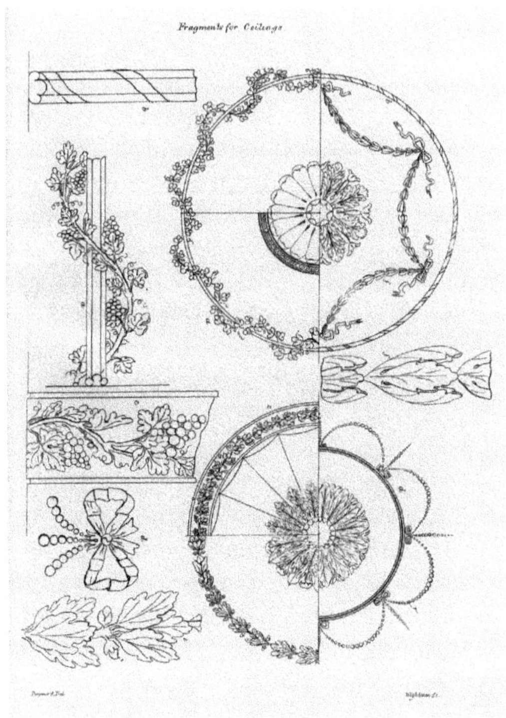

3.11 Designs for 'ornamental stucco ceilings' (plate 27) from Asher Benjamin and Daniel Raynerd, *The American builder's companion* (Boston, 1806).

The craftsman as agent of taste

Having established the character of artisanal neoclassicism and some of its different iterations in towns and cities cross the British Atlantic world, we now turn our attention to how that taste was effectively introduced and transmitted. Here we must remind ourselves of the spatial and cultural distances between Britain and Ireland and between Britain and North America. While Ireland encountered neoclassicism through direct patronage of Robert Adam and other architects based in England, through the work of English architects and artisans resident in Ireland and through subscription networks to English architectural and pattern books, the Federal style blossomed only with the arrival of composition ornament manufacturers from England and Ireland during the 1790s. Only then did the interiors of houses in metropolitan centres like Boston and Philadelphia approximate the level of embroidered enrichment already ubiquitous in the terraces of London and Dublin. That said, the present narrative is concerned not with reiterating outmoded appraisals of the supposedly adaptive failure of Adam neoclassicism in America – once dismissed as 'little more than a few delicate neo-classical motifs grafted on to the provincial styles' – but rather with emphasizing its dependence on the immigrant artisan as an agent of that taste.[51]

This section will consider the working context of English plasterer Edward Robbins in Ireland, and the English ornament manufacturer Robert Wellford in early national America. Although largely absent from the admittedly limited literature on eighteenth-century interior decoration in Ireland, Robbins's professional milieu in fact placed him among the progenitors of the neoclassical movement in Dublin. Wellford, on the other hand, has recently been the subject of a monograph which unambiguously underlines his role as a pivotal figure for the development of the Federal style across British North America. Just as design histories have problematized traditional 'trickle down' theories of reception and emulation, so the introduction of new and/or marginalized names from the historical record contributes layers of meaning and complexity to our deepening understanding of British neoclassicism.

British agents of the Irish Adamesque

In a notice published in the *Dublin Journal* of 4 April 1769, Thomas Weston, recently arrived from London and 'versed in the Stucco Art', announced his proficiency in the 'Antique Taste', having worked 'some Years under the Designs of Mess. Adams, Chambers and Stewart [*sic*]'.[52] His timing was far from coincidental: less than a month earlier the premium for the design of the Royal Exchange in Dublin (now City Hall) – a building 'at the cutting edge of British Neoclassicism' – had been awarded to the English architect Thomas Cooley.[53] Just as 'enlightened' Irish architectural discourse had deemed the employment of an English architect for this particular project as being 'too obvious to be insisted upon' – the competition generated no fewer than thirty-three British submissions (or 60 per cent of the total number of competitors) – so it would appear that Weston had identified an opportunity to establish himself in Ireland as an unrivalled exponent of the neoclassical style.[54] Some weeks later, on 27 April, Weston amended his original advertisement to record that he had 'served his Apprenticeship to Mr. Rose of London'.[55]

Although Thomas Weston's name does not appear in the records of apprentices taken by Joseph Rose & Co. during the 1750s and 1760s, he clearly sought to profit by this association.[56] These particulars aside, the fact that the Rose name was invoked in this manner in a Dublin newspaper is of special importance for our narrative: not only does this announcement predate Robert and James Adam's public endorsement of Rose's abilities in the early numbers of *The works in architecture* in 1773/74, but it suggests a familiarity with the Rose firm beyond the perimeter of London.[57] Indeed, while Weston's advertising rhetoric was clearly aimed at the Irish nobility and gentry, this reference to Rose suggests that he may in fact have been looking to claim a position of authority within Dublin's burgeoning decorating trade. The significance of this is easily overlooked. While architects like Adam and Chambers enjoyed Irish patronage from early in their careers, the 1760s was the decade when 'hundreds of fine passages of rococo plasterwork' were executed in stair halls and drawing rooms of elite town houses across Dublin, a phenomenon that finds no parallel in British cities.[58] Although no record of his work in Ireland has so far come to light, and he was certainly back in England by 1780, Weston doubtless sought to turn his London experience, and his knowledge of the newly fashionable Adam style, to his advantage.[59]

Others effected a more substantial contribution to the character of the Irish neoclassical interior: of these, Scottish author and designer George Richardson (1737/38–c. 1813) is one of the most significant. Described by Howard Colvin as 'an accomplished draughtsman and designer of internal decoration in the Adam style', Richardson enjoyed a long association with the Adam architectural practice before embarking on an independent career in 1769: he was in fact one of the British entrants to the Dublin competition for the Royal Exchange in that year, and had already begun exhibiting his own architectural and decorative designs at the Society of Artists in London from 1765.[60] In spite of a career in architectural publishing that spanned more than thirty years, however, Eileen Harris argues that 'Richardson's own designs are less important than his engravings of the executed works of other late eighteenth-century architects'.[61] But this of course is to ignore the wider geographical reach of his designs: as we have seen, his *Ceilings*, originally issued in eight 'numbers' of six plates apiece between 1774 and 1776, represented an important source for house decorators in Ireland and was recognized as an important pedagogical tool within the drawing

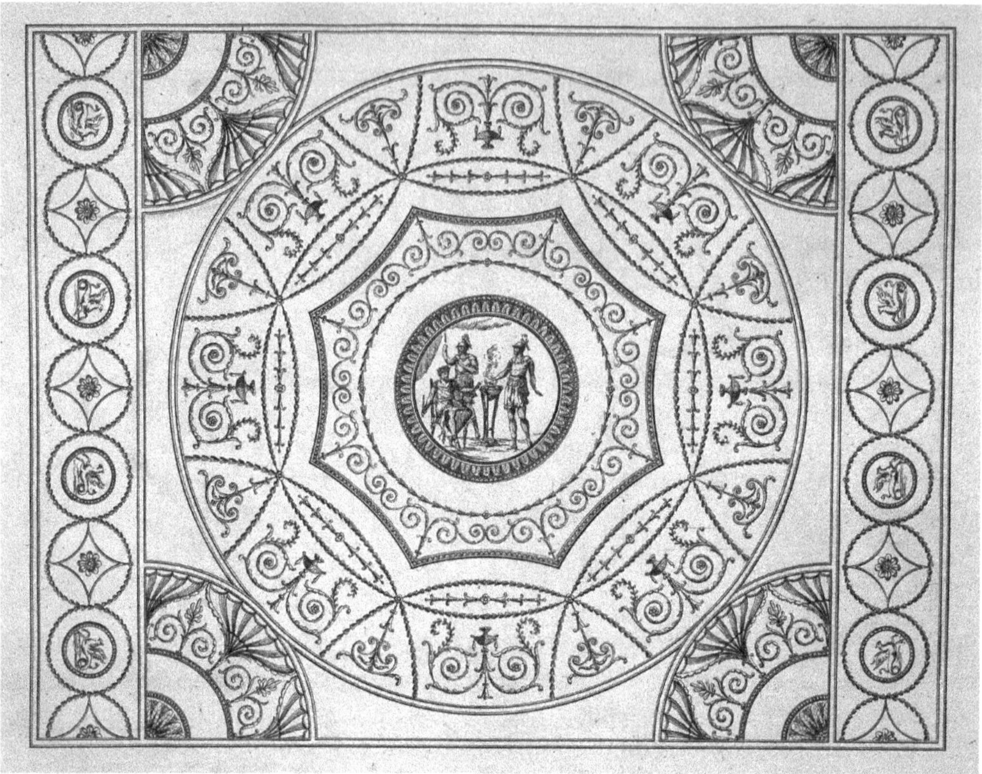

3.12 George Richardson, ceiling design for an 'anti-chamber' (plate 20) from *A book of ceilings in the stile of the antique grotesque* (London, 1776).

schools that operated under the aegis of the Dublin Society (Figure 3.12 and Plate 16). Of particular significance was the number of Irish subscribers to the bound volume. Although the Irish nobility and gentry subscribed to English architectural treatises and pattern books throughout the eighteenth century, the unprecedented interest in Ireland for the *Ceilings* is noteworthy: it was one of only two English architectural titles, the other being Robert Wood's *Ruins of Palmyra* (1753), that were actively promoted and publicized by the Dublin book trade.[62] Moreover, despite accounting for only thirteen of the 217 subscriptions, fully one third of these were plasterers.[63] Bearing in mind that the average industrial wage of a skilled plasterer in Dublin during this period amounted to 12s. per week, the pledge to purchase the complete book at a cost of £3 4s. represented a considerable economic investment.[64]

Richardson's astute marketing of his books of designs made much of his long tenure with the Adam practice; according to Eileen Harris, of the numerous pattern books of neoclassical ornament issued during the early 1770s, Richardson's *Ceilings* represented 'the most damaging to the novelty and exclusivity of the *Works*'.[65] With this in mind, it is perhaps significant that the Irish distributor of the *Works in architecture*, William Wilson of Dame Street, was one of two distributors secured for Richardson's *Ceilings*. Indeed, although the Adam brothers' advertisements for the first numbers of the *Works* claimed that it would contain designs 'invented and executed by them in Great Britain and Ireland'[66] – an attempt, no doubt, to broaden their Irish client base – this never in fact transpired. Richardson, on the other hand, when advertising the bound volume of the *Ceilings* in 1776, was able to declare that several of his designs had been 'executed in different parts of Great Britain and Ireland'.[67] Although cost was certainly a factor in the relative success of these titles within building circles – a guinea for one number of the *Works* compared with 8s. for one number of the *Ceilings* – Richardson's advice that artisans innovate freely from the printed source (noted above) no doubt held greater appeal for the aspiring designer than the *Works in architecture*, Adam's 'publicity brochure' of already executed designs.[68] Indeed, while Richardson's text is clearly at pains to address the broadest demographic concerned with architecture, from the grand tourist to the building tradesman, it is the plasterer who is accorded the greatest attention: not only would the plasterer, 'in particular', benefit from the book's plates in practice, the designs were specifically 'intended in general to be of stucco'.[69] Moreover, Richardson also identified those individuals who had, by the date of publication in November 1776, executed his designs 'in town and country'. In the 'Explanation of the pictures and bas-reliefs', describing each design and its apposite location, he identifies a number of plasterers, including Thomas Clayton and John Coney at Sir Laurence Dundas's House, St Andrew's Square, Edinburgh; and Edward Robbins at Lord Montalt's House in St Stephen's Green, Dublin. (All named individuals, it should be noted, were subscribers to the bound edition published in 1776.) Not only did this promote their efficacy in realizing these designs – acting as a type of exclusive directory of competent practitioners – but it also served to underline the critical role of the plasterer in realizing the neoclassical decorative style.[70]

Although he does not feature prominently in C.P. Curran's seminal *Dublin decorative plasterwork* (1967) and is known principally for the mention of his work in the *A book of ceilings*, notices in the *Hibernian Journal* throughout 1775–76 indicate that Edward Robbins (*fl.* 1774–91) was in fact the original agent for Richardson's designs in Ireland. When the publication of the fourth fascicle of the *Ceilings* in March 1775 was announced, Irish readers were advised of its availability from Robbins's premises in St Stephen's Green alone.[71] With this in mind, it seems certain that the unprecedented number of Irish subscribers to the *Ceilings* must be attributed, at least in part, to Robbins's agency. Indeed, it would appear that it was only with the publication of the bound edition of the *Ceilings* that Richardson secured distribution from book and print sellers outside of London: one apiece in Bath, Oxford and Edinburgh, but two in Dublin.[72] This is all the more significant when one considers that provincial booksellers and publishers across Britain and Ireland generally were cautious about their architectural stock and its market appeal.[73]

Robbins's biography remains frustratingly incomplete and does not concern us here, but one important fact requires elucidation: his national identity. Based on a Dublin newspaper notice of October 1782, when he returned his thanks to the nobility and gentry of Ireland for 'the many favours since he came into this kingdom', it is clear that Robbins was neither born nor educated in Ireland.[74] While a number of plasterers and masons variously from Bath and London share the same family name, no information concerning his apprenticeship, his formative years in practice or the purpose or date of his arrival in Ireland has come to light. (He was certainly in Dublin by March of 1775, the date of the first Irish newspaper advertisement concerning the *A book of ceilings*.) Unique in the building industry as both agent and practitioner of Richardson's Adamesque decorative style, Robbins enjoyed the patronage of Ireland's nobility and gentry such as Wills Hill, Earl of Hillsborough, and the 'nabob' James Alexander, later Earl of Caledon. In fact, although overshadowed in the literature on eighteenth-century interior decoration by his Irish-born contemporaries, Robbins's professional association with George Richardson unequivocally places him in a very significant position with respect to the development of the Adam decorative style in Dublin. By 1775, Dublin's house decorators were already using the most progressive printed matter from London booksellers: the initial phase of interior decoration at Powerscourt House, South William Street, for example, completed by the stuccoists James McCullagh and Michael Reynolds in 1774, utilized the first pattern books devoted to the 'antique grotesque' style; the ceiling and mural decorations of the stair hall are transcribed from plates in Matthias Darly's *The ornamental architect* (1769) and N. Wallis's *A book of ornaments in the Palmyrene taste* (1771).[75] Today, the formal contrast between this decoration and that in the principal reception rooms, undertaken by Michael Stapleton in 1778–80, reveals that a more appreciably Adamesque manner – or should that be *Richardsonian* manner – had been established in Dublin in the interim.[76]

British and Irish agents of the American Adamesque

Just as the historiography of Irish neoclassical architecture has long acknowledged its profound debt to British architectural authority – it has for example been argued that the style unambiguously signified the Irish political administration's colonial relationship to Britain – so the American Adamesque is typically understood in similar, strictly British terms.[77] Dell Upton and Amy Henderson have shown how American elites created a sense of exclusivity and a shared social identity through importing British architectural goods and styles from chimneypieces to fanlights,[78] while Gabrielle Lanier and Bernard Herman have commented on how 'avowedly' American artisans and designers, like Asher Benjamin, 'failed to escape the tyranny of European tastes'.[79] Others, paradoxically, have described the Federal style as 'the first national style', despite recognizing its dependence on a specifically Adam interpretation of neoclassicism.[80] But this in fact accords with recent scholarship on the British Atlantic world which emphasizes cultural hybridity as opposed to simple dichotomies based on oversimplified theories of centre and periphery: while neoclassicism signified a shared architectural identity between Britain and North America, there were manifest differences in materials, ornament and even ideology.[81] As we shall see, a specifically American vocabulary of figurative classical ornament was developed in the first decades of the nineteenth century.

The origins of the Adam style in America are difficult to discern: American elites did not customarily solicit designs from English architects, relying instead on an artisan class with varying degrees of knowledge and experience.[82] It is also understood to have developed at different times in different locations. Early 'evidence' in cities like Annapolis remains questionable: the interiors of the Chase Lloyd House (built 1769–74), although indisputably the work of artisans 'late from London', are neoclassical only if we admit a very generic use of the term – their visual equivalence with Adam's decorative manner representing 'a question of interpretation rather than of declaration'.[83] More convincing are the interiors of The Solitude (in terms of applied decoration) and Woodlands (in terms of plan), built on the outskirts of Philadelphia in the late 1780s – though, like the work of Adam and Chambers in Dublin in the early 1760s, neither appears to have had any immediate influence on interior decoration in that city (Figure 3.13). In Boston a more credible Adamesque was introduced by amateur architect Charles Bulfinch, whose first essays in the style date from the early 1790s and were of singular importance for an entire generation of New England artisans, including Samuel McIntire.[84]

English books and their American counterparts have traditionally been regarded as the 'primary influence' on the dissemination of the British neoclassical style in America:[85] while colonial craftsmen are generally understood to have innovated from the printed page – precise copies from pattern books sources being 'relatively rare' – the American expression of the neoclassical style 'often followed English prototypes more closely'.[86] Recent scholarship, however, has reasserted the importance of the peripatetic artisan. Curiously, this position complements the established narratives of indentured craftsmen in the colonial era and an imported (typically English) craft tradition, while simultaneously embracing new Atlantic world narratives with their focus on complex systems of cultural

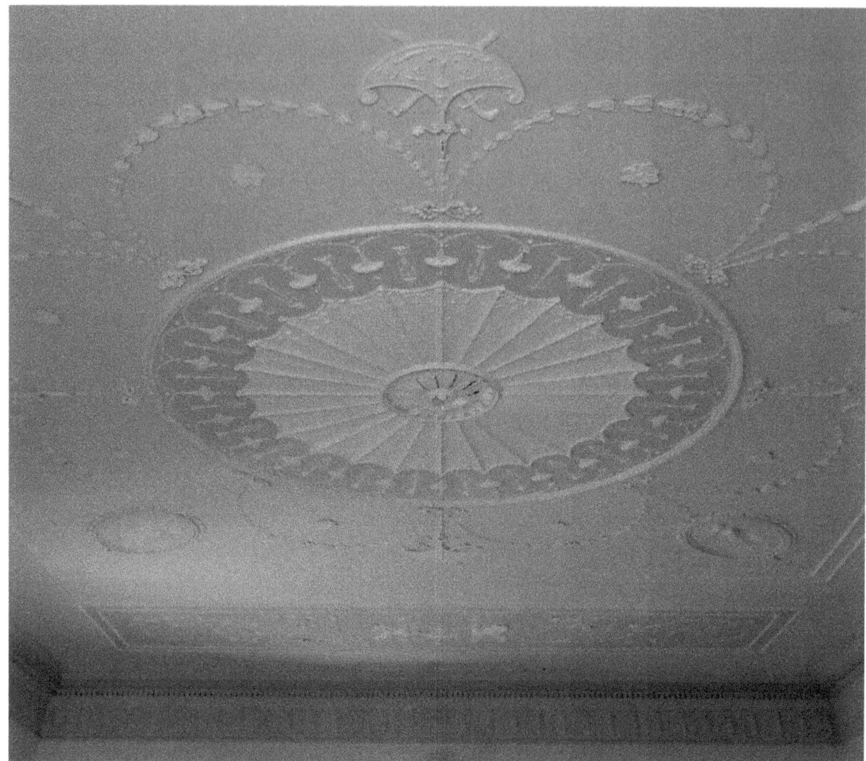

3.13 Ceiling plasterwork in the dining-room at The Solitude, Philadelphia, c. 1788.

exchange. In his account of the design process among building operatives across the towns and cities of the Chesapeake Bay, Carl Lounsbury has described the immigrant artisan as the 'first and foremost' conduit for architectural tastes between Britain and America, affording the book a more subsidiary role.[87] Mark Reinberger has likewise identified émigré ornament manufacturer Robert Wellford as 'a major vehicle for the transatlantic transfer of neoclassicism to America and its adaptation to American themes'.[88] Indeed, given the character of the architectural literature circulating among American building communities at this time, described above, the immigrant artisan as the pre-eminent agent of fashionable tastes represents the more convincing thesis.

Although a decorated ceiling was 'often the key' to Robert Adam's interior schemes, and *de rigueur* for the better sort of artisan-built town house in cities across Britain and Ireland, such enrichments were uncommon in American domestic architecture generally.[89] British and Irish plasterers were, nonetheless, already advertising 'ornaments on ceilings' and 'Plain or Inriched Cornices' from Philadelphia to Charleston at mid-century.[90] In 1771, John Rawlins and James Barnes, originally

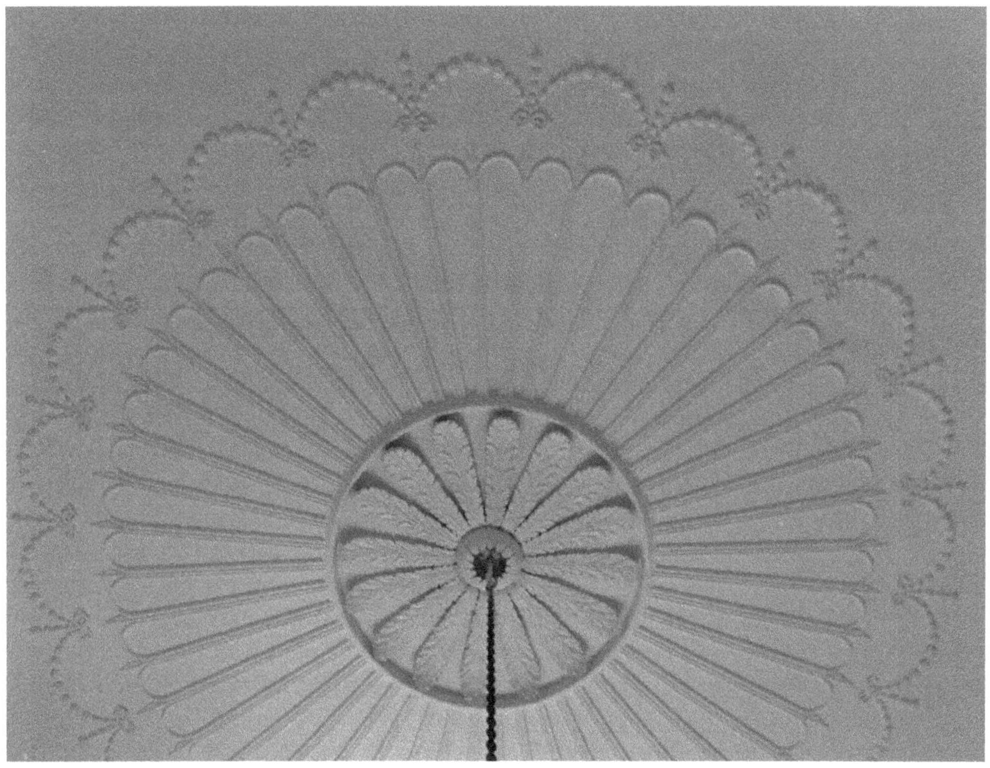

3.14 Ceiling plasterwork in the hall at Joseph Manigault House, Charleston, c. 1803.

of London, announced the commencement of their 'Plaistering and Carving in Stucco' business in Annapolis, and by the mid-1780s had worked in different parts of Maryland and Virginia. Although 'designs for Ceilings' were a feature of their practice it is, however, difficult to discern their influence on decorative tastes; as indeed it is of Joseph Kennedy of Dublin, who in 1789 was working 'in the most approved and latest Fashions' but whose sole documented work at Mount Clare, Baltimore is similar to work in Annapolis of the mid 1770s (and in Dublin of the mid-1740s).[91] That said, the Adamesque decorative plasterwork at Willow Brook (1799) and Clifton Mansion in the same city (1803), with its combination of classical and foliate ornaments – similar to the work of Michael Stapleton in Dublin (described above) – has been reasonably attributed to Irish hands and 'their love of naturalistic details'.[92] Notable examples of the neoclassical style in Charleston, including the Gaillard-Bennett House (1802) and the Joseph Manigault House (1803), are consistent with the presence in that city of individuals such as John Fallon, described as 'a native of Ireland' and 'an artist in the Stucco and Plaistering line' (Figure 3.14).[93]

These singular examples of decorative plasterwork aside, the chimneypiece remained the foremost architectural ornament of the American house and the principal signifier of elite classical taste throughout the Federal era. While carved marble and scagliola inlay constituted the materials of choice for elite town houses in London and Dublin, the timber and composition chimneypiece was associated with the 'top rung of Federal period houses'.[94] London carpenter and builder Matthew Armour was, it seems, first to advertise 'full enriched composition chimney pieces' in Philadelphia in 1785, stimulating a flourishing trade in imported English manufactures from printed catalogues.[95] By the mid-1790s, 'Complete setts' of ornaments for 'interior architecture' were offered by a number of retail merchants across the city, often with 'Great allowance made to Builders'.[96] The question of supply and demand is complex and difficult to disentangle, but the flourishing of the Federal style from the mid-1790s into the 1810s certainly coincided with the arrival in Philadelphia in 1797 of English ornament maker Robert Wellford, and in New York a year earlier of George Andrews, a Dublin statuary.[97] Here, the agency of the immigrant artisan was paramount. By 1800, houses far from the major metropolitan centres, in towns such as Lancaster, Pennsylvania and Salisbury, North Carolina, customarily featured a mantel enriched with composition ornaments in the classical idiom.[98]

Robert Wellford, like McIntire, enjoys a significant place in the history of interior decoration in America.[99] Apprenticed to John Jaques, one of the prominent London manufactories of synthetic 'stone' that were such a distinguishing feature of the English building industry of the early 1770s, he took advantage of the emerging demand for Adamesque decoration in America just as it was in decline in England. Working initially with established Philadelphia companies, by 1801 Wellford was in trade independently and quickly became one of the few manufacturers operating on a national scale. In 1807, he rechristened his business 'Robert Wellford's Original American Manufactory of Composition Ornaments', a title that reflected a shift from making products with an English pedigree – derived from commonly used printed sources and/or inherited moulds – towards ornaments that tapped into a burgeoning political consciousness. Patriotic figurative scenes for chimneypiece tablets, such as his autographed 'Goddess of Liberty' and 'Battle of Lake Erie' ornaments, were created in the wake of the 1812 war with Britain, and have been interpreted as a sign of his sympathies for Republican nationalism and the democratization of domestically produced luxury goods (Figure 3.15). In this respect he has been favourably compared with Josiah Wedgwood, Matthew Boulton and other champions of industrialized capitalism.

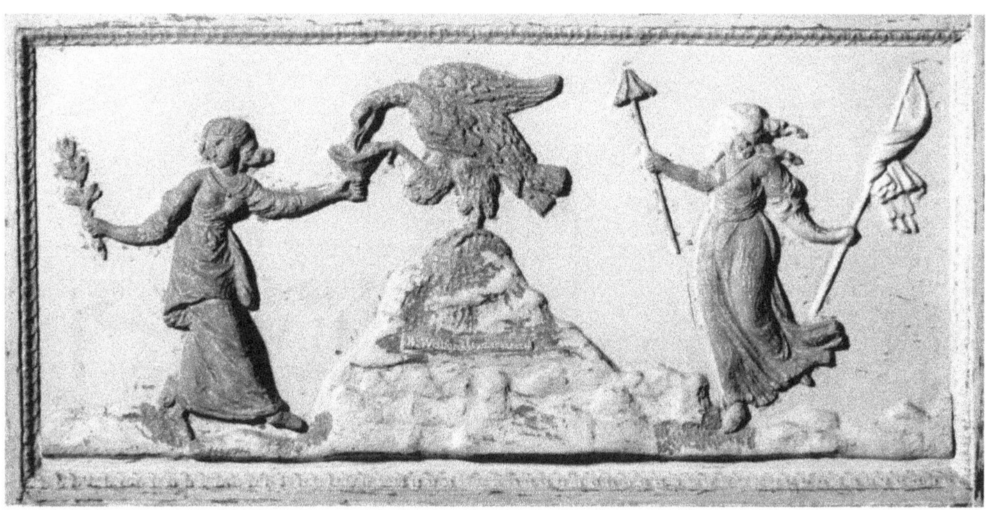

3.15 Robert Wellford, 'Goddess of Liberty' composition ornament.

Wellford's creation of a decidedly American decorative repertoire in the first decades of the nineteenth century was also commercially shrewd. As traditional craft practice and skilled piecework came under threat from serial production and unskilled wage labour, artisans adapted to changing markets by developing new products and by taking advantage of advertising and marketing strategies in the form of trade cards and newspaper advertisements. Wellford, it seems, preferred the handbill as it allowed him the space – literally and figuratively – to distinguish his ornaments from the 'rudely constructed' ornaments of his competitors, and to underline the significance of decoration for architectural 'magnificence'.[100] Using established trade links along both inland and coastal routes, Wellford developed a network of agents and distributors from New Jersey to South Carolina (Figure 1.24).

But while ornament manufactories were certainly 'an important conduit for neoclassical imagery from England to America', they did not supersede the creative capacity of indigenous craftsmen.[101] Ironically, as interiors became more ostensibly 'English' (Adamesque) they also became more 'American' (Federal). A distinctive dialect of the Federal style, known as 'punch-and-gouge' decoration, has long been admired for its 'local' character and its 'decorative and coloristic effects'.[102] Ostensibly a timber joiner's approximation of the Adam neoclassical vocabulary, and sometimes referred to as 'Carpenter's Adam' without the pejorative associations that such a designation might suggest, it was often used in combination with composition ornaments (Figure 3.16).[103]

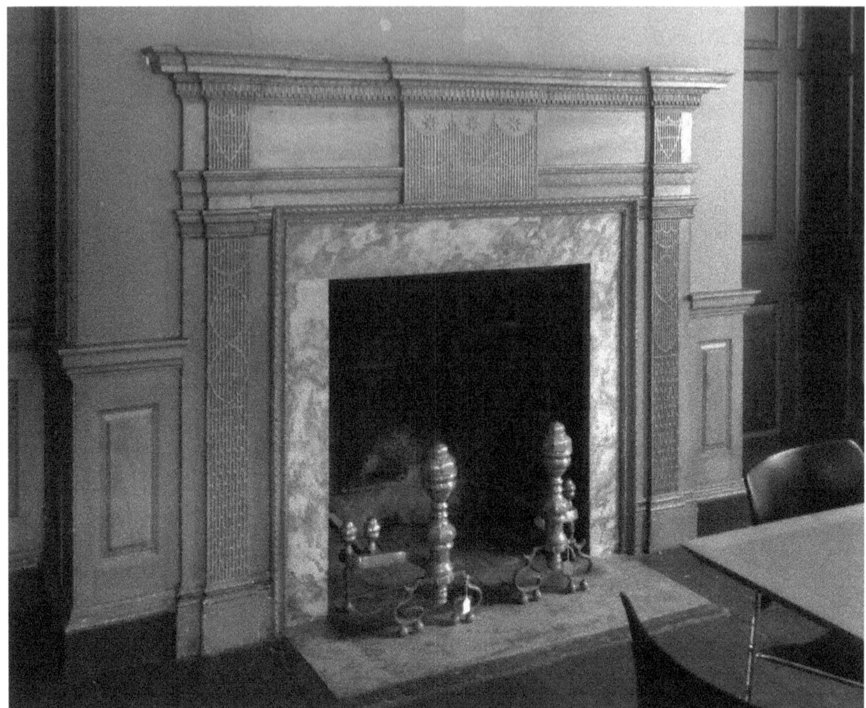

3.16 Punch and gouge chimneypiece at Upsala, Philadelphia, c. 1800.

The business of interior decoration

The dichotomy between plain exteriors and richly decorated interiors is frequently characterized as a manifestation of the early modern distinction between building as a commercial enterprise and decorating as a signifier of taste and social and cultural identity; respectively, the province of the builder and the consumer. However, it is becoming increasingly clear that decoration formed an integral part of property speculation in cities throughout the British Atlantic world. This section examines the business of house decorating, considering the impact of standardization within the building industry, and the implications arising from the house builder as an autonomous agent of neoclassicism.

Just as the unarticulated brick elevation became *de rigueur* for elite domestic architecture, so other spatial and visual elements of the town house were subject to similar processes of standardization. Composed of an axially aligned entrance hall and stair hall, flanked by a front and rear parlour, the so-called 'two-room' plan type was ubiquitous in cities across the Atlantic world by the beginning of the nineteenth century. While its widespread adoption may be understood in terms of the economic motivations of a largely speculative building industry, its popularity must also be understood in terms of the demands of the elite consumer market where both convenience and display were paramount. A survey of plan typologies at Parnell Square in Dublin, built between 1755 and 1785 and the city's foremost aristocratic enclave throughout the entire eighteenth century, reveals that forty-seven of the fifty-five surviving houses (85 per cent) were built to this rear-stair, two-room model.[104] Peter Guillery, drawing on the research of Elizabeth McKellar and Frank Kelsall, has identified the pattern book and the scale of speculative building as the 'effective agents' of this plan type in the aristocratic estates of London's West End by 1800, and it was certainly favoured for the better class of bespoke house erected in American cities, such as the Powel House in Philadelphia (1765) and 1621 Thames Street in Baltimore (c. 1790), and indeed of the better sort of row houses erected in those same cities in the first decades of the nineteenth century.[105] One way to create spatial distinction with this rear-stair type was to terminate the formal staircase at the first floor, emphasizing the social performativity of the *piano nobile*. At 42 North Great George's Street, Dublin (built 1786–88) the stonemason and property developer Henry Darley utilized this configuration for a house with a wide street frontage (41 feet); in numbers 39 (27 feet) and 41 (32 feet) on the same street, which he built in the same years, the stair rises from ground to second floor and so may have been intended for a different demographic (dispensing with the necessity of a concealed service stair). Indeed, while the architect Robert Adam had imaginatively introduced a variety of plan types and room shapes for his bespoke town houses in London – criticizing 'modern architects [who], by paying too little regard to the example of the Ancients in this point, are apt to fatigue us with a dull succession of similar apartments' – his speculatively built houses in that city typically conformed to more practical archetypes.[106] At the Adelphi, Adam employed the centre-stair plan, a type habitually used for plots of narrow frontage when space was at a premium; examples at Queen Anne's Gate, London (20 feet frontage) and at Sansom's Row, Philadelphia (18 feet frontage) confirm its general appeal to builder and consumer alike. Universally, it seems that the choice of architectural plan was a decidedly pragmatic one, where 'flexibility and adaptability transcended aesthetic ideals'.[107]

While interior space might be enhanced in a variety of ways – bowed and canted rear elevations to form distinctive room shapes; columnar screens to create picturesque scenographic effects; and barrel-vaulted ceilings *all'antica* – the chief method employed to create visual interest in the increasingly standardized apartments of the typical town house was through applied decoration: for this reason the protean nature of fashionable eighteenth-century architectural taste – from Palladianism via rococo and Chinoiserie to neoclassicism – is best appreciated in ornamented ceilings and chimneypieces rather than in elevation or plan. While degrees of enrichment differed across the British Atlantic world, by 1800 the better sort of speculatively built house customarily featured a high level of interior finish; a finish, moreover, dictated by house builders and their contractors. Indeed, through the commercial imperative of a burgeoning consumer economy – and paraphrasing Neil McKendrick – the decorated interior went from a luxury to a decency to a necessity over the course of the eighteenth century.[108]

Here we must address the historiography on urban domestic architecture generally, as the received wisdom continues to advance a distinction between the processes of building and decorating the urban house: the brick envelope representing the province of the builder/developer, and the decorative interior embodying the owner/occupier's concerns with fashionable taste and cultural capital. Sir John Summerson regarded the work of London's speculative house builders as being concerned exclusively with erecting 'the carcase of a house – simply a brick shell with floors and a roof', before offering it for sale.[109] The interior would then be completed to suit the taste and purse of the consumer. Elizabeth McKellar, describing an earlier period, has recently presented corroborating evidence supporting this position, identifying particular individuals 'customising' their houses and concluding that 'even with speculative developments consumers had some choice and control over the interior fitting-out of the building'.[110] However, in describing now demolished houses built by the developer Nicholas Barbon between 1670 and 1700, Summerson found the interiors 'all very much alike, economically planned to the point of meanness', and further observed that 'The design of panelling and staircases of his houses never varies.'[111] In response to this, McKellar raised the question as to why choices about interior finishes were not available in houses built by Barbon, wondering if they were aimed at a different market or if their appeal was based 'on the price reduction that standardisation might bring'.[112] Indeed, while recent histories of the elite London house have tended to uncritically reiterate verbatim Summerson's original position, it is now becoming more widely appreciated that builders rather than consumers dictated architectural form and ornament, both inside and out. But while Peter Guillery is correct to suggest that the interior fitting-out of a property by speculative builders encouraged standardization and uniformity, it is also true that builders often took the opportunity to create interiors of greater enrichment and refinement in order to claim a share of the potentially lucrative housing market.[113] So, while the decorating of houses prior to sale might be read as the material sign of a determinedly economic approach to architectural ornament, it might also be taken to express the competing claims of those individuals who aspired to the improved status of tastemakers. In many instances such enrichments formed a key part of the advertising and marketing of houses in the public press (the subject of the next chapter). The drawing-rooms of a tenement building in Rose Street, Edinburgh built by mason James Hill and decorated for him by plasterer James Dickie in 1789, for example, were evidently abundant with plasterwork ornament in the form of festoons, roses and 'Gothick' ogee mouldings: in his recent account of the city's building industry, Anthony Lewis has suggested that this may have acted as 'an appealing advert for those wanting to live in the New Town'.[114]

As noted in the previous chapter, the town house aesthetic relied on the repetition of regular forms and patterns for its effect, from skirting boards and newel posts to doors and window frames, and evidence of this type of standardized production for timber construction in London has been dated to the early Georgian period.[115] Coade's Artificial Stone Manufactory in Lambeth, London, founded in 1769, is also recognized as an important step towards system building, one that was paralleled in cities across Britain and Ireland: ornamental fanlights, stair balustrades and related stock in 'patent metal', for example, were available from the firms of Joseph Lowe and Player & Co. in Dublin during the 1780s and 1790s.[116] This standardisation of the material components of the house unsurprisingly extended to decoration, and the commercial sculpture produced by the plaster shops of London and Dublin evidences the growing commodification of the architectural interior. William Salmon, a statuary of Anglesea Street, Dublin advertised in 1779 'a new and curious Collection of Bass-reliefs, well adapted for all Kinds of Ceilings, Dining Parlours, Stair Cases, Halls, &c.', and the catalogue of John Harris in The Strand, London (c. 1790) extends to twelve pages of pre-prepared ornament from statues, chimneypieces and busts to 'Brackets, Vases, Urns, &c. of different Sizes and Patterns'.[117] As well as innumerable references to 'blocks', paterae and rosettes of various sizes, the daybook of Philadelphia ornament maker Edward Evans records the sale of an apparently ready-made 'Glory & Clouds' to plasterer William Thackara, Jr on three separate occasions in 1812.[118] As we have seen, plasterwork was recognized as the medium by which fashionable, decorative taste was routinely effected throughout the period under review: in Joseph Collyer's *Parent and guardian's directory* (1761), plasterwork was an 'ingenious art, that requires taste';[119] and as late as 1831, John Nicholson's *The operative mechanic* described the plasterer as 'a workman to whom the decorative part of architecture owes a considerable portion of its effect, and whose art is requisite in every kind of building'.[120] Drawings in the Stapleton Collection further confirm the standardization of much stuccoed enrichment: designs for ceilings and room elevations often include illustrations of identifiable stock-in-trade bas-reliefs available from plaster shops; sheets of frieze designs, often two or three to a single folio and individually numbered, suggest that they once formed part of a manuscript catalogue of compositions presented to potential clients for their consideration (Figure 3.17). On the other hand, the absence of cast plaster ornament in late eighteenth-century Salem prompted carver and joiner Samuel McIntire to approximate the Adam lexicon of trophies, drapery and festoons in timber.[121]

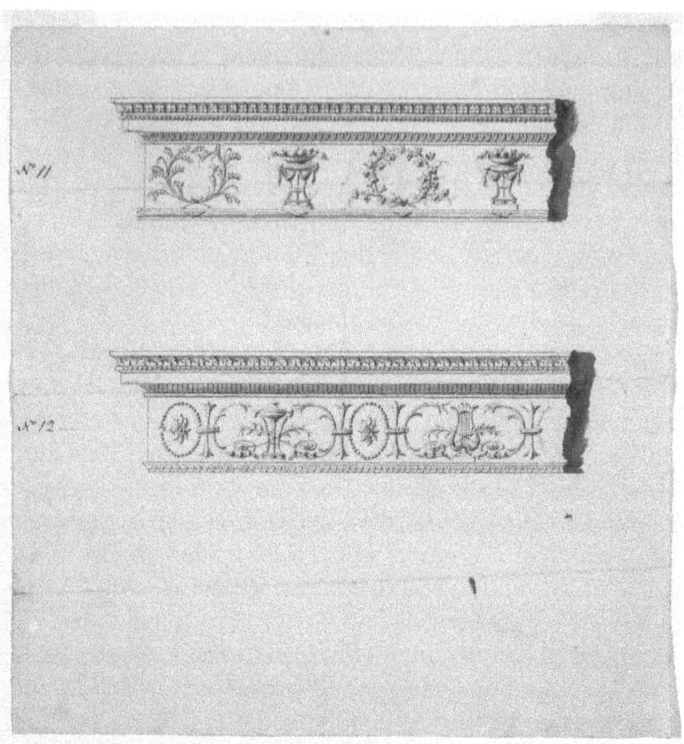

3.17 Numbered designs for plasterwork friezes from the Stapleton Collection.

By the late eighteenth-century, books of building mensuration, or 'estimators', included prices for increasingly standardized interior finishes such as plasterwork cornices and friezes, as well as more specific enrichments: while Philip Levi Hodgson's *The modern measurer* (Dublin, 1793) refers to a 'Cove Cornice of the first Magnitude, completely ornamented and enriched', priced at 3s. per running foot, *The builder's price book* (London, 1789) itemized costs for an 'Apollo's head and rays' (£1 1s.) and 'A fable of the fox and crane' (£1 5s.).[122] This proto-industrial process of decorating also informed the literature in more prescriptive ways and reveals the degree of embellishment expected of the typical, spec-built house by the beginning of the nineteenth century: William Fuller Pocock's *Modern finishing for rooms* (1811) illustrated the 'suitable ornaments, enrichments, and mouldings' for the reception rooms of the typical London house; an estimate for the cost of labour and materials for a 'substantial house' in Dublin, published in the *Irish builder's guide* (1813), included provision for 'good marble chimney-pieces' in the parlours and drawing-room and 'fancy' cornices with 'a frieze enriched with composition flowers, &c'.[123] The public endorsement of Robert Wellford's ornament manufactory by eighteen of Philadelphia's foremost house carpenters in 1811 is further testament to the importance of pre-prepared ornament for the housing market in that city.[124]

Given the largely speculative nature of domestic architecture and the growing standardisation of both the construction and decorating trades, it is perhaps unsurprising that the practice of decorating houses as a concomitant part of a property venture emerged during the last decades of the eighteenth century in Britain and Ireland, and in the cities of America around 1800. The evidence provided by the built environment in the form of houses built in pairs with equivalent interior schemes reveals the range of professional and commercial motivations that gave rise to this phenomenon. They also unequivocally situate the house builder as an agent of neoclassical taste, especially in provincial towns and cities. With this in mind it is interesting, if not entirely surprising, to note how well established the practice was in Dublin, a city where specialist decorative plasterers, or 'stuccoworkers', were apparently more numerous than in other British cities, and where the plasterer/stuccoworker was a more conspicuous property developer. At Mountjoy Square, laid out from 1789, the original leaseholders included the plastering firms of James Butler (two lots), James McCullagh (four lots), Michael Stapleton (three lots) and Charles Thorp (six lots) and the statuary and supplier of cast ornament William Salmon (two lots).[125] In mid-1770s London, the plasterer John Johnson played 'a fairly significant role' in the design and decoration of speculatively built houses in Harley Street;[126] in Boston, speculative building played 'a major role' in the career of Daniel Raynerd, 'the leading stucco worker' in that city during the 1790s.[127] In other instances, builders and decorators formed mutually beneficial house-building partnerships, such as that between John Morgan, carpenter, and Mark Fowles, plasterer, at Camden Crescent in Bath (begun 1788).[128]

Decoration and property speculation

Confirmation that the business of decorating was a constituent part of the business of building by at least the 1780s is provided by extensive material and documentary evidence. At the outset, and considering the speculative building industry in its entirety, it is clear that in the last decades of the eighteenth century master builders – either within or without the building trades – customarily decorated their properties in advance of introducing them onto the real estate market. In August 1790, William Crosbie, a silk manufacturer of Dublin, let three adjoining lots of ground on the south side of Gardiner Place and the corner of Temple Street, corresponding to the present 33–35 Gardiner Place, to a John Hayes Esq.[129] In November 1791, the site of 35 Gardiner Place 'together with all buildings and improvements' was sold to Charity Smith, widow, and in April 1792 the interest in the 'Brick House' at 33 Gardiner Place, described as 'lately erected' by Hayes, was acquired by the Rt Hon. Lady Martha Saunders.[130] Built to the standard

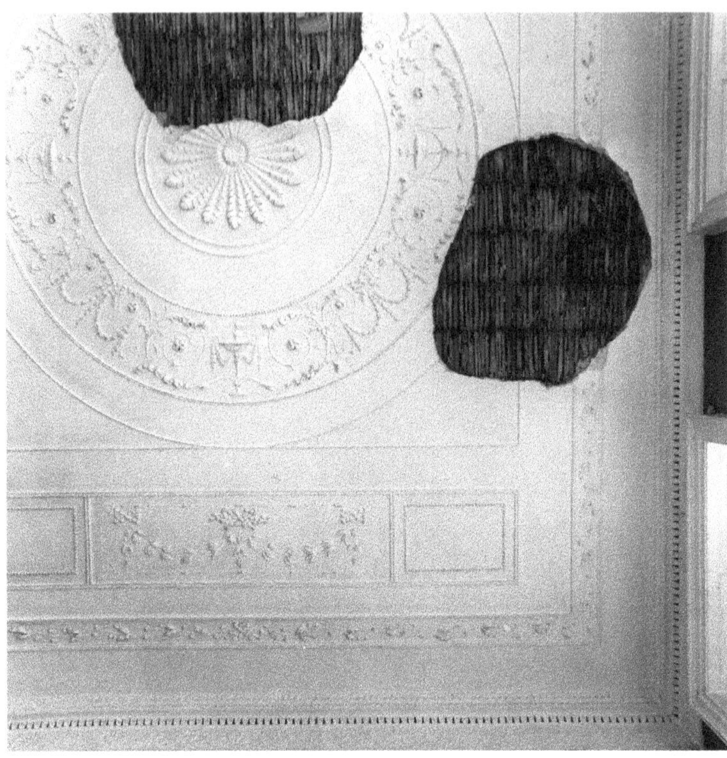

3.18 Ceiling plasterwork in front drawing-room at 59 Mountjoy Square (dem.), Dublin, c. 1795.

two-room, rear-stair plan, with identical Ionic doorcases, the interior decoration was evidently part of the building programme, seen in the identical plasterwork ceilings to the front drawing rooms and entrance halls in both houses (number 34 likely contains identical enrichments but is at present inaccessible). Nearby, on Mountjoy Square West, on ground owned and developed by the distiller Christopher Nihill, numbers 59 (dem.) and 60 were leased to Sir Francis Hopkins and the Rev. Joseph Pratt in 1797 and 1795 respectively; the adjoining house (58 Mountjoy Square, dem.) was described in 1800 as the 'dwelling house of Nihill Esq'.[131] The identical ceilings to the front and rear drawing-rooms and ground-floor dining-rooms in all three houses, of which only one survives intact (number 60), indicates that all three were planned and executed concurrently (Figures 3.18 and 3.19). Of course, the decision to fit properties with identical stuccoed interiors is fully comprehensible when capital risk and the practice of sub-contracting are taken into account: the duplication of a decorative scheme across two or more houses necessarily made less creative and technical demand on the contracted decorator, and so represented a smaller financial outlay for the real estate investor. Although clearly modelled by hand, the front and rear drawing-room ceilings at 64 and 65

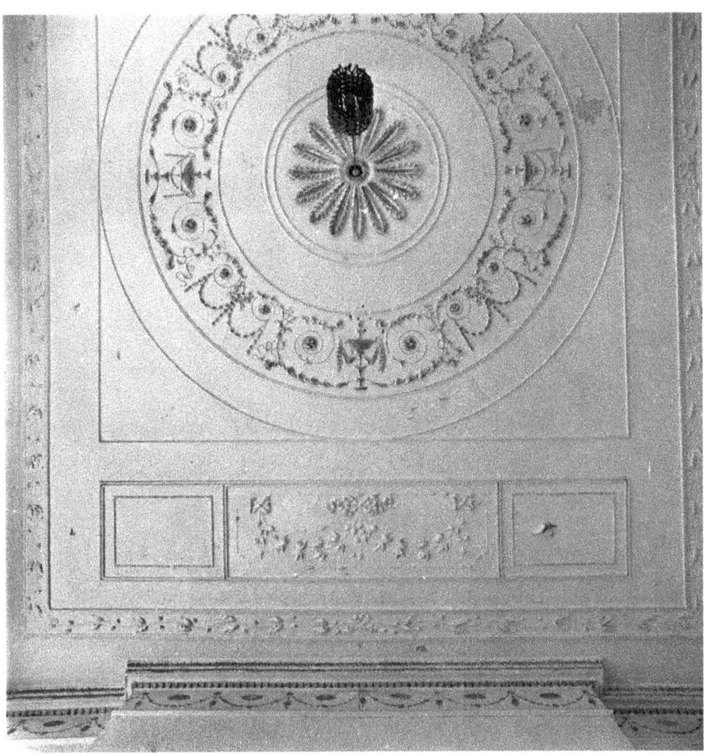

3.19 Ceiling plasterwork in front drawing-room at 60 Mountjoy Square, Dublin, c. 1795.

Merrion Square, built on ground originally leased to Hall Lamb Esq. in 1787, are similarly equivalent in composition and detail: a corresponding design in the Stapleton Collection suggests a role for drawings in determining decorating contracts of this nature.[132] The building of Waterloo Row in Baltimore, a terrace of twelve houses designed by the architect Robert Mills in 1816 (dem.), involved a consortium of building tradesmen and suppliers who each received the title deeds to one property. Unique in that city in terms of its monumental, regular elevation and refined Federal-style detailing, the terrace's interiors were identical in plan, construction and decoration.[133]

Needless to say, speculative houses undertaken by building tradesmen reveal a similar approach to decorating pairs of houses. At 53 and 54 Mountjoy Square, built on ground leased to the bricklayer William Pemberton in 1790, the surviving original decoration in both entrance halls is identical, with simple tripartite ceiling compositions and plaster friezes.[134] The interiors of the present 36–40 Merrion Square, built on ground leased to the architect Samuel Sproule and the paper-stainer George Kent in 1786, though now altered to varying degrees, also have much in common with one another.[135] Evidently built as a block – each individual house boasting the same parapet height, pattern of fenestration and tripartite Adamesque doorcase – there are numerous consonances with the surviving plasterwork decoration across all five properties: the rear drawing-room ceiling at 36 corresponds with that at 37; the friezes in the entrance halls of 37 and 38 were evidently cast from the same mould; and the stair halls of numbers 36–40 inclusive share an identical barrel-vaulted ceiling ornamented with an elegant diaper motif. A corresponding practice in London is represented by a number of houses in Bedford Square, decorated to designs by the architect and speculative builder Thomas Leverton. As well as designing the interiors of 6 and 13 Bedford Square, for which he obtained a lease in 1781, it seems that Leverton's 'principal concern in promoting the finishing' of the houses involved 'several of my own account', now identified as numbers 1 and 10. The ceiling of the rear drawing-room at 10 Bedford Square is identical to that in the corresponding room at 1 Bedford Square – including the repetition of figurative inset panels – while the ceilings of the front drawing-rooms at 10 and 13 Bedford Square, composed of circular and semi-circular compartments, are also equivalent in form and ornament.[136] While such duplications and repetitions were recorded in the *Survey of London* (1914) – observing that it was 'a fact which points to one controlling influence in the decorative treatment of these houses' – the notion that there existed in the eighteenth century a wider culture of system decorating, equivalent to system building, was not entertained.[137]

Extensive documentary evidence provided by the surviving accounts of Dublin 'measurer' or quantity surveyor Bryan Bolger (*fl.* 1787–1818), now held at the National Archives of Ireland, and the records of Philadelphia property insurance companies such as the Mutual Assurance Company and the Philadelphia Contributionship provides further clues to the extent of decorative work undertaken by speculative builders across the Atlantic world. Plasterer's work by George Potter for pairs of houses in Mountjoy Place and Temple Street in Dublin, during the course of 1790/91, included enriched friezes and cornices, 'stucco flowers' for hall ceilings, and 'Ornamental Stucco centers' over the sideboard recesses in dining-rooms.[138] In 1792, the carpenter's work executed by John Low for Hall Kirchoffer's two new-built houses in Temple Street included '86 Cartouce Brackets & puting on Composition', referring to the ornamentation of the tread ends of the principal staircases in both properties, a practice confirmed by comparing the composition ornaments in houses built in pairs across the city (Figures 3.20 and 3.21).[139] Fire insurance surveys for 257–263 South Fourth Street, Philadelphia, a row of four houses built by carpenter Jacob Vogdes between 1810 and 1812 – and leased variously to two merchants, a doctor and a 'gentleman' – reveal that the interiors were fitted with floors of 'best yellow pine', indoor shutters of 'the best kind', stucco cornices, mahogany doors and marble chimneypieces (Figure I.2).[140] The fine material and decorative finishes of 425–427 Spruce Street in the same city, built between 1790 and

3.20 Composition ornament at 53 Mountjoy Square, Dublin, c. 1791.

1792 by house carpenter William Williams, almost certainly contributed to the increased insurance rates issued for both properties in 1793/94.[141]

Plasterers turned property developers routinely decorated their houses as part of a speculative venture, a practice particularly common in Dublin. Indeed, the gauging of traditional lime plaster with gypsum (plaster of Paris or casting plaster) from mid-century onwards increased the rate of production and facilitated the greater degree of plaster enrichment found in houses of the 1780s and 1790s: the neoclassical style with its insistence on repetition and shallow relief was certainly best suited to this process; this in turn created a market distinction for the house decorator turned house builder. (That said, earlier examples of system decoration apparently predate the introduction of these new plaster technologies: the rococo plasterwork in the present numbers 1 and 2 Great Denmark Street, built on ground leased in 1768 to carpenter Thomas Browne, includes almost identical drawing-room overdoors featuring hand-modelled cartouches of floral and rocaille ornament.[142]) Built by 'painter and plaisterer' Francis Ryan and leased in 1784 to the Hon. Valentine Browne (later 1st Earl of Kenmare), 35 North Great George's Street boasts one of the most comprehensive

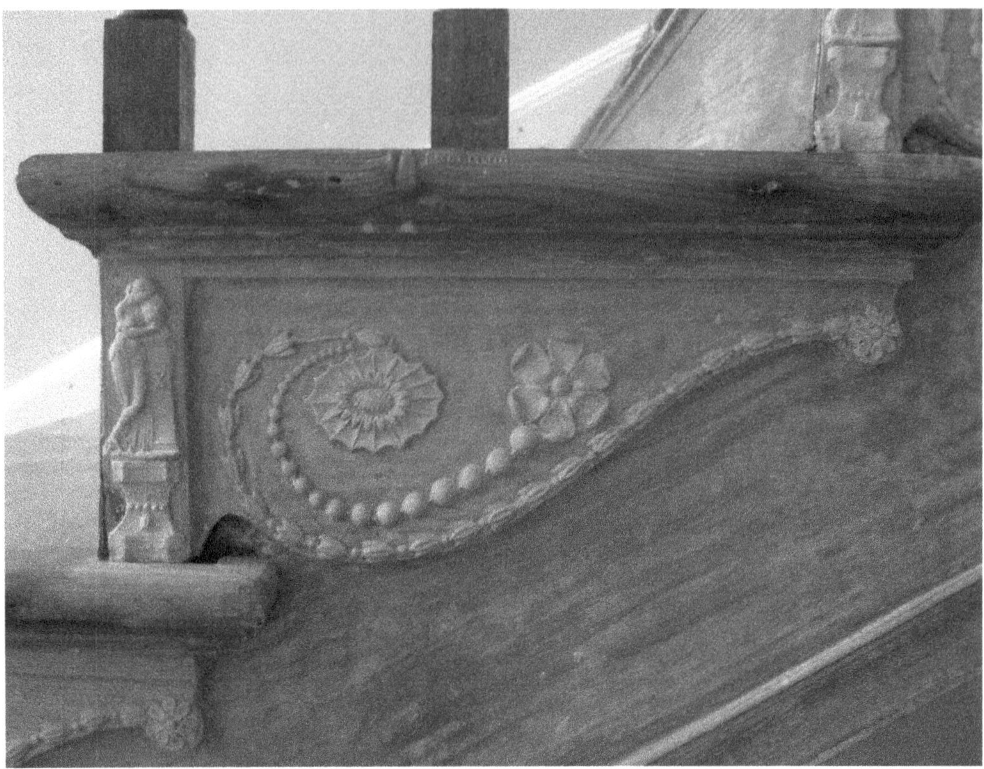

3.21 Composition ornament at 54 Mountjoy Square, Dublin, c. 1791.

decorative schemes found in a 'typical' three-bay terraced house, with enriched ceilings and mural decorations throughout all of its principal reception rooms and circulation spaces. Photographs of the interiors at 43–45 Mountjoy Square (all now demolished), erected by Michael Stapleton in 1789–90, confirm that prominent elements of the decoration in each house, including the tympanum over the door leading to the front drawing-room, were equivalent in composition and ornament.[143] Houses built by the plasterer Charles Thorp also illustrate the same practice, seen in the repeated use of a simple design of concentric circles in the drawing-rooms of his speculative ventures in Hume Street and North Great George's Street (built 1777–90), and of painted ceiling centrepieces of Apollo in a phaeton after a published design of Michelangelo Pergolesi in many of the same properties (Figure 3.22). In Bedford Square, London, houses built on speculation by plasterers turned property developers similarly boast a higher concentration of decorative enrichment while betraying the same concerns with economic pragmatism: houses erected by Thomas Utterton (numbers 16, 17, 31 and 47) and Robert Philips (number 9), are unsurprisingly among the most richly decorated.[144] Edinburgh plasterer James Nisbet appears to have repeated the same decorative scheme at his self-built properties

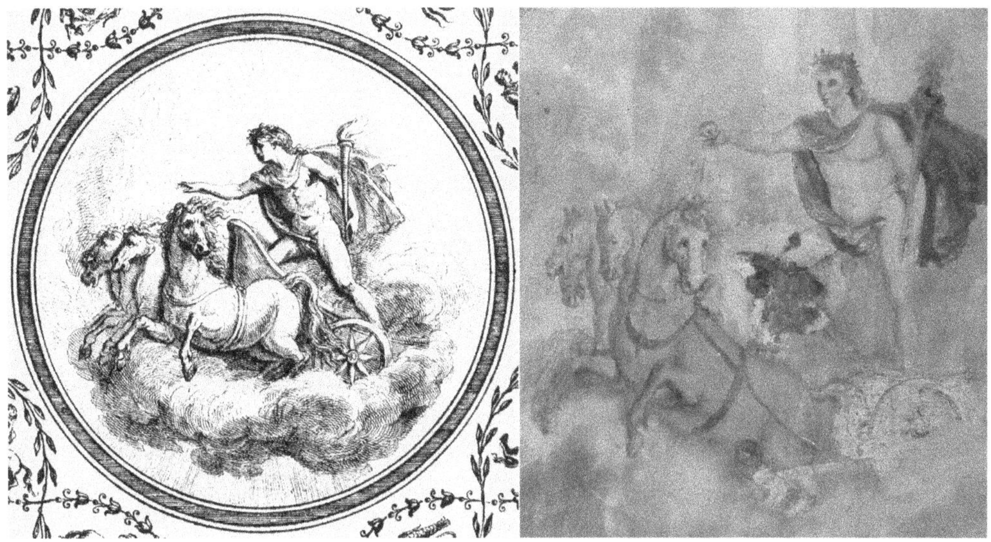

3.22 Ceiling painting in rear drawing-room at 10 Hume Street, Dublin, c. 1787, and plate 21, fig. 88 from Michelangelo Pergolesi, *Original designs of vases, figures, medallions, pilasters, and other ornaments in the Etruscan and grotesque styles* (1777–92).

in George and Queen Streets during the 1790s.[145] Nor was the practice confined to the major metropolitan centres: 5 Royal Crescent in Bath, built as speculation by the plasterer Charles Coles, is one of the few houses in that celebrated development to feature ornamental ceilings in its principal reception rooms.[146]

Evidence for a similar practice in American cities generally dates from the first decades of the nineteenth century, when the building of monumental terraces or rows first became economically viable. In September 1812, 'measurer of plastering' Edward Evans valued work by plasterer William Jones on two adjoining houses in Fourth Street, Philadelphia that included 'ornamental work' over the folding doors in the front parlours of both properties.[147] Indeed, while decorative plasterwork was not a medium that enjoyed much purchase in colonial or early national America, the standardizing of interior ornament was facilitated through other means. In Philadelphia, for example, refined decorative finishes were an increasingly common feature of houses built for sale or rent by the early nineteenth century. Built speculatively in 1800–2, the uniform size and spatial organization of the twenty-two houses of Sansom Street, between Seventh and Eighth Streets (now much altered), evidently extended to identical interior finishes including 'ornamented mantels' on both first and second floors.[148] Houses lower down the social scale, such as 233–241 Delancey Street, built speculatively by businessman Joseph Wetherill in 1810–11, were also 'fashionably finished inside', being enriched with carved joinery, cornices and decorated chimneypieces that exhibited some variety within a standardized system.[149]

Ornament manufactories also took advantage of the serial decoration of speculative houses by builders and decorators. Robert Wellford's house and shop in Tenth Street, Philadelphia, built in 1810, constituted what Mark Reinberger has described as 'a three-dimensional catalog of his work and a sampler of [the] ways compo[sition] could be used in a house': the hall and front parlour likely comprised the public area of the shop and so served as a sort of show home for prospective clients.[150] Dublin ornament supplier William Salmon's speculative houses in Mountjoy Square (built 1789–91) may also have acted in this capacity: from composition ornament on skirting boards, stair treads and door and window architraves, to plaster bas-reliefs as the focal point of plasterwork ceilings and overdoors, the interiors ostensibly formed a conspectus of the sort of off-the-peg decorations available from his commercial premises in Anglesea Street.[151]

Given the ubiquity of the two-room plan, the availability of ready-made ornaments in timber and plaster, and the necessary sub-contracting of specialist trades, the interiors of town houses became as much the 'refined industrial products' of the capitalized building industry as the brick terrace itself.[152] But there are other ways to think about this phenomenon. In response to the sizeable quantity of first-rate terraced housing erected in cities throughout Britain, Ireland and North America in the eighteenth and early nineteenth centuries, an already decorated speculatively built house represented a distinct commercial advantage in a competitive marketplace, augmenting a builder's potential revenue and reputation – the subject of our next chapter.[153]

Conclusion

With respect to the foregoing material and documentary evidence regarding builder- as opposed to consumer-driven decoration, an important corollary requires elucidation: while such a commercially driven approach to interior decoration necessarily encouraged standardization of form and ornament, it also placed the builder/developer in the vanguard of disseminating the taste for the Adam decorative style, a role that has typically been the preserve of the patron, architect and manufacturer of luxury goods in the historiography of eighteenth-century architecture and decorative arts. If less important from a strictly teleological perspective of neoclassicism when compared with the designs of James 'Athenian' Stuart, Robert Adam or George Richardson, the artisanal network involved in erecting and decorating speculative row houses nevertheless emerges as a creative agent of architectural taste in its own right. This position also represents a challenge to the supposition that as drawings assumed an increasingly important role in architectural practice generally, 'The centre of gravity of the design process was moving closer to the architect, away from the craftworker and the site.'[154]

While erudite British and Irish patrons may have recognized the degree to which the 'remnants of antiquity' had become, in the words of Dana Arnold, 'part of a currency of material culture disembodied from their original context but with related sets of meanings', it is clear that the artisan negotiated neoclassicism in complex ways.[155] As Barbara Arciszewska and Elizabeth McKellar have recently argued, 'the reception and spread of classicism in the eighteenth century suggests ... overlapping spheres of influence between the national and the provincial, the classical and the non-classical, the elite and the everyday'.[156] If we accept that the neoclassical appearance of the town house interior was increasingly dictated by an artisan class of plasterers, joiners and ornament makers, then its interpretation of that idiom demands a reading germane to the circumstances contingent on its realization: less a mismanaged simulacrum of classical antique prototypes and their literary significations, and rather a credible and regionally diverse adaptation of a shared architectural culture.

Notes

1 Daniel Maudlin and Bernard L. Herman, 'Introduction', in Daniel Maudlin and Bernard L. Herman (eds), *Building the British Atlantic world: spaces, places and material culture, 1600–1850* (Chapel Hill: University of North Carolina Press, 2016), pp. 3–7.
2 Alistair Rowan, *Robert Adam: catalogues of architectural drawings in the Victoria and Albert Museum* (London: Victoria and Albert Museum, 1988), p. 21.
3 Geoffrey Beard, 'Robert Adam's craftsmen', in Giles Worsely (ed.) *Adam in context: Georgian Group symposium* (London: Georgian Group, 1992), p. 27.
4 Maudlin and Herman, 'Introduction', p. 7.
5 Conor Lucey, *The Stapleton Collection: designs for the Irish neoclassical interior* (Tralee: Churchill House Press, 2007); Dean Lahikainen, *Samuel McIntire: carving an American style* (Salem, MA: Peabody Essex Museum and University of New England Press, 2007).
6 Albert Boime, *Art in an age of revolution, 1750–1800* (Chicago: University of Chicago Press, 1987) p. 60.
7 Joseph Rykwert, *Robert and James Adam* (London: Collins, 1985), p. 98.
8 C.P. Curran, *Dublin decorative plasterwork of the seventeenth and eighteenth centuries* (London: Tiranti, 1967), p. 71.
9 Howard Davis, *The culture of building* (Oxford: Oxford University Press, 2006), p. 13.
10 Kjetil Fallan, *Design history: understanding theory and method* (London: Bloomsbury Academic, 2014), p. 61.
11 For a recent account of this phenomenon see Dana Arnold, 'The illusion of grandeur? Antiquity, grand tourism and the country house', in Dana Arnold (ed.), *The Georgian country house: architecture, landscape and society* (Stroud: Sutton, 2003), pp. 100–16.
12 Robert and James Adam, *The works in architecture*, vol. 1, part 1 (London, 1773), p. i.
13 Viccy Coltman, *Fabricating the antique: neoclassicism in Britain, 1760–1800* (Chicago: University of Chicago Press, 2006), pp. 11–16.
14 Anne Puetz, 'Design instruction for artisans in eighteenth-century Britain', *Journal of Design History* 12:3 (1999): 222–3.

15 John Turpin, *A school of art in Dublin since the eighteenth century: a history of the National College of Art and Design* (Dublin: Gill & Macmillan, 1995), p. 52, 61.
16 Pierre Bourdieu, *Distinction: a social critique of the judgment of taste* (Cambridge, MA: Harvard University Press, 1984), p. 2. Referring to the neo-classical products of manufacturers like Matthew Boulton and Josiah Wedgwood, Viccy Coltman notes that 'the inventive fabrications' of archaeological volumes such as Sir William Hamilton's *Collection of Etruscan, Greek and Roman antiquities*, were 'stamped with the prestige of the collector and his collection of ancient artefacts: a prestige that the craftsmen literally subscribed to in their reproductive craft'. Coltman, *Fabricating the antique*, p. 77.
17 Coltman, *Fabricating the antique*, p. 45.
18 Michael Snodin and Maurice Howard, *Ornament: a social history since 1450* (New Haven and London: Yale University Press, 1996), pp. 54–5. See also Peter Thornton, *Form and decoration: innovation in the decorative arts 1470–1870* (London: Weidenfeld & Nicolson, 1998), p. 180.
19 Abigail Harrison-Moore, introduction to 'Part I: knowledge, taste, and sublimity, c.1750–1830', in Abigail Harrison-Moore and Dorothy C. Rowe (eds), *Architecture and design in Europe and America 1750–2000* (Oxford: Blackwell Publishing, 2006), p. 32.
20 Christie's Archive, London, *A catalogue of the valuable collection of architectural drawings and designs; Library of architectural and other books ... The property of the late ingenious artist Mr Joseph Rose, decd.*, 12 April 1799.
21 Irish Architectural Archive, Curran collection, 77/6.
22 Matthias Darly, *The ornamental architect or young artist's instructor* (London, 1769), t.p.
23 William Pain, *The practical builder* (London, 1774), p. 3.
24 Puetz, 'Design instruction for artisans', 220.
25 The ceiling was also intended to incorporate a figurative medallion featuring characters from Shakespeare's *Timon of Athens*, including Phrynia and Timandra (IV, iii). For a summary of the original bill see National Library of Ireland, *J.F. Ainsworth reports on private collections*, vol. 2, Report No. 29, 'Powerscourt Papers', p. 500.
26 Richardson describes iconology as being 'derived from two Greek words, which signify speaking pictures, or discourse of images'. George Richardson, *Iconology; or a collection of emblematical figures*, 2 vols (London, 1779), vol. 1, p. i.
27 *The builder's magazine* (London, 1774–78), plate XXII, figs 1–3.
28 Asher Benjamin and Daniel Raynerd, *The American builder's companion* (Boston, 1806), p. 47.
29 From a design-historical perspective, 'the way things look is, in the broadest sense, a result of the conditions of their making'. Adrian Forty, *Objects of desire: design and society since 1750* (London: Thames & Hudson, 1987), p. 7.
30 Much research to date has focused on identifying the engraved sources used by plasterers. For the period under review see Joseph McDonnell, *Irish eighteenth-century stuccowork and its European sources* (Dublin: National Gallery of Ireland, 1991).
31 The Stapleton Collection of drawings is held at the National Library of Ireland, Dublin; the 'Sketch Book of Rose' is held at Harewood House, Yorkshire; the bound 'Sketches of Ornamented Frizes' is in the collections of the Royal Institute of British Architects, London.
32 The drawings are numbered AD 2214–2371.
33 Eugenie Carr, 'A catalogue of the Stapleton family collection of drawings in the National Library of Ireland', MA diss., National University of Ireland, 1985, p. 3.
34 *A catalogue of the valuable collection*, *passim*.

35 Beard, 'Robert Adam's craftsmen', p. 26. A more recent overview of Joseph Rose's career fails to address this important aspect of their practice. See Ashleigh Murray, 'Joseph Rose and company', *Georgian Group Journal* 20 (2012): 103–18.
36 Eileen Harris, *The genius of Robert Adam: his interiors* (New Haven and London: Yale University Press, 2001): Kedleston Hall, pp. 22–3 (figs 20–1); Harewood, pp. 141, 149 (figs 203–4); Osterley Park, pp. 163–4 (figs 235–6).
37 Once part of the Stapleton Collection, it is illustrated in C.P. Curran, 'Dublin plaster work', *Journal of the Royal Society of Antiquaries of Ireland* 70:1 (1940), plate IX.
38 *Ibid.*
39 McDonnell, *Irish Eighteenth-century stuccowork*, pp. 28–9, and plates 150–9.
40 George Richardson, *A book of ceilings in the stile of the antique grotesque* (London, 1776), p. i.
41 Puetz, 'Design instruction for artisans', 221.
42 Robert and James Adam, *Works in architecture*, vol. 1, part 1, preface. The volumes of Adam drawings in Sir John Soane's Museum contain unpublished designs by for a 'British Order' and a 'Scottish Order' (Adam vol. 7, nos. 69 and 163).
43 Curran, *Dublin decorative plasterwork*, p. 87.
44 C.H. Reilly, 'Bath I', *Country Life* (21 October 1922): 515.
45 Herman and Maudlin, 'Introduction', p. 24.
46 Damie Stillman, 'Homewood: an American villa and its sources', *Building Homewood, vision for a villa 1802–2002*, exh. cat. (Baltimore: Johns Hopkins University, 2002), pp. 12, 14–15.
47 Janice G. Schimmelmann, *Architectural books in early America: architectural treatises and handbooks available in American libraries and bookstores through 1800* (New Castle, DE: Oak Knoll Press, 1999).
48 Lahikainen, *Carving an American style*, pp. 36–7, citing Paul F. Norton, 'Samuel McIntire of Salem: the drawings and papers of the architect/carver and his family, 1988', unpublished MS (photocopy).
49 Biddle, *Young carpenter's assistant*, pp. 3–4.
50 Schimmelman, *Architectural books*, pp. 16–18. Columbani's titles appear in the catalogues of booksellers in Boston, New York and Philadelphia from 1796 onwards.
51 Alistair Rowan, 'New York and Philadelphia. Robert Adam and the Concorsi Clementini', *Burlington Magazine* 124:950 (1982): 322.
52 *Dublin Journal*, 4–6 April 1769.
53 Christine Casey, *Dublin*. Buildings of Ireland 3 (New Haven and London: Yale University Press, 2005), p. 362.
54 *Freeman's Journal*, 13–16 August 1768, cited in Edward McParland, 'James Gandon and the Royal Exchange competition, 1768–69', *Journal of the Royal Society of Antiquaries of Ireland* 102 (1972): 58–75.
55 *Dublin Journal* of 4–6 April 1769. The amended advertisement, noting the apprenticeship to Rose, appeared first on 27–29 April.
56 London, Guildhall Library, MS 6122/3, Plaisterers Company court minutes 1698–1761. For the Rose apprentices, see Geoffrey Beard, *Decorative plasterwork in Great Britain* (London: Phaidon, 1975), pp. 237–44.
57 Robert and James Adam, *Works in architecture*, vol. 1, part 1 (July 1773) and part 2 (May 1774).
58 Timothy Mowl and Brian Earnshaw, *An insular rococo: architecture, politics and society in Ireland and England, 1710–1770* (London: Reaktion, 1999), p. 180.
59 *Oxford Journal*, 25 March 1780.
60 For a biographical overview see Howard Colvin, *A biographical dictionary of British architects 1600–1840*, 3rd edn (New Haven and London: Yale University Press, 1995), pp. 810–11.

61 Eileen Harris, *British architectural books and writers, 1556–1785* (Cambridge: Cambridge University Press, 1990), p. 388.
62 Christine Casey, 'Books and builders: a bibliographical approach to Irish 18th-century architecture', PhD diss., Trinity College Dublin, 1991, p. 28.
63 These were Michael Maguire, Edward Robbins, Francis Ryan and Robert West. On Irish subscriptions to architectural books see Casey, 'Books and builders', pp. 30–1.
64 F.A. D'Arcy, 'Wages of skilled workers in the Dublin building industry 1667–1918', *Saothar* 13 (1990): 21–37. The wage of 12s. per week is based on an average rate of 2s. (24d.) per day over a six-day working week. This is calculated for the period 1741–68, for which figures are readily available.
65 Harris, *British architectural books*, p. 86.
66 *Hibernian Journal*, 12–15 November 1773; *Public Advertiser*, 5 January 1774; *Caledonian Mercury*, 11 September 1773.
67 *Gazetteer and New Daily Advertiser*, 19 November 1776.
68 Harris, *British architectural books*, p. 71.
69 Richardson, *Ceilings*, p. i.
70 The commercial incentive for tradesmen as subscribers is noted in John Archer, *The literature of British domestic architecture, 1715–1842* (Cambridge, MA: MIT Press, 1985), p. 10. English plasterers who subscribed to the *Ceilings* included Richard Cox of London and William Roberts of Oxford.
71 Three of the fascicles of Richardson's *Ceilings* were announced in the *Hibernian Journal* on 24–27 March 1775 (number IV), 13–15 November 1775 (number VI) and 19–21 June 1776 (number VIII). All were available from Robbins's premises in St Stephen's Green, Dublin.
72 *Gazetteer and New Daily Advertiser*, 19 November 1776.
73 Archer, *Literature of British domestic architecture*, p. 17.
74 *Dublin Evening Post*, 29 October 1782.
75 Conor Lucey, 'Pattern books and pedagogies: neoclassicism and the Dublin artisan', in Lynda Mulvin (ed.), *The fusion of neoclassical principles* (Dublin: Wordwell, 2011), pp. 141–2, figs 10–11.
76 The plasterwork by McCullagh and Reynolds was described as 'somewhat antiquated' in the accompanying textual description to plate 31 in James Malton, *A picturesque & descriptive view of the city of Dublin* (London, 1799). Malton more favourably described Stapleton's work in the first-floor reception rooms as being 'well worthy of notice ... particularly the ball and drawing rooms'.
77 Murray Fraser, 'Public building and colonial policy in Dublin', *Architectural History* 28 (1995): 102–23.
78 Dell Upton, *Architecture in the United States* (Oxford: Oxford University Press, 1998), pp. 33–4; Amy Henderson, 'A family affair: the design and decoration of 321 South Fourth Street, Philadelphia', in John Styles and Amanda Vickery (eds), *Gender, taste, and material culture in Britain and North America, 1700–1830* (New Haven and London: Yale University Press, 2006), pp. 267–91.
79 Gabrielle M. Lanier and Bernard L. Herman, *Everyday architecture of the mid-Atlantic: looking at buildings and landscapes* (Baltimore: Johns Hopkins University Press, 1997), p. 127.
80 Sterling Boyd, *The Adam style in America 1770–1820* (New York and London: Garland Publishing, 1985), p. 5.
81 Maudlin and Herman, 'Introduction', pp. 7–8.
82 While the Bingham Mansion (dem.) on Third Street, Philadelphia, built in 1789 to designs of English architect John Plaw, was the exception to this rule, '[it] did not have much immediate influence on the architecture of its own city'. Beatrice B. Garvan, *Federal Philadelphia: the Athens of the western world*, exh. cat. (Philadelphia: Philadelphia Museum of Art, 1987), p. 38.

83 Boyd, *Adam style in America*, p. 176.
84 Harold and James Kirker, *Bulfinch's Boston 1787–1817* (Oxford: Oxford University Press, 1964), pp. 50–1; Lahikainen, *Carving an American style*, p. 219; Kimball, *Samuel McIntire, carver: the architect of Salem* (Portland, ME: Southworth-Anthoensen Press, 1940), pp. 10–11.
85 Boyd, *Adam style in America*, p. 171.
86 Kevin M Sweeney, 'High-style vernacular: lifestyles of the colonial elite', in Cary Carson, Ronald Hoffman and P.J. Albert (eds), *Of consuming interests: the style of life in the eighteenth century* (Charlottesville: University Press of Virginia, 1994), pp. 41, 54.
87 Carl Lounsbury, 'Design process', in Cary Carson and Carl R. Lounsbury (eds), *The Chesapeake house: architectural investigation by Colonial Williamsburg* (Chapel Hill: University of North Carolina Press, 2013), p. 79.
88 Mark Reinberger, *Utility and beauty: Robert Wellford and composition ornament in America* (Newark: University of Delaware Press, 2003), p. 49.
89 Damie Stillman, *The decorative work of Robert Adam* (London: Academy Editions, 1973), p. 10. On the rarity of decorative plasterwork ceilings in America see Willie Graham, 'Interior finishes', in Carson and Lounsbury (eds), *The Chesapeake House*, pp. 324–5.
90 *Pennsylvania Journal*, 29 December 1763; *South Carolina and American General Gazette*, 28 October 1774.
91 Robert L. Raley, 'Early Maryland plasterwork and stuccowork', *Journal of the Society of Architectural Historians* 20:3 (1961): 131–5.
92 *Ibid.*, 134.
93 Frances H. Ford, 'The design and fabrication of the plastered cornices of the Gaillard-Bennett House, 60 Montagu Street, Charleston, SC', MSc diss., University of Pennsylvania, 2006, p. 40, citing unpublished research by Richard Marks, 'Case studies of Charleston's ornamental plaster work' (1994).
94 Reinberger, *Utility and beauty*, p. 102; Lanier and Herman, *Everyday architecture of the mid-Atlantic*, pp. 127–38.
95 *Pennsylvania Packet*, 15 March 1785.
96 *Pennsylvania Packet*, 6 December 1793; *Federal Gazette*, 3 September 1795.
97 For Andrews see Reinberger, *Utility and beauty*, pp. 89–90; Nancy Davis, 'George Andrews' composition ornament in the early Federal period', *The 1988 Washington Antiques Show*, exh. cat. (Washington, DC, 1988), pp. 145–7; Orlando Ridout, *Building the Octagon* (Washington, DC: American Institute of Architects Press, 1989), pp. 91, 123. Andrews was established in Dublin by at least 1790, when he advertised composition mouldings and ornaments in 'the newest stile', and boasted of their superiority 'both in design and execution, to any ever done in this kingdom, or in England'. *Dublin Evening Post*, 11 September 1790.
98 The inventory of Samuel McIntire's estate in 1811 itemized composition ornaments valued at $35, described as 'the most valuable item in the shop inventory'. Lahikainen, *Carving an American style*, p. 230.
99 The following précis of Wellford's career is indebted to Mark Reinberger's exemplary monograph.
100 'To the Public', handbill published 6 April 1801.
101 Reinberger, *Utility and beauty*, p. 15.
102 Boyd, *Adam style in America*, p. 255.
103 Reinberger, *Utility and beauty*, p. 104.
104 Anthony Duggan, 'Parnell Square: an analysis of house types', *Bulletin of the Irish Georgian Society* 38 (1995): 16–24.
105 Peter Guillery, *The small house in eighteenth-century London* (New Haven and London: Yale University Press, 2004), p. 69.

106 Robert Adam, *Ruins of the palace of the emperor Diocletian at Spalatro* (London, 1764), p. 9.
107 Guillery, *Small house*, p. 69.
108 Neil McKendrick, 'The consumer revolution of eighteenth-century England', in Neil McKendrick, John Brewer and J.H. Plumb (eds), *The birth of a consumer society: the commercialization of eighteenth-century England* (Bloomington: Indiana University Press, 1982), p. 10.
109 John Summerson, *Georgian London* (London: Pleiades Books, 1945; repr. New Haven and London: Yale University Press, 2003), p. 78. For later reiterations of this position see Dan Cruickshank and Neil Burton, *Life in the Georgian city* (London: Viking, 1990), p. 115; and Rachel Stewart, *The town house in Georgian London* (New Haven and London: Yale University Press, 2009), p. 117.
110 Elizabeth McKellar, *The birth of modern London: the development and design of the city, 1660–1720* (Manchester: Manchester University Press, 1999), pp. 172–3, 178.
111 Summerson, *Georgian London*, p. 45.
112 McKellar, *Birth of modern London*, p. 173.
113 Guillery, *Small house*, p. 285.
114 A.R. Lewis, 'The builders of Edinburgh New Town', PhD dissertation, University of Edinburgh, 2006, p. 207.
115 McKellar, *Birth of modern London*, p. 78.
116 *Dublin Journal*, 7 May 1754; *Dublin Journal*, 12 August 1780; *Hibernian Journal*, 13 August 1794.
117 Conor Lucey, 'Statuaries and plaster shops in eighteenth-century Dublin', in Paula Murphy (ed.), *Sculptors and sculpture 1600–2000*. Art and architecture of Ireland 3 (London: Yale University Press, 2014), pp. 518–20; Timothy Clifford, 'The plaster shops of the rococo and neoclassical era in Britain', *Journal of the History of Collections* 4:1 (1992): 39–65.
118 Historical Society of Pennsylvania (hereafter HSP), 'Daybook of Edward Evans 1812–18', pp. 14, 18, 22. Throughout this period Evans variously described his trade as plasterer, measurer of plastering and 'caster of ornamental stucco work'.
119 Joseph Collyer, *Parent and guardian's directory* (London, 1769), p. 266. This echoes Robert Campbell, who in 1747 had described 'Stucco Workers', as a 'genteel and profitable' branch of the plastering trade requiring 'Judgment and Education'. Robert Campbell, *The London tradesman* (London, 1747), p. 141.
120 John Nicholson, *The operative mechanic, and British machinist*, 2 vols (London, 1831), vol. 2, p. 168.
121 Kimball, *Samuel McIntire, carver*, pp. 45–7.
122 P.L. Hodgson, *The modern measurer* (Dublin, 1793), p. 111; *The builder's price book* (London, 1789), p. 124.
123 W.F. Pocock, *Modern finishing for rooms* (London, 1811); Thomas Humphreys, *Irish builder's guide* (Dublin, 1813), pp. 209, 213.
124 Reinberger, *Utility and beauty*, p. 111.
125 Conor Lucey, 'The scale of plasterwork production in the metropolitan centres of Britain and Ireland', in Christine Casey and Lucey (eds), *Decorative plasterwork in Ireland and Europe: ornament and the early modern interior* (Dublin: Four Courts Press, 2012), pp. 194–218.
126 'Harley Street', in Philip Temple and Colin Thom, *Survey of London*, vols 51 and 52: *South-East Marylebone* (London: Yale University Press, 2017), available online at www.ucl.ac.uk/bartlett/architecture/sites/bartlett/files/chapter12_harley_street.pdf, p. 6, accessed 13 June 2017.
127 J. Quinan, 'Daniel Raynerd, stucco worker', *Old-Time New England* 65:3–4 (1975): 1–21.
128 Lucey, 'The scale of plasterwork production', pp. 211–12.

129 Registry of Deeds, Dublin (hereafter RD) 422/550/277144, 425/301/277146 and 416/306/277145.
130 RD, 442/8/285711 and 451/259/289795.
131 RD, 492/31/318983, 511/82/330346, 528/452/347321.
132 RD, 427/327/278972, 430/79/278973.
133 Mary Ellen Hayward and Charles Belfoure, *The Baltimore rowhouse* (New York: Princeton Architectural Press, 1999), pp. 30–1.
134 RD, 448/382/288134 and 444/197/288135.
135 National Archives of Ireland (hereafter NAI), Pembroke Papers, 97/46/2. See also Casey, *Dublin*, p. 585.
136 Andrew Byrne, *Bedford Square: an architectural study* (London and Atlantic Highlands, NJ: Athlone Press, 1990), pp. 73, 95.
137 W. Edward Riley and Laurence Gomme (eds), *Survey of London*, vol. 5: *Parish of St Giles in the Field, part II* (London: LCC, 1914), p. 153.
138 NAI, Bryan Bolger Papers, bundle 'R'.
139 NAI, Bryan Bolger Papers, bundle 'K'.
140 Philadelphia Contributionship Archives, policy no. 2517; Historical Society of Pennsylvania, Mutual Assurance Company (Green Tree) records, policy no. 3641.
141 Anthony Garvan (ed.), *The architectural surveys 1784–1794: the Mutual Assurance Company papers*, vol. 1 (Philadelphia: Mutual Assurance Company, 1976), pp. 256–67, 306.
142 RD, 280/177/181183, 282/40/181184.
143 Lucey, *Stapleton Collection*, pp. 77–86.
144 Byrne, *Bedford Square*, pp. 93–4, 104–7, 118, 132.
145 Lewis, 'Builders of Edinburgh New Town', p. 130–1.
146 See Michael Forsyth, *Bath*. Pevsner Architectural Guides (New Haven and London: Yale University Press, 2003), pp. 146–50; and Ayres, *Building the Georgian City*, fig. 36.
147 HSP, 'Edward Evans Day Book', 3, 10 and 14 September 1812, pp. 26–8. The properties are described as 'Pratts 4th St N. house' and 'Pratts 4th St South house'. For a description of this manuscript see Mark Reinberger, 'A plasterer's daybook attributed to Edward Evans', *Pennsylvania Magazine of History and Biography* 117:4 (1993): 331–8.
148 Philadelphia Contributionship (Archives), 'Survey Book 1794–1809', Insurance Surveys 3116 and 3117, and 3120 and 3121.
149 Reinberger, *Utility and beauty*, pp. 107–11.
150 *Ibid.*, p. 23.
151 Lucey, *Stapleton Collection*, pp. 37–8.
152 Steen Eiler Rasmussen, *London, the unique city* (London: Jonathan Cape, 1934, repr. 1960), p. 224.
153 For a similar view concerning speculative building and its relationship to interior decoration in Georgian Bath, see Christopher Woodward, *The building of Bath* (Bath: Building of Bath Museum, n.d.,), p. 35.
154 Richard Hill, *Designs and their consequences* (New Haven and London: Yale University Press, 1999), p. 18.
155 Arnold, 'The illusion of grandeur?', p. 109.
156 Preface to Barbara Arciszewska and Elizabeth McKellar (eds), *Articulating British classicism: new approaches to eighteenth-century architecture* (Aldershot: Ashgate, 2004), p. xxiii. On the perceived threat that commercialization posed to the early nineteenth century architectural profession, see Abramson, 'Commercialization and backlash in late Georgian architecture', pp. 143–61, in the same volume.

4

Building sales: advertising and the property market

Asked about the most expedient way to dispose of a London town house in 1770, the British architect Sir William Chambers counselled, 'the Surest way is to advertise'.[1] Nonetheless, despite decades of scholarship devoted to the production and consumption of eighteenth-century urban domestic architecture, the marketing and advertising of town houses has received only limited attention.[2] The processes of designing and decorating houses now having been considered, this chapter will explore how builders marketed and sold their properties, principally through the medium of the newspaper. Beginning with an account of real estate advertising in the eighteenth and early nineteenth centuries, the focus is on how builders advertised their own property portfolios and negotiated the language of auctioneers and other polite retailers. Particular consideration is given to how issues such as location, quality of structural and decorative finish, convenience and decorum were reflected in, and dependent on, the socio-economic order in cities across the Atlantic world.

While a well-appointed town house was a mark of social status in London, Dublin and Philadelphia, the character of elite urban housing in the British Isles and in British North America requires reiteration here. As we have seen, despite the potential affront to social order the upper classes of London and Dublin often took an undistinguished, speculatively built terraced house for their pied-à-terre (or built one in a similar style). Forming a constituent part of exclusively designed residential streets and squares, these houses appealed to those who often preferred to lease properties for short periods rather than enter into the expense of building or purchasing a house. A survey of occupancy rates in Grosvenor Square, London for the period 1730–1830 indicates an average tenure of a mere twelve to thirteen years,[3] and houses in Dublin's fashionable residential quarters were evidently available for similar limited periods: in 1780 a furnished house 'in the neighbourhood of St Stephen's Green or Merrion Street' was 'wanted for six months'; two houses in Merrion Square were available furnished or unfurnished 'by the week, month, or year' in November 1797.[4] By contrast, the merchant elite of Philadelphia and other American cities loudly announced their social distinction through larger, freestanding buildings. Thus, while the Powel House on South Third Street (built 1765) approaches, in scale, spatial organization and interior finish, the 'typical' aristocratic town house in London and Dublin, it was not conceived as part of an enclave strictly devoted to the homes of the politer classes. Not until the 1790s, with Charles Bulfinch's design for the Tontine Crescent in Boston, was the idea of grouping private residences into urban complexes introduced to America.

Advertising and the genteel consumer

By the mid-eighteenth century, newspaper advertising was both a ubiquitous and highly specialized literary sub-genre, and a daily paper 'might contain about fifty advertisements of increasing specialization'.[5] While the cost of newspapers rose steadily during the Georgian era, and 'was probably a major factor restricting readership' among certain classes of the polity,[6] advertising had the potential to reach a broad audience, a fact recognized by astute printers and publishers across the English-speaking world. Robert Munter's history of the Irish newspaper industry suggests that 'in its early stages of development, [it] catered primarily to the Dublin upper classes',[7] and contemporary American observers acknowledged that advertisements were 'the Life of a Paper'.[8] A typical newspaper of the Georgian period consisted of four pages, of which one page (at least) was devoted to advertisements: by mid-century, advertising was 'a financial mainstay for most newspapers', and by the 1790s 'most were almost entirely filled with the boxes and block cuts of advertising notices and designs'.[9] While some papers specialized in particular goods – in the late 1730s, for example, the *Dublin Journal* enjoyed a veritable monopoly on announcements for rental accommodation for sale or lease – such specialisms decreased as advertising grew exponentially.[10] This corresponds with Jeremy Black's account of the growth of advertising in the English press between the 1720s and 1780s, and how advertising generally occupied 'a larger and more prominent proportion of the papers'.[11] In the American colonies after 1760, some publishers 'issued special supplements that were overwhelmingly devoted to commercial notices'.[12]

Concerns about the ethical dimensions of advertising rhetoric were raised early. Already at mid-century, Dr Johnson was moved to comment: 'Whatever is common is despised. Advertisements are so numerous that they are very negligently perused, and it is therefore become necessary to gain attention by magnificence of promises and by eloquence sometimes sublime and sometimes pathetic.'[13] Against the backdrop of an increasingly literate consumer class, recent scholarship has highlighted the sophisticated marketing strategies utilized by retailers and manufacturers, suggesting that the language of advertising deliberately responded to distinctions in politeness and to signifiers of gentility. In her study of advertising and marketing strategies in Georgian London, for example, Claire Walsh has argued that the shop environment itself emerged as the prime means of marketing for retailers throughout the century, and that many luxury goods manufacturers, such as Josiah Wedgwood, loudly decried the vulgarity of newspaper advertising and its 'association with lower-class retailing'.[14] In deference to the strictures of social decorum, Walsh further argues that middle-class consumers 'shied away from overt references to commercialism', favouring more 'genteel' methods such as shop displays and exhibitions.[15]

Similarly 'polite' methods of purchase and acquisition were available to the consumer of real estate in the urban centres of Britain and Ireland. Responding to the fashion for evening promenades, architect Sir William Chambers described the advantage of a neighbourhood perambulation for scouting houses eligible for sale or lease, advising a client in 1773, 'I see bills upon every window.'[16] Word of mouth, or the advice and assistance of architects and friends, represented other methods preferred by the upper classes for either finding houses or attracting the better sort of tenant.[17] Chambers and Robert Mylne were often prevailed upon by their clients to source a suitable pied-à-terre in London: Mylne advised Lord Abingdon on the purchase of a house in Grosvenor Place in 1773 and looked at several properties in Lower Grosvenor Street and Bond Street on behalf of Lady St Aubyn in 1779.[18] For the sale of Lady Catherine Toole's house in Gardiner's Row, Dublin in 1782, interested parties were advised to make 'application' to Sir Frederick Flood at his house in Merrion Square.[19] Others elected to appraise potential tenants without intermediaries: in Dublin in the 1770s, the sale of houses belonging to the Knight of Kerry, the Viscountess Kingsland and the Dowager Countess of Shelburne were all based on 'proposals' received directly by the distinguished residents themselves.[20] In 1800, buildings lots in Hamilton Village, on the west banks of the Schuylkill River in Philadelphia, were available on request to William Hamilton, the proprietor of the estate.[21]

In fact, despite the taint of 'pushy commercialism', R.B. Walker's pioneering research on London newspaper advertising in the first half of the eighteenth century found that 'a high social class of readership correlated positively with book and real estate advertisements', and papers aimed at the upper classes carried a higher proportion of real estate notices than other dailies.[22] Indeed, notices for the sale or lease of houses and land counted among the earliest newspaper advertisements.[23] Although in 1700 property advertising amounted to less than 6 per cent of revenue taken by the *London Gazette*, then the largest circulating title in the city, a new breed of paper devoted to commercial publicity, commencing with the launch of the *Daily Advertiser* in 1730 (quickly followed in Dublin by the *General Advertiser* in 1736), inaugurated what has been described as 'the Age of the *Advertisers*'.[24] While announcements of house sales remained proportionally small when compared with books, patent medicines and lotteries – accounting for only 8.5 per cent of advertisements in the *London Evening Post* in 1749/50 for example – and in the cheaper dailies (the so-called 'halfpenny readers') was confined to rental properties only, selling houses through newspapers was, by the latter half of the eighteenth century, 'the most popular option for buyers and sellers, lessors and lessees'.[25] Moreover, anxieties about breaching decorum appear not to have troubled the real estate market in American cities: Emma Hart, reflecting on commonalities and differences in advertising between Britain and the colonies, has recently argued that 'the relatively flat social structure of the colonies meant that retailers had few qualms about using the newspaper as [a] means of publicity'.[26] Hart further argues that the more polite means of advertising in British cities – such as handbills and trade cards – were options not routinely available to the colonial retailer and manufacturer.[27]

By the end of the eighteenth century, visual materials, in the form of architectural drawings and engravings, increasingly formed part of the publicity material utilized by landowners, surveyors, architects and builders. Dublin's planning authority, the Commission for Wide and Convenient Streets, customarily ordered plans and elevations of new streets and squares, including Beresford Place (1790) and North Frederick Street (1793), to be posted in the Royal Exchange Coffee House for public appraisal.[28] In 1815, Irish-born architect James O'Donnell prepared and advertised a master plan for row houses on State Street, New York: a year later, during the course of construction, this was exhibited for public consumption.[29] As part of the promotion for their extensive speculative Adelphi scheme in London, architects Robert and James Adam published an engraving of the Royal Terrace, its principal ornament; an impressively-scaled drawing of the scheme, measuring almost 9 feet long, was on display in both the design offices in Grosvenor Street and in the building company's premises in New Bond Street (Figure 4.1).[30] These, together with a series of finely executed presentation drawings illustrating the

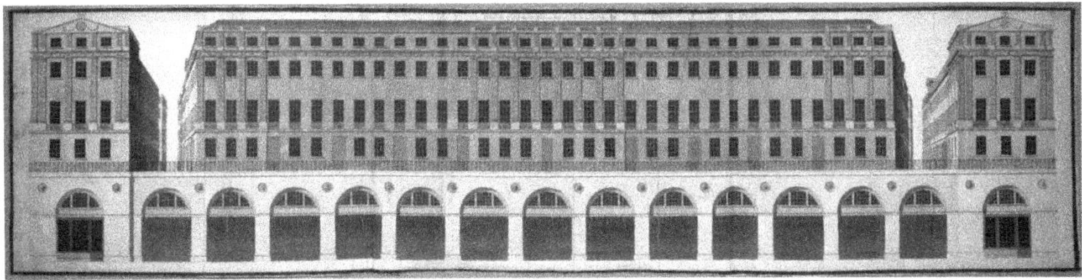

4.1 Robert and James Adam, elevation of the Royal Terrace at the Adelphi, London, c. 1768–69.

spatial organization of one of these houses, in plan and section, were prepared to attract the better sort of tenant. (Ever the pragmatists, the Adam firm was eventually forced to sell the venture in a lottery, for which a published eight-page catalogue and lottery tickets survive.) Dublin surveyor Thomas Sherrard's elevation and plan of Mountjoy Square in 1787 was evidently created for the purpose of advertising ground 'to be Let for Building' in this proposed scheme (Figure 4.2); a similar motivation to generate interest among builder-speculators was behind the publication of Charles Bulfinch's design for the Tontine Crescent in Boston in the *Massachusetts Magazine* in 1794 (Figure 4.3). In other instances it appears

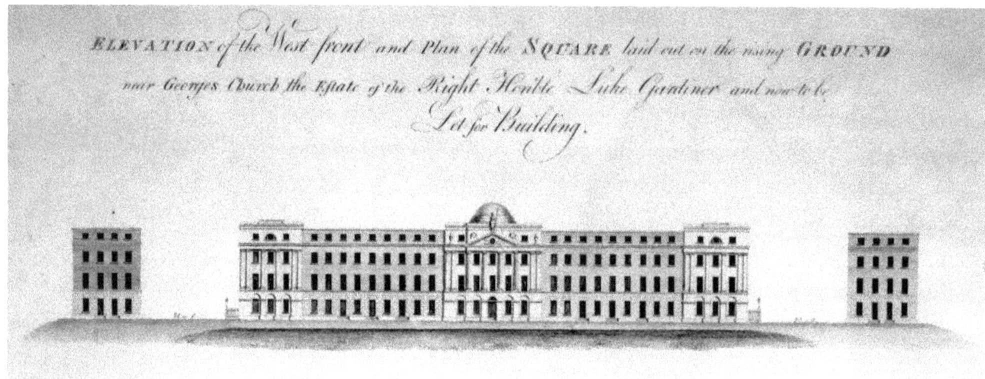

4.2 Thomas Sherrard, proposal for west side of Mountjoy Square, Dublin (detail), 1787.

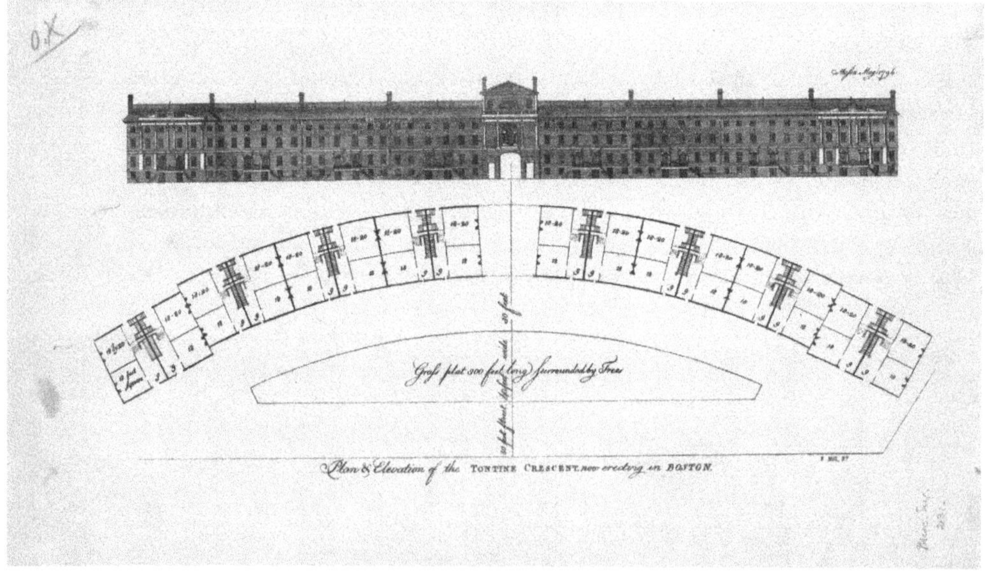

4.3 Charles Bulfinch, design for Tontine Crescent, Boston from the *Massachusetts Magazine*, vol. 6, February 1794.

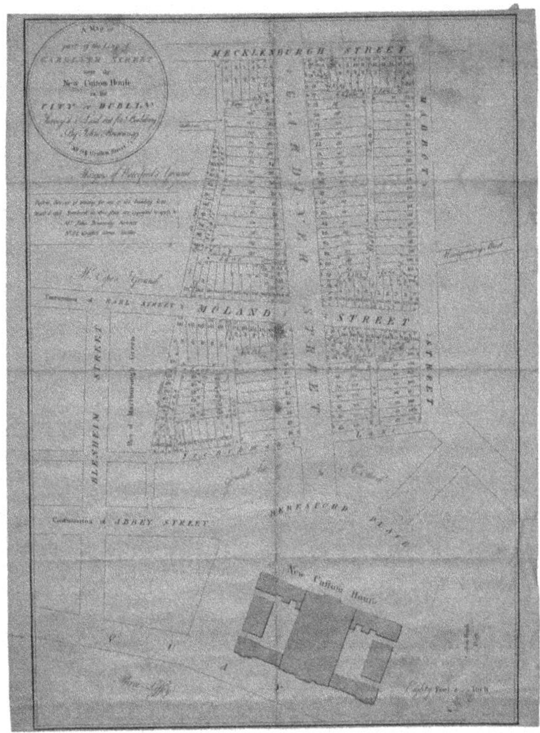

4.4 John Brownrigg, plan of building ground to let at Gardiner Street, Dublin, c. 1790.

that a model or show house was used in conjunction with plan drawings in order to solicit capital investment from developers. In 1787, newspaper notices for building lots in Lansdown Crescent, Bath advised builders that:

> A plan is now making, to be laid before the principal builders, for their approbation at an early day, of which they will have previous notice; in the mean time it is request, that they will take a survey of the ground, and house already built on the spot, to be the better prepared to form a right judgment of the plan when submitted to their consideration.[31]

This more pragmatic approach to the realization of 'enlightened' urban design is represented by 'A map of part of the line of Gardiner Street, Dublin, near the new Custom House', published c. 1790; parties 'desirous of treating' for any of the numbered building lots were requested to direct enquiries to the surveyor John Brownrigg (Figure 4.4).

The language of real estate advertising

Independent research regarding the advertising of town houses in London and Dublin newspapers has to date focused on the elite consumer: perhaps unsurprisingly, the nobility and gentry in those cities demanded houses with a good situation (that is, quality of air and prospect, but also proximity to centres of commerce and to places of resort), the most up-to-date domestic conveniences (such as water closets and powdering rooms), good stabling and coach houses and fashionable, commodious interiors.[32] With these criteria foremost in the consumer mind, house vendors developed a vocabulary designed specifically to appeal to a 'polite' audience. In fact, Hannah Barker points to evidence that those advertising goods and services in late eighteenth-century London 'may have targeted only a section of the capital's newspaper readership': advertising in the *Gazetteer* – a paper with an audience largely drawn from those lower down the social scale – was periodically 'out of step with its circulation levels', indicating that advertisers 'intended to appeal to a select and richer proportion of its readership; that is, those whose residence in London continued to be determined by the social season'.[33] In his account of shopping and advertising in Colonial America, however, Richard Bushman makes the important point that gentility was a signifier to attract anyone with the money to pay, and that one created a genteel audience by simply addressing advertisements for the attention of 'ladies and gentlemen'.[34] As early as 1710, Joseph Addison identified 'the great skill in an advertiser' as being 'chiefly seen in the style which he makes use of. He is to mention the *Universal Esteem*, or *General Reputation* of things that were never heard of ... *for the information of the Nobility and Gentry*.'[35]

The most common descriptor for patrician housing in London and Dublin throughout the Georgian era was 'elegant' (referring to beauty with propriety), followed by 'convenient' (meaning suitable or proper), both of which hint at the role of the house as an agent of social capital: in 1795, a house in Buckingham Street, Dublin was described as 'a most fashionable, convenient, and well finished house', being decorated 'in the most superb stile of the present fashion'.[36] Collectively, degrees of appropriateness for members of the upper classes are evidenced by references to 'capital mansions', and to houses 'fit for a Nobleman or Gentleman',[37] or 'fit for the immediate reception of a genteel family'.[38] In one remarkable instance in Dublin in 1765, the location of the house was withheld entirely and readers were advised only that 'none but Persons of Fashion need apply'.[39] Rachel Stewart's illuminating account of London's real estate market acknowledges the problem of interpreting terms like 'mansion' to describe properties of a particular scale, noting the difference between its designation in the 1667 Act for Rebuilding the City of London and the more casual use of the term by property vendors and auctioneers.[40] This problem of interpretation further extends to a comparison of real estate advertising between different cities throughout the British Atlantic world: in 1797, a description of the 'mansion house' of British Minister Robert Liston in Arch Street, Philadelphia was clearly predicated on its size;[41] a reference to 'first rate' houses in Park Street, Boston in 1810 was likely a generic use of the term, meaning of the best class or quality, rather than a reference to the London system of house rates introduced in that city in 1774. In fact, it seems clear that property advertising was adapted specifically to address the demands of localized consumer markets. In the early decades of Washington's development, following its foundation in 1790, frame buildings outnumbered brick houses two to one. With less demand for the type of refined housing stock found in Boston or Philadelphia, building standardization was not limited to the brick house, and kit-houses were available into the early 1800s: the firm of Munroe and Connor, carpenters, offered frame houses of various dimensions from their shop in nearby Alexandria.[42] This had an impact on the description of genteel property in regional newspapers: in 1796, for example, a timber frame two-storey house in Georgetown was described as 'elegant', a term usually reserved for the better class of brick house in more established American cities.[43]

Just as Claire Walsh noted a general restraint in the language of retail advertising aimed at the politer classes, so the description of real estate occasionally reached the limits of a somewhat restricted vocabulary. In 1794, for example, a 'spacious *elegant* house' in Portman Square, London, boasted an '*elegant* Hall' and 'spacious *elegant* rooms' on its principal storeys; the purchaser was further advised that the '*elegant* household furniture' was available at a valuation.[44] Taken together, these notices evidence what John Styles has identified as the complex methods of association employed in marketing and advertising all types of commodities, and the 'considerable significance' attached to 'considerations of novelty, fashion and the taste of the metropolitan elite'.[45]

An association with a distinguished member of the nobility was long an important selling feature for city residences in London and Dublin: in 1774, the leasehold interest in a house in Granby Row, Dublin, 'in which Sir Edward Newenham lived, and lately belonging to and lived in by the Right Hon. Lord Sydney', was offered on favourable terms;[46] in 1775, a 'convenient' house in Mayfair, London was 'many Years in the Occupation of the late Earl of Eglinton'.[47] Sarah Drumm has also remarked upon the impact of the vice-regal court and the parliamentary season on Dublin's elite real estate market, noting 'a surge in demanded for fashionable housing' in the wake of the requirement, established in 1765, for the viceroy (the king's representative in Ireland) to take up fulltime residence in the city for the duration of his term of office. In December 1768, without a seat in government, and *ergo* no need for a town house, the Hon. Edward Augustus Stratford (later 2nd Earl Aldborough) advertised the lease of a house in Marlborough Street 'during the continuance of the present Parliament'.[48] Indeed, the movement of aristocratic families between the British Isles influenced the markets in both Dublin and London: in 1774, a 'well furnished' house in 'an airy part' of Bath, England, was offered for a ten-month period 'in exchange' for a house in Dublin;[49] while in 1787, 'genteel and pleasant furnished Apartments' in the polite London suburb of Richmond were advertised in the Irish newspapers.[50] Houses adjacent to a prestigious street or square could also take advantage from a 'borrowed' view of a more fashionable address. In 1784, a house in an unidentified part of London was 'situated in a genteel Street, in the neighbourhood of two of the best Squares at the West End of the Town';[51] a house in Upper Titchfield Street was described in 1793 as being but 'a few paces from Fitzroy Square'.[52] In 1796, an undeveloped site in Fitzwilliam Street was described as 'the most eligible lot of ground in Dublin', being 'nearly central to Fitzwilliam and Merrion-squares', while a house in nearby Mount Street Upper was located in 'one of the most delightful situations in Dublin, commanding a view of nearly the whole of Merrion-square'.[53] The builder Nicholas Kildahl's economically worded property advertisement in 1797 – a mere twenty-three words in total – prioritized this advantage alone: 'A House in the neighbourhood of Merrion-square – the fine and rent reasonable'.[54]

Philadelphia, on the other hand, had neither an indigenous aristocracy nor class-dictated residential areas specifically designed to cultivate social exclusivity, and so references to a property's suitability to certain classes of consumer – such as nobleman, gentleman, lady or merchant – are unusual. In her review of real estate advertising in Philadelphia newspapers, Elizabeth Gray Kogen Spera noted that 'The residential areas are vague, in a private and somewhat exclusive fashion, as to their location but clear as to the qualities of the area: airy, polite, pleasing and quiet, near to but not on the market; and as to the requirements of any prospective tenants: respectable family, sober, and orderly.'[55] This is corroborated by advertisements of singular brevity. John Styles attaches considerable significance to what he calls the 'verbal language of visual description' that operated within the commercial axes of production and consumption, noting in particular the use of specialist vocabularies that could be every bit as potent as the printed image.[56] This almost certainly explains the typically laconic description of Philadelphia town houses in newspaper advertising to 1800, where the apparently concise term 'brick house' in fact spoke a multitude. Nonetheless, occasionally longer, more descriptive notices were used to make clear distinctions in terms of finish or accommodation, or to derive commercial advantage within the market. In a city dominated by mixed-use properties (often both commercial and residential), terms such as 'elegant' and 'genteel' signified houses of some pretension and were clearly invoked to attract members of the new Federal Government and the so-called 'Republican Court'; related phrases like 'commodious', 'handsome' and 'finished in the best manner' indicate an appreciation of discriminating consumer tastes in general. Indeed, in the teeth of debates about probity and luxury, and the social virtues of the early republic, proximity to prestigious neighbours, or the distinguished standing of a property's current occupant, remained a desirable quality in early national American real estate. In October 1791, the sole advertised advantage of a property in Fourth Street was its 'fronting the Garden' of William Bingham's house, then the most distinguished residence in the city (the Bingham house itself fronted on Third Street).[57] Some months later the public auction of a 'large elegant' house in High (now Market) Street was described as being 'in the possession of the Hon. Pearce [*sic*] Butler, senator from South Carolina'. That the house was 'almost new and finished in the modern stile' was obviously an advantage here, but its high-ranking association with one of the founding fathers was patently its most immediately marketable commodity.[58] In other instances, the reputation of the location was evidently deemed sufficient in and of itself: advertisements for the Seven Buildings on Pennsylvania Avenue in Washington, built from 1796 and one of the city's most prestigious addresses, offer no description of the houses but noted the eligibility of the location and the social standing of the tenant.[59] In 1803, the 'elegant' house in Washington 'in which the Secretary of State now resides' was 'within one square of the President's House'.[60]

In a period when the urban house was increasingly subject to architectural theorizing – being a private concern with a public obligation to the civic milieu – it is interesting to note that elevation of a house, its presentation to the street, was rarely mentioned in advertisements. Rachel Stewart discovered 'a notable absence of remarks of both the exterior condition and decoration of houses' in London property notices during the 1770s, finding references only to houses designed by the architect Robert Adam, specifically 20 Soho Square ('the Elevation is superb') and Chandos House ('beautiful stone front').[61] In Dublin in 1771, the sale details of the Dowager Countess of Shelburne's house in St Stephen's Green boasted 'three fine Fronts', but here the emphasis was on its advantageous orientation to fashionable streets rather than to its architectural composition.[62] Materials alone often distinguished a property, and the frequent references to houses with a 'brick front' in American newspapers confirm this as an important signifier for the better sort of house: in 1764, a 'Very commodious new Dwelling house' in Cherry Street, New York, boasted a 'yellow Brick Front'.[63]

In fact, while uniformity and palace front designs gained currency in architectural discourse throughout the century, it is rare to find this as a selling point in contemporary property advertising throughout the Atlantic world. This is true even of Bath, long celebrated as the epitome of genteel urban planning. In 1787, the sale of a house in the Circus, begun in 1754 to designs of architect John Wood, made no mention of its exceptional architectural elevation, focusing instead on how its 'four garrets, three attic rooms, two drawing-rooms, and two parlours' contained 'every convenience for a family'.[64] Advertisements for houses in the Royal Crescent, arguably the paragon of eighteenth-century terrace design, also privileged the concerns of the householder rather than the architectural connoisseur: between 1787 and 1789, a number of houses became available for sale or lease, although none made reference to its celebrated modular design.[65] A rare example where architectural uniformity was posited as a desirable asset relates to the sale of three 'capital' houses in London in 1794, described as 'adjoining together, and forming part of the elegant and uniform Range of Buildings on the West Side of Great Cumberland Place'.[66] In 1790, 'capital, brick-built, well erected Houses' in Alfred Place, a residential enclave designed by architect George Dance the younger, were described as 'uniform, well built, and finished in a costly stile' (Plate 1).[67] Given the bespoke character of elite house production in Federal-era Philadelphia, speculatively built houses of 'architectural' character appeared only in the early nineteenth century. In 1804, a 'well-finished house' on Twelfth between Market and Filbert Streets was 'situate in a handsome row'.[68] Four 'new and elegant three story brick dwelling houses' on Race Street were described in 1810 as 'built in the best style of modern architecture, with marble steps, &c. and wreath tablets, as exterior enrichments'; adjoining this, on the corner of Race and Ninth Streets, was a house whose 'principal front' was 'particularly neat, and in a new and correct style of architecture'.[69]

The value of the 'typical' London house might also be improved by employing an architect to adapt or augment its elevation, room distribution and/or interior decoration: as we have seen, important figures like Robert Adam and Sir William Chambers worked within the plain brick idiom of the speculatively built terrace. In such instances, the architect's name might be invoked, or the interior apartments described in superlative terms; being built in 'an expensive and uncommonly substantial manner' or 'finished in a style of singular elegance'.[70] In 1783, a 'nearly finished' house on the north side of Bedford Square was distinguished by being built 'from the designs, and under the immediate inspection of Mr. James Wyatt'; no doubt the architect's reputation contributed to its classification as a 'capital leasehold'.[71] In 1792, the announcement of the auction of the former home of the Dublin architect Thomas Penrose, an otherwise undistinguished mid-terrace house in Baggot Street Lower, noted that:

> As this house was designed for the residence of Mr. Penrose, it has been built with the greatest durability as well as elegance, and many conveniences have been attended to, not usual in the common-style of building, which those who were acquainted with the taste of the late proprietor must be sensible of on survey of the premises.[72]

While references to the number and types of room became increasingly common (described below), references to the architectural plan *per se* were also rare and habitually reserved for bespoke properties. The sale of the Earl of Mornington's house in Upper Merrion Street, Dublin in 1777, for example, described it as 'built upon the best Plan of any Brick House in Ireland'.[73] In the same year, Belvedere House, Great Denmark Street, though only half-finished, was built 'upon a most elegant and approved Plan'.[74] While both of these houses were larger than the typical terraced house in Dublin, and their spatial distribution arguably warranted special mention, the particular qualities of the standard 'two-room' plan could also be enhanced with clever phrasing. In 1794, a typical three-bay house in Mountjoy Square was built 'on a much approved plan'; two unfinished houses in Merrion Square in the same year were 'constructed on the best plan of modern architecture'.[75] Such sophisticated manipulation of language is a hallmark of auctioneers' notices generally, readily adapted to distinguish properties of all grades.

More common was the description of interior architecture, particularly spatial organisation (number and type of rooms), the dimensions of individual rooms (particularly dining parlours and drawing-rooms) and decorative finish. Collectively, such detail confirms the way in which houses in London and Dublin were used: references to 'drawing rooms', 'principal apartments' or, in the case of 1 Mansfield Street, a house designed by architect Robert Adam, the 'Two Suites of Apartments' which occupied the 'principal Story'.[76] In 1790, an 'Elegant New House' in Dominick Street, Dublin boasted rooms 'finished in the best stile, with ornamented ceilings, &c.', including an 'eating Parlour, 16 feet by 17 feet, bowed in the rere'.[77] Announcements for properties in Portland Square, Bristol customarily referred to room dimensions: in 1812, the middle house on the south side boasted a front parlour 20 feet × 22 feet and a drawing-room 21 feet × 27 feet; in 1814, the house on the northeast corner had a front parlour 21 feet × 25 feet and a drawing-room 20 feet × 25 feet.[78]

Advertisements for Philadelphia houses, on the other hand, were less descriptive generally and correspondingly less prescriptive about the use of individual storeys. As noted in Chapter 2, the ground floor was typically reserved for the best parlours in American town houses, and only a few of the very grandest residents adopted the aristocratic manner of elevating the drawing-room storey above ground level. (With this in mind, it's interesting to note that one of the few Philadelphia advertisements to mention an 'upstairs' drawing-room refers to an 'elegant' house built (and marketed) by a carpenter.[79]) References to particular features or interior flourishes were typically reserved for outstanding properties: in 1799, a house on the northwest corner of Chestnut and Eighth Streets, almost certainly the notoriously unfinished mansion designed for founding father Robert Morris, boasted 'a large hall laid with marble' and 'a public and private mahogany staircase, one of which is lighted by a Venetian window';[80] an advertisement for the sale of Chief Justice Benjamin Chew's house in South Third Street described it in terms that distinguished it from the common stock, being 'large and excellent' and 'unusually finished with handsome wainscoating throughout the two lower stories'.[81] More representative is the announcement of a 'new, elegant and superior' house at the northeast corner of Race and Ninth in 1810, described as being 'excellently well planned and arranged' with interiors finished 'in a rich manner'.[82] However, while there are certainly fewer references to specific room designations or decorative finishes in American property advertisements before 1800, there were other modern conveniences available to the consumer: in 1775, a three-storey brick house in Arch Street was fully 'insured and electrised'; that is, fitted with a lightning conductor.[83] In a city where fire insurance increasingly dictated building design and construction, such moves towards safety were both prescient and commercially astute.

An important determinant concerning the textual length of property notices was related to, and subject to, advertising costs. By the 1730s, a rate of 2s. for 2 inches of a column (in a three-column newspaper) was standard in English papers.[84] In 1734, for example, the *Daily Courant* charged 2s. for 'advertisements of a moderate length, and which require no preference, or particular character'.[85] Almost this exact wording was echoed in a 1736 edition of the *Dublin Daily Advertiser*, which further added that 'advertisements may be inserted at a cheap Rate, [which] has been much wanting in this City'.[86] As advertising became a more conspicuous part of the daily papers, what constituted a 'cheap rate' or a 'moderate length' was evidently subject to a range of variables: in 1755, an advertisement of 155 words length in the *Dublin Journal* cost the Irish MP Richard Edgeworth 7s. 7d. (approximately ½d. per word).[87] By the end of the century, in Dublin at least, the standard rate had risen exponentially: in 1795, an advertisement for the sale of a house in *Saunders's News-letter* cost 8s. 8d. for a mere twenty-two words (or 4½d. per word).[88] These elevated costs clearly informed the economy of language typical of many real estate announcements in Dublin at this time, and may have encouraged the creative design of advertising copy generally.[89] Serial advertising, on the other hand, represented better value for money given the reductions offered by some publishers for booking advertisements by the quarter: the *Flying Post*, for example, appears to have offered one free advertisement for every eight booked.[90] In the late 1810s, the *Aurora* group of newspapers in Philadelphia offered a range of group rates per 'each square of twenty lines', including the attractive price of one dollar for three insertions as opposed to fifty cents for one insertion (Figure 4.5). Given that a house might remain on the market for a lengthy period of time, being subject to varying degrees of legal

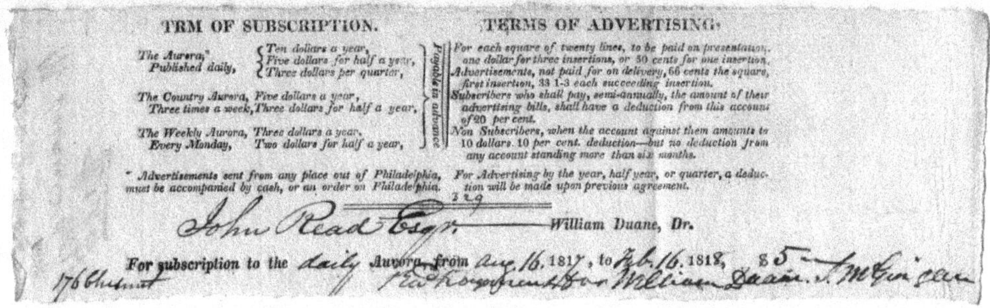

TRM OF SUBSCRIPTION.

The Aurora, Published daily,* — *Ten dollars a year, Five dollars for half a year, Three dollars per quarter,*

The Country Aurora, Three times a week, — *Five dollars a year, Three dollars for half a year,*

The Weekly Aurora, Every Monday, — *Three dollars a year, Two dollars for half a year,*

Payable in advance.

** Advertisements sent from any place out of Philadelphia, must be accompanied by cash, or an order on Philadelphia.*

TERMS OF ADVERTISING.

For each square of twenty lines, to be paid on presentation, one dollar for three insertions, or 50 cents for one insertion. Advertisements, not paid for on delivery, 66 cents the square, first insertion, 33 1-3 each succeeding insertion. Subscribers who shall pay, semi-annually, the amount of their advertising bills, shall have a deduction from this account of 20 per cent. Non Subscribers, when the account against them amounts to 10 dollars. 10 per cent. deduction—but no deduction from any account standing more than six months.

For Advertising by the year, half year, or quarter, a deduction will be made upon previous agreement.

John Read Esqr. ——— **William Duane, Dr.**

For subscription to the daily **Aurora, from** Aug. 16. 1817, to Feb. 16. 1818, $ 5 –

176 Chestnut

4.5 Advertising rates for the *Aurora* newspaper (Philadelphia), 1817–18.

and administrative bureaucracy, such an arrangement likely appealed to house vendors. In 1787, the notice of the leasehold interest in a number of houses in Hume Street and North Great George's Street, Dublin, built by plasterer and builder-speculator Charles Thorp, appeared repeatedly in editions of *Saunders's News-letter*; first on 2 January, then again on 16 February, 27 February and 2 March.

Visual strategies

John Strachan's analysis of the advertising culture of the late Georgian era describes it as 'a time of real significance … in terms of technical innovation', specifically emphasizing 'the use of display copy most particularly'.[91] Proselytizing in 1710, Joseph Addison commented that 'the great art in writing Advertisements, is the finding out a proper method to catch the Reader's Eye', describing the 'asterisks and hands' and 'Cuts and Figures' that constituted an already conventional repertoire of visual motifs.[92] The use of images in newspaper advertising was, however, rare during the eighteenth century: relying on a different relief printing technique – woodcut as opposed to movable metal type – it was both expensive and regarded as an impediment to the letterpress printing process generally.[93] Robert Munter's history of the Irish newspaper industry argues that while the introduction of illustrations in the 1720s was a signal part of the growing sophistication of advertising forms generally, the 'constant pressure of finding space' was key to many journals abandoning woodcut illustrations around 1740.[94] Raymond Williams's account of the English advertising industry also notes the proliferation of 'devices of emphasis' before mid-century – namely 'the hand, the asterisk, the NB' – but attributes their decline to their overuse.[95] More significant, perhaps, was an early association with the makers of quack medicines – among the first to use illustrated notices – which likely limited their appeal for those seeking to attract the politer end of the consumer market.[96]

TO LET,
A Genteel Dwelling House, near the Rev. Dr. Elliots meeting House, Love lane, 3 ſtories high, 3 rooms on a floor in good repair with a yard garden, rain water Ciſtern and pump.
Enquire of the Printer.
Boſton, Aug. 26, 1798.

4.6 House advertisement, *Independent Chronicle* (Boston), 15 October 1798.

Just as Maxine Berg and Helen Clifford have described how newspapers 'did not build on the opportunities for illustrated advertisement',[97] so there are few illustrated real estate notices before 1800 (Figure 4.6). Moreover, of those that have come to light, the veracity of what they represent remains open to question and misinterpretation. An example from the *New York Journal* in 1767 represents such a case in point: here the textual description of a modest, two-storey row house of 17 feet frontage is depicted as a freestanding, three-storey building of five bays' width (Figure 4.7).[98] A few examples from the *Hibernian Journal* (Dublin) are equally difficult to appraise: an advertisement of 1791 for 'a small convenient house' wanted in the vicinity of a number of the city's principal arteries is obviously accompanied by a generic illustration given that there is no particular property in question; on the other hand, the image accompanying an announcement of the leasehold interest of a house in Fishamble Street on the same page more likely approximates its formal appearance (Figure 4.8).[99] A rare example in Philadelphia before 1800 was prompted by the singular fame of the former occupant, Benjamin Franklin, whose 'mansion house' was announced in the *General Advertiser* throughout 1792: a comparison made between different editions of the paper, however, reveals the use of different images for the same house; evidently selected for what they signified ('mansion') rather than what they represented (the actual property) (Figures 4.9).[100] By the mid-1810s, the *Franklin Gazette* fully embraced the woodcut illustration at a time

To be Sold, or Let,

On the Premiſes, at public Vendue, at 10 o'Clock, on Friday the 5th Day of June next, or by private Agreement any Time before:

A Houſe and Lot, now in the Occupation of Mr. John Bryant, Maſon, formerly belonging to Mr. Tenus Rapalje, on Ferry-Street, adjoining on one Side to Mr. John Burger, on the other to Mr. Willet. The Front of the Lot on the Street is 17 Feet 4 Inches, and runs 53 Feet Back. The Houſe is new, has a Brick Front, is 2 Stories high, and has 3 Rooms with Fire-places: In the Yard is a good Ciſtern—An indiſputable Title will be given to the Purchaſer, by

JAMES SEACORD,
At Iſaac Blank's, Shoemaker, Ferry-Street.

4.7 House advertisement, *New York Journal*, 7 May 1767.

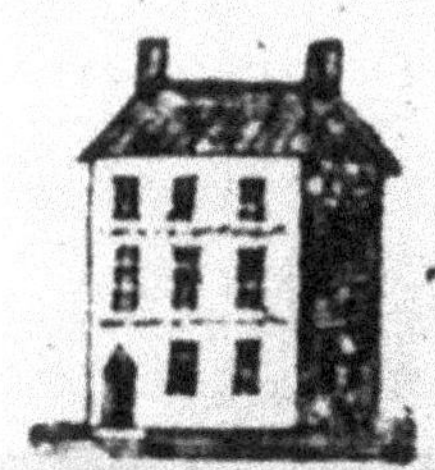

TO BE LET,
THE HOUSE, No. 42,
IN FISHAMBLE STREET.
THE RENT AND TAXES ARE LOW,
AND IT IS AN EXCELLENT
STANDING FOR ANY BUSINESS.

WANTED IMMEDIATELY,

IN the Neighbourhood of Capel-ſtreet, Dorſet-ſtreet, Henry-ſtreet, Grafton-ſtreet, Aungier ſtreet, or Camden-ſtreet,, or in any healthy Situation Eaſt of Capel-ſtreet or Bride ſtreet, a ſmall convenient Houſe, with a Yard, Coach-houſe, and Stabling for two or three Horſes.—A Fine will be given if neceſſary; or, unfurniſhed Lodgings.—Apply to Mr M Can, No. 2, Bridge-ſtreet, or the Printer hereof.

☞ Five Hundred Pounds to be lent, on approved Security, apply as above.

4.8 House advertisement, *Dublin Journal*, 5 September 1791.

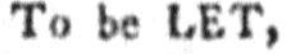

To be LET,

The Mansion House,

Formerly occupied by B. FRANKLIN, now deceafed, with Ice-Houfe and Out-Houfes.

For further particulars apply to RICHARD BACHE, up Franklin Court, in Market, between Third and Fourth Streets.

March 22.

TO BE LET,

The Mansion HOUSE

Of the late Dr. FRANKLIN.

Its central and retired fituation is well known.

Enquire of the Editor of the General Advertifer.

4.9 Benjamin Franklin's house advertised in *General Advertiser* (Philadelphia), 22 March 1792 and 18 July 1792.

when the textual description of houses was becoming more sophisticated. By this date, images were employed by the printer largely to create visual interest on the page and to group common elements together, such as property sales and auctions: the same 'stock' illustration, for example, appears in advertisements for various auctioneering firms between 1818 and 1820 (Figure 4.10). (This is underlined by closer inspection of the text describing particular properties: the stock image created for this purpose – of a rather grand, three storey, double-fronted house – often bears no formal comparison to the 'two story Brick House' or to the 'Frame Building' it accompanies.) The unusual method undertaken by the *Dublin Intelligence* newspaper in the 1710s, of printing real estate notices perpendicular to the main columns in the margins of the front and back pages, may represent an early example of creating visual distinction on the printed page or, more likely, pressure from the demand for advertising space.[101]

More typical were designs that worked within the limitations of the graphic conventions of newspaper column inches, employing simple

REAL ESTATE.

On Tuesday, the 6th of April, at 7 o'clock in the evening, at the Merchants' Coffee-house,

Two lots of ground, situate in Cherry-street, at the northwest corner of Schuylkill Sixth street—the lots are 99 feet front on Cherry street, by 54 feet deep on Sixth street. The improvements are a double two story frame house, with a two story kitchen to each—a fire place in each room, garret, plastered cellar under the front of the house, pumps of good water in the yard.—The house is built so that it lets for two tenements, and is now tenanted at the rent of $143, per year, payable quarterly. One half of the purchase money may stand for one or two years if required, with bond and mortgage secured on the same, with interest from the day of sale. Sold clear of all incumbrance.

Passmore & Sparhawk,

March 27—3t Auctioneers.

TO BE SOLD

On Tuesday evening, the 6th of April next, at half past seven o'clock, at the Merchant's Coffee-House,

Two Three Story Brick Houses, the south west corner of High and Schuylkill, Eighth street, together forty feet front, on High Street, by forty-five feet deep, with a one story Brick Kitchen adjoining. The lot is 40 feet front on High Street, by 118 feet deep on Schuylkill Eighth Street, to an 8 feet alley, with the priviledge thereof.

ALSO,

Two Three Story Brick and Frame Houses, No 67 and 69, North Fifth Street, together 36 feet front, by 17 feet inches deep, with kitchens adjoining. The lot is 36 feet front on Fifth street, by 50 feet deep. Additional particulars given at the time of sale. By order of the assignee of George Flomerfelt.

Peirsol & Greland,

Auctioneers, No. 51, North Front-St.

March 29—dts

4.10 Real estate section (detail) from *Franklin Gazette* (Philadelphia), 6 April 1819.

typographic emphases to catch the reader's attention. This was of course a symptom of the rise in advertising copy generally, which saw printers enlarge the sheet dimensions while simultaneously reducing the type size. As a measure of his success in attracting repeat business, George Faulkner, printer of the *Dublin Journal*, reduced the size of his type in 1729, in 1735 and again in 1741.[102] It also coincided with the development of mastheads and dividing space lines – arranging advertisements into separate, made-up blocks – and the corresponding use of section headings with titles such as 'Sales by Auction', 'Valuable Real Estate' and 'Lands and Houses' (Figure 4.11). By mid-century, quality newspapers across the British Isles adopted a system of 'regimented blocks of notices, cleanly positioned within the columns'.[103]

The principal typographical device used in property advertising was the use of all caps for keywords throughout the body of the text, specifically those related to location, scale and finish ('elegant' or 'capital'), to terms (either lease or sale) and conveniences. In 1777, an advertisement for a house in Bloomsbury, London, for example, capitalized the words 'SPACIOUS' and 'ELEGANT', but also 'COACH HOUSES', 'OFFICES'

Lands and Houſes.

TO BE LET,

FOR a long Term of Years, in HARCOURT-STREET, near End to STEPHEN's-GREEN, TWO HOUSES, completely finiſhed in a neat elegant Stile, (Stable and Coach-Houſe to one Houſe only) commanding a moſt pleaſing View of Lord Earlsfort's beautiful Improvements, and Wicklow Mountains, &c. and eſteemed the beſt Situation for Air in Dublin.

Application to be made at ſaid Houſe, or to Michael Stapleton, No. 80, Marlborough ſtreet.

4.11 'Land and Houses' section heading, *Hibernian Journal* (Dublin), 7 July 1788.

and 'LEASEHOLD'.[104] Some of the most interesting examples are found in the Philadelphia papers, enhancing the customary brevity of textual description common before 1800. Here the use of different point sizes and weights, as well as typesetting techniques like kerning (character spacing), tracking (word spacing) and leading (vertical line spacing), occasionally produced designs of striking visual impact. Advertisements throughout the 1780s and 1790s illustrate how a relatively short textual description might, through the simple yet creative manipulation of scale (small caps), fonts (roman and italic) and colour (the interplay of printed text and white space), command attention on even the busiest page.[105] In a city where frame buildings were prohibited only in 1796, the emphasis on 'brick house' in many of these advertisements arguably represents a localized response to a stubbornly prevailing building tradition (Figure 4.12).[106] A rare example of a Philadelphia property advertisement aimed specifically at a gentleman, published in May 1782, manages to be both visually arresting and textually succinct, with its bold emphasis on a single word ('house') and references to status, elegance of finish and prospect.[107]

To be Let,
A genteel, convenient three ſtory
BRICK HOUSE,
IN SPRUCE STREET, (no. 64)
THIS houſe has been newly papered and painted, and was not occupied during laſt fever.
feb. 12. d§t af. eo tf.

TO BE LET,
A convenient three ſtory brick
H O U S E,
IN UNION-STREET.
Alſo, a ſmall TENEMENT in Pine-ſtreet.
The preſent tenants term will expire on the 25th September next. Enquire of the Printers.
1ſt Auguſt, 1787. 3awtf

HOUSE. Any gentleman inclining to purchaſe a fine, large, elegant, and well finiſhed THREE STORY BRICK HOUSE ſituated in a healthy part of the town, and commands a delightful proſpect, may hear of ſuch a one to be SOLD, by inquiring of the printer.

4.12 Illustrated house advertisements, *Pennsylvania Evening Post*, 7 May 1782; *Pennsylvania Packet*, 13 August 1787; and *Gazette of the United States*, 11 March 1799.

Selling houses

The sale or lease of property was customarily handled by auctioneers – although the most astute builder-speculators, as we shall see, soon embraced the practice – and print media played a key role. The modish trade card of English auctioneer John Riddell, based in Morpeth, Northumberland, notes that he 'Sells Houses and Estates' and prepares 'Leases Securities', an aspect of his business amplified by the accompanying illustration, which features a scrivener's desk with documents variously inscribed 'A Plan of an Estate' and 'This indenture witnesseth' (Figure 4.13). During the 1770s and 1780s, Langford's of Covent Garden and Christie's of Pall Mall dominated the genteel market in London; in

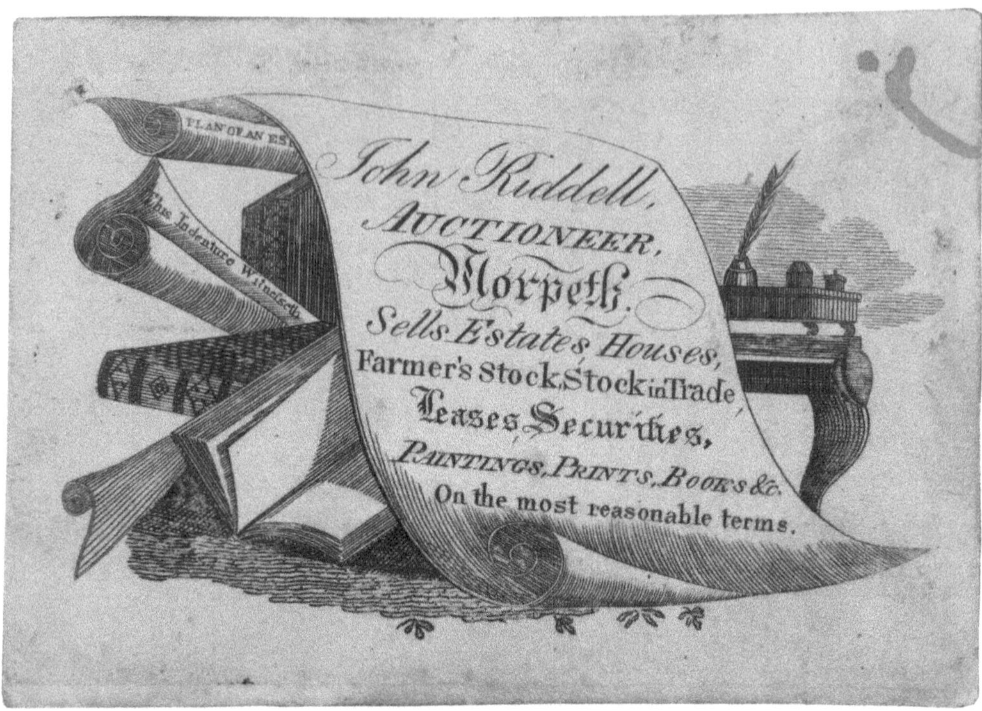

4.13 Trade card of John Riddell, auctioneer of Morpeth, Northumberland.

early nineteenth-century Philadelphia, the most prominent firms included Shannon & Poalk, T.B. Freeman and Peirsol & Grelaud. Ironically, of course, the very same auctioneers advertised their impending sales in the real estate pages of the daily and weekly newspapers. Emma Hart has recently described 'the synergy between the auction as a method of sale and the newspaper as an instrument of publicity', and how by the 1760s in America, 'the newspaper advertisement and the auction were locked in a mutually sustaining relationship'.[108] Richard Pue, the proprietor of Dick's Coffee House, the foremost venue for real estate auctions in 1730s Dublin, was also the publisher of *Pue's Occurrences*, a title that enjoyed a 'near monopoly of large estate and property advertisements'.[109]

The best houses were viewed by appointment only: in May 1778, Langford's announcement of the impending auction of a 'capital mansion' in Bedford Square, London, noted that it could be 'viewed by tickets'; in the same year in Dublin, 'Ladies and Gentlemen' interested in a house in fashionable Henrietta Street would be 'admitted between the Hours of Twelve and Three, on sending Notice of their Intention on the preceding Day, to the Housekeeper'.[110] Houses were sold or let by 'private contract' or public auction, and 'printed particulars' describing a property were typically available in advance by application to the tenant or to the auctioneer.

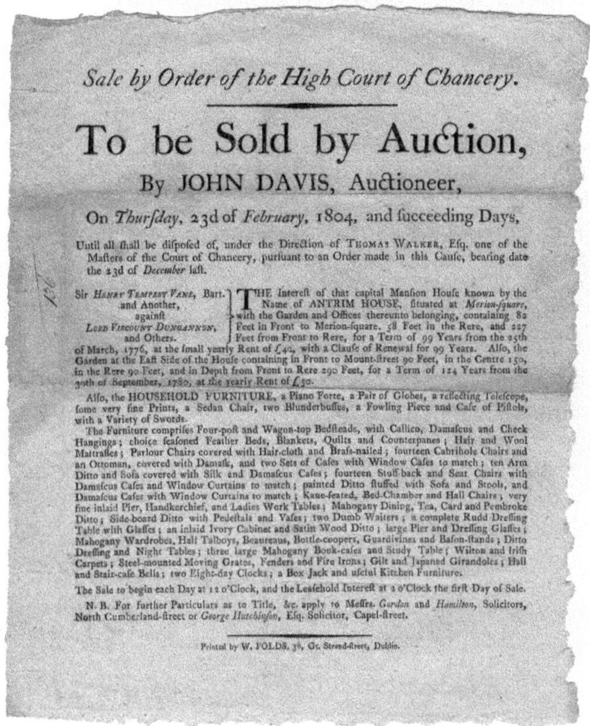

Sale by Order of the High Court of Chancery.

To be Sold by Auction,

By JOHN DAVIS, Auctioneer,

On *Thurſday*, 23d of *February*, 1804, and ſucceeding Days,

Until all ſhall be diſpoſed of, under the Direction of THOMAS WALKER, Eſq. one of the Maſters of the Court of Chancery, purſuant to an Order made in this Cauſe, bearing date the 23d of *December* laſt.

Sir *Henry Tempest Vane*, Bart. and Another, againſt *Lord Viscount Dungannon*, and Others.

THE Intereſt of that capital Manſion Houſe known by the Name of ANTRIM HOUSE, ſituated at *Merion-ſquare*, with the Garden and Offices thereunto belonging, containing 82 Feet in Front to Merion-ſquare, 58 Feet in the Rere, and 227 Feet from Front to Rere, for a Term of 99 Years from the 25th of March, 1776, at the ſmall yearly Rent of £40, with a Clauſe of Renewal for 99 Years. Alſo, the Garden at the Eaſt Side of the Houſe containing in Front to Mount-ſtreet 90 Feet, in the Centre 150, in the Rere 90 Feet, and in Depth from Front to Rere 290 Feet, for a Term of 124 Years from the 30th of September, 1780, at the yearly Rent of £50.

Alſo, the HOUSEHOLD FURNITURE, a Piano Forte, a Pair of Globes, a reflecting Teleſcope, ſome very fine Prints, a Sedan Chair, two Blunderbuſſes, a Fowling Piece and Caſe of Piſtols, with a Variety of Swords.

The Furniture compriſes Four-poſt and Wagon-top Bedſteads, with Callico, Damaſcus and Check Hangings; choice ſeaſoned Feather Beds, Blankets, Quilts and Counterpanes; Hair and Wool Mattraſſes; Parlour Chairs covered with Hair-cloth and Braſs-nailed; fourteen Cabriholc Chairs and an Ottoman, covered with Damaſk, and two Sets of Caſes with Window Caſes to match; ten Arm Ditto and Sofa covered with Silk and Damaſcus Caſes; fourteen Stuff-back and Seat Chairs with Damaſcus Caſes and Window Curtains to match; painted Ditto ſtuffed with Sofa and Stools, and Damaſcus Caſes with Window Curtains to match; Kane-ſeated, Bed-Chamber and Hall Chairs; very fine inlaid Pier, Handkerchief, and Ladies Work Tables; Mahogany Dining, Tea, Card and Pembroke Ditto; Side-board Ditto with Pedeſtals and Vaſes; two Dumb Waiters; a complete Rudd Dreſſing Table with Glaſſes; an inlaid Ivory Cabinet and Satin Wood Ditto; large Pier and Dreſſing Glaſſes; Mahogany Wardrobes, Hall Talboys, Beaureaus, Bottle-coopers, Guardivines and Baſon-ſtands; Ditto Dreſſing and Night Tables; three large Mahogany Book-caſes and Study Table; Wilton and Iriſh Carpets; Steel-mounted Moving Grates, Fenders and Fire Irons; Gilt and Japanned Girandoles; Hall and Stair-caſe Bells; two Eight-day Clocks; a Box Jack and uſeful Kitchen Furniture.

The Sale to begin each Day at 12 o'Clock, and the Leaſehold Intereſt at 2 o'Clock the firſt Day of Sale.

N. B. For further Particulars as to Title, &c. apply to Meſſrs. *Gordon* and *Hamilton*, Solicitors, North Cumberland-ſtreet or *George Hutchinſon*, Eſq. Solicitor, Capel-ſtreet.

Printed by W. FOLDS, 38, Gt. Strand-ſtreet, Dublin.

4.14 Bill of sale for Antrim House, Dublin, 1804.

A handbill announcing the sale of Antrim House in Dublin was produced by the auctioneer John Davis in 1804: here the dimensions of the 'capital Mansion House' and its grounds are present and correct, as well as the terms of lease and ground rent (Figure 4.14). The emphasis on the contents of the house, however, from the sedan chair to the 'Hall and Staircase Bells', was evidently predicated on the enforced sale of the property by the Court of Chancery.[111] The volume of transactions and sales that might constitute a typical working day in a successful late eighteenth-century London firm is glimpsed in the real estate section of the *Oracle and Public Advertiser* for 10 January 1795: here, the auctioneer Edward Smith of Broad Street announced the impending auctions, held simultaneously on 15 January at twelve noon, of three houses in Russell Place (in separate lots), a house in Finsbury Square, a house in Newman Street (near Oxford Street) and a 'set of genteel chambers' in 2 James's Street, the Adelphi.[112]

Despite being more agreeable to the upper and middling classes, the auctioneer was not above suspicion or reproach. A satirical verse poem of c. 1787, entitled 'On a certain Auctioneer', mocks the hyperbolic language used in property auctions and is instructive in terms of how this apparently elevated profession was perceived in popular terms. Opening with the observation that an auction was 'a whimsical thing', the author continues:

> If it's Houses he sells, or a pretty Estate,
> In both I am sure he's exceedingly great!
> Let's first take the House, which is *ample* and *large*,
> Tho's close to the River, the *noise* of a Barge
> Don't affect it at all, 'tis an *elegant Place*,
> And gives up to none that I ever could trace!
> It's *spacious*, *commodious*, *convenient*, and fit,
> I think on my Conscience you could not have hit
> On so *charming* an *House*, see the *beauties around*,
> Which appear to your view in the *adjacent ground!*
> The *Rooms* are all *lofty*, the *Floors nicely laid*,
> I know they were done by the *best in the Trade*,
> What say ye? 'tis going for four thousand pound,
> Don't miss it I beg – there can never be found
> Such a Bargin – indeed 'tis sold for a Song!
> I'll wait 'till the Bidders approach in a throng![113]

Another popular option was the upholder (or upholsterer), the forerunner of the modern interior decorator (Figure 4.15). Possessed of 'Taste in the Fashions' and 'a Connoisseur in every Article that belongs to a

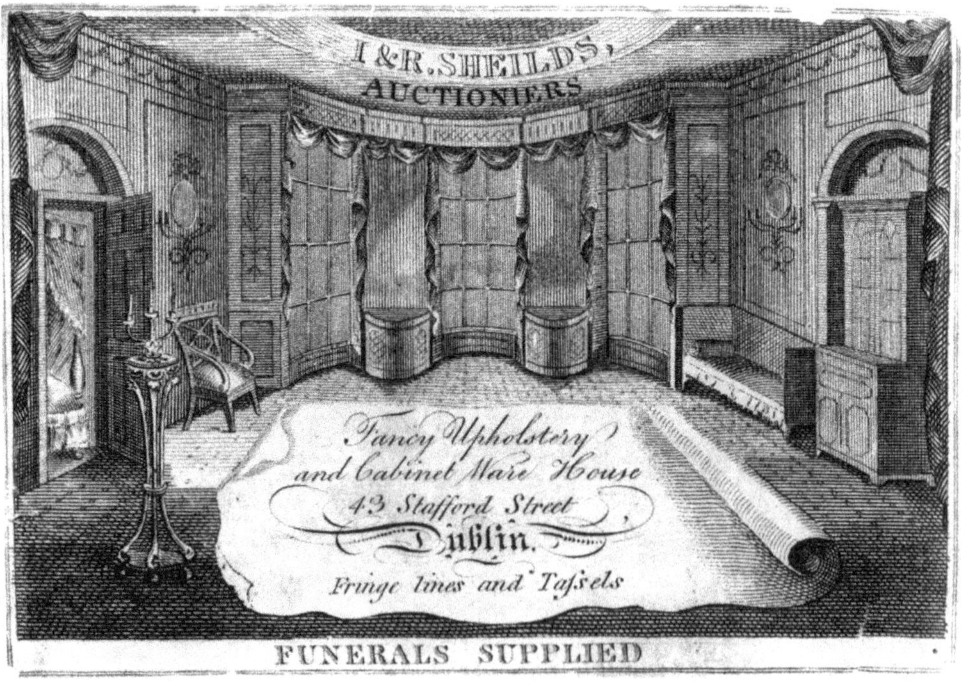

4.15 Trade card of I. Shields, auctioneer of Stafford Street, Dublin.

House', the upholsterer frequently acted as an appraiser of real property and was thus well placed to identify those architectural features of a house that might appeal to a particular social demographic.[114] In many such cases the character and quality of interior finish was foremost in the description of the house. In 1758, a house in Dawson Street, Dublin was described by William Hanna, upholsterer of Chequer Lane, as being 'in Good Repair, with Silk Damask and Paper Hangings'.[115] On the other hand, when Nicholas Higly, upholder of Lower Ormond Quay, advertised a 'very good modern well built House' in Marlborough Street in 1771, he focused exclusively on architectural novelty ('Back Rooms bowed to the Attic Story') and convenience ('Coach-house for two Carriages, a Stable for six Horses, a Loft for 40 Loads of Hay').[116] In London in 1773, the renowned firm of Ince and Mayhew, upholsterers and cabinetmakers, offered houses to let in Argyll Street and Grafton Street.[117] More interesting still was the career of Dublin upholsterer Gabriel Whistler, who evidently showed properties to potential customers on behalf of other vendors but soon became a building speculator in his own right.[118] In 1786 he took leases on three lots of ground in fashionable Merrion Square; in 1797, one of the newly built houses was advertised to let for six months, being 'completely fitted up, with every convenience necessary for the immediate reception of a family'.[119]

Houses were also disposed of through the intercession of brokers, solicitors or public notaries, a reminder that the sale or lease of a property was often a complex legal transaction involving mortgage settlements, hereditary entailments and other covenants and codicils. In early nineteenth-century Philadelphia, John Bonsall, conveyancer (a lawyer who specializes in the legal aspects of buying and selling real property), assisted a number of building mechanics with the sale of their properties; his services often extended into the realm of finances, procuring a mortgage of $1,000 on behalf of carpenter and house builder Thomas Carstairs.[120] William Shannon, a public notary in Dublin, witnessed legal transactions on behalf of the Fitzwilliam Estate during the 1790s, but also had his own portfolio of houses in Dame Street, Capel Street and Merrion Square.[121] Such specialists became an increasingly visible component in property markets across the Atlantic world, and by the end of the eighteenth century offered services now associated with the modern commercial real estate agent. For the sale of a house in Second Street in Philadelphia in 1782, interested parties were requested to attend to George Meade 'at his Office for Sale of Real Estates', situated opposite the Friends' Meeting House on Pine Street.[122] In London, Crosby's House Agency Office specialized in 'the engagement or disposal of Houses or Estates, either in Town or Country'. Located in Bruton Street, adjacent to Berkeley Square, they evidently catered to both the upper and middling sorts: in three separate notices in the 3 October 1789 edition of *The World* newspaper, they advertised a 'handsome' house in Berners Street, a 'commodious Family House' near Grosvenor Square and two houses 'situate in the vicinity of St. James's'.[123]

Builders selling houses

Just as the purpose of this book is to consider the relationship of the building mechanic to the world of architectural taste and elite consumption, so we now turn our attention to how builders marketed and sold their houses. Here, however, we arrive at a conundrum. Although carpenters, bricklayers and other operatives assumed every responsibility related to the house-building process – from raising capital to purchasing materials and contracting labour – the sale or lease of real estate throughout the eighteenth century Atlantic world was, as we have seen, typically handled by auctioneers, valuers and estate agents. While property speculation demanded a good business head and a proficiency in managerial and financial matters, there are in fact comparatively few instances of builders selling houses. Having built the house, the builder then needed to dispose of it: why was there an apparent reluctance to sell the house directly to the consumer?

Leaving aside the obvious advantage of employing professional auctioneers, the prudence of builders selling houses was in many ways discouraged in the eighteenth-century social imaginary. Although builders enjoyed varying degrees of design and financial autonomy throughout the period, as mechanics they belonged to a lower social rank generally. Associated with the related worlds of building economics and productive effort, their stock did not run high among a consumer society obsessed with gentility. Indeed, while titled landowners acknowledged the importance of house builders and real estate speculators to the generation of capital from their estates, contemporary criticism of the building world came from many directions and in many guises: as we have seen, John Gwynn took exception to the products of the building industry, decrying the 'depraved tastes of builders', and Matthew Darly added the 'Macaroni bricklayer' to his gallery of risible modern types. Moreover, viewed against the emergence of the architectural profession, which codified the distinction between the polite and vulgar aspects of building process, house builders as house vendors might not have been deemed commercially shrewd. That said, it seems that architects, too, were reticent about promoting their own building projects: there is no evidence, for example, of Sir William Chambers advertising his speculatively built houses in Berners Street,[124] and the commercial announcement in 1772 of 'Several Houses' at the Royal Terrace, the Adelphi, described as 'the property of Mess. Adams and … executed after their Designs', was almost certainly compelled by the impending collapse of the Adams' building business.[125] The Adam brothers, though never shy of publicity, appear always to have relied on Christie's for the disposal of their houses. An exception to this rule was the sale of a house in Mansfield Street in 1773, which was by direct application to 'Mr. John Grierson, at Mess. Adams's, in the Adelphi' (although here the transaction was in fact through the intercession of an office clerk).[126]

What encouraged those builders who did advertise in the real estate pages of newspapers in London, Dublin and Philadelphia? Aside from the possibility of raising one's professional profile, the impetus for builders marketing and selling their own houses was economic but also pragmatic: at its most basic level, there was no building business without building sales. While auctioneers and real estate agents might handle the sale or auction of multiple properties at any given time, some builders clearly recognized an opportunity to create a positive distinction in the real estate market. Success in the house building business evidently inspired market confidence, and the scale of individual real estate portfolios, and by extension the relative prosperity of individual enterprises, can often be determined by reference to the 'For Sale' and 'To Let' sections of eighteenth-century newspapers. In Dublin in 1787, plasterer turned developer Charles Thorp was offering 'elegant new Houses of different Dimensions' in Hume Street and North Great George's Street, all of which were 'ready for the immediate Reception of Families'.[127] Throughout the course of 1792, Edinburgh builder Daniel Lamb advertised houses in George Street, South Frederick Street and Hill Street in the New Town.[128] In 1802, the Philadelphia house carpenter William Hamilton had seven houses 'now finishing' on the south side of Chestnut between Seventh and Eighth Streets.[129]

Instances of builders selling their own houses appear towards the end of the eighteenth century, concurrent with what John Strachan has defined as 'a time of much resourceful and highly imaginative advertising' and related to innovations in marketing methods and techniques.[130] In a period when the urban house was increasingly subject to architectural theorizing – yet remained the province of the speculative building industry – how did builders negotiate the sensibilities of a genteel audience? What, if anything, was peculiar about their advertising strategies?

While builders generally followed the tone and content developed by auctioneers, upholsterers and real estate brokers – announcing a range of genteel, elegant and convenient houses from London to Baltimore – they also had the opportunity to capitalize on their particular knowledge of architectural tastes and fashions. This was particularly pronounced in Dublin, a city where, as we have seen, house decorators emerged as key figures in property development in the last decades of the eighteenth century. At the outset, however, the intimate relationship with the business of building is one of the most immediately tangible differences in builder-led advertising. A good case in point is the career of carpenter Robert Grews, one of the principal builder/contractors at Bedford Square, London (built 1775–83). In 1788, Grews advertised a new house in Harley Street: described as being 'finished in an elegant style', it boasted marble chimneypieces and 'ornament ceilings' as well as modern conveniences in the form of 'compleat hot and cold baths' and water closets. However, while references to decorative finishes, spatial dimensions and room types were relatively common at this time, particularly for those parts of the house that witnessed the most social traffic, Grews's inventory of the house is singular in its fastidious enumeration of almost every room on every storey – noting, for example, that the first floor comprised, '3 large rooms, dressing room and water closet, i.e. front drawing room, 34-6 by 22 feet, back ditto, 23-6 by 20-6 feet, the third room, 16-6 by 15 feet'.[131] No doubt anxious to draw attention to the particular merits of the property in a competitive environment, Grews may also have wished to expedite the sale. As a builder of some standing, he was keenly aware of the capital risks involved in speculative development: Bedford Square had been built in the economic slump that arose during the American War of Independence, and he later admitted that it had

> so severely affected many of the persons concerned under us [i.e. the individual building speculators], that some were compelled to stop, and we found ourselves under the unfortunate necessity of taking back the Ground, and completing houses thereon … several of which when finished we were obliged to sell for less than they cost us, and to let others considerably under the value.[132]

With such difficulties in mind, the careful delineation of the house dimensions and distribution of apartments – augmenting a format common to Christie's, Langford's and other auctioneers – makes sense from the perspective of someone involved in the business of house building. Similarly worded advertisements in other cities may have arisen from concerns with the disposal of speculatively built properties in uncertain markets. In 1794, with mounting arrears in ground rents on the Fitzwilliam Estate in Dublin, due to financial concerns arising from the French wars, the enumeration of room widths and story heights of a number of 'joisted and slated' houses in Merrion Square (requiring 'about 300l. to finish each house') was clearly intended to attract potential developers to the imminent auction.[133] Philadelphia carpenter William Powell's equally precise account of a property in Arch near Ninth Street in 1796, against a backdrop of political and economic instability, was predicated on his desire to dispose of a house that he described as being 'about two-thirds finished'.[134] In 1794, the spectacular failure at Cornwallis Crescent, described as 'one of the most ambitious schemes undertaken during the heyday of speculative building in Bristol', occasioned the sale of a number of unfinished houses, advertised in that year as 'Nos. 1, 2 and 9 roofed in with timber; Nos. 3 to 6, built up to withdrawing-room floor; No. 7, built up to the attic story; No. 8, built up to the garret floor'.[135]

Given that a financial competence and a head for business were necessary skills for a successful career in house building and property development, it is perhaps unsurprising that some of the most distinguished and entrepreneurial building operatives chose to dispense with auctioneers, brokers and solicitors, electing to advertise their own property portfolios directly to the market. Here, the different degrees of business *nous* are made plain in both advertising rhetoric and in the marketing strategies adopted by individual vendors. A good example is the Philadelphia house carpenter Jacob Vogdes (d. 1816), who in 1803 was selling two houses adjacent to the newly improving Washington Square. Maximizing the sale potential by advertising in two different newspapers simultaneously, Vogdes's advertisement is practically indistinguishable from that of a polite London auctioneer:

> **HOUSES FOR SALE**
>
> For sale on reasonable terms, two houses, one on Eighth, and the other on Little Seventh street, a little south of Walnut street – the former is a large new building, with lofty stories, built of the best materials, and in a handsome stile of modern architecture, together with a coach house, stables and ice house, &c. &c. The latter is a handsome well finished house, on the west side of the public square, into which the occupant has a fine view. The contemplated improvements on the public square, when completed, will add much to the value of those houses. For further information enquire of JACOB VOGDES.
>
> N.B. If the Eighth street house in not sold in short time, it will be rented to a genteel tenant.[136]

Elsewhere, individuals embraced different aspects of the more polite advertising methods preferred by upper and middling sorts. For a house in Hill Street near Berkeley Square, London in 1772, for example, interested parties were invited to make application to builder and speculator Edward Gray directly, but were also advised of 'A Bill on the Window'.[137] Between 1808 and 1809, the Boston plasterer turned builder Joseph Batson variously advertised his houses in Charles Street as 'very convenient', 'large and elegant' and 'genteel.'[138] Batson's compatriot, the stucco worker Daniel Raynerd, utilized a number of techniques to sell a property in Charlestown, Massachusetts: in December 1802 the house was described as 'elegant' and 'finished in a modern and expensive style'; a few months later, in April 1803, the property was 'calculated for a genteel family' and accompanied by a woodcut illustration (Figure 4.16).[139]

Not all were as perspicacious. Having removed to a new house and workshop premises in the spring of 1801, the celebrated carpenter turned author Owen Biddle attempted to dispose of his first property speculation, the present 525 Delancey Street in Philadelphia (built 1799–1800). In contrast to the succinct yet considered wording of American real estate notices, Biddle advertised his property simply as 'A New Three story brick House'.[140] Appearing repeatedly in newspapers between April and August of that year, this terse notice evidently did not elicit a positive response and Biddle sought the professional advice of

Valuable Real Eſtate For Sale.

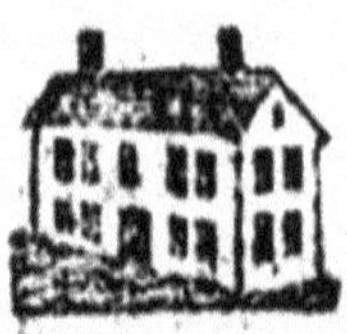

SITUATED in Charleſton, on the main ſtreet, one mile from the bridge and directly oppoſite the Mill Pond, which will be the outlet of the Middleſex Canal—conſiſting of an elegant and well finiſhed Houſe, with Coach-Houſe, Stable, & one acre of Land, laid out in an ornamental Garden and Nurſery, which contains a variety of fruit trees of the beſt kind.

Alſo—one acre of Land adjoining, planted with young fruit trees. The ſituation is delightful, and calculated for the reſidence of a genteel family. For terms, apply to

DENIEL RAYNERD,

April 13. on the Premiſes.

4.16 House advertisement, *Gazetteer* (Boston), 13 April 1803.

Shannon & Poalk, auctioneers in Market Street. Under their guidance, the location and the dimensions of the building and lot were itemized at length, and the house itself was then described as both 'convenient' and 'well-finished'.[141] A successful advertisement, however, need not necessarily be so verbose. In 1799, the house carpenter Joseph Corbit's notice for the sale of a property in Fifth Street was brief but to the point, describing the house as being both 'well finished' and 'in a good situation'.[142] Later, in 1804, and then boasting a substantial property portfolio, Corbit advertised a house in Sansom Street that was 'built of the best materials and finished in a very handsome stile'.[143] While some of his earlier notices clearly benefited from association with conveyancer Edward Bonsall, Corbit was soon capable of conducting his own affairs – the sale of properties in 1804 being by application to him alone. Jonathan Corbit, presumably a relative, shared similar marketing skills: a house on Locust Street in 1811, 'for convenience and superiority of style', was described as 'exceeded by none'.[144]

In Dublin, seasoned builders fully embraced the opportunities afforded by direct advertising in newspapers: plasterers like Charles Thorp and

Two elegant Houſes,

TO be let, in the Eaſt end of Glouceſter-ſtreet, by CHARLES THARP, No. 10, North Cumberland-ſtreet, Stucco-plaiſterer and painter.——Every branch in theſe buildings are executed in modern taſte, and in the moſt maſterly manner; the walls, cielings, &c. ornamented, the painting and ſtaining entirely new, and cannot be excelled in this kingdom. No expence has been ſpared in finiſhing them to the higheſt perfection As the builder has had the honour of compleating the moſt capital buildings in this kingdom, he flatters himſelf that on inſpection, theſe houſes (for convenience and taſte) will be found to anſwer every expectation of the judicious and refined artiſt.

4.17 House advertisement, *Freeman's Journal* (Dublin), 1 March 1781.

Michael Stapleton, key figures in the city's building industry – or, more specifically, building and decorating industries – frequently announced the sale of their own speculatively built properties. Well versed in the changing modes of interior decoration, but also, crucially, shrewd business entrepreneurs, they embraced one of the key marketing strategies of eighteenth-century retailing – product branding. Noting the rise of brands in the world of late Georgian consumption generally, John Strachan finds an equivalence with the emerging cultural emphasis on individual rather than universal agency:

> With the increasing emphasis on brands comes an attendant focus on their proprietors, who become figures of some celebrity … If the wider culture of the Romantic period places great stress upon the creative power of the individual genius, then the cult of the individual is certainly apparent in the publicity efforts mounted on behalf of contemporary advertisers.[145]

Thorp is a particular case in point. Contracted to decorate some of the most important public buildings erected in Dublin during the 1770s – including the Royal Exchange (1768–79) – he subsequently undertook an assiduous rise through the ranks of local government in the decades that followed (becoming Lord Mayor in 1800). Confident of his position within the city's building industry, Thorp frequently invoked his professional credentials as a means of singling out his houses within an expanding marketplace (Figure 4.17). In 1780, describing a pair of houses in Gloucester Street,

Thorp, then Master of the Guild of St Bartholomew (for bricklayers and plasterers), noted that:

> Every branch in these buildings are executed in modern taste, and in a masterly Manner, under his own Inspection, particularly the Plastering, Stucco Work, and Painting, the ornament Cielings, &c. entirely new, and *cannot be excelled in this Kingdom*. No Expence has been wanting in finishing them to the highest Perfection. The builder has had *the Honour of compleating the most capital Buildings in this Kingdom*, and flatters himself, that on Inspection, these Houses will be found to answer the Expectation of *the most refined Architect*.[146]

While 'modern taste' and 'masterly manner' are quintessential terms commonly invoked by auctioneers at this time, and 'cannot be excelled in this kingdom' is also somewhat typical of inflated advertising puff, Thorp's description of himself (only *his* name appears in all caps) as 'a refined Architect' is significant: here he both proclaims his knowledge of contemporary architectural taste – specifically interior architecture and decoration – and correspondingly joins the ranks of what Strachan has identified as 'an entertaining cast of resourceful self-publicists'.[147] This approach was further underscored when, in 1787, he came to dispose of his own house in North Great George's Street: with a simple headline announcing 'an elegant new house to let', Thorp felt it 'unnecessary to say more in its Favour, than that it is the most complete one he has built, and the best Judges must allow (on Inspection) it is the most elegant finished of the Dimensions in the Kingdom'. To further distinguish his property, and attract the better sorts, he added 'it is requested that none will apply but Principals'.[148]

Although typically less verbose, Michael Stapleton's promotional notices were arguably more astute. While early advertisements predictably focused on finish and prestigious neighbours – describing a pair of houses in Harcourt Street in 1788 as being built in a 'neat elegant stile' and commanding 'a most pleasing View of Lord Earlsfort's beautiful Improvements'[149] – later notices presented these same qualities through the lens of his building reputation. An advertisement for a house in Mountjoy Square in 1793, though economical in detail, admirably meets all consumer criteria:

> A House to be let in this beautiful situation, finished in the most elegant style of taste – no expence has been spared to render it convenient and permanent, being built under the immediate inspection of the proprietor. Apply to Michael Stapleton, said Square.[150]

Here, situation, style, convenience and permanence are duly noted. However, with a subtle shift in textual emphasis from brazen self-promotion to mindful supervision – being 'built under the immediate inspection of the proprietor' – Stapleton, although clearly linking the building's elegance and sound construction to his own reputation, arguably remained more closely within the boundaries of decorum. In 1787, Anthony O'Reilly, 'carpenter and architect' of Dublin, had three houses 'almost fit for Reception' to let: by shrewdly announcing 'his most sincere Thanks to his generous Patrons for all past Favours, particularly *since his Return from London*', O'Reilly makes quiet, almost casual reference to that most ubiquitous signifier of style and fashion – a London partnership, training or business connection/licence – and thus, by implication, elevates his properties above the common stock.[151] A more subtle approach was to allow the house to 'speak' for itself. The developer John Scott's announcement of a property in Mountjoy Square, Dublin suggested that the 'house and premises will best recommend themselves on inspection'.[152] Despite the less than fortuitous circumstances under which it appeared on the property market, when stucco worker Joseph Batson's house in Boston was offered for sale in 1811, the advertisement claimed it was 'too well known to need commendation'.[153]

Interestingly, Stapleton and Thorp's counterparts in the decorating businesses across London, Boston, Philadelphia and elsewhere appear to have been more reticent when it came to marketing houses.[154] Joseph Rose & Co., the plastering firm favoured by Robert Adam, speculated in Mansfield Street and Portland Place in the 1770s, and the plasterer William Collins was partner to Sir William Chambers at Berners Street in the 1760s; neither appears to have advertised these properties directly, and likely secured more genteel means to dispose of their houses based on their association with these distinguished architects. Those decorators turned property developers who did advertise apparently sought no advantage from their professional station as arbiters of decorative tastes. In 1784, Thomas Utterton, plasterer and builder-speculator of a number of houses in Bedford Square, London, described a house in adjacent Gower Street simply as a 'handsome new house' with 'three rooms on a floor, stone stair-case, and large garden'.[155] Equally, when William Thackara, Jr came to dispose of his property in Powell (Delancey) Street, Philadelphia, in 1804, it was described simply as a 'convenient three story brick house', with no allusions, for example, to his role as decorator of the Senate Chamber of Congress Hall (built 1787–89), seat of the United States Congress between 1790 and 1800.[156] Here, however, the character of these particular properties likely dictated their description: while Utterton's houses on Bedford Square are among the most richly decorated in that development, houses in Gower Street house were smaller and more economically built. Equally, Powell Street, although within the vicinity of some of Philadelphia's more prestigious neighbourhoods, was a street of houses distinctly aimed at the middling sorts.[157]

Related to this was the practice of system decorating (as described in Chapter 3). Advertisements for elite Dublin real estate in the 1780s and 1790s make plain that houses were increasingly decorated prior to sale or lease, confirming the increasing standardization in the building and decorating of urban domestic architecture in that city before 1800. Here, descriptions of Charles Thorp's houses in Gloucester Street as finished 'to the highest perfection', or to Michael Stapleton's Harcourt Street houses as 'completely finished in a neat elegant Stile', underline the practice and confirm the desirability of already-decorated properties within the aristocratic housing market. In 1790, 'Two Elegant Houses To be Let at the upper end of Merrion-square' were described as 'well finished' and 'strongly built in the modern taste ... fit for immediate occupation'.[158] Other advertisements record specific details regarding the degree of decoration available: in 1793, a 'stone fronted house' in Gloucester Street boasted rooms furnished with 'handsome marble chimney pieces' and 'enriched with stucco friezes';[159] in February 1794, a 'New House' in Eccles Street was already 'papered, painted, and elegantly finished'.[160] Evidence of builders decorating houses prior to sale in other cities throughout the Atlantic world is determined by close reading: in Philadelphia in 1810, four houses in Race Street were 'newly painted, papered, &c. with handsome fireplaces, cornices and stairways'.[161] When carpenter James Lyndall came to sell his three speculative properties in Third Street in the same city in April 1815, they were 'built in the modern style' of 'good materials'.[162] In an era of increasing standardization – in terms of architectural form, spatial distribution and decorative finish – the Dublin builder John Russell's announcement in 1797 that a house 'now finishing' in Belvedere Place could be 'done to the purchaser's fancy' was perhaps directed towards a more discerning class of consumer.[163]

With the above in mind, it is clear that builders across the British Atlantic world embraced the full complement of available methods and strategies for selling houses. In 1762, Bristol carpenter Peter Prigg advertised a 'very neat Strong-built House' in King Square; in tandem with the structural qualities of the building's timber construction, Prigg was keen to emphasize the decorative qualities of its joinery describing the 'two Handsome Parlours, and a large Dining-Room' as being 'neatly wainscotted and ornamented with enriched Cornishes'.[164] Dublin carpenter James Bowden's announcement of the leasehold interest in a 'Fashionable and well built house' in Gloucester Street in 1793 was economical in detail, but didn't neglect to describe the property as 'next adjoining to Lady Anne Fitzgerald's', widow of the Knight of Kerry.[165] And in the same year, the building partnership of Hendy and Gibson of Baggot Street turned what might have been deemed a commercial disadvantage into a proper virtue, noting that a corner house in Hume Street 'not having coach-house and stable to pay for, must certainly be an object to those who do not want such – with the advantage of residing in one of the best parts of the city'.[166] Indeed, just as houses were built to different specifications and consumer economies, so builders created different textual emphases where appropriate: in January 1803, Philadelphia carpenter Joseph Corbit described a property in Seventh Street, then a relatively undeveloped part of the city, as simply a 'new three-story house'; later that year, a 'three story brick house' in Lombard Street, 'between Third and Fourth Streets', one of the more desirable residential neighbourhoods, was described as 'handsome' and 'well-finished'.[167] Indeed, some of the most successful entrepreneurs were the most reticent. A terse notice placed by the London builder James Burton in *The Times* for 20 September 1797 represents a case in point.

> To be SOLD, the LEASE of a very Capital FAMILY HOUSE, in Bloomsbury-place, Bloomsbury-square. For particulars, apply to Mr. James Burton, Southampton-terrace, Bloomsbury.[168]

Created in the 1660s by the Earl of Southampton, Bloomsbury Square remained one of the foremost aristocratic squares in London, and so perhaps the address was deemed sufficient in and of itself – the house requiring no other particular recommendation than the ambiguous moniker of 'very Capital'. But more importantly, this short advertisement provides no clue as to Burton's extraordinary business acumen: between 1785 and 1823, it has been estimated that he built 2,366 houses across London, including some 586 houses during the 'difficult' years of 1792–1802.[169]

Conclusion

Self-promoting house builders emerged in competition with professional house sellers and quickly adopted their vocabulary of 'elegant', 'handsome' and 'commodious' properties to bolster commercial interest. But one size did not fit all. The higher proportion of upper-class housing in cities like London and Dublin throughout the eighteenth century demanded a more sophisticated approach to marketing in the daily newspapers, hence the greater proportion of advertisements describing genteel decorative finishes and convenient fixtures and fittings. By way of contrast, the flatter social order in the American colonies fostered a different type of housing stock and informed a more reticent form of advertising. Nonetheless, in the wake of revolution, coupled with the exponential growth of American cities after 1800, an increasingly wide stratum of society created a demand for houses of distinction. Correspondingly, we find an increase in advertisements catering for socially mobile audiences in the first decades of the nineteenth century. T.H. Breen's account of post-Revolutionary consumer politics describes a situation where 'the lexicon of the consumer marketplace became more complex; challenging both buyers and sellers to keep up with a changing commercial vocabulary'.[170]

As we have seen, some of the most successful building entrepreneurs in these cities – like Joseph Corbit in Philadelphia or Michael Stapleton in Dublin – elected to bypass the services offered by brokers and auctioneers, and sold their own houses directly through the medium of newspaper advertising. But aside from ruling out the middleman, and so reducing legal fees and associated administrative costs, what other professional advantages accrued to those who navigated the world of elite real estate sales? In concert with his own speculative building projects in Mayfair and Marylebone, builder Edward Gray was the liaison for the sale of Sir John

Rouse's house in Hill Street, Berkeley Square in 1772 and for Lady Harriet Vernon's 'capital elegant villa' in Thames Ditton in 1780.[171] As agent for these premises he was no doubt remunerated for his time and services, but it may also have served to elevate his professional reputation – and by extension his property – above the ordinary class of house builder. Such concerns with personal and professional reputation likely encouraged Michael Stapleton to note that 'all possible pains' had been taken to render a house 'convenient and elegant' in Mountjoy Square in 1795.[172]

While house building and house selling were principally economic activities, the evidence from property advertisements reveals that builders were cognizant of the semantics of advertising rhetoric and capitalized on performance and reputation as a means of distinguishing their properties from the common stock of speculatively built houses. More significantly, it confirms a professional confidence with respect to consumer tastes among the burgeoning building classes. House builders patently understood what appealed to house buyers.

Notes

1 Quoted in Rachel Stewart, *The town house in Georgian London* (London: Yale University Press, 2009), p. 76.
2 To date, the advertising of town houses has focused on the consumer viewpoint. See Stewart, *Town house*, pp. 76–89; Sarah Drumm, '"None but persons of fashion need apply": Dublin townhouses of the Irish MPs', MLitt thesis, University College Dublin, 2007. Drumm selectively chooses from a single newspaper over a long period (1726–1780) in Dublin, while Stewart offers a sustained look at a single year (1775) in London. On property advertising in the towns and cities of northern England, and 'at the more modest end of the scale', see Hannah Barker, *Family and business during the Industrial Revolution* (Oxford: Oxford University Press, 2017), pp. 166–79.
3 M.H. Port, 'West End palaces: the aristocratic town house in London, 1730–1830', *London Journal* 20:1 (1995): 27.
4 *Dublin Evening Post*, 24 October 1780 and 30 November 1797.
5 Claire Walsh, 'The advertising and marketing of consumer goods in eighteenth-century London', in Clemens Wischermann and Elliott Shore (eds), *Advertising and the European city: historical perspectives* (Aldershot: Ashgate, 2000), p. 81.
6 Jeremy Black, *The English press in the eighteenth century* (Philadelphia: University of Pennsylvania Press, 1987), pp. 106–8.
7 Robert Munter, *The history of the Irish newspaper, 1685–1760* (Cambridge: Cambridge University Press, 1967), p. 113.
8 T.H. Breen, *The marketplace of revolution: how consumer politics shaped American Independence* (Oxford: Oxford University Press, 2005), p. 54.
9 James Raven, 'Serial advertisement in 18th-century Britain and Ireland', in Robin Myers and Michael Harris (eds), *Serials and their readers 1620–1914* (New Castle, DE: Oak Knoll Press, 1993), pp. 105–6.
10 Munter, *History of the Irish newspaper*, p. 60.
11 Black, *The English press*, p. 26. See also Raven, 'Serial advertisement', pp. 106–7.
12 Breen, *Marketplace of revolution*, p. 55.
13 *The Idler*, 20 January 1761, quoted in Blanche B. Elliott, *A history of English advertising* (London: B.T. Batsford, 1962), p. 109. See also Raymond Williams,

Problems in materialism and culture: selected essays (London: Verso, 1980), p. 172.
14 Walsh, 'The advertising and marketing of consumer goods', pp. 89–91. This position, however, did not preclude Wedgwood advertising in newspapers. See Raven, 'Serial advertisement', p. 108.
15 Walsh, 'The advertising and marketing of consumer goods', p. 83; Munter, *History of the Irish newspaper*, p. 56. Munter notes a similar reticence among merchants in Dublin.
16 Stewart, *Town house*, p. 73.
17 *Ibid*., p. 75; Drumm, '"None but persons of fashion"', p. 74.
18 Stewart, *Town house*, pp. 74, 218, n. 19.
19 *Dublin Evening Post*, 26 February 1782.
20 *Dublin Journal*, 11–13 June 1771; *Dublin Journal*, 5–8 March, 1774; *Dublin Journal*, 3–5 January 1775.
21 *Gazette of the United States*, 9 July 1800.
22 R.B. Walker 'Advertising in London newspapers, 1650–1750', *Business History* 15:2 (1973): 112–30.
23 Raven, 'Serial advertisement', p. 103.
24 Lucyle Werkmeister, *The London daily press 1772–1792* (Lincoln: University of Nebraska Press, 1963), p. 2; Munter, *History of the Irish newspaper*, p. 61.
25 Stewart, *Town house*, p. 76.
26 Emma Hart, 'A British Atlantic world of advertising? Colonial American "For Sale" notices in comparative context', *American Periodicals* 24:2 (2014): 114–15.
27 *Ibid*., 112.
28 Dublin City Archives, WSC/Mins/11, 4 May 1792–19 July 1793, p. 274.
29 *Evening Post* (New York), 31 May 1815. See Franklin Toker, 'James O'Donnell: an Irish Georgian in America', *Journal of the Society of Architectural Historians* 29:2 (1970): 132–43.
30 Alistair Rowan, *Vaulting ambition: the Adam brothers, contractors to the metropolis in the reign of George III* (London: Sir John Soane's Museum, 2007), pp. 14, 52.
31 *Bath Chronicle*, 11 January 1787.
32 Stewart, *Town house*; Drumm, '"None but persons of fashion"'.
33 Hannah Barker, *Newspapers, politics, and public opinion in late eighteenth-century England* (Oxford: Clarendon Press, 1998), p. 33.
34 Richard L. Bushman, 'Shopping and advertising in Colonial America', in Cary Carson, Ronald Hoffman and Peter J. Albert (eds), *Of consuming interests: the style of life in the eighteenth century* (Charlottesville: University of Virginia Press, 1994), p. 248.
35 *The Tatler*, 12 April 1710, quoted in Elliott, *History of English advertising*, p. 105.
36 *Dublin Evening Post*, 13 June 1795.
37 *Ibid*., 30 November 1782.
38 *Parker's General Advertiser and Morning Intelligencer*, 2 July 1783.
39 Cited in Drumm, '"None but persons of fashion"', p. 69.
40 Stewart, *Town house*, p. 77.
41 *Philadelphia Gazette*, 21 June 1797.
42 *Columbia Mirror and Alexandria Gazette*, 15 October 1796. Cited in Orlando Ridout, *Building the Octagon* (Washington, DC: American Institute of Architects Press, 1989), p. 32.
43 *Centinel of Liberty*, 8 July 1796.
44 *The World*, 22 January 1794.
45 John Styles, 'Manufacturing, consumption and design in eighteenth-century England', in John Brewer and Roy Porter (eds), *Consumption and the world of goods* (London: Routledge, 1993), p. 541.

46 *Faulkner's Dublin Journal*, 12–14 April 1774.
47 *Daily Advertiser*, 12 December 1772.
48 Sarah Drumm, '"Fine rooms increase wants": town houses of Irish MPs', in Christine Casey (ed.), *The eighteenth-century Dublin town house* (Dublin: Four Courts Press, 2010), pp. 138–48.
49 *Faulkner's Dublin Journal*, 19–22 March 1774.
50 *Saunders's News-letter*, 25 May 1787.
51 *Morning Post and Daily Advertiser*, 8 November 1784.
52 *Morning Post*, 19 November 1793.
53 *Saunders's News-letter*, 28 March 1796 and 4 May 1796. In the same year, the lease of a house at the corner of Gardiner's Row and North Frederick Street noted that it commanded 'the most extensive and pleasing prospect of any house in Rutland-square of the Square and Hospital Gardens, and that without being in any degree subject to the tax for lighting or securing the rails round the garden'. *Saunders's News-letter*, 1 April 1794.
54 *Ibid.*, 20 May 1797.
55 Elizabeth Gray Kogen Spera, 'Building for business: the impact of commerce on the city plan and architecture of the city of Philadelphia, 1750–1800', PhD diss., University of Pennsylvania, 1980, p. 49. This is based on a review of advertisements from the *Pennsylvania Gazette* for the years 1749/50, 1760, 1770, 1780 and 1789/90; and *Claypoole's Daily Advertiser* for 1799/1800.
56 Styles, 'Manufacturing, consumption and design in eighteenth century England', p. 545.
57 *Federal Gazette*, 21 October 1791.
58 *Dunlap's American Daily Advertiser*, 28 February 1792.
59 James M. Goode, *Capital losses: a cultural history of Washington's destroyed buildings*, 2nd edn (Washington, DC: Smithsonian Institution Press, 2003), p. 169.
60 *Washington Federalist*, 7 January 1803.
61 Stewart, *Town house*, pp. 84–5. Although limited to one newspaper (*Daily Advertiser*) for one calendar year (1775), Stewart's assessment would appear to hold true: a wider search undertaken by the present author has yielded no new notices.
62 *Faulkner's Dublin Journal*, 11–13 June 1771.
63 *New York Gazette*, 23 February 1764.
64 *Bath Chronicle*, 15 November 1787.
65 *Ibid.*, 6 March 1788.
66 *The World*, 22 January 1794.
67 *Gazzetteer and New Daily Advertiser*, 8 March 1790.
68 *Poulson's American Daily Advertiser*, 29 September 1804.
69 *Ibid.*, 21 June 1810.
70 *The World*, 13 June 1789; *Saunders's News-letter*, 22 March 1793.
71 *Morning Herald*, 17 December 1783. It is not clear which house is being referred to (Bedford Square North is at present numbers 12 to 25). No mention of Wyatt's involvement at Bedford Square appears in Andrew Byrne, *Bedford Square: an architectural history* (London and New Jersey: Athlone Press, 1990); or John Martin Robinson, *James Wyatt 1746–1813: architect to George III* (New Haven and London: Yale University Press, 2012).
72 *Dublin Evening Post*, 10 November 1792.
73 *Dublin Journal*, 9–11 August 1777, cited in Drumm, '"None but persons of fashion"', p. 75.
74 *Dublin Journal*, 11–13 November 1777.
75 *Saunders's News-letter*, 28 February 1794 and 1 May 1794.
76 *St James's Chronicle or the British Evening Post*, 20 December 1773–1 January 1774.
77 *Dublin Evening Post*, 2 January 1790.

78 Walter Ison, *The Georgian buildings of Bristol* (London: Faber and Faber, 1952), p. 221.
79 *Gazette of the United States*, 2 February 1796.
80 *Aurora General Advertiser*, 8 June 1799.
81 Historical Society of Pennsylvania (hereafter HSP), Chew Family Papers, Box 131, Folder 23, undated newspaper advertisement, c. 1819.
82 *Poulson's American Daily Advertiser*, 21 June 1810.
83 *Pennsylvania Packet*, 20 March 1775. In 1795, a 'genteel residence' in Finsbury Square, London was 'finished in a superior style of taste and safety', having been 'secured in every part from fire by patent iron plates'. *Oracle and Public Advertiser*, 10 January 1795.
84 James Tierney, 'Advertisements for books in London newspapers, 1760–1785', *Studies in Eighteenth-Century Culture* 30 (2001): 159. The standard charge for a newspaper advertisement in late seventeenth-century London was 2s. 2d.
85 Black, *The English press*, p. 62. See also Elliott, *History of English advertising*, p. 97.
86 The paper announced that 'Advertisements that require no particular Place or Character and are of moderate Length, are taken in at Two Shillings each.' Cited in Munter, *History of the Irish newspaper*, pp. 61–3. He further observes that advertising costs 'were seldom listed'.
87 National Library of Ireland, Edgeworth Accounts, MS 1522, f. 27.
88 Public Record Office of Northern Ireland (hereafter PRONI), Staples Papers, D/1567/E/1/3. Receipt dated 23 May 1795. Cited in Drumm, '"None but persons of fashion"', p. 57.
89 Munter suggests that a four- or five-line advertisement constituted a moderate length notice before 1760. Munter, *History of the Irish newspaper*, p. 63.
90 Raven, 'Serial advertisement', pp. 109–10.
91 John Strachan, *Advertising and satirical culture in the romantic period* (Cambridge: Cambridge University Press, 2007), p. 3.
92 *The Tatler*, 12 April 1710, quoted in Elliott, *History of English advertising*, pp. 104–5.
93 On the use of images in newspaper advertising see Raven, 'Serial advertisement', pp. 100–20.
94 Munter, *History of the Irish newspaper*, p. 60. A more consistent use of illustration in Irish newspapers has been attributed to the lack of advertising duty. Raven, 'Serial advertisement', p. 115.
95 Williams, *Problems in materialism and culture*, p. 172. On this point see also John Styles, 'Manufacturing, consumption and design', p. 541.
96 Walker, 'Advertising in London newspapers', p. 127.
97 Maxine Berg and Helen Clifford, 'Selling consumption in the eighteenth century: advertising and the trade card in Britain and France', *Cultural and Social History* 4:2 (2007): 146.
98 *New York Journal*, 7 May 1767.
99 *Hibernian Journal*, 22 August 1791 and 7 September 1791.
100 Note that one of these images was used for a house on the northeast corner of Walnut and Fourth Streets. *General Advertiser*, 7 May 1791.
101 Raven, 'Serial advertisement', p. 109.
102 Munter, *History of the Irish newspaper*, p. 59. Earlier devices like the factotum (an ornamental printing block designed to carry an outsized capital letter) and illustrations were abandoned at this time. In Britain, the Stamp Acts of 1712 and 1725 also contributed to the reduction in type size. See Raven, 'Serial advertisement', p. 112.
103 Raven, 'Serial advertisement', p. 117.
104 *Morning Post and Daily Advertiser*, 21 May 1777.
105 *Pennsylvania Journal*, 31 January 1787; *Pennsylvania Packet*, 18 August 1787.

106 A 1796 ordinance had prohibited the erection of timber structures on pain of a $500 fine. William J. Novak, *The people's welfare: law and regulation in nineteenth-century America* (Chapel Hill: University of North Carolina Press, 1996), p. 67.
107 *Pennsylvania Evening Post*, 7 May 1782.
108 Hart, 'A British Atlantic world of advertising?', 116–17.
109 Munter, *History of the Irish newspaper*, p. 159.
110 *Dublin Evening Post*, 19 September 1778.
111 PRONI, Antrim Papers D2977/5/9/1/3001.
112 *Oracle and Public Advertiser*, 10 January 1795. Other properties offered by Smith in this same edition included freehold estates in Warwick, Buckinghamshire and Worcester.
113 George Villiers (attrib.), 'On a certain Auctioneer' (London, c. 1787).
114 Robert Campbell, *The London tradesman* (London, 1747), pp. 169–70.
115 *Faulkner's Dublin Journal*, 25–29 April 1758.
116 *Faulkner's Dublin Journal*, 2–5 March 1771.
117 *St James's Chronicle or the British Evening Post*, 30 December 1773–1 January 1774.
118 For the sale or lease of a house in Dominick Street in 1786, potential buyers were advised to contact Whistler, who 'will show the Concerns'. *Dublin Evening Post*, 25 February 1786.
119 Registry of Deeds, Dublin, 419/517/274913. This recites the transfer of Whistler's interest in three lots of ground of 30 feet frontage each to William Warren, merchant, in 1790. See also *Dublin Evening Post*, 19 December 1797.
120 Donna Rilling, *Making houses, crafting capitalism: builders in Philadelphia, 1790–1850* (Philadelphia: University of Pennsylvania Press, 2001), p. 58.
121 Conor Lucey, 'To be let', *Journal of the Royal Society of Antiquaries of Ireland* 139 (2009): 121–3.
122 *Independent Gazette*, 14 September 1782.
123 *The World (1787)*, 3 October 1789.
124 The architect's reputation was, however, used as a selling point for his own house in Berners Street when it was described as having been 'built by the late Sir William Chambers, for his own residence'. *Morning Post*, 5 October 1814.
125 *Public Advertiser*, 26 September 1772.
126 *St James's Chronicle or the British Evening Post*, 30 December 1773–1 January 1774. While some of the draughtsmen employed by Adam have been identified, the names of those who worked in a different capacity have yet to be established.
127 *Saunders's News-letter*, 2 January 1787.
128 A.R. Lewis, 'The builders of Edinburgh's New Town, 1767–1795', PhD diss., University of Edinburgh, 2006, p. 250.
129 *Philadelphia Gazette*, 23 December 1802.
130 Strachan, *Advertising and satirical culture*, p. 27.
131 *The World*, 22 November 1788.
132 Quoted in Byrne, *Bedford Square*, p. 154.
133 *Saunders's News-letter*, 1 May 1794.
134 *Gazette of the United States*, 2 February 1796.
135 Ison, *Georgian Bristol*, pp. 231–2. The same houses were being offered for sale in 1809 and 1824.
136 *Aurora General Advertiser*, 8 November 1803; *Gazette of the United States*, 21 December 1803.
137 *Daily Advertiser*, 21 March 1772.
138 *Columbian Centinel*, 30 March 1808; 1 November 1809.
139 *Ibid.*, 8 December 1802; *Gazetteer*, 13 April 1803. Quoted in Jack Quinan, 'Daniel Raynerd, stucco worker', *Old-Time New England* 65:3–4 (1975): 1–21.
140 *Poulson's American Daily Advertiser*, 17 April 1801.

141 *Philadelphia Gazette*, 21 October 1801.
142 *Ibid.*, 30 November 1799.
143 *Poulson's American Daily Advertiser*, 29 September 1804.
144 *Ibid.*, 22 July 1811.
145 Strachan, *Advertising and satirical culture*, p. 15.
146 *Saunders's News-letter*, 24 June 1780. Author's emphasis.
147 Strachan, *Advertising and satirical culture*, p. 7. These houses were still 'to let' in early 1781, and the copy was slightly revised: interestingly, 'refined architect' was replaced with 'refined artist' (*Freeman's Journal*, 1 March 1781). See Conor Lucey, 'Decoration and property speculation: newspaper advertisements from Michael Stapleton and Charles Thorp', *Irish Architectural and Decorative Studies* 10 (2007): 266–71.
148 *Saunders's News-letter*, 16 November 1787.
149 *Freeman's Journal*, 7 July 1788.
150 *Saunders's News-letter*, 8 May 1793.
151 *Ibid.*, 31 March 1787.
152 *Ibid.*, 11 March 1793.
153 *Columbian Centinel*, 9 March 1811. Quoted in Quinan, 'Daniel Raynerd'.
154 Anthony Lewis offers the tantalizing proposal that advertisements for houses in Edinburgh's New Town 'usually carried claims that the plasterwork and decoration made each the most elegant in the area', without providing any examples. Anthony Lewis, *The builders of Edinburgh New Town 1767–1795* (Reading: Spire Books, 2014), p. 138.
155 In February 1784 the property was described simply as a 'house'; by July, it was a 'handsome New House' and in October a 'Neat New Compact house'. *Gazetteer and New Daily Advertiser*, 14 February 1784; *Morning Herald and Daily Advertiser*, 31 July 1784; *Morning Herald and Daily Advertiser*, 15 October 1784.
156 *Poulson's American Daily Advertiser*, 6 February 1804.
157 Conor Lucey, 'Owen Biddle and Philadelphia's real estate market, 1798–1806', *Journal of the Society of Architectural Historians* 75:1 (2016): 30.
158 *Dublin Evening Post*, 9 March 1790. The houses referred to evidently stood between Antrim House (dem.) and the present 64 Lower Mount Street, built by Samuel Sproule for George Putland in 1783. 'Sproule, Samuel', in *Dictionary of Irish architects 1720–1940*, online, www.dia.ie, accessed 1 March 2015.
159 *Saunders's News-letter*, 22 March 1793.
160 *Hibernian Journal*, 17 February 1794.
161 *Poulson's American Daily Advertiser*, 21 June 1810.
162 *American Daily Advertiser*, 18 April 1815.
163 *Saunders's News-letter*, 25 February 1797.
164 Ison, *Georgian Bristol*, p. 174. The entrance hall was 'panell'd'.
165 *Saunders's News-letter*, 15 March 1793.
166 *Ibid.*, 17 December, 1793.
167 *Poulson's American Daily Advertiser*, 22 January and 5 March 1803.
168 *The Times*, 20 September 1797.
169 Roger Bowdler, 'Burton [Haliburton], James (1761–1837)', in the *Oxford dictionary of national biography*, online, www.oxforddnb.com.elib.tcd.ie/view/article/50182?docPos=1, accessed 28 January 2015.
170 Breen, *Marketplace of revolution*, p. 56.
171 *Daily Advertiser*, 21 March 1772; *Gazetteer and New Daily Advertiser*, 6 March 1780.
172 *Saunders's News-letter*, 27 April 1795.

Conclusion: the builder rehabilitated?

In a satirical postscript to the preface of *The architectural remembrancer* (1751), concerning 'the peculiar Fondness of Novelty, which reigns at present', author Robert Morris announced a new publication on behalf of 'a Friend':

> There is now in the Press, and speedily will be published, *A Treatise on Country Five Barr'd Gates, Stiles, and Wickets, elegant Pig-styes, beautiful Henhouses, and delightful Cow-Cribs, superb Cart Houses, magnificent Barn Doors, variegated Barn Racks and admirable Sheep-Folds; according to the* Turkish *and* Persian *Manner; a work never* (till now) *attempted.*
>
> To which are added, some Designs of *Fly-Traps, Bees Palaces*, and *Emmet Houses* in the *Muscovite* and *Arabian* Architecture; all adapted to the *Latitude* and *Genius* of *England*. The whole entirely new, and inimitably designed in Two Parts, on Forty Pewter Plates, under the immediate Inspection of *Don Gulielmus De Demi Je ne scai Quoi*, Chief Architect to the *Grand Signior*. Originally printed in the Seraglio at Constantinople, and now translated into *English* by *Jeremy Gymp*.[1]

As a very pointed satire about contemporary books of architectural design, bearing titles such as *New designs for Chinese bridges, temples, triumphal arches, garden seats, palings, obelisks, termini's, &c.* (1750), this spoke directly to the link between modernity and novelty; the humour residing in the improper use of exotic, non-classical decorative styles and their signifying or representative capacities.[2] That this was not an entirely facetious parody is borne out by an advertisement published in the *New York Mercury* of 25 September 1758:

> Theophilus Hardenbrook, surveyor, designs all sorts of buildings well suited to both town and country, Pavillions, Summer Rooms, Seats for Gardens, all sorts of Rooms after the taste of the Arabian, Chinese, Persian, Gothic, Muscovite, Paladian, Roman, Vitruvian and Egyptian.[3]

The question of how we interpret this appraisal of the artisan's competence – as evidence of a general architectural illiteracy or of a creatively adroit and commercially astute pragmatism – has been a leitmotif of this study.

The rich and complex histories of urban domestic architecture in eighteenth- and early nineteenth-century Britain and North America have typically emphasized building production at the expense of building design. The economic and managerial proficiency of the bricklayers, carpenters and plasterers responsible for the streets and squares of London and Philadelphia has consequently been prioritized, and the town house aesthetic correspondingly understood primarily as the visual and material expression of the relational effects between urbanization, contracted labour and industrialized capitalism. That house building in the early modern era was equal parts commercial enterprise and creative endeavour cannot be refuted, and design, as we have seen, was informed by a multitude of social, cultural and economic factors. Irish architect James O'Donnell's houses in State Street, New York, built 1815–17 (dem.), serve as a potent reminder that domestic architecture was a delicate balancing act between producer and consumer. Although an early account of his career suggested that the façades 'corresponded to the style he had acquired in Ireland', the houses were resolutely in the American Federal style in terms of scale, proportion and ornament: O'Donnell unequivocally responded to the prevailing tastes of New York's real estate market.[4] Nonetheless, while clearly informed by an emerging standardization in construction and materials production, by regulations instituted by private landowners and city councils and by the financial risks involved in running a business, the capital return from speculative housing was not the sole motivation of the eighteenth-century house builder – in other words, a concern with building economics did not necessarily preclude a concern with building aesthetics. By considering the tradesman's engagement with the processes of architectural design – focusing on drawing schools and builders' academies, artisan-authored pattern books and portfolios of designs – it is clear that some artisans were concerned as much with making design (architecture) as with making profits (building). With this in mind, Sir John Summerson's characteristically withering comment that, with the rise of free market economics, 'any clown of a bricklayer with some spare cash in hand could plunge into the speculative business' demands qualification:[5] while individual 'clowns' certainly operated throughout the period under review – contemporary newspaper editorials decrying the collapse of poorly built houses in London are undoubtedly a testament to sharp practice among some members of the building community – the fine brick terraces of Fitzwilliam Square in Dublin (laid out in 1792) and Louisburg Square in Boston (begun 1826), both of which have sustained exclusive private residences down to the present day, speak to a different class of artisan-led building practice at the upper end of the property market (Figure C.1).[6]

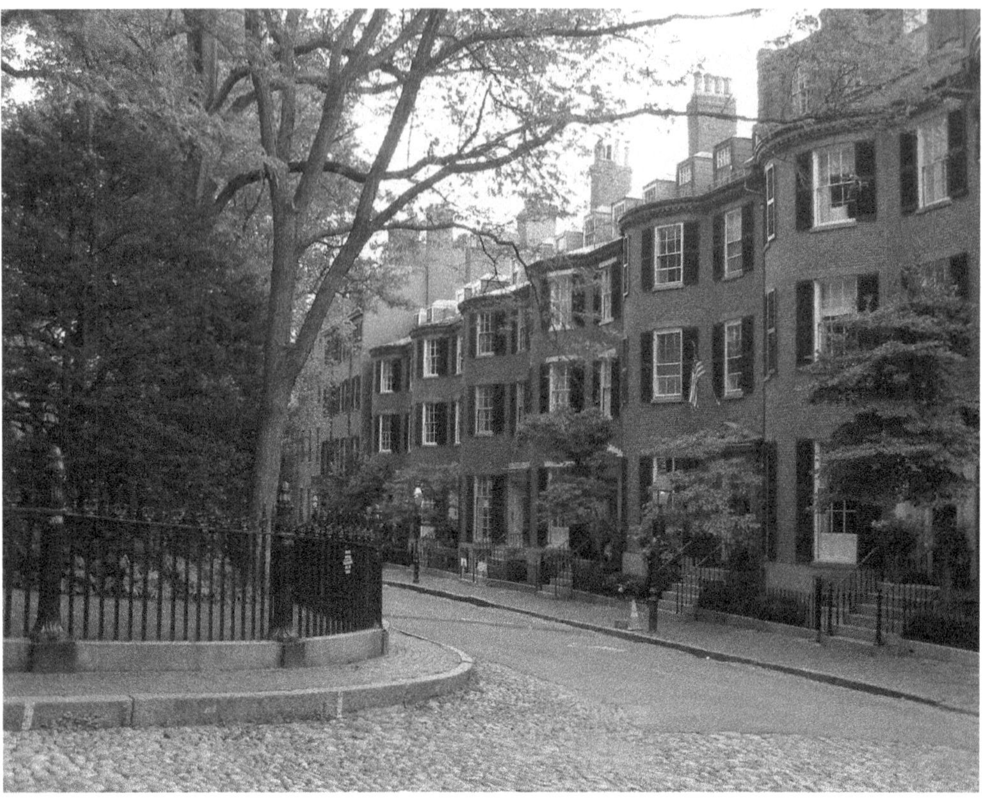

C.1 Louisburg Square, Boston, begun 1826.

The separation of house building and house decorating in the historiography of the terraced town house, still prevalent in the recent literatures on eighteenth-century domestic life and the material cultures of house and home, has also been detrimental to our understanding of the urban house, specifically the character of the urban interior. This is particularly true of Britain and Ireland, where the widespread use of pattern books and serially produced plaster ornament has been habitually regarded as a shortcoming of the neoclassical style of decoration generally, and of the artisan interpretation of Adamesque classicism particularly. (The American literature, by contrast, has long understood the importance of the artisan as an agent of architectural and decorative tastes, although studies of the Federal interior have been almost exclusively concerned with the bespoke mansion as opposed to the row house.[7]) Recognizing that decoration formed a constituent part of speculative building, the form and character of elite town house interiors in London, Dublin and Philadelphia is here ascribed to an artisan class of plasterers, carpenters and joiners rather than the enlightened tastes of the aristocratic and gentry classes who inhabited them. And although indebted to an established and burgeoning print culture devoted to the classical idiom, the tradesman's creative adaptation from these printed sources fostered distinct vocabularies and dialects of neoclassical design and ornament across the Atlantic world that contradict the received notion of a universal acquiescence to architectural authority: the 'personal Adamesque manner' of plasterer John Johnson's interiors in Harley Street, London and the distinctively American vocabulary of 'punch and gouge' decoration in houses from Philadelphia to Charleston, for example, are diverse and stylistically innovative responses to the classical paradigm at the heart of early modern 'British' architectural taste.[8]

Reflecting on the broader social and cultural contexts of the eighteenth- and early nineteenth-century building tradesman – embracing the wider discourses concerning gentility, social performativity and professional mobility; appraising the textual and visual representations of the building trades in contemporary print media – a more complex picture of his working life appears. While the profit margin was a primary incentive for building mechanics to invest in real estate, the evidence from newspaper advertisements, trade cards and other print media reveals that builders were cognizant of the semantics of marketing and advertising rhetoric, and employed a sophisticated vocabulary that emulated luxury goods manufacturers, auctioneers and polite retailers. Although writing for an earlier period, James Farr has cautioned against assuming a strictly 'production-centred definition' when considering the complex, multivalent identity of the early modern artisan.[9] Edinburgh cabinet-maker and housewright Francis Brodie's premises 'at the sign of Palladio's head' within the city's mercantile Lawnmarket district, coupled with his transcription of the portrait of Palladio from the frontispiece to Giacomo Leoni's *The architecture of A. Palladio, in four books* (1715) for his commercial billhead, unambiguously signalled such a concern for creating professional distinction.[10]

Daniel Defoe's 'working trades' might at first glance fit the description of Michael Stapleton, Asher Benjamin, Joseph Rose and other individuals encountered in the preceding chapters of this book; but his qualifying statement that they 'feel no want' hardly accounts for the social and economic mobility that might have allowed him to 'live well', a state attributed by Defoe to the 'middle sort' who populated the social stratum above the artisan.[11] Occupying a professional space between journeyman tradesman and architect, the characters that have peopled this narrative, although necessarily confined to a minority of the artisan workforce involved in the construction industry at any one time, evidently aspired to make a success of their house-building businesses in both creative and commercial terms. Key to success was performance, and performance operated within an increasingly visualized semiotic field: as John Brewer has argued, 'access to culture and social performance' was 'a vital means of maintaining or attaining social status and of establishing social distinctions'.[12] Professional pre-eminence was indeed often concurrent with social prestige. Described in 1790 as 'an intelligent sober & industrious young Mechanic', John McComb, Jr established himself as the one of the most distinguished builders and designers in early nineteenth-century New York; a position paralleled by his trajectory through the ranks of the General Society of Mechanics and Tradesman, from secretary in 1787 to president in 1818.[13]

This returns us neatly to the 'Macaroni bricklayer', that conspicuous figure of architectural modernity. Here, the conflicting signs of aspiring gentility (dress) and vulgar formation in trade (trowel) provided the source of amusement for the contemporary viewer. But with an understanding of building construction and management formed on site and in apprenticeship, a taste for design fostered through drawing classes and pattern books, and an aptitude for the nuanced language of marketing and advertising, the building artisan was clearly a less ridiculous character than he might at first appear. As we have seen, the apparent dichotomy between the manual and intellectual dimensions of eighteenth-century building/architecture, manifested in the caricature of the 'Macaroni bricklayer', does not withstand scrutiny: all aspects of building production and building design clearly remained within the judicious artisan's reach. And just as his business competence has been restored in academic scholarship, so his facility for design and decoration, and his knowledge and appreciation of fashionable consumer tastes, must follow.

Notes

1 Robert Morris, *The architectural remembrancer* (London, 1751), pp. xv–xvi.
2 William Halfpenny, the author of this particular book, produced many similar titles during the 1750s.
3 *New York Mercury*, 25 September 1758. Hardenbrook remains a shadowy figure, although he is known to have designed the Bridewell workhouse and debtors' prison in New York in 1775.
4 Franklin Toker, 'James O'Donnell: an Irish Georgian in America', *Journal of the Society of Architectural Historians* 29:2 (1970): 134. Toker acknowledges that O'Donnell's style corresponded to the 'conservative tastes' of New York society, but his suggestion that 'with a few modifications they might have been found among the rows of Regency [*sic*] houses on Kildare [*sic*] or Merrion Squares in Dublin' undermines the integrity of the town house typology long established in America.
5 John Summerson, *Georgian London* (London: Pleiades Books, 1945; repr. New Haven and London: Yale University Press, 2003), p. 53.
6 For a retrospective view of editorial responses to building malpractices in eighteenth-century London, see James Peller Malcolm, *Anecdotes of the manners and customs of London*, 2 vols (London, 1810), vol. 2, pp. 390–1.
7 A recent example is Alexandra A. Kirtley and Peggy A. Olley, *Classical splendor: painted furniture for a grand Philadelphia house* (New Haven and London: Yale University Press, 2017).
8 'Harley Street', in Philip Temple and Colin Thom, *Survey of London*, vols 51 and 52: *South-East Marylebone* (London: Yale University Press, 2017), available online at

www.ucl.ac.uk/bartlett/architecture/sites/bartlett/files/chapter12_harley_street.pdf, p. 6, accessed 13 June 2017.

9 James R. Farr, 'Cultural analysis and early modern artisans', in Geoffrey Crossick (ed.), *The artisan and the European town, 1500–1900* (Aldershot: Ashgate, 1997), p. 56. On the other hand, a more rigidly hierarchical contemporary view of the division of responsibilities on the late Georgian building site is represented in Peter Nicholson's *The architectural dictionary* (1819): here, the architect was the person 'skilled in the art of building, who forms and estimates designs of edifices, directs the workmen, conducts the work, and measures and values the whole' (p. 23); the builder was one 'who contracts to build, or rear up edifices' (p. 139).

10 Francis Bamford, 'Dictionary of Edinburgh wrights and furniture makers, 1660–1840', *Furniture History* 19 (1983): 49. See also Sebastian Pryke, 'The extraordinary billhead of Francis Brodie', *Regional Furniture* 4 (1990): 81–99.

11 Daniel Defoe, *The Review*, 25 June 1709.

12 John Brewer, '"The most polite age and the most vicious": attitudes towards culture as a commodity, 1600–1800', in Ann Bermingham and Brewer (eds), *The consumption of culture: word, image, and object in the seventeenth and eighteenth centuries* (London: Routledge, 1995), p. 348.

13 Harold C. Syrett, *The papers of Alexander Hamilton*, vol. 7: *September 1790–January 1791* (New York: Columbia University Press, 1963), p. 376.

Select bibliography

Contemporary secondary sources and treatises

Anecdotes of the manners and customs of London, during the eighteenth century, 2 vols (London, 1810).

Adam, Robert. *The ruins of the palace of the emperor Diocletian at Spalatro* (London, 1764).

Adam, Robert and James. *The works in architecture*, 2 vols (London, 1774/79).

Adams, George. *Geometrical and graphical essays* (London, 1791).

Articles of the carpenters company of the city and county of Philadelphia (Philadelphia, 1805).

Benjamin, Asher. *Country builder's assistant* (Boston, 1798).

Benjamin, Asher. *The builder's assistant* (Greenfield, MA, 1800).

Benjamin, Asher and Daniel Raynerd. *The American builder's companion* (Boston, 1806).

Biddle, Owen. *The young carpenter's assistant* (Philadelphia, 1805).

Bottomley, J. *A book of designs* (London, 1793).

The builder's dictionary or gentleman and architect's companion, 2 vols (London, 1734).

The builder's magazine (London, 1774–78).

The builder's price book (London, 1789).

Campbell, Robert. *The London tradesman* (London, 1747).

A catalogue of the capital and extensive collection of architectural models the property of the late ingenious artist Mr Joseph Rose (London, 1799).

A catalogue of the statues, bass reliefs, bustos, &c. of Charles Harris, statuary (London, n.d.).

A catalogue of the valuable collection of architectural drawings and designs; library of architectural and other books; … the property of the late ingenious artist Mr Joseph Rose (London, 1799).

Chambers, William. *A treatise on civil architecture* (London, 1759).

Collyer, Joseph. *The parent and guardian's directory* (London, 1761).

Columbani, Placido. *A new book of ornaments* (London 1775).

Columbani, Placido. *Vases and tripods* (London, 1775–76).

Columbani, Placido. *A variety of capitals, freezes and corniches* (London, 1776).
Crunden, John. *Convenient and ornamental architecture* (London, 1767).
Darly, Matthias. *The ornamental architect, or young artist's instructor* (London, 1769).
Defoe, Daniel. *The complete English tradesman* (London, 1726).
Elmes, James. *Lectures on architecture* (London, 1823).
Gwynn, John. *An essay on design* (London, 1749).
Gwynn, John. *London and Westminster improved* (London, 1766).
Halfpenny, William. *Practical architecture* (London, 1724).
Haviland, John. *An improved and enlarged edition of Biddle's young carpenter's assistant* (Philadelphia, 1833).
Hawney, William. *The compleat measurer* (Dublin, 1730).
Hodgson, P.L. *A set of tables of solid and superficial measure* (Dublin, 1774).
Hodgson, P.L. *The modern measurer* (Dublin, 1793).
Humphreys, Thomas. *The Irish builder's guide* (Dublin, 1813).
Jacques, John. [illustrated catalogue] (London, c.1785–98).
Jee & Eginton. *List of ornaments, manufactured by Jee, Eginton, and Co.* (Birmingham, n.d.).
Jee & Eginton. *Twelve designs of chimney pieces* (Birmingham, n.d.).
Langley, Batty. *The builder's chest book; or a complete key to the five orders of columns in architecture* (London, 1727).
Langley, Batty. *The city and country builder's and workman's treasury of designs* (London, 1740).
Leadbeater, John. *The gentleman and tradesman's compleat assistant* (London, 1770).
Mac Packe, Jose [James Peacock]. *Oikidia, or nutshells: being ichnographic distributions for small villas; chiefly upon oeconomical principles* (London, 1785).
Morris, Robert. *An essay in defence of ancient architecture* (London, 1728).
Morris, Robert. *Rural architecture* (London, 1750).
Morrison, Richard. *Useful and ornamental designs in architecture* (Dublin, 1793).
Moxon, Joseph. *Mechanick exercises: or, the doctrine of handy works* (London, 1703).
Neve, Richard. *The city and countrey purchaser, and builder's dictionary* (London, 1703).
Nicholson, John. *The operative mechanic, and British machinist*, 2 vols (London, 1831).
Nicholson, Peter. *The new practical builder, and workman's companion* (London, 1823).
Nicholson, Peter. *An architectural dictionary, containing a correct nomenclature and derivation of the terms employed by architects, builders, and workmen*, 2 vols (London, 1819).
Pain, William. *The builder's companion, and workman's general assistant* (London, 1769).
Pain, William. *The practical builder, or workman's general assistant* (London, 1774).
Pain, William. *The builder's golden rule, or the youth's sure guide* (London, 1781).
Pain, William. *The practical house carpenter* (London, 1790).
Pain, William. *The builder's pocket treasure* (Boston, 1794).
Pain, William. *The practical house carpenter* (Boston, 1796).
Pain, William. *The practical house carpenter* (Philadelphia, 1797).
Pain, William and James Pain. *Pain's British Palladio* (London, 1786).
Pergolesi, Michelangelo. *A great variety of original designs of vases, figures, medallions, friezes, pilasters, pannels and other ornaments, in the Etruscan and grotesque Style* (London, 1777–85).

Phillips, Richard. *The book of English trades; and library of the useful arts* (London, 1818).

Pocock, W.F. *Modern finishing for rooms* (London, 1811).

Price, Francis. *The builder's guide* (Dublin, 1758).

Richardson, George. *A book of ceilings, composed in the stile of the antique grotesque* (London, 1774–76).

Richardson, George. *Iconology; or, a collection of emblematical figures*, 2 vols (London, 1779).

Richardson, George. *A new collection of chimney pieces, ornamented in the style of the Etruscan, Greek, and Roman architecture* (London 1781).

Richardson, George. *New designs in architecture* (London, 1792).

Salmon, William. *The London and country builder's vade mecum* (London, 1760)

Stewart, John. *Critical observations on the buildings and improvements of London* (London, 1771).

Stitt, William. *The practical architect's ready assistant* (Dublin, 1819).

Swan, Abraham. *A collection of designs in architecture* (London, 1757).

Swan, Abraham. *The British architect, or the builder's treasury of staircases* (London, 1758).

Thomas, William. *Original designs in architecture* (London, 1783).

Wallis, N. *A book of ornaments in the Palmyrene taste* (London, 1771).

Wallis, N. *The carpenter's treasure* (London, 1773).

Ware, Isaac. *A complete body of architecture* (London, 1756–57).

Secondary sources

Abramson, Daniel M. 'Commercialization and backlash in late Georgian architecture', in Barbara Arciszewska and Elizabeth McKellar (eds), *Articulating British classicism: new approaches to eighteenth-century architecture* (Aldershot: Ashgate, 2004).

Adamson, Glenn. *Thinking through craft* (Oxford and New York: Berg, 2007).

Alexander, Christopher. *A pattern language: towns, buildings, construction* (New York: Oxford University Press 1977).

Ames, Kenneth. 'Robert Mills and the Philadelphia row house', *Journal of the Society of Architectural Historians* 27:2 (1968): 140–6.

Archer, John. *The literature of British domestic architecture, 1715–1842* (Cambridge, MA: MIT Press, 1985).

Arnold, Dana. 'The illusion of grandeur? Antiquity, grand tourism and the country house', in Dana Arnold (ed.), *The Georgian country house: architecture, landscape and society* (Stroud: Sutton, 2003).

Ayres, James. *Building the Georgian city* (New Haven and London: Yale University Press, 1996).

Baer, W.C. 'Is speculative building underappreciated in urban history?', *Urban History* 34:2 (2007): 296–316.

Ballantyne, Andrew. 'Architecture as evidence', in Dana Arnold, Elvan Altan Ergut and Belgin Turan Özkaya (eds), *Rethinking architectural historiography* (London and New York: Routledge, 2006).

Barker, Hannah. *Newspapers, politics, and public opinion in late eighteenth-century England* (Oxford: Clarendon Press, 1998).

Barker, Hannah. *Family and business during the Industrial Revolution* (Oxford: Oxford University Press, 2017).

Barnard, Toby. *Making the grand figure: lives and possessions in Ireland 1641–1770* (New Haven and London: Yale University Press, 2004).

Beard, Geoffrey. *Decorative plasterwork in Great Britain* (London: Phaidon, 1975).

Beard, Geoffrey. *Craftsmen and interior decoration in England, 1660–1820* (New York: Holmes and Meier, 1981).

Beard, Geoffrey. *Stucco and decorative plasterwork in Europe* (London: Harper & Row, 1983).

Beard, Geoffrey. 'Robert Adam's craftsmen', in Giles Worsley (ed.), *Adam in context: Georgian Group symposium* (London: Georgian Group, 1992).

Bell, Dorothy. *Edinburgh Old Town: the forgotten nature of an urban form* (Edinburgh: Tholis Publishing, 2008).

Berg, Maxine and Helen Clifford. 'Commerce and the commodity: graphic display and selling new consumer goods in eighteenth-century England', in Michael North and David Ormrod (eds), *Art markets in Europe 1400–1800* (Aldershot: Ashgate, 1998).

Berg, Maxine and Helen Clifford. 'Selling consumption in the eighteenth century: advertising and the trade card in Britain and France', *Cultural and Social History* 4:2 (2007): 145–70.

Bermingham, Ann. 'Introduction. The consumption of culture: image, object, text', in Ann Bermingham and John Brewer (eds), *The consumption of culture: word, image, and object in the seventeenth and eighteenth centuries* (London: Routledge, 1995).

Binney, Marcus. *Town houses: evolution and innovation in 800 years of urban domestic architecture* (London: Mitchell Beazley, 1998).

Black, Jeremy. *The English press in the eighteenth century* (Philadelphia: University of Pennsylvania Press, 1987).

Blackmar, Elizabeth. *Manhattan for rent, 1785–1850* (Ithaca, NY: Cornell University Press, 1989).

Blumin, Stuart M. *The emergence of the middle class: social experience in the American city, 1760–1900* (Cambridge: Cambridge University Press, 1989).

Blythe Gerson, M. 'A glossary of Robert Adam's neo-classical ornament', *Architectural History* 24 (1981): 59–82.

Boime, Albert. *Art in an age of revolution, 1750–1800* (Chicago: University of Chicago Press, 1987).

Bold, John. 'The design of a house for a merchant, 1724', *Architectural History* 33 (1990): 75–82.

Bonehill, John. '"The centre of pleasure and magnificence": Paul and Thomas Sandby's London', *Huntington Library Quarterly* 75:3 (2012): 365–92.

Bonwitt, W. *Michael Searles: a Georgian architect and surveyor* (London: Society of Architectural Historians of Great Britain, 1987).

Borsay, Peter. *The English urban renaissance: culture and society in the provincial town 1680–1770* (Oxford: Clarendon Press, 1989).

Borsay, Peter. 'The English urban renaissance: the development of provincial urban culture c.1680–c.1760', in Peter Borsay (ed.), *The eighteenth-century town: a reader in English urban history 1688–1820* (London: Longman, 1990).

Borsay, Peter. 'Why are houses interesting?', *Urban History* 34:2 (2007): 338–46.

Boyd, Sterling. *The Adam style in America 1770–1820* (New York: Garland Publishing, 1985).

Boyer, M. Christine. *Dreaming the rational city: the myth of American planning* (Cambridge, MA: MIT Press, 1983).

Breen, T.H. *The marketplace of revolution: how consumer politics shaped American independence* (Oxford: Oxford University Press, 2005).

Brewer, John. '"The most polite age and the most vicious": attitudes towards culture as a commodity, 1660–1800', in Ann Bermingham and John Brewer (eds), *The consumption of culture: word, image, and object in the seventeenth and eighteenth Centuries* (London: Routledge, 1995).

Brewer, John. *The pleasures of the imagination: English culture in the eighteenth century* (London: HarperCollins, 1997).

Bridenbaugh, Carl. *Cities in the wilderness: the first century of urban life in America, 1625–1742*, 2nd edn (New York: Knopf, 1955).

Bridenbaugh, Carl. *The colonial craftsmen* (Chicago: University of Chicago Press, 1966).

Briggs, Peter M. '"News from the little world": a critical glance at eighteenth-century British advertising', *Studies in Eighteenth-Century Culture* 23 (1994): 29–45.

Burke, Nuala T. 'Dublin 1600–1800: a study in urban morphogenesis', PhD diss., Trinity College Dublin, 1972.

Burton, Neil (ed.). *Georgian vernacular: papers given at the 1995 Georgian Group symposium* (London: Georgian Group, 1996).

Burton, Neil and Peter Guillery. *Behind the façade: London house plans 1660–1840* (Reading: Spire Books, 2006).

Bushman, Richard L. *The refinement of America: persons, houses, cities* (New York: Knopf, 1992).

Bushman, Richard L. 'Shopping and advertising in Colonial America', in Cary Carson, Ronald Hoffman and Peter J. Albert (eds), *Of consuming interests: the style of life in the eighteenth century* (Charlottesville: University of Virginia Press, 1994).

Byrne, Andrew. *Bedford Square: an architectural study* (London and Atlantic Highlands, NJ: Athlone Press, 1990).

Cannadine, David. *Class in Britain* (New Haven and London: Yale University Press, 1998).

Casey, Christine. 'Architectural books in eighteenth-century Ireland', *Eighteenth-Century Ireland/Iris an Dá Chultúr* 3 (1988): 105–13.

Casey, Christine. 'Books and builders: a bibliographical approach to Irish 18th century architecture', PhD diss., Trinity College Dublin, 1992.

Casey, Christine. *Dublin*. Buildings of Ireland (New Haven and London: Yale University Press, 2005).

Casey, Christine (ed.). *The eighteenth-century Dublin town house* (Dublin: Four Courts Press, 2010).

Chalklin, C.W. *The provincial towns of Georgian England: a study of the building process, 1740–1820* (Montreal: McGill-Queen's University Press, 1974).

Clarke, Linda. *Building capitalism: historical change and the labour process in the production of the built environment* (London and New York: Routledge, 1992).

Clifford, Timothy. 'The plaster shops of the rococo and neoclassical era in Britain', *Journal of the History of Collections* 4:1 (1992): 39–65.

Cohen, Jeffrey A. 'Early American architectural drawings and Philadelphia, 1730–1860', in James F. O'Gorman, Jeffrey A. Cohen, George E. Thomas, and G. Holmes Perkins (eds), *Drawing toward building: Philadelphia architectural graphics, 1732–1986* (Philadelphia: University of Pennsylvania Press, 1986).

Cohen, Jeffrey A. 'Building a discipline: early institutional settings for architectural education in Philadelphia, 1804–1890', *Journal of the Society of Architectural Historians* 53:2 (1994): 139–83.

Cohen, Jeffrey A. 'Place, time and architecture: materialized memory and the moment of Latrobe's Waln House', in Alexandra Alevizatos Kirtley and Peggy A. Olley, *Classical splendor: painted furniture for a grand Philadelphia house* (New Haven and London: Yale University Press, 2016).

Collins, Peter. *Changing ideals in modern architecture, 1750–1950* (Montreal: McGill-Queen's University Press, 1965).

Coltman, Viccy. *Fabricating the antique: neoclassicism in Britain, 1760–1800* (Chicago: University of Chicago Press, 2006).

Colvin, Howard. 'The beginnings of the architectural profession in Scotland', *Architectural History* 29 (1986): 68–182.

Colvin, Howard. 'The practice of architecture, 1600–1840', in Howard Colvin, *A biographical dictionary of British architects 1600–1840*, 4th edn (New Haven and London: Yale University Press, 2008).

Connolly, S.J. 'Eighteenth-century Ireland: colony or ancien-régime?', in D.G. Boyce and Alan O'Day (eds), *The making of modern Irish history: revisionism and the revisionist controversy* (London: Routledge, 1996).

Corfield, Penelope. 'Class by name and number in eighteenth-century England', *History* 72:234 (1987): 38–61, repr. in Penelope Corfield (ed.), *Language, history and class* (Oxford: Blackwell, 1991).

Craig, Lee A. and Douglas Fisher. *The European macroeconomy: growth, integration and cycles 1500–1913* (Cheltenham and Northampton, MA: Edward Elgar, 2000).

Craig, Maurice. *Dublin 1660–1860* (London: Cresset, 1952).

Craig, Maurice. *The architecture of Ireland* (London: Batsford, 1982).

Craske, Matthew. 'Plan and control: design and the competitive spirit in early and mid-eighteenth-century England', *Journal of Design History* 12:3 (1999): 187–216.

Crinson, Mark and Jules Lubbock. *Architecture: art of profession? 300 years of architectural education in Britain* (Manchester: Manchester University Press, 1994).

Crompton, Robert Donald. 'William Thackara, Jr., master plasterer of early Philadelphia', *Plastering Industries* 46:3 (1960): 27–37.

Cruickshank, Dan. 'Queen Anne's Gate', *Georgian Group Journal* 2 (1992): 56–67.

Cruickshank, Dan and Neil Burton. *Life in the Georgian city* (London: Viking, 1990).

Cruickshank, Dan and Peter Wyld. *London: the art of Georgian building* (London: Architectural Press, 1975).

Curran, C.P. *Dublin decorative plasterwork of the seventeenth and eighteenth centuries* (London: Tiranti, 1967).

D'Arcy, F.A. 'Wages of skilled workers in the Dublin building industry 1667–1918', *Saothar* 15 (1990): 21–37.

Davis, Deering, Stephen P. Dorsey and Ralph Cole Hall. *Georgetown houses of the Federal period, Washington D.C. 1780–1830* (New York: Architectural Book Publishing Co., 1944).

Davis, Howard. *The culture of building* (Oxford: Oxford University Press, 2006).

Davis, Nancy. 'George Andrews' composition ornament in the early Federal period', *The 1988 Washington Antiques Show*, exh. cat. (Washington, DC, 1988).

Diamonstein-Spielvogel, Barbaralee. *The landmarks of New York* (Albany: State University of New York Press, 2011).

Dickson, David. 'Large-scale developers and the growth of eighteenth-century Irish cities', in Paul Butel and L.M. Cullen (eds), *Cities and merchants: French and Irish perspectives on urban development, 1500–1900* (Dublin: Trinity College Dublin, 1986).

Dickson, David. 'Second city syndrome: reflections on three Irish cases', in S.J. Connolly (ed.), *Kingdoms united? Great Britain and Ireland since 1500: integration and diversity* (Dublin: Four Courts Press, 1999).

Dickson, David. *Dublin: the making of a capital city* (London: Profile Books, 2014).

Dixon, Caroline Wyche. 'The Miles Brewton house: Ezra Waite's architectural books and other possible design sources', *South Carolina Historical Magazine* 28:2 (1981): 118–42.

Donald, Diana. *The age of caricature: satirical prints in the reign of George III* (New Haven and London: Yale University Press, 1996).

Drumm, Sarah. '"None but persons of fashion need apply": Dublin townhouses of the Irish MPs 1750–1800', MLitt diss., National University of Ireland, 2007.

Drumm, Sarah. '"Fine rooms increase wants": town houses of Irish MPs', in Christine Casey (ed.), *The eighteenth-century Dublin town house* (Dublin: Four Courts Press, 2010).

Drury, P.J. 'Joseph Rose senior's site workshop at Audley End, Essex: aspects of the development of decorative plasterwork technology in Britain during the eighteenth century', *Antiquaries Journal* 64:1 (1984): 62–83.

Duggan, Anthony. 'Parnell Square: an analysis of house types', *Bulletin of the Irish Georgian Society* 38 (1995): 16–24.

Eco, Umberto. 'Function and sign: the semiotics of architecture' (1986), in Neil Leach (ed.), *Rethinking architecture: a reader in cultural theory* (New York: Routledge, 1997).

Elliott, Blanche B. *A history of English advertising* (London: B.T. Batsford, 1962).

Epstein, S.R. 'Craft guilds, apprenticeship, and technological change in pre-industrial Europe', *Journal of Economic History* 58:3 (1998): 684–713.

Evans, Robin. *Translations from drawing to building, and other essays* (Cambridge, MA: MIT Press, 1997).

Fallan, Kjetil. 'Architecture in action: travelling with Actor-Network Theory in the land of architectural research', *Architectural Theory Review* 13:1 (2008): 80–96.

Farr, James. 'Cultural analysis and early modern artisans', in Geoffrey Crossick (ed.), *The artisan and the European town, 1500–1900* (Aldershot: Ashgate, 1997).

FitzGerald, Desmond. 'Early Irish trade-cards and other eighteenth-century ephemera', *Eighteenth-Century Ireland/Iris an Dá Chultúr* 2 (1987): 115–32.

Foglesong, Richard E. *Planning the capitalist city: the colonial era to the 1920s* (Princeton, NJ: Princeton University Press, 1986).

Foner, Eric. *Tom Paine and Revolutionary America* (New York: Oxford University Press, 1976).

Ford, Frances H. 'The design and fabrication of the plastered cornices of the Gaillard-Bennett House, 60 Montagu Street, Charleston, SC', MSc diss., University of Pennsylvania, 2006.

Forty, Adrian. *Objects of desire: design and society since 1750* (London: Thames & Hudson, 1987).

Foyle, Andrew. *Bristol*. Pevsner Architectural Guides (New Haven and London: Yale University Press, 2004).

Fraser, Murray. 'Public building and colonial policy in Dublin', *Architectural History* 28 (1995): 102–23.

Friedman, Alice T. 'The way you do the things you do: writing the history of houses and housing', *Journal of Society of Architectural Historians* 58:3 (1999): 406–13.

Fries, Sylvia Doughty. *The urban idea in colonial America* (Philadelphia: Temple University Press, 1977).

Garnier, Richard. 'Speculative housing in 1750s London', *Georgian Group Journal* 12 (2002): 163–214.

Garnier, Richard. 'Grafton Street, Mayfair', *Georgian Group Journal* 13 (2003): 201–72.

Garrison, J. Ritchie. *Two carpenters: architecture and building in early New England, 1799–1859* (Knoxville: University of Tennessee Press, 2006).

Garvan, Anthony (ed.). *The architectural surveys 1784–1794: the Mutual Assurance Company papers*, vol. 1 (Philadelphia: Mutual Assurance Company, 1976).

Garvan, Beatrice B. *Federal Philadelphia: the Athens of the western world* (Philadelphia: Philadelphia Museum of Art, 1987).

Gentry, Thomas Samuel. 'Specialized residential and business districts: Philadelphia in an age of change, 1785–1800', MA diss., Montana State University, 1988.

George, Mary Dorothy. *Catalogue of the political and personal satires preserved in the department of prints and drawings in the British Museum*, vol. 5: *1771–1783* (London: British Museum, 1935).

The Georgian Society records of eighteenth century domestic architecture and decoration in Dublin, 4 vols (Dublin, 1909–12).

Gibney, Arthur. 'Studies in eighteenth-century building history', PhD diss., Trinity College Dublin, 1997.

Gilchrist, Agnes Addison. 'Notes for a catalogue of the John McComb (1763–1853) collection of architectural drawings in the New-York Historical Society', *Journal of the Society of Architectural Historians* 28:3 (1969): 201–10.

Gilchrist, Agnes Addison. 'John McComb, Sr. and Jr., in New York, 1784–1799', *Journal of the Society of Architectural Historians* 31:1 (1972): 10–21.

Gilje, Paul A. 'Identity and independence: the American artisan, 1750–1850', in Howard B. Rock, Paul A. Gilje and Robert Asher (eds), *American artisans: crafting social identity, 1750–1850* (Baltimore: John Hopkins University Press, 1995).

Girouard, Mark. *The English town: a history of urban life* (New Haven and London: Yale University Press, 1990).

Glaab, Charles N. *The American city, a documentary history* (Homewood, IL: Dorsey Press, 1963).

Glaab, Charles N. *A history of urban America* (New York: Macmillan, 1967).

Glennie, Paul. 'Consumption, consumerism and urban form: historical perspectives', *Urban Studies* 35:5–6 (1998): 927–51.

Gomme, A.H., Michael Jenner and Bryan D.G. Little, *Bristol, an architectural history* (Bristol: Lund Humphries, 1979).

Goode, James M. *Capital losses: a cultural history of Washington's destroyed buildings* (Washington, DC: Smithsonian Institution Press, 2003).

Goodman, Phebe S. *The garden squares of Boston* (Hanover, NH: University Press of New England, 2003).

Gough, Robert J. 'The Philadelphia economic elite at the end of the eighteenth century', in Catherine E. Hutchins (ed.), *Shaping a national culture: the Philadelphia experience, 1750–1800* (Winterthur, DE: H.F. du Pont Winterthur Museum, 1994).

Graham, Willie. 'Interior finishes', in Cary Carson and Carl Lounsbury (eds), *The Chesapeake house: architectural investigation by Colonial Williamsburg* (Chapel Hill: University of North Carolina Press, 2013).

Greenhalgh, Paul (ed.). *The persistence of craft: the applied arts today* (New Brunswick, NJ: Rutgers University Press, 2003).

Gregory, Stacia. '"In the most approved and latest fashions": ornamental plasterwork in Philadelphia 1760–1840', unpublished paper, H.F. du Pont Winterthur Museum (10 December 1985).

Greig, Hannah. *The beau monde: fashionable society in Georgian London* (Oxford: Oxford University Press, 2013).

Griffin, David. 'The building and furnishing of a Dublin townhouse in the 18th century', *Bulletin of the Irish Georgian Society* 38 (1996–97): 24–39.

Guillery, Peter. *The small house in eighteenth-century London* (New Haven and London: Yale University Press, 2004).

Guillery, Peter. 'Introduction: vernacular studies and British architectural history', in Guillery (ed.), *Built from below: British architecture and the vernacular* (London: Routledge, 2011).

Guillery, Peter. 'Georgian: builders' classicism', in Denna Jones (ed.), *Architecture: the whole story* (London: Thames & Hudson, 2014).

Hafertepe, Kenneth. '*The country builder's assistant*: text and context', in Kenneth Hafertepe and James F. O'Gorman (eds), *American architects and their books, 1840–1915* (Amherst: University of Massachusetts Press, 2007).

Hanson, Brian. *Architects and the 'building world' from Chambers to Ruskin: constructing authority* (Cambridge: Cambridge University Press, 2003).

Harris, Eileen. *The genius of Robert Adam: his interiors* (New Haven and London: Yale University Press, 2001).

Harris, Eileen and Nicholas Savage, *British architectural books and writers, 1556–1785* (Cambridge: Cambridge University Press, 1990).

Hart, Emma. *Building Charleston: town and society in the eighteenth-century British Atlantic world* (Charlottesville: University of Virginia Press, 2010).

Hart, Emma. 'A British Atlantic world of advertising? Colonial American "For Sale" notices in comparative context', *American Periodicals* 24:2 (2014): 110–27.

Hastings, William. 'Philadelphia microcosm', *Pennsylvania Magazine of History and Biography* 19:2 (1967): 164–80.

Hayward, Mary Ellen. 'Urban vernacular architecture in nineteenth-century Baltimore', *Winterthur Portfolio* 16:1 (1981): 33–63.

Hayward, Mary Ellen and Charles Belfoure. *The Baltimore rowhouse* (New York: Princeton Architectural Press, 1999).

Hayward, Mary Ellen and Frank R. Shivers, Jr (eds). *The architecture of Baltimore: an illustrated history* (Baltimore: Johns Hopkins University Press, 2004).

Heal, Ambrose. *London tradesmen's cards of the XVIII century: an account of their origin and use* (New York: Dover Publications, 1968).

Henderson, Amy H. 'A family affair: the design and decoration of 321 South Fourth Street, Philadelphia', in John Styles and Amanda Vickery (eds), *Gender, taste, and material culture in Britain and North America, 1700–1830* (New Haven and London: Yale University Press, 2006).

Henderson, Amy H. 'Furnishing the Republican Court: building and decorating Philadelphia homes, 1790–1800', PhD diss., University of Delaware, 2008.

Herman, Bernard L. *Town house: architecture and material life in the early American city, 1780–1830* (Chapel Hill: University of North Carolina Press, 2005).

Herman, Bernard L. and Peter Guillery. 'Negotiating classicism in eighteenth-century Deptford and Philadelphia', in Barbara Arciszewska and Elizabeth McKellar (eds), *Articulating British classicism: new approaches to eighteenth-century architecture* (Aldershot: Ashgate, 2004).

Hill, Richard. *Designs and their consequences* (New Haven and London: Yale University Press, 1999).

Hitchcock, Henry Russell. *American architectural books: a list of books, portfolios, and pamphlets on architecture and related subjects published in America before 1895* (Minneapolis: University of Minnesota Press, 1962).

Hobsbawm, E.J. 'The tramping artisan', *Economic History Review* (NS) 3 (1950–51): 299–320.

Hoppit, Julian. 'Attitudes to credit in Britain, 1680–1790', *Historical Journal* 33:2 (1990): 305–22.

Hubbard, Philippa. 'Trade cards in 18th-century consumer culture: movement, circulation, and exchange in commercial and collecting spaces', *Material Culture Review*, 74–75 (Spring 2012): 30–46.

Ison, Walter. *The Georgian buildings of Bath from 1700 to 1830* (London: Faber and Faber, 1948).

Ison, Walter. *The Georgian buildings of Bristol* (Bath: Kingsmead Press, 1952).

Jackson, A. 'The façade of Sir John Soane's Museum: a study in contextualisation', *Journal of the Society of Architectural Historians* 51:4 (1992): 417–29.

Jacobus, Laura. 'On "whether a man could see before him and behind him both at once": the role of drawing in the design of interior space in England c.1600–1800', *Architectural History* 31 (1988): 148–59.

Jay, Robert. *The trade card in nineteenth-century America* (Columbia: University of Missouri Press, 1987).

Jeacle, Ingrid. 'Accounting and the construction of the standard house', *Accounting, Auditing and Accountability Journal* 16:4 (2003): 582–605.

Joyce, Patrick (ed.), The historical meanings of work (Cambridge: Cambridge University Press, 1987).

Kelsall, Frank. 'The architect as speculator', in Giles Worsley (ed.), *Georgian architectural practice: papers given at the Georgian Group symposium 1991* (London: Georgian Group, 1992).

Kimball, Fiske. *Samuel McIntire, carver, the architect of Salem* (Portland, ME: Southworth-Anthoensen Press, 1940).

Kirker, Harold and James Kirker. *Bulfinch's Boston 1787–1817* (Oxford: Oxford University Press, 1964).

Klee, Jeffrey. 'Civic order on Beacon Hill', *Buildings and Landscapes: Journal of the Vernacular Architecture Forum* 15 (2008): 43–57.

Klein, Lawrence. 'Politeness for plebes: some social identities in early eighteenth-century England', in Ann Bermingham and John Brewer (eds), *The consumption of culture: word, image, and object in the seventeenth and eighteenth centuries* (London: Routledge, 1995).

Knowles, C.C. and P.H. Pitt. *The history of building regulation in London 1189–1972* (London: Architectural Press, 1972).

Kostof, Spiro. *The city shaped: urban patterns and meanings through history* 2nd edn (London and New York: Thames & Hudson, 1999).

Kostof, Spiro. *The city assembled: elements of urban form through history*, 2nd edn (London and New York: Thames & Hudson, 2005).

Kostof, Spiro (ed.). *The architect: chapters in the history of the profession* (Oxford: Oxford University Press, 1977).

Kuykendall, Erin E. 'Philadelphia carpenters, cabinetmakers and captains: the working world of Thomas Nevell 1762–1784', MA diss., University of Delaware, 2011.

Lahikainen, Dean. *Samuel McIntire: carving an American style* (Salem, MA: Peabody Essex Museum, 2007).

Lane, Fintan. 'William Thompson, class and his Irish context, 1755–1833', in Fintan Lane (ed.), *Politics, society and the middle class in modern Ireland* (Basingstoke: Palgrave Macmillan, 2010).

Langford, Paul. *A polite and commercial people: England 1727–1783* (Oxford: Clarendon Press, 1989).

Lanier, Gabrielle M. and Bernard L. Herman. *Everyday architecture of the mid-Atlantic: looking at buildings and landscapes* (Baltimore: Johns Hopkins University Press, 1997).

Leech, Roger H. *The town house in medieval and early modern Bristol* (Swindon: Historic England, 2014).

Lees-Maffei, Grace and Linda Sandino, 'Dangerous liaisons: relationships between design, craft and art', *Journal of Design History* 17:3 (2004): 207–19.

Lewis, A.R. 'The builders of Edinburgh New Town 1765–1795', PhD diss., University of Edinburgh, 2006.

Lewis, Anthony. *The builders of Edinburgh New Town 1765–1795* (Reading: Spire Books, 2014).

Lewis, Michael J. 'Owen Biddle and *The young carpenter's assistant*', in Kenneth Hafertepe and James F. O'Gorman (eds), *American architects and their books to 1848* (Amherst: University of Massachusetts Press, 2001).

Lewis, Michael J. 'William Birch and the culture of architecture in Philadelphia', *Studies in the History of Gardens and Designed Landscapes* 32:1 (2012): 35–49.

Lockwood, Charles. *Bricks and brownstone: the New York row house, 1783–1929, an architectural and social history* (New York: McGraw-Hill, 1972).

Longmore, Jane. 'Residential patterns of the Liverpool elite, c.1660–1800', in John Dunne and Paul Janssens (eds), *Living in the city: elites and their residences, 1500–1900* (Turnhout: Brepols, 2008): 175–92.

Lounsbury, Carl. '"An elegant and commodious building": William Buckland and the design of the Prince William County courthouse', *Journal of the Society of Architectural Historians* 46:3 (1987): 228–40.

Lounsbury, Carl. *Essays in early American architectural history: a view from the Chesapeake* (Charlottesville: University of Virginia Press, 2011).

Lounsbury, Carl R. 'Design process', in Cary Carson and Carl R. Lounsbury (eds), *The Chesapeake house: architectural investigation by Colonial Williamsburg* (Chapel Hill: University of North Carolina Press, 2013).

Lowe, Patricia Ann. 'Volumes that speak: the architectural books of the Drayton library catalog and the design of Drayton Hall', Master's diss., Clemson University and the College of Charleston, 2010.

Lubbock, Jules. *The tyranny of taste: the politics of architecture and design in Britain 1550–1960* (New Haven and London: Yale University Press, 1995).

Lucey, Conor. *The Stapleton Collection: designs for the Irish neoclassical interior* (Tralee: Churchill House Press, 2007).

Lucey, Conor. 'Classicism or commerce? The town house interior as commodity', in Christine Casey (ed.), *The eighteenth-century Dublin town house* (Dublin: Four Courts Press, 2010).

Lucey, Conor. 'Building dialectics: negotiating urban scenography in late Georgian Dublin', in Gillian O'Brien and Finola O'Kane (eds), *Portraits of the city: Dublin and the wider world* (Dublin: Four Courts Press, 2012).

Lucey, Conor. 'The scale of plasterwork production in the metropolitan centres of Britain and Ireland', in Christine Casey and Conor Lucey (eds), *Decorative plasterwork in Ireland and Europe: ornament and the early modern interior* (Dublin: Four Courts Press, 2012).

Lucey, Conor. 'British agents of the Irish Adamesque', *Architectural History* 53 (2013): 135–70.

Lucey, Conor. 'Statuaries and plaster shops in eighteenth-century Dublin', in Paula Murphy (ed.), *Sculptors and sculpture 1600–2000. Art and architecture of Ireland* vol. 3 (London: Yale University Press, 2014).

Lucey, Conor. 'Owen Biddle and Philadelphia's real estate market, 1798–1806', *Journal of the Society of Architectural Historians* 75:1 (2016): 25–47.

McAulay, Eve. 'Some problems in building on the Fitzwilliam estate during the agency of Barbara Verschoyle', *Irish Architectural and Decorative Studies* 2 (1999): 98–117.

McAulay, Eve. 'The origins and early development of the Pembroke estate beyond the Grand Canal, 1816–1880', PhD diss., Trinity College Dublin, 2003.

McCullough, Niall. *Dublin: an urban history* (Dublin: Anne Street Press, 1989).

McDonnell, Joseph. *Irish eighteenth-century stuccowork and its European sources* (Dublin: National Gallery of Ireland, 1991).

McKean, Charles. 'The incivility of Edinburgh's New Town', in W.A. Brogden (ed.), *The neo-classical town: Scottish contributions to urban design since 1750* (Edinburgh: Rutland Press, 1996).

McKellar, Elizabeth. *The birth of modern London: the development and design of the city 1660–1720* (Manchester: Manchester University Press, 1999).

McKellar, Elizabeth. 'Populism versus professionalism: John Summerson and the twentieth-century creation of the "Georgian"', in Barbara Arciszewska and Elizabeth McKellar (eds), *Articulating British classicism: new approaches to eighteenth-century architecture* (Aldershot: Ashgate, 2004).

McKendrick, Neil. 'The commercialization of fashion', in Neil McKendrick, John Brewer and J.H. Plumb (eds), *The birth of a consumer society: the commercialization of eighteenth-century England* (Bloomington: Indiana University Press, 1982).

McKendrick, Neil. 'The consumer revolution of eighteenth-century England', in Neil McKendrick, John Brewer and J.H. Plumb (eds), *The birth of a consumer society: the commercialization of eighteenth-century England* (Bloomington: Indiana University Press, 1982).

McLeod, Richard Alan. 'The Philadelphia artisan 1828–1850', PhD diss., University of Missouri, 1971.

McParland, Edward. 'The papers of Bryan Bolger, measurer', *Dublin Historical Record* 25:4 (1972): 120–31.

McParland, Edward. 'The Wide Streets Commissioners: their importance for Dublin architecture in the late 18th and early 19th centuries', *Bulletin of the Irish Georgian Society* 15:1 (1972): 1–50.

McParland, Edward: 'Strategy in the planning of Dublin', in Paul Butel and L.M. Cullen (eds), *Cities and merchants: French and Irish perspectives on urban development, 1500–1900* (Dublin: Trinity College Dublin, 1986).

McWilliam, Colin, David Walker and John Gifford. *Edinburgh*. Buildings of Scotland (New Haven and London: Yale University Press 1984).

Massey, Doreen. 'Space-time and the politics of location', in Alan Read (ed.), *Architecturally speaking: practices of art, architecture and the everyday* (London: Routledge, 2000).

Matthews, Christopher N. 'Part of a "polished society": style and ideology in Annapolis's Georgian architecture', in Paul A. Shackel, Paul R. Mullins and Mark S. Warner (eds), *Annapolis pasts: historical archaeology in Annapolis, Maryland* (Knoxville: University of Tennessee Press, 1998).

Maudlin, Daniel. 'Introduction', in Daniel Maudlin and Robin Peel (eds), *The materials of exchange between Britain and North East America, 1750–1900* (Farnham: Ashgate, 2013).

Maudlin, Daniel and Bernard L. Herman (eds). *Building the British Atlantic world: spaces, places, and material culture, 1600–1850* (Chapel Hill: University of North Carolina Press, 2016).

Maynard, W. Barksdale. *Architecture in the United States 1800–1850* (New Haven and London: Yale University Press, 2002).

Maynard, W. Barksdale. *Buildings of Delaware* (Charlottesville: University of Virginia Press, 2008).

Morgan, Keith N. *Buildings of Massachusetts: metropolitan Boston* (Charlottesville: University of Virginia Press, 2009).

Morrison, Hugh. *Early American architecture: from the first colonial settlements to the national period* (Oxford: Oxford University Press, 1987).

Moss, Jr., Roger W. 'Master builders: a history of the colonial Philadelphia building trades', PhD diss., University of Delaware, 1972.

Moss, Jr., Roger W. 'The origins of the Carpenters' Company of Philadelphia', in Charles E. Peterson (ed.), *Building early America: contributions toward the history of a great industry* (Radnor, PA: Chilton Book Co., 1976).

Mowat, Ian R.M. 'Adam Square: an Edinburgh architectural first', *Book of the Old Edinburgh Club* (NS) 5 (2002): 93–101.

Mowl, Timothy. *To build the second city: architects and craftsmen of Georgian Bristol* (Bristol: Redcliff, 1991).

Mowl, Timothy and Brian Earnshaw. *An insular rococo: architecture, politics and society in Ireland and England, 1710–1770* (London: Reaktion, 1999).

Munter, Robert. *The history of the Irish newspaper, 1685–1760* (Cambridge: Cambridge University Press, 1967).

Murray, Ashleigh. 'Joseph Rose and company', *Georgian Group Journal* 20 (2012): 103–18.

Murtagh, William John. 'The Philadelphia row House', *Journal of the Society of Architectural Historians* 16:4 (1957): 8–13.

Muthesius, Stefan. *The English terraced house* (New Haven: Yale University Press, 1982).

Nash, Gary B. 'City planning and political tension in the seventeenth century: the case of Philadelphia', *Proceedings of the American Philosophical Society* 112:1 (1968): 54–73.

Nash, Gary B. 'A historical perspective on early American artisans', in Francis J. Puig and Michael Conforti (eds), *The American craftsman and the European tradition 1620–1820* (Minneapolis: Minneapolis Institute of Arts, 1989).

Nenadic, Stana. 'Necessities: food and clothing in the long eighteenth century', in Elizabeth Foyster and Christopher A. Whatley (eds), *A history of everyday life in Scotland 1600–1800* (Edinburgh: Edinburgh University Press, 2010).

Nenadic, Stana. 'Architect-builders in London and Edinburgh, c.1750–1800, and the market for expertise', *Historical Journal* 55:3 (2012): 597–617.

Norton, Paul F. 'Samuel McIntire of Salem: the drawings and papers of the architect/carver and his Family, 1988', unpublished MS (photocopy), Phillips Library, Peabody Essex Museum, Salem, MA.

Novak, William J. *The people's welfare: law and regulation in nineteenth-century America* (Chapel Hill: University of North Carolina Press, 1996).

O'Brien, Gillian and Finola O'Kane (eds). *Portraits of the city: Dublin and the wider world* (Dublin: Four Courts Press, 2012).

O'Driscoll, Sally. 'What kind of man do the clothes make? Print culture and the meanings of macaroni effeminacy', in Kevin Murphy and Sally O'Driscoll (eds), *Studies in ephemera: text and image in eighteenth-century print* (Lewisburg, PA and Lanham, MD: Bucknell University Press, 2013).

O'Gorman, James F. 'The Philadelphia architectural drawing in its historical context: an overview', in James F. O'Gorman, Jeffrey A. Cohen, George E. Thomas and G. Holmes Perkins (eds), *Drawing toward building: Philadelphia architectural graphics 1732–1986* (Philadelphia: University of Pennsylvania Press, 1986).

O'Gorman, James F. 'Some architects' portraits in nineteenth-century America: personifying the evolving profession', *Transactions of the American Philosophical Society* 103:4 (2013): 1–94.

O'Kane, Finola. '"Bargains in view": the Fitzwilliam family's development of Merrion Square', in Christine Casey (ed.), *The eighteenth-century Dublin town house* (Dublin: Four Courts Press).

O'Neal, William B. 'Pattern books in American architecture', in Mario di Valmarana (ed.), *Building by the book* (Charlottesville: University Press of Virginia, 1984).

Ogborn, Miles. *Spaces of modernity: London's geographies 1680–1780* (New York and London: Guildford Press, 1998).

Ogborn, Miles. 'Designs on the city: John Gwynn's plans for Georgian London', *Journal of British Studies* 43 (2004): 15–39.

Olsen, D.J. *Town planning in London: the eighteenth and nineteenth centuries* (New Haven and London: Yale University Press, 1964).

Park, Helen. 'A list of architectural books available in America before the Revolution', *Journal of the Society of Architectural Historians* 20:3 (1961): 115–30.

Peterson, Charles E. (ed.). *Building early America* (Mendham, NJ: Astragal Press, 1976).

Pollard, Mary. *Dublin's trade in books 1550–1800* (Oxford: Clarendon Press, 1986).

Port, M.H. 'West End palaces: the aristocratic town house in London, 1730–1830', *London Journal* 20:1 (1995): 117–38.

Porter, Roy. 'Enlightenment London and urbanity', in T.D. Hemming, E. Freeman, David Meakin and Haydn Trevor Mason (eds), *The secular city: studies in the Enlightenment* (Exeter: University of Exeter Press, 1994).

Powel, Martyn J. *The politics of consumption in eighteenth-century Ireland* (Basingstoke: Palgrave Macmillan, 2005).

Powell, Christopher. 'Cobing and helling: a Georgian building firm at work', *Construction History* 15 (1999): 3–14.

Power, Garrrett. 'Entail in two cities: a comparative study of long term leases in Birmingham, England and Baltimore, Maryland, 1700–1900', *Journal of Architectural and Planning Research* 9:4 (1992): 315–24.

Puetz, Anne. 'Design instruction for artisans in eighteenth-century Britain', *Journal of Design History* 12:3 (1999): 217–39.

Quimby, Ian M. (ed.). *The craftsman in early America* (New York: W.W. Norton, 1984).

Quinan, Jack. 'Daniel Raynerd, stucco worker', *Old-Time New England* 65:3–4 (1975): 1–21.

Quinan, Jack. 'Some aspects of the development of the architectural profession in Boston between 1800 and 1830', *Old-Time New England* 68:1–2 (1977): 32–8.

Raley, Robert L. 'Early Maryland plasterwork and stuccowork', *Journal of the Society of Architectural Historians* 20:3 (1961): 131–5.

Rasmussen, Steen Eiler. *London, the unique city* (Cambridge, MA and London: MIT Press, 1982).

Rauser, Amelia F. 'Hair, authenticity, and the self-made macaroni', *Eighteenth-Century Studies* 38:1 (2004): 101–17.

Raven, James. 'Serial advertisement in 18th-century Britain and Ireland', in Robin Myers and Michael Harris (eds), *Serials and their readers 1620–1914* (New Castle, DE: Oak Knoll Press, 1993).

Rawson, Michael. 'The march of bricks and mortar', *Environmental History* 17 (2012): 844–51.

Rees, Helen. 'Patterns of making: thinking and making in industrial design', in Peter Dormer (ed.), *The culture of craft: status and future* (Manchester: Manchester University Press, 1997).

Reiff, Daniel D. *Houses from books: treatises, pattern books, and catalogs in American architecture, 1738–1950* (University Park, PA: Pennsylvania State University Press, 2000).

Reinberger, Mark. 'A plasterer's daybook attributed to Edward Evans', *Pennsylvania Magazine of History and Biography* 117:4 (1993): 331–8.

Reinberger, Mark. *Utility and beauty: Robert Wellford and composition ornament in America* (Newark: University of Delaware Press, 2003).

Ridout, Orlando. *Building the Octagon* (Washington, DC: American Institute of Architects Press, 1989).

Rilling, Donna. *Making houses, crafting capitalism: builders in Philadelphia, 1790–1850* (Philadelphia: University of Pennsylvania Press, 2001).

Roach, Hannah Benner. 'Thomas Nevel (1721–1797): carpenter, educator, patriot', *Journal of the Society of Architectural Historians* 24:2 (1965): 153–64.

Rock, Howard B. (ed.). *The New York City artisan, 1789–1825: a documentary history* (Albany: State University of New York Press, 1989).

Rowan, Alistair. *Vaulting ambition: the Adam brothers, contractors to the metropolis in the reign of George III* (London: Sir John Soane's Museum, 2007).

Rowan, Alistair. 'Edinburgh: the town house in the capital of North Britain', in Christine Casey (ed.), *The eighteenth-century Dublin town house* (Dublin: Four Courts Press, 2010).

Rubenstein, Harry R. 'With hammer in hand: working-class occupational portraits', in Howard B. Rock, Paul A. Gilje and Robert Asher (eds), *American artisans: crafting social identity, 1750–1850* (Baltimore: Johns Hopkins University Press, 1995).

Rykwert, Joseph. *The first moderns: the architects of the eighteenth century* (Cambridge, MA: MIT Press, 1980).

Rykwert, Joseph and Anne Rykwert. *Robert and James Adam* (London: Collins, 1985).

Salinger, Sharon V. 'Spaces, inside and outside, in eighteenth-century Philadelphia', *Journal of Interdisciplinary History* 26:1 (1995): 1–31.

Saumarez-Smith, Charles. *Eighteenth-century decoration: design and the domestic interior in England* (London: Weidenfeld & Nicolson, 1993).

Schimmelmann, Janice G. *Architectural books in early America: architectural treatises and handbooks available in American libraries and bookstores through 1800* (New Castle, DE: Oak Knoll Press, 1999).

Schweitzer, Mary M. 'The spatial organization of Federalist Philadelphia, 1790', *Journal of Interdisciplinary History* 24:1 (1993): 31–57.

Scott, Katie. 'The Waddesdon trade cards: more than one history', *Journal of Design History* 17:1 (2004): 91–100.

Scott, Mel. *American city planning since 1890* (Berkeley, Los Angeles and London: University of California Press, 1971).

Sennett, Richard. *The craftsman* (London: Penguin Books, 2008).

Sharples, Joseph. *Liverpool*. Pevsner Architectural Guides (New Haven and London: Yale University Press, 2004).

Sheridan, Edel. 'Designing the capital city: Dublin, c.1600–1810', in John Brady and Anngret Simms (eds), *Dublin through space and time* (Dublin: Four Courts Press, 2001).

Shivers, Natalie W. *Those placid old rows: the aesthetic and development of the Baltimore rowhouse* (Baltimore: Maclay & Associates, 1981).

Siddle, David. *Migration, mobility, and modernization* (Liverpool: Liverpool University Press, 2000).

Smith, Billy G. *The 'lower sort': Philadelphia's laboring people, 1750–1800* (Ithaca, NY: Cornell University Press, 1990).

Smith, Margaret Supplee and John C. Moorhouse, 'Architecture and the housing market: nineteenth century row housing in Boston's South End', *Journal of the Society of Architectural Historians* 52:2 (1993): 159–78.

Smith, Ryan K. *Robert Morris's folly: the architectural and financial failures of an American founder* (New Haven: Yale University Press, 2014).

Smyth, Jim. 'The men of property: politics and the language of class in the 1790s', in Fintan Lane (ed.), *Politics, society and the middle class in modern Ireland* (Basingstoke: Palgrave Macmillan, 2010).

Snodin, Michael. 'Trade cards and English rococo', in Charles Hind (ed.), *The rococo in England: a symposium* (London: Victoria and Albert Museum, 1986).

Snodin, Michael and Maurice Howard. *Ornament: a social history since 1450* (New Haven and London: Yale University Press, 1996).

Snodin, Michael and John Styles. *Design and the decorative arts: Georgian Britain, 1714–1837* (London: Victoria and Albert Museum, 2004).

Spann, Edward K. 'The greatest grid: the New York Plan of 1811', in Daniel Schaffer (ed.), *Two centuries of American planning* (Baltimore: Johns Hopkins University Press, 1988).

Spera, Elizabeth Gray Kogen. 'Building for business: the impact of commerce on the city plan and architecture of the city of Philadelphia, 1750–1800', PhD diss., University of Pennsylvania, 1980.

Stanton, Phoebe. 'The sources of Pugin's *Contrasts*', in John Summerson (ed.), *Concerning architecture: essays on architectural writers and writing presented to Nikolaus Pevsner* (London: Allen Lane, 1968).

Stewart, Rachel. 'The West End house c.1765–1785: a gamble and forfeit', *Georgian Group Journal* 12 (2002): 135–48.

Stewart, Rachel. *The town house in Georgian London* (New Haven and London: Yale University Press, 2009).

Stieber, Nancy. 'Space, time, and architectural history', in Dana Arnold, Elvan Altan Ergut and Belgin Turan Özkaya (eds), *Rethinking architectural historiography* (London and New York: Routledge, 2006).

Stillman, Damie. *The decorative work of Robert Adam* (London: Academy Editions, 1973).

Stillman, Damie. *English neoclassical architecture*, 2 vols (London: Zwemmer, 1988).

Stillman, Damie. 'City living, Federal style', in Catherine E. Hutchins (ed.), *Everyday life in the early Republic* (Winterthur, DE: H.F. du Pont Winterthur Museum, 1994).

Stillman, Damie. 'Architectural books in New York: from McComb to Lafever', in Kenneth Hafertepe and James O'Gorman (eds), *American architects and their books to 1848* (Amherst: University of Massachusetts Press, 2007).

Strachan, John. *Advertising and satirical culture in the romantic period* (Cambridge: hCambridge University Press, 2007).

Styles, John. 'Manufacturing, consumption and design in eighteenth-century England', in John Brewer and Roy Porter (eds), *Consumption and the world of goods* (London: Routledge, 1993).

Styles, John and Amanda Vickery (eds). *Gender, taste, and material culture in Britain and North America, 1700–1830* (New Haven and London: Yale University Press, 2006).

Summerson, John. *Georgian London* (London: Pleiades Books, 1945).

Summerson, John. *Architecture in Britain, 1530–1830* (London: Penguin Books, 1953).

Sutcliffe, Anthony. *Towards the planned city: Germany, Britain, the United States and France 1780–1914* (Oxford: Blackwell, 1981).

Sweeney, Kevin M. 'High-style vernacular: lifestyles of the colonial elite', in Cary Carson, Ronald Hoffman and P.J. Albert (eds), *Of consuming interests: the style of life in the eighteenth century* (Charlottesville: University Press of Virginia, 1994).

Tatum, George B. *Penn's great town: 250 years of Philadelphia architecture illustrated in prints and drawings* (Philadelphia: University of Pennsylvania Press, 1961).

Tatum, George B. *Philadelphia Georgian: the city house of Samuel Powel and some of its eighteenth-century neighbors* (Middletown, CT: Wesleyan University Press, 1976).

Taylor, Charles. *Modern social imaginaries* (Durham, NC: Duke University Press, 2004).

Temple, Philip (ed.). *Survey of London*, vol. 47: *Northern Clerkenwell and Pentonville* (London: Yale University Press, 2008).

Thompson, E.P. *The making of the English working class* (London: Pantheon Books, 1964).

Thompson, F.M.L. *Gentrification and the enterprise culture, Britain 1780–1980* (Oxford: Oxford University Press, 2001).

Thornton, Peter. *Form and decoration: innovation in the decorative arts 1470–1870* (London: Weidenfeld & Nicolson, 1998).

Toker, Franklin. 'James O'Donnell: an Irish Georgian in America', *Journal of the Society of Architectural Historians* 29:2 (1970): 132–43.

Trentmann, Frank. 'Materiality in the future of history: things, practices, and politics', *Journal of British Studies* 48:2 (2009): 283–307.

Turner, Olivia Horsfall (ed.). *'The mirror of Great Britain': national identity in seventeenth-century British architecture* (Reading: Spire Books, 2012).

Turpin, John. *A school of art in Dublin since the eighteenth century* (Dublin: Gill & Macmillan, 1995).
Twomey, Brendan. *Smithfield and the parish of St. Paul, Dublin, 1698–1750* (Dublin: Four Courts Press, 2005).
Upton, Dell. 'Pattern books and professionalism: aspects of the transformation of domestic architecture in America, 1800–1860', *Winterthur Portfolio* 19:2–3 (1984): 107–50.
Upton, Dell. *Architecture in the United States* (Oxford: Oxford University Press, 1998).
Upton, Dell. *Another city: urban life and urban spaces in the new American republic* (New Haven and London: Yale University Press, 2008).
Usher, Robin. *Protestant Dublin, 1660–1760: architecture and iconography* (Basingstoke: Palgrave Macmillan, 2012).
Van Horn, Jennifer. *The power of objects in eighteenth-century British America* (Chapel Hill, NC: University of North Carolina Press, 2017).
Vickery, Amanda. *Behind closed doors: at home in Georgian England* (New Haven and London: Yale University Press, 2009).
Wainwright, Nicholas B. *A Philadelphia story: the Philadelphia Contributionship for the Insurance of Houses from Loss by Fire* (Philadelphia: Philadelphia Contributionship, 1952).
Wainwright, Nicholas B. *Colonial grandeur in Philadelphia: the house and furniture of General John Cadwalader* (Historical Society of Pennsylvania: Philadelphia, 1964).
Walker, R.B. 'Advertising in London newspapers, 1650–1750', *Business History* 15:2 (1973): 112–30.
Walsh, Claire. 'The advertising and marketing of consumer goods in eighteenth-century London', in Clemens Wischermann and Elliott Shore (eds), *Advertising and the European city: historical perspectives* (Aldershot: Ashgate, 2000).
Ward, J.R. 'Speculative building at Bristol and Clifton, 1783–1793', *Business History* 20:1 (1978): 3–18.
Watkin, David (ed.). *Sir John Soane: the Royal Academy Lectures* (Cambridge: Cambridge University Press, 2000).
Werkmeister, Lucyle. *The London daily press 1772–1792* (Lincoln: University of Nebraska Press, 1963).
West, Shearer. 'The Darly macaroni prints and the politics of "Private Man"', *Eighteenth-Century Life* 25 (2001): 170–82.
Whitehill, Walter Muir. *Boston, a topographical history* (Cambridge, MA: Harvard University Press, 1968).
Wilkenfeld, Bruce M. 'New York City neighborhoods, 1730', *New York History* 57:2 (1976): 165–82.
Williams, Raymond. *Problems in materialism and culture: selected essays* (London: Verso, 1980).
Wilton-Ely, John. 'The rise of the professional architect in England', in Spiro Kostof (ed.), *The architect: chapters in the history of the profession* (New York: Oxford University Press, 1976).
Wittman, Richard. *Architecture, print culture, and the public sphere in eighteenth-century France* (New York and London: Routledge, 2007).
Woods, Mary N. *From craft to profession: the practice of architecture in nineteenth-century America* (Berkeley: University of California Press, 1999).

Woodward, Christopher. '"In the jelly mould": craft and commerce in 18th century Bath', in Neil Burton (ed.), *Georgian vernacular: papers given at the Georgian Group Symposium, 28 October 1995* (London: Georgian Group, 1996).

Yeomans, David T. 'Early carpenter's manuals 1592–1820', *Construction History* 2 (1986): 13–33.

Yeomans, David T. 'Managing eighteenth-century building', *Construction History* 4 (1988): 3–20.

Youngson, A.J. *The making of classical Edinburgh* (Edinburgh: Edinburgh University Press, 1966).

Index

Page numbers in italics relate to information found in figures.

EU authorised representative for GPSR:
Easy Access System Europe, Mustamäe tee 50,
10621 Tallinn, Estonia
gpsr.requests@easproject.com

www.ingramcontent.com/pod-product-compliance
Lightning Source LLC
LaVergne TN
LVHW060622110826
845147LV00015B/915

* 9 7 8 1 5 2 6 1 5 9 5 7 1 *